C000260512

Risk and Survival in Ancient Greece

To Ma and Dad
&
Mary

Risk and Survival in Ancient Greece

Reconstructing the Rural Domestic Economy

Thomas W. Gallant

Stanford University Press
Stanford, California
1991

Stanford University Press
Stanford, California

© 1991 Thomas W. Gallant

Originating publisher: Polity Press, Cambridge in association with
Basil Blackwell, Oxford
First published in the U.S.A. by Stanford University Press, 1991

Printed in Great Britain

ISBN 0-8047-1857-1

LC 90-70905

This book is printed on acid-free paper

Contents

Figures

Tables

Preface

My central aim in this study is to elucidate the key adaptive mechanisms and survival strategies embedded in the domestic economy of ancient Greek households which enabled them to cope with climatically induced fluctuations in food production. Confronted with a capricious natural environment and armed with a rudimentary technology, Greek peasants developed an extensive but delicate web of risk-management strategies. I argue that the efficacy of these coping mechanisms was directly linked to wider social, political, and economic factors and that changes occurred which altered the fragile equilibrium between them, thereby rendering the peasantry more vulnerable to subsistence risk and even famine. Thus, while the primary focus of the book is ancient Greece, it addresses issues of importance and interest to anthropologists, agricultural economists, geographers, and historians of other areas and epochs.

Methodologically, I employ an explicitly cross-cultural, comparative approach and draw on evidence from medieval and early modern Europe, India, China, Latin America, and Africa. On the one hand, I utilize these materials to frame research questions and to construct working hypotheses against which the empirical data from ancient Greece can be tested, and on the other, as a basis for generalizing about the similarities and differences between Greek peasants and peasants elsewhere. In addition, wherever possible, I have applied quantitative analyses and computer simulation as a means of constructing models which can guide our discussion of the ancient domestic economy.

The work stands at the intersection of three important theoretical debates. The first concerns the causes of famines. My argument is predicated on the theory that famines are the result of cultural systemic failures, not "natural disasters," and that in order to comprehend fully why famines do or do not occur we need first to analyze the fragile set of mechanisms peasants develop for ensuring an entitlement to subsistence. The burden of this book is to reconstruct the systems of coping mechanisms devised and employed in ancient Greek for managing risk. The second debate concerns the nature of the ancient economy. On this issue, my work follows a school of thought most closely associated with Moses Finley. The "moral economy–political economy" debate provides the third one of interest. I find many points of contact between the two positions and attempt to demonstrate their complementariness.

Four works in particular have exerted a powerful influence over this study. James Scott's *The Moral Economy of the Peasant: Rebellion and Subsistence in Southeast Asia* still represents one of the most evocative and provocative studies of peasant domestic economy and subsistence risk, and my indebtedness to it is evident throughout. Amartya Sen's *Poverty and Famines: An Essay on Entitlement and Deprivation* presents a powerful statement on the social and economic foundations of famine. I have been influenced in particular by his "entitlement" theory, and while I only rarely employ it directly, its imprint is pervasive. Michael Watts's *Silent Violence: Food, Famine and Peasantry in Northern Nigeria* is to my mind the most successful attempt at combining the essential points of both Scott's and Sen's works into a holistic analysis of the political economy of a single region. I have tried to model my study on this book and to do in a modest way for the peasantry of ancient Greece what Watts does for Hausan peasants. Peter Garnsey's pioneering *Famine and Food Supply in the Graeco-Roman World* introduces many of the issues discussed here, and this study is intended to complement his.

Peasants perpetually have had to confront challenges to their subsistence entitlement posed by the ravages of climatic perturbations and the demands imposed by external agencies. Through a detailed analysis of how peasants in one pre-industrial, agrarian society, that of ancient Greece, attempted to deal with those challenges, this book aims to contribute to the critically important debate on the perennial problem of how peasants cope with uncertainty.

Chapter 1 provides an introduction to the theoretical and methodological basis of the book. The first part of the chapter establishes the framework of the argument and discusses the methodology on which it is based. The second part sets the work into its broader historiographical context, focussing in particular on the literature concerning the relationship between peasant domestic economy, subsistence crises, famines, and risk-management, and the works on the moral economy–political economy debate.

Chapter 2 contains a systematic reconstruction of the life cycle of the modal ancient Greek household. Given the primacy of the household as the unit of production and consumption in peasant societies, a firm understanding of its development over time is a critical prerequisite for a detailed examination of the domestic economy. After an assessment of the ancient documentary sources, the available osteological material, and demographic studies of comparable pre-industrial societies, I present a model of the life cycle of the ancient Greek household. The model provides the basis for many of the analyses conducted in later chapters.

In Chapter 3, after a discussion of the theory that agricultural systems represent a set of adaptive mechanisms geared to certain environmental and socio-economic conditions, I analyze the strategies embedded in the agricultural system which Greek peasants employed to cope with crop yield variability and to buffer themselves against the possibility of dearth. I end the chapter by indicating how structural constraints, some generated internally by the households and others imposed by the shifting demands of external agencies, could place limitations on the potential efficacy of these prophylactic measures.

I present in Chapter 4 a computer simulation model of the domestic economy. As a necessary precursor to this task, I examine the role of the household as both consumer and producer, in addition to other structural constraints such as farm size, crop storage technology, and the role of the market. Based on this discussion and the observations drawn in the previous two chapters, I construct a computer simulation model which assesses the performance of ancient farms over the course of the life cycle. I incorporate into the program the action of climatically-induced crop yield variability. The dominant conclusion drawn from this exercise is that the average ancient peasant household existed on the very edge of viability. Moreover, due to the action of the "vulnerability cycle", the household was more at risk during certain phases of its life cycle. This sets the state for an extended discussion in the next chapters of the various strategies which Greek households devised for coping with the frequent occasions when their food supply ran short.

Households were not defenseless in the face of their capricious climate, and in Chapter 5 I analyze the primary-order response strategies open to them. Some were based on the exploitation of natural resources, while others entailed the manipulation, and often the irrevocable loss, of both animate and inanimate resources belonging to the household. I argue that the former were able to provide only minor assistance and that while the latter were effective in allaying food shortages in the short term, in the long term they reduced the household's resiliency, or ability to recover once a subsistence crisis has passed. In turn, this made it more vulnerable to subsistence risk.

In Chapter 6 I examine the ways in which interpersonal relations acted as risk-buffering mechanisms. I begin by disccusing the ideological basis of interpersonal relations. I argue that in cultures where they are structured according to an ideology based on an ethos of obligation, we also find well-developed systems of both kin- and non-kin-based inter-household support networks and clientism; the last underlying both elite–elite and elite–peasant bonds. I contend that there was a communally held belief that members of the upper class should provide subsistence insurance for the remainder of the community. Based on the results of this discussion, the rest of the chapter explores the role of interpersonal obligations as risk-buffering strategies.

Taking up some of the themes outlined in Chapter 6, in Chapter 7 I analyze the ways by which communal level organizations and institutions operated to reduce subsistence risk and to provide needed assistance during crises. After an examination of inter-household food-sharing groups, religious organizations, and associations as redistributors of food, I conclude that they played only a limited, secondary role. I argue that the community effectively abrogated its role as an agent of subsistence relief to private, wealthy individuals. This placed a greater burden on inter-class relations. The latter sections of the chapter are devoted to an extended discussion of the impact on the peasants' domestic economy of changes in the political economy of the elite. In particular, the formation of large imperial states and the accompanying demands they imposed led to a re-evaluation and a redefinition of the moral obligation of the elite to provide subsistence support. The end result of these developments was an irrevocable alteration in the ability of the peasant household to manage subsistence risk, leading to dependency, chronic indebtedness, and immiseration.

Acknowledgements

My debts to the scholars and friends who shaped my thinking on so many of the issues addressed in this book are numerous. Like many ancient peasants, I shall never be able to repay all of my debts.

First and foremost, I want to thank Peter Garnsey. During the years of our fruitful collaboration, I have learned from him much about the craft of the historian. Further, he has been a source of unflagging encouragement through both the fat and the lean times. He has commented on this work at all stages of its production and in each case his advice has been sound, incisive, and thought-provoking. This work is envisaged as the second installment of our joint study of food supply and food shortages in the ancient Mediterranean.

The following people have done yeoman's service by reading and commenting on earlier drafts of the book either in part or in total: Jeff Adler, Mary Bussey, Ian Morris, Cynthia Patterson, Allan Silverman, and David Whitehead. Their careful eyes and keen minds kept me from making too many errors of both fact and fancy. Needless to say, any slips of logic or grammar which remain are exclusively mine.

Over the long period of this work's gestation, I profited greatly by working alongside, talking with, and being criticized by John Bennet, Richard Catling, John Cherry, Patrick Geary, Paul Halstead, Glynis Jones, Bob McMahon, Dave Small, and Anthony Snodgrass. I want to thank David Colburn, in particular, and my other colleagues, in general, for making my time as a novice in the History Department at the University of Florida less stressful than it might otherwise have been. Special thanks go to Jim Amelang, Anita Rutman, and Darrett Rutman. From them I have learned more about history and writing than I can ever convey.

This book was written in its entirety during my tenure as a Junior Fellow at the Center for Hellenic Studies in Washington DC. My thanks to the Senior Fellows for giving me the opportunity to write in such amenable surroundings and to the Director and Mrs Stewart and the Staff of the Center for making my stay a pleasant one. Allan Silverman, Annie Silverman, Andrea Berlin, and Doug Olson made the task of writing this book much more bearable, and Franklin, Eleanor, and Theodore provided critical comic relief.

Funding for the early stages of the research leading to this book was provided by the Economic and Social Research Council of the United Kingdom.

Finally, this book is dedicated to three special people: To my parents, Robert and Kassiani Gallant, who instilled in me from youth a love of learning which I shall treasure always, and to Mary Bussey who endured far more than she deserved to while I toiled on this work and who showed the stoutness of heart to drag me away from it when necessary.

List of Abbreviations

Ailian *NA*   De natura animalium
  VH   Varia historia
Aineias Taktikos   *How to Survive under Siege*
Alexis   *Comic Fragments*, cited in Athenaios
Antiphon   *Orations*
Archytas   Fragment 437 in Diels-Kranz (1934/7)
Aristophanes *Ach*   *Acharnians*
  Ec   *Ekklesiazousai*
  Pl   *Ploutos*
Aristotle *Ath*   *Athenaion Politeia*
  Mete   *Meteorologika*
  NE   *Nichomachean Ethics*
  Pol   *Politics*
  Pr   *Problems*
Athenaios   *Deipnosophistai*
Demokritos   Fragment 255 in Diels-Kranz (1934/7)
Demosthenes   *Orations*
DGI   *Sammlung der griechischen Dialekt Inschriften*
Diodoros Sikeliotes   *World History*
Galen   *On Diet*
Herakleides Kretikos   *Periplous*
Herodotos   *The History*
Herodas   *The Mimes*
Hesiod *WD*   *Works and Days*
Hipponax   Fragments 5–11 in West (1972)
Homer *OD*   *Odyssey*
IG   *Inscriptiones Graecae*
Isaios   *Orations*
Isokrates *Arch*   *Archidamos*
  Demon   *Demonidas*
  Pan   *Panegyrikos*
  Phi   *Philippos*
Lysias   *Orations*
OGIS   *Orientis Graeci inscriptiones selectae*
Philo   *On Siege Warfare*
Plato *Lg*   *Laws*
  R   *Republic*

Plutarch *Kim*   *Life of Kimon*
   Mor   *Moralia*
   Per   *Life of Perikles*
Polyaninos   *On Strategy*
Pseudo-Aristotle   *Economics*
Pseudo-Demosthenes   *Orations*
Pseudo-Xenophon   *Athenaion Politeia*
SEG   *Supplementum epigraphicum Graecum*
SIG   *Sylloge inscriptionum Graecarum*
Theophrastos *Char*   *Characters*
   CP   *De Causis Plantarum*
   HP   *Historia Plantarum*
Thoukydides   *The Peloponnesian War*
Xenophon *Ana*   *Anabasis*
   Hell   *Hellenika*
   Kyn   *Kynegetikos*
   LP   *Lakadaimon Politeia*
   Mem   *Memorabilia*
   Oik   *Oikonomikos*
   Sym   *Symposium*

1   Introduction: The Domestic Economy and Subsistence Risk

> The persistent fear of hunger, the recurrent threat of starvation, reinforced by the periodic visitations of famine itself, have profoundly influenced human society throughout the ages and helped fashion elaborate strategies for survival, subsistence and collective security.
>
> David Arnold

The specter of famine still haunts many regions of the globe and so controversy continues to rage over the causes of famines and the ways they can be prevented. Often the burden placed on history is to provide a context in which to assess developments in the modern world. And, indeed, historians can contribute to these debates by analyzing how cultures in the past coped with the problem of ensuring the availability of an adequate food supply when confronted with uncertain environments and mutable economies (Rabb 1983, 62–5). This books aims to contribute to the current debate by presenting a detailed explication of the "elaborate strategies for survival, subsistence and collective security" developed by ancient Greek peasants, and by elucidating the reasons why those strategies changed over time and the consequences of those transformations.

Comparative Approaches to the Past

Before embarking on the narrative, I want to set out the theoretical and methodological basis of the work.

There has been much discussion recently about the desirability of greater dialogue between history and other social sciences. A reflection of this ferment has been the increase in the number of appellations given to such ventures, for example "historical anthropology," "historical sociology," "historical geography," "ethnohistory," "historical ethnography," "comparative history," and "anthropological history." My own approach has been deeply influenced by this literature and I think it not only commendable but necessary that there be greater contact between history and these other disciplines. Common to the discussion on all of these in varying degrees are the following: (1) the question of the role and use of theory; (2) the need and function of model-building and testing; (3) the use of cross-cultural comparisons. In particular, attention, has focused on the question of the role of theory (Rutman 1986, 120–1). On this I find myself substantially in agreement with E. P. Thompson when he observes that "history is not a factory for the manufacture of Grand Theory, like some Concorde of the global air; nor is it an assembly-line for the production of midget theories in series. Nor yet is it some gigantic experimental station in which theory of foreign manufacture can be "applied," "tested," and "confirmed." That is not its business at all. Its business is to recover, to "explain" and to "understand" its object: real history" (Thompson 1978, 46).

We may write history for the present but the past has its own autonomy and integrity as well and we need to understand it on its terms as far as possible. There is a uniqueness to each culture and to the methods it employs to survive that needs to be appreciated and analyzed. Obviously, we should not lapse into historical particularism and deny the possibility and the desirability of drawing generalizations. On the contrary, a study such as this one has to be based explicitly on a cross-cultural comparative methodology. My contention is that the attaining of a deeper understanding of the systems for coping with uncertainty devised by a past society is a legitimate and valid exercise in itself. Thus, while infused by current debates on the theory of peasant economy and the causes of famine, I hope to have produced a "real history" of the ancient Greek peasant economy as well.

I address then two different though not mutually exclusive audiences. I hope that anthropologists, agrarian economists, political scientists, and historians concerned with other peasant societies will come away from it with a better understanding of the interconnectedness between domestic economy and risk-management strategies, and the need to examine these at the levels of the household, the community, and the state in a holistic framework. Though this is widely accepted in theory, in practice there are very few case studies which have adopted such an approach. It is my aim as well to offer to ancient historians a novel view of the Greek world based on an approach different from the one many of them traditionally employ. I risk, therefore, antagonizing practitioners of not one but many disciplines.

Some social scientists will bridle at my extensive use of "soft" data, the deficiencies of my discussion of current debates in their fields, and my reluctance to draw as explicitly as they might wish the lessons of the past for the present. Some ancient historians will be deeply suspicious of my use of comparative material for the application of probabilistic arguments based on analogies, feeling that I am imposing on ancient Greece a view shaped too much by my perceptions of the more recent past and the modern world. Others might wish that I had delved more deeply into certain problems of interest specifically to ancient historians and suppose that I do not go far enough in my analysis of ancient Greece exclusively.

To some extent, any interdisciplinary and comparative endeavor runs the risk of being criticized for superficiality either because it does not extend the analysis far enough into a single culture or because it does not draw on enough of the literature in the other disciplines. A fine line has to be walked between emphasizing the uniqueness of each culture to the point of precluding any meaningful comparisons and highlighting the general resemblance between cultures to the point of inferential banality.

In using comparative evidence as the basis for drawing analogies, I have borne in mind two key points. The first deals with the quesiton of context. Is there sufficient comparability between the overall context from which the two analogues are drawn? As Fredrickson argued "simulitude must first be established to make comparison meaningful – it is essential to show that one is dealing with the same type or category of phenomena in each case, and that the larger historical contexts are sufficiently alike to make comparison more than forced analogy or obvious contrast." (Fredrickson 1981, xv). This can be accomplished either by setting out a broad array of similarities between two entities or by demonstrating a smaller number of similarities between a larger number of cultures. The former demonstrates that the resemblance is unlikely to be merely fortuitous because the referent and the analogue share so many features and the latter that a more general pattern of behaviour characteristic of a cross-culturally meaningul category (gender or peasant, for example) is being identified. In sum, the relevance to the analogue has to be carefully examined.

The second point of importance pertains to causality. By causality I refer to the processes which produced – or "caused" – the pattern we observe in the historical record. If we are not careful in drawing analogies, we may end up merely gauging the degree of similarity or difference between two or more perceptible patterns. Yet often what we seek is greater understanding of the processes which produced the pattern. In order to attain a better understanding of the relationship between pattern and process, a type of *relational analogy* is required. An example clarifies what I mean by this term.

Suppose we wish to draw comparisons between certain aspects of two cultures. Let us call the perceived pattern of the referent A and the analogue A^1. In the case of the referent we can also determine with a fair degree of certainty the actual behavior and logic behind that behavior which produced pattern A; we can call this process B. Having demonstrated the relevance of the referent, we can then turn to the evidence from the analogue, define a range of possible processes or B^1, and assess the probability of each on the basis of our knowledge of the A:B relationship. To be sure, we do not prove that a specified B^1 is correct or historically "true", but no matter which methodology we employ we shall never be able to accomplish that. We attempt to reconstruct and to understand the past by weighing the likelihood of variant inferences and suggestions about it.

I employ throughout the comparative method outlined above and try in particular to pay careful attention to both context and causality when drawing analogies. I endeavor to show explicitly the relevance of the referents. A consequence of this is that I frequently spend as much time discussing the comparative material as I do the data from ancient Greece. In terms of presentation, I have deliberately kept separate the discussion of the comparative material and its implications and the evidence from ancient Greece so that the reader may be better able to judge the validity of the analogies and the inferences I draw from them.

Before continuing, one last methodological point requires comment. The central topic of this book is the domestic economy of ancient Greek peasants. This proposition rests on two assumptions which we need ·to explore and has certain implications which require comment. The two assumptions are that 'peasant' represents a meaningful analytical category and that there were ancient Greeks who can be identified as peasants. Both assumptions are well-founded and acceptable. In anthropology the concept of peasant has a widely accepted, specified comparative meaning (Silverman 1986, 125). Among the defining characteristics of peasants are: (1) the peasantry represents only one sector in large, complex, stratified societies; (2) peasants orientate their economic strategies toward production for subsistence utilizing primarily labor derived from within the household; (3) the surplus extracted from peasant producers supports the other social strata (E. R. Wolf 1966; Gamst 1974; Dalton 1971; Arnold 1988; 50–1). All of these traits describe accurately the vast majority of ancient Greeks (Finley 1985; Garnsey 1988a, 39–42) and so the second assumption made above has merit as well.

A further note of caution is required here. The peasantry in any culture is never monolithic. A wide range of diversity has always characterized peasant cultures. There were differences based on family size and household wealth. Moreover, only a fluid line separated rich and poor peasant households. This generation's wealthy household could be impoverished in the next generation by any one of many potential hazards. We need accordingly to be aware of these gradations and to appreciate that different options and strategies may have been available to some but not others. There were distinctions related to geographical and environmental factors as well. Unfortunately, the nature of the ancient sources is such that many differences between various peasant groups in ancient Greece or the boundaries between groups based on wealth are blurred or invisible. And so we can only infer or suggest how the differential access to opportunities would have affected peasant household production strategies and coping mechanisms. Indeed, given the ancients' predilection for avoiding discussion of anything to do with the peasantry and the village, reconstructing the world of the peasant in general terms is a difficult enough task (Snodgrss 1987, 62–92, esp. 88; Garnsey 1988a, 46–7).

One significant implication flows from the observations made above. Because the focus is on the peasantry, I nowhere undertake a systematic examination of the plight of the various segements of urban society – the artisans, the laborers, and the poor. This is regretable but explicable. The inclusion of these groups would have substantially expanded an already large piece of work and would have taken us down an analytical path rather different from the one carved in this study as it stands.

I want to turn next to a brief discussion of the two theoretical debates which have helped to shape the theoretical framework on which this study is based. The first of these centers of the problématique concerning the causes of famines.

The Causes of Subsistence Crises and Famines

This work is not directly concerned with famine in the sense that it is not my intention to examine specific episodes of "destitution, hunger and death" caused by catastrophic food shortages in ancient Greece (Arnold 1988, 6). Yet the shadow of famine looms large, not as an event but as a deeply ingrained structural feature of pre-industrial peasant socieites. My approach to the problem is predicated on the theory that famines represent the failure of a social-political-economic system to cope with a traumatic shock which adversely affects the production and distribution of vital food supplies.[1]

Often analysts have attempted to identify *the cause* of famines: for some, the primary causal agency is a radical imbalance between population and resources; for others, the main culprit is a mean and fickle climate. Any unicausal theory of famine is unsatisfactory. While a traumatic event, such as droughts, floods, or warfare for example, is *necessary* for the occurrence of a famine, it can never be a *sufficient explanation*.

The connection between any single factor and a famine is neither simple nor direct. With regard to drought, van Apeldoorn concluded:

> . . . famine is certainly not the natural outcome of drought. There is no automatic link; the connection between the two is mediated by the political and economic arrangements of the society that comes under their threat. Disasters should be analyzed not in isolation but as extreme situations that are implicit in the everyday conditions of the population. They must be placed in the context of the entire social system in which they occur. (van Apeldoorn 1981, ix–x)

Garcia put it more succinctly: "Droughts *do not* generate disequilibrium, they merely *reveal* a pre-existing one" (Garcia 1981, 185). On this view, hazards may initiate subsistence crises but famines are caused by systemic failures (J. Mayer 1974, 100). The inability of the social, economic, and political systems to cope with this short-fall in production allows the crisis conditions to deteriorate further. Famines are caused by a multiplicity of factors (Arnold 1988, 42; Lofchie 1987, 85–6; Baker

1987, 49–53; Cummings 1987, 111–17; Shaw 1987, 127; Vaughan 1987, 157–9).

Not only must an acceptable theory of famine be multicausal, it should be, Kates's terms, "interactive" as well (Kates 1985a, 12). Many models of famine, even some of the multicausal ones, portray human cultures as mere passive victims. Such a view underestimates the capacity of groups to adapt to changing conditions regardless of whether those changes are political, demographic, or environmental. Adopting concepts and terms from systems theory, Kates defines a number of interactive feedback models (Kates 1985a, 12–30). Underlying all of the models is the notion that societies develop systems of survival strategies which enable them to cope with food shortages and that there is a continual process of interaction between those systems and other environmental and cultural factors. In other words, interposed between the traumas and hazards on one side and famine conditions on the other is a system of culturally constructed coping mechanisms. Combined these determine a society's *vulnerability* to a given hazard or level of risk (Timmerman 1981, 17–36). An increase in the level of risk or a detrimental change in the web of coping mechanisms would alter a society's ability to manage successfully a subsistence crisis.

In sum, the best theory of famines stresses multiple causality, emphasizes the interaction between societies and those causes, and focuses attention on the systems of survival strategies cultures develop for coping with food shortages. This theory has strongly influenced my research and one of the aims of this book is to provide a case study.

One other theoretical construct has helped to shape my approach to the subject: Amartya Sen's theory of "exchange entitlement" (Sen 1977; 1981). Briefly, Sen's argument is that many famines occur through the maldistribution of foodstuffs rather than a shortfall in production. The entitlement approach concentrates on the ability of people through legal and legitimate means to command food by direct production, trade, and labor, or through welfarist policies by the state (Sen 1981, 6–7, 45). People construct dense networks of exchange relations which entitle them to access to resources. Sen refers to these networks as "E[ntitlement]-maps" (Sen 1981, 45–6). The theory forces us to confront and to explain the obvious fact that only some people starve in a famine, and his own re-examination of three well-known famines demonstrates its utility (Sen 1977; 1980; 1981; for other case studies, see Greenough 1982; L. Tilly 1983).

The drawbacks to the entitlement approach are: first, on its own it is an insufficient explanation of famines, other factors have to be included as well (Arnold 1988, 44); second, its emphasis on exchange has made it more useful in analyzing the plight of wage earners in market situations than of subsistence-oriented peasants (Vaughan 1987, 110; Arnold 1988; 45). The first point need not concern us, the second one should. It seems to me that this criticism relates more to the way the theory has been applied than to the theory itself. Construed most widely, the theory of entitlement points to the heart of the relationship between the domestic economy and subsistence risk: peasants endeavor to maximize their ability to command access (thus, entitlement) to food through various production strategies and by means of exchange relations with other individuals and with the collectivity of which they are a part. Defined in this manner, entitlement provides a key cog in the theoretical framework on which this study is built.

Perspective on Peasant Domestic Economy

In writing this book, I have been influenced by and hope to contribute to the current debate between the "moral economy" and the "political economy" approaches to the study of peasant economy. The works by James Scott (1976) and Samuel Popkin (1979) adumbrate the central tenets of each position. The debate focuses essentially on three related issues: the explanation for peasant revolts, the production ethic of the subsistence peasant, and the dominant idology of interpersonal social and economic relations in peasant villages. For our purposes, the last two points are most important, and in the remainder of this section, I confine my comments to them. I agree with many of the arguments made by each side, and in line with recent works by Huang (1985, 3–9) and Watts (1983, 16–17) on Chinese and Nigerian peasants respectively, I find the two approaches to be complementary rather than strictly contradictory.

At the center of the moral economy lay the belief that "the need for . . . reliable subsistence [is] the primordial goal of the peasant cultivator" (Scott 1976, 5). Since most peasants exist much of the time on the very margin of viability anyway, they consistently and predictably select production strategies which enable them to lessen the risk of production failures. They opt for *Safety-first*. In Scott's view, this "means that the cultivator prefers to minimize the probability of having a disaster rather than maximizing his average return" (Scott 1976, 18). Consequently, peasants are averse to undertakings which put their subsistence at risk, or to phrase it another way, they actively seek to minimize subsistence risk and so avoid activities which would increase the level of risk.

The political economy approach contends that "although poor and close to the margin . . . there are still many occasions when peasants do have some surplus and do make risky investments: the fact that they are poor and risk averse does not imply, either logically or factually, that they do not make investments" (Popkin 1979, 18). Peasants are constantly implementing strategies selected from a wide range of options. They make their choices with an eye to both the short term and the long-term risks and benefits. In this way the peasant household is analogous to a corporation, and so an approach based on decision-making theory borrowed from micro-economics might provide a more appropriate basis from which to analyze peasant economy (Popkin 1979, 4).

The two positions are not incompatible. Compare the following passages: "Peasants often are willing to gamble on innovations *when their position is secure against the loss* and when a success could measurably improve their position. There are times when a small loss would mean a big fall, but there are also times when a small loss would mean little and a win would move the peasant up one level" (Popkin 1979, 21; my italics). "The safety-first principle thus does not imply that peasants are creatures of custom who never take risks they can avoid. . . What safety-first does imply, however, is that there is a defensive perimeter around subsistence routines within which risks are avoided as potentially catastrophic and outside of which a more bourgeois calculus of profit prevails. . . We are therefore confronted with a dichotomy between swash-buckling capitalist risk-taking on the one hand and immovable peasant conservatism on the other. The subsistence peasant is more accurately seen as something of a limiting case in risk-management" (J. Scott 1976, 24–5).

Common to both views is the notion that in the matrix of factors which influence the decision-making process, the primary one is the assurance of subsistence. If, for example, the previous harvest has been bountiful and the weather signs were favorable, peasants readily implement different, more risky, production strategies than they would if the last harvest had been lean, if the storage bins were running low, or if the portends predicted drought. Production decisions are thus contextually sensitive and contingent on a number of factors. Central among these was the impulse to minimize subsistence risk above all. In sum, the argument that "safety-first" is a vital element in, if not the cornerstone of, peasant domestic economy is logical, compatible with a political economy approach, and well documented (Watts 1983, 17; Huang 1985, 190; Greenough 1982, 46–8; McCann 1987a, 100).

"Moral economy concentrates on the system of rights and obligations that surround interpersonal and interclass relations in rural societies" (Guggenheim and Weller 1982, 3). Undoubtedly it is this aspect which has sparked the most controversy. Scott borrowed the term "moral economy" from E. P. Thompson's classic essay on bread-riots in eighteenth-century England (1971) and expanded its connotations. Essentially Scott employs it to describe an ideological construct found in peasant societies which states that the collectivity as a whole and the elite in particular were obligated to guarantee the "right to subsistence" of each member of the group. "The operating assumption of the 'right to subsistence' is that all members of a community have a presumptive right

[handwritten marginalia at top: "What is compatible moral assumption re 'life'? Who-will-love-give-me more?"]

to a living so far as local resources allow" (Scott 1976, 176). When yields were bountiful, elites and "rich peasants were expected to be charitable, to sponsor more lavish celebrations, to help out temporarily indigent kin and neighbors, to give generously to local shrines and temples" (Scott 1976, 5); when dearth prevailed, they were expected to be lenient landlords, secure sources of sustenance, and openhanded givers (Scott 1976, 40–4). On this view, the pre-industrial village was organized on the principles of obligation and reciprocity with the elite and the patrons agreeing to guarantee a "right to subsistence" for all in exchange for honors, gifts, dutiful clients, and the legitimate right to appropriate the peasant's surplus production.

[handwritten marginalia at right: "expectations of support – 'let down'"]

Moral economy, according to the political economists, romanticizes the pre-industrial village (Popkin 1979, 28–9; Skocpol 1982; Guggenheim and Weller 1982, 5–6; Arnold 1988, 81). In their view, "both conflict and cooperation, both power struggles and widespread benefits, are inherent in village patterns of distribution and collective action" (Popkin 1979, 26). Peasant villages were rife with tension as households and kingroups competed for access to resources, vied with one another for prestige and honor, and contended for status. There was no automatic guarantee of a "right to subsistence." "Rights" such as this were won through intense bargaining in a dialectical process between peasants and patrons. Rather than being fixed, the "norms [of interclass relations] are malleable, renegotiated and shifting in accord with considerations of power and strategic interaction among individuals. There are always tradeoffs between conflicting and inconsistent norms" (Popkin 1979, 22). Where moral economy focuses on consensus and the action of collectivities, political economy emphasizes conflict, competition, and the ways in which individuals can act to buffer themselves from subsistence risk.

I do not want to change one unacceptable stereotype for another. Neither "dog-eat-dog" nor "all-for-one and one-for-all" was the code of the pre-industrial village. There is an element of truth in both these images. Individuals constructed elaborate networks of relations and they were members of a number of groups – household, kingroup, associations, villages, factions, and states. Depending on the context, there was always ample scope for both competition and co-operation between these entities. We need to appreciate the complexity of social relations and the duties and obligations attached to them.

Moral economy and political economy describe two sides of the same coin. As a depiction of a belief widely held by peasants, moral economy is accurate. Peasants do contend that patrons and communal leaders are obligated to assist them in a crisis and to prevent food shortages from degenerating into famines (Wasserstrom 1982; 43; Thaxton 1982, 138–43; Watts 1983, 122–7; 1987, 132–3; McCann 1987a, 97–102; Greenough 1982, 48; G. Evans 1988; 233; Wylie 1989, 173). Peasants do accept a certain amount of exploitation as legitimate so long as those exploiting them reciprocate by providing subsistence insurance (Scott and Kerkvliet 1977, 441–9; G. Evans 1988, 248–9; on peasant exploitation, see Dalton 1974; 1975 and 1977; Newcomer and Rubenstein 1975; Newcomer 1977; Derman and Levin 1977). Yet it must be borne in mind that moral economy is essentially an ideological construct.

It is political economy which may portray more closely actual behavior. In practice, interclass relations, especially patron–client bonds, may be more accurately viewed as "self-reinforcing, dyadic relations beneficial to both parties and the exchanges, while governed by norms and constrained by the subsistence needs of the weaker party, are based on the relative bargaining power of the parties" (Popkin 1979, 27). Following on from this, I would argue that it is political accountability in its widest sense rather than a shared moral code which determines the premium that peasants must pay for their subsistence insurance. The line between what peasants expect from the elite (the moral economy) and what they will accept (the political economy) is subject to constant reassessment and negotiation. The two theories, then, are not incompatible but rather complementary, and in the last two chapters of the book I examine the interplay between them in detail using data from ancient Greece.

2 Ancient Households and their Life Cycle

> The household is the association established by nature for the supply of people's everyday wants, and the co-members of it are called by Charondas "those who share the same storeroom" and by Epimenides of Crete "those who eat from the same table."
>
> Aristotle, *Politics*

When we attempt to analyze the domestic economy of ancient Greece, what unit of study is optimal? Is it the family, the village, the region, or the state? All are important and all are related to the domestic economy. For Aristotle, the answer was simple: *household*.

Any investigation of the ancient Greek household must focus on the issues of size, composition, and longitudinal development of coresidential groups in households. We need to ask: Just how large was the "average" ancient household? How many mouths were there that had to be fed from the larder? How much man-power could be called on to work the household's land? And most important, how did this change over the course of the household's *life cycle*. We need answers to these questions if we are to understand why ancient peasants made the economic choices they did. It makes a world of difference if a household could call on the labor of numerous adult males and females, in say a multiple household of the *zadruga* type (Hammel 1972; 1980a; 1980b; Halpern 1958; Gavazzi 1982; Wheaton 1975; for Italian examples of multiple households, see; Kertzer 1984; 1985; and 1989), or only on the labor of a single adult couple. But simply to define a single static type of average household would be misleading. Instead we have to introduce the notion of the household as an entity constantly in a state of flux, changing over time to the rhythm of the life cycle.

The dominant aim of this chapter is to construct a working model of the average Greek peasant household life cycle. As with any model, it represents a simplified version of reality. Not every family in ancient Greece developed in precisely the manner described here. Exceptions can always be found. What the model is intended to do is to portray the life cycle with reference to a specified set of demographic parameters, legal requirements, and social customs if no other extraneous factors or circumstances intervened to preclude its full operation. The end result of the exercise should approximate the "modal" (the most frequently occurring type) ancient household. This model provides the basis for the much more sophisticated computer simulations of the domestic economy presented in Chapter 4.

The Primacy of the Household

Most students of the ancient household have utilized almost exclusively literary sources and have either adopted a narrow legalistic viewpoint or produced functionalist analyses of kinship terminology (Wolff 1944; Harrison 1968; Schaps 1979; MacDowell 1989; Humphreys 1983; Littman 1979). Much of the growing body of literature on women and gender has focused on women in isolation, outside of the context of the household. Yet in an agrarian pre-industrial society, women's productive and reproductive roles were integrally bound up with those of their household (Foxhall 1989). Historians have concluded or simply taken for granted that ancient families were nuclear and practiced neolocal residence. In such studies the dynamics of the life cycle are overlooked; two different aspects of domestic relations, kinship and residence, are conflated (e.g., as in MacDowell 1989); and the assumption is made that neolocal, nuclear households were independent of wider socially and economically co-operating units, what Laslett refers to as the "collectivity" (Laslett 1984a; 1988). Comparative evidence throws doubt on these suppositions (e.g. Segalen 1984; Le Roy Ladurie 1979, 23–30, 47–8; O'Neill 1987; Rutman and Rutman 1984, 121–7; Chaytor 1980, 27–8; B. L. Foster 1984; O. Harris 1982, 144).[2] Furthermore, other important, non-kin members of the household, such as slaves or hired laborers, are neglected: an obvious shortcoming if one is interested in the labor supply and productive capacity of the group. Finally, the works cited above fail to take into account the influence of class and wealth differences on the composition of the domestic group. Clearly another approach, utilizing a wider data base is needed if we are to draw any useful conclusions on ancient domestic units. Unfortunately we cannot go into detail on all of these matters here. All we can do is skim the surface of many of them and extract the main points required to construct our model.

The limitations imposed by the use of the family as the analytical unit have led social historians to shift their research orientation to the *household*, leading to its recognition as the central focus of both social and economic life in peasant societies. The household is the focal point for socialization of the young, the place where sex roles, norms of behavior, and kinship are primarily defined. "The household is a fundamental social unit. Households are more than groups of dyadic pairs. They have emergent character that makes them more than the sum of their parts. They are the primary arena for the expression of age and sex roles, kinship, socialization, and economic cooperation where the very stuff of culture is mediated and transformed into action" (Netting, Wilk, and Arnould 1984, xxii).

Furthermore, most historians accept that the household is the single most important economic unit in peasant societies, as the following makes clear: "pooling and sharing of resources, food processing, cooking, eating, and sheltering from the elements tend to take place in the household, which has therefore become *the standard unit of analysis for ecological and economic purposes*" (Netting, Wilk, and Arnould, 1984, xxii; emphasis mine); but in addition, "the household is a product of a strategy for meeting diverse functional requirements, and this strategy is always a compromise" (Wilk and Rathje 1982, 631). I think this last point in particular requires emphasis. The important decisions regarding the selection of crops, the scheduling of labor, and the disposition of the final product are all made within the household (Wilk and Rathje 1982, 622; Wilk and Netting, 1984, 6–11). In the last instance, the household stands as an individual's primary focus of allegiance and affection vis-a-vis the rest of society and the most flexible and responsive unit to socio-economic change (Wheaton 1975; Netting 1981, 39–58; Laslett 1984a; Chaytor 1980; Crummet 1987).

Appreciating the importance of the household as an analytical unit in the abstract has proved far easier than identifying it in reality (Hammel 1984; Yanagisako 1979; 1984; Anthony T. Carter 1984; Cornell 1986; Stone 1981, 64). Obviously kinship alone is insufficient because relatives may reside far away from one another (Hesiod *WD* 344–5). Nor does the introduction of "family" get us very far as the term itself is susceptible to numerous definitions. Coresidence would seem to be one of the best criteria, but it too has deficiencies. How, for example, does one deal with boarders or slaves kept in separate slave-quarters. Are they part of the "household"? A more functionally orientated approach based on economic co-operation drew quick criticism from Africanists who found that frequently members of two different residential units worked together, and that not infrequently they were kin, sometimes even husbands and wives (Vaughan 1982; 1983; Arnould 1984; Lianres 1984). Following Wilk and Netting, the working definition for household accepted here emphasizes four aspects – coresidence, kinship, commensality, and economic co-operation (Wilk and Netting 1984). Alone, each is insufficient; together, they can help us to identify households.

The Household Life Cycle: A Definition

The economic implications of change in the age composition and size of the family are expressed in the ratio of supply and demand, in the level of earnings and numbers of earners, and in the number of dependents, young and old. The lifetime course of the family economy is thus intimately linked to changes in the age of the household head, to change in the number and age of children, and to loss of productive family members through death, disability, divorce, and the formation of new family units.   (Edler 1978, 50)

This statement aptly captures the rationale for adopting a methodology which emphasizes change over time. One of the major criticisms of the approach employed by family historians in the 1960s and 1970s was that by focusing their attention primarily on the mean household size, they reduced an essentially dynamic entity, the household, into a static one (Vinovskis 1977, 283; Yanagisako 1979; Hareven 1978, 1; Kertzer and Bretell 1987, 101–8; Elder 1987, 186–7). As Stone noted, "the major and insuperable objection to most aspects of this work on households derives from a realization that family size and composition are not fixed over time, but oscillate throughout the family life cycle"; and he likens this static approach to viewing a single frame excerpted from a movie: interesting and accurate, but not the whole picture (Stone 1981, 63).

As early as 1949 Meyer Fortes introduced the concept of the development cycle into the anthropologist's toolkit (Fortes 1949). It was utilized most visibly by Jack Goody (Goody 1958; 1976). Amongst social historians, its currency can be dated to the publication of Berkner's seminal essay on the family and the development cycle of the Austrian peasant household (Berkner 1972). Since then it has been widely applied (Wheaton 1975; Medick 1976; Plakans 1984; Kertzer 1984; R. M. Smith 1984; Wall 1984; Wolf 1984; Segalen 1987). The development cycle approach compels us to recognize that the morphology of the household unit is constantly changing over time as new members are introduced and others leave. Alternative methodologies for applying such an approach have been proposed. Elder has emphasized the need not to lose sight of the individual in our quest to chart the development of the collectivity. On this view, we should examine the interlocking trajectories of events and developmental phases affecting individual members of the family and the household (Elder 1978; 1987). Anthony Carter recommends much the same with his "household history" approach (Carter 1984).

Obviously the best way to observe the life cycle in operation is to analyze long runs of serial data in conjunction with detailed "biographies" of individual members of the household. For antiquity, this is impossible. Instead what we can do is to elucidate the major factors which affected the life cycle and then by using comparative evidence draw some inferences as to their probable impact on ancient Greece. We can then turn to more biographical data contained in the forensic speeches in order to gain some impressions as to validity of the picture drawn from the other sources.

The Sources

When we turn to the ancient Greek household, we are confronted by an insurmountable problem: lack of data. The sources on the life cycle of ancient families are sparse. Unavailable is the wide range of sources, such as censuses or parish registers and the like, used to great advantage by historians and anthropologists working in other parts of Europe at different time (for examples, see, Kertzer and Bretell 1987, 89–91; Plakans 1984). Nonetheless armed with comparative evidence from the Mediterranean and other parts of Europe during the pre-industrial period, we can make some sense of the ancient evidence. The final intention is a better understanding of the full range of different household configurations in ancient Greece and the construction of a model of the "average" household and its life cycle, around which the arguments in the remainder of the chapter will be built.

I begin with an assessment of the ancient sources. The small-scale polities of the Classical period (490–323 BC) and even the cumbrous empires of the Hellenistic period (323–146 BC) never developed the type of bureaucratic mentality or centralized administration which leads to the creation of detailed census records or tax registers like those found in early modern and modern Europe. In the Classical period, the size of the political units was so small and the level of internal taxation so minimal that records of this nature were unnecessary, and in the Hellenistic period the practice of corporate taxation did not require the state to keep detailed records of individuals in subject territories because for the fisc's purposes it was sufficient to note only the lump sum owed to the treasury by each administrative district. Occasionally, ancient *poleis* drew up land registers (Pseudo-Aristotle 1346b3; 1350a1–6; Klaffenbach 1960) and certain corporate associations established lists of their members. In the first case, none survive, and in the second, the register contains only lists of individual males (Hedrick 1989). So they provide us with little help. Instead we must turn to other, less satisfactory types of sources to study the composition of the ancient household.

The single largest body of material at our disposal refers to legal proceedings and court cases from Athens and, accordingly, we must be cautious in drawing generalizations from it. Land, property, and inheritance were, predictably, subjects close to every agriculturalists' heart and the source of constant dispute. Such disputes generated two main categories of documents: forensic speeches and publicly displayed law decrees, usually written on stone. The problems with the speeches are:

1   We have only one side of the story – the speeches were intended to persuade a jury to find in favor of the writer's client, not to record a accurate picture of the household.

2   The thrust of the case referred to inheritance and control of property and thus any comments about the composition and functioning of the household are incidental to the main concern of the speech. Thus, while the speeches are an excellent source on inheritance and kinship, when it comes down to discerning household composition, we have to drag snippets of information from the background to the foreground.

Published laws and decrees throw pinpoints of light into the household, but because of the vagaries of survival and the lack of supporting documentation, we cannot set these decrees into a specific historical context; in other words, we cannot elucidate with any clarity why at a certain point it was necessary to restate publicly the laws and rules of inheritance. Nevertheless, these two categories will provide the bulk of our evidence.

The next type of documentary evidence is found in the writings of the philosophers Plato (*Lg* and *R*) and Aristotle (*Pol*). These can provide some useful tidbits of information, but it is necessary for us to remember at all times that these works were prescriptive not descriptive, and as such require careful handling. For example, it is impossible to penetrate to the social reality behind Plato's preference for small, nuclear families in the *Laws*. Differentiating cultural norms from the personal views of the philosophers presents us with problems. Once again there is information there to be had, but we must tread warily.

Other types of documentary sources at our disposal are historical works, political pamphlets, and literary pieces such as plays and poems. With the first two categories we have to deal with the fact that when households appear they do so as a backdrop to the author's main subject. The writings of antiquity were orientated to the political, not the social sphere. Once again we confront the problem of differentiating social norms from an individual's personal perceptions. With literary works, the problems are more acute, even though masterpieces such as Athenian tragedies and comedies have the family firmly on center stage. The former are set in a mythical past with characters larger than life, the latter are intended to mock society and parody real life. In either case, social reality is presented through a distorting lens (Goldhill 1986).

Material remains brought to light by the archaeologist's trowel provide our last category of ancient evidence. Recently certain archaeologists have become preoccupied with the problem of assessing population, household composition and function from the analysis of excavated houses. Through the calculation of floor space, overall house size, and spatial analyses of the rooms, in conjunction with comparative ethnographic material, considerable strides have been made in the study of households (Kramer 1982a; 1982b; Horne 1982). There are problems, however, with using the archaeological data. For a start, archaeological excavations until recently have not been concerned with the issue raised here; indeed most of the writing on the "ancient house" has been preoccupied with it as an architectural entity, paying scant attention to the people who actually inhabited the structures. Similarly excavators have not always paid as careful attention to the finds from within the houses as one would like. As well, there are the problems raised by the fact that archaeological deposits are subject to various pre- and post-depositional processes which can render their interpretation difficult, the problems involved with precisely dating archaeological deposits, and the difficulties raised when trying to interpret dynamic process from an essentially static record. Nonetheless archaeological evidence does provide us with information on aspects of the household unavailable from any other sources, and accordingly, in this chapter as elsewhere, use will be made of archaeological data whenever possible.

All the ancient sources, then, have limitations which present us with difficulties of interpretation and completeness. Each category has its owns set of strengths and weaknesses when it comes to shedding light on the form and function of ancient households. Accordingly, it seems to me that the best way to proceed is as follows. Based on comparative evidence, a series of expectations will be established, providing us with a number of test hypotheses. If we then pull together the ancient evidence, drawing on the strengths of each category of sources – while cognizant of its weaknesses – and judiciously compare the pictures presented in them with the historical and anthropological data I think that we can arrive at an accurate understanding in general terms of the form, functions, and life cycle of ancient households.

The Demographic Parameters

Some of the primary factors determining the development cycle of the family are male and female ages at marriage, mortality rates, fecundity rates, the length of the interval between births, the level of infant mortality, and residence pattern of children when they wed. Information on some, but unfortunately not all, of these is available from ancient Greece.

Age at Marriage and Marriage Order

According to many students of family history, the age at which men and women married for the first time is critically important in shaping the structure of the household (e.g. Modell and Hareven 1978, 250). Indeed it provided one of the main criteria on which Hajnal based his cross-cultural categories for marriage and household structure (Hajnal 1965;

1983). He distinguished a Mediterranean Marriage Pattern characterized by a high age at marriage for men and early age at marriage for women. Studies of Mediterranean communities in recent times have produced sound data which call this pattern into question (e.g. Bell 1979, 86; Kenna 1976b, 29). For this reason, some have urged caution because age at marriage is a feature of society which can change quickly and for a variety of reasons (Laslett 1984b, 81–2). A wide range of factors can affect the age at marriage. For example if property is devolved at the death of the head of the natal household, then sons may have to marry later because they lack the necessary wherewithal to establish their own households. If it is incumbent on brothers to delay their own marrriage until they have married off their sisters in the event of their father's death, then here again they will probably marry at a later age.

The monumental study of a fifteenth-century Florentine *Catasto* indicated that the modal age at marriage for men was 28 and for women 18 (Herlihy and Klapisch-Zuber 1985, 202–19). Rheubottam's recent study of members of the Ragusan elite found that the average ages there were 33 for men and 19 for women (Rheubottam 1988, 363).

Two excellent quantitative studies of ages at marriage for men and women in various sectors of the Roman world during the first two centuries AD indicated that men married on average in their late twenties to early thirties (Saller 1987, 25–30) and that women were wed usually in their late teens (B. Shaw 1987; see also Hopkins 1965).

The prescriptive evidence from ancient Greece indicates that it was expected, or least recommended, that a man marry at around age 30 (Hesiod *WD* 700–1; Plato *Lg* 721b, 785b; *R* 460e; Aristotle *Pol* 1335a6). There was no hard and fast rule. Simply it was expected that a man, particularly if he was the eldest son, would take a bride either after the death of his father or when his father was ready to hand control of the household over to him. We can postulate that the average Greek man would marry sometime between the ages of 25 and 30 if he could.

Several sources suggest that girls were ripe for marriage at menarche, roughly 14 (Amundson and Diers 1969) and they should be wed shortly after that (Hesiod *WD* 696–8; Aristotle *Pol* 1335a6; Xenophon *Oik* 7.42). In the Gortyn law code, it is specified that a girl could be married at 12 if she was a *patroiko* (i.e. a brotherless orphan). Even more so than with the age at marriage for men, we need to be wary of a discrepancy between cultural prescriptions and actual practice (Laslett 1984b, 81–90). Also, we should bear in mind that excessively early age at marriage for girls may be a practice restricted to the upper classes. The evidence from Greece resembles that from the Roman period and the early modern period in southern Europe. While this does not prove that on average Greek girls married in their middle to late teens, it does make it more likely. For the purpose of the model proposed at the end of this chapter, I propose to use a range of ages from 16 to 19 as the age at marriage for the average ancient Greek girl.

We can employ another method as a means of assessing the likelihood of these figures. That is to determine if the factors causing these age differentials in the comparative material existed in Greece as well. If we can demonstrate that there is a structural similarity, then the analogy gains in probability.

Rheubottam argues that the order of marriage has a significant impact on age at marriage (Rheubottam, 1988; see also Hammel and Wachter 1977). He contends that if brothers have to delay their own marriages until most or all of their sisters have been wed, then the average age at marriage for men will be elevated considerably. Using data from fifteenth-century Ragusa and a computer simulation, he demonstrates the linkage decisively (Rheubottam 1988).

Our best evidence refers to the more well-to-do from ancient Athens. Cox has determined from her study of the available genealogical data that by a margin of 3:1 daughters were married before their brothers (Cox 1988, 386). Moreover, it seems to have been accepted and expected that if the father had died before all the children were married (a very common occurrence as we shall see), then the sons were not to marry until husbands had been found for all their sisters. "Having thus found matches for ours sisters, men of the jury, . . ." two brothers tell how they went off to fight (Isaios 2.6). By including this snippet of information, they were attempting to vouchsafe their character by demonstrating that they were men of probity. Furthermore, If Isager is correct that in case of the father's death, sons could not marry until their mother was safely remarried – if she desired to remarry (Isager 1981–2) – this would push back the age at marriage for men even further. There are sound reasons then for accepting that in general the Mediterranean Marriage Pattern as defined by Hajnal held true in ancient Greece.

Adult Mortality Rates and Life Expectancy

We need to know next how long the couple could have expected to remain together.

Life expectancy and mortality rates in Greece seem to resemble those found in a number of other pre-industrial societies. Turning first to the ancient evidence, our main source of information is derived from the detailed examination of human skeletal remains. There has been much controversy recently over the methodological bases of paleodemography in general and the use of skeletal material for answering the kinds of questions raised here in particular (Bocquet-Appel and Masset 1982; van Gerven and Armelagos 1983; Buikstra and Konigsberg 1985). My own view tends toward the more optimistic assessment; nevertheless, care needs to be taken when drawing inferences about the demographic structure and development of a society on the basis of skeletal material alone.

Angel found that average age at death for adult males during the Classical period was 45.0 (N – 91) and 42.4 for the Hellenistic period (N – 91); for females the corresponding figures were 36.2 years (N – 55) and 36.5 (N – 36) (Angel 1975, Table). Bisel's results for Athens and Akanthos are rather different (Bisel 1980, 66). She found that women at Athens during the Classical period lived until 47.0 – but this was based on a sample of two; during the Hellenistic this fell to 44.3 (N – 15). For men she recorded ages of 49.7 (N –7) and 44.3 (N – 15). At Akanthos in northern Greece, samples were drawn only for the Classical period, and the results there were ages of 35.5 for men (N – 10) and 42.1 for women (N – 7). These samples are simply too small to allow us to draw any firm conclusions. A likely assumption, and the one opted for here, is that average age at death for men would have been 40 years and for women approximately 38.

Another approach would be to use life tables, like those produced by Coale and Demeny (1966), as a means of approximating life expectancy at birth. Hopkins and Burton employed this method in their demographic analysis of the Roman aristocracy. They found the average life expectancy among the aristocracy to be 25 years (Hopkins and Burton 1983, 73). We might expect for Greek peasants, then, a figure closer to 20 years given the lower nutritional levels likely with a "peasant diet", the lower end of the range typical of pre-industrial societies (Hopkins and Burton 1983, 71).

Compared to comparable societies elsewhere, the figures presented here do seem somewhat high but not totally out of line (Laslett 1984b, 111–13; Wrigley 1987, 200–206; Frier 1982; 1983; Zanetti 1982; and 1977). Female mortality during the prime childbearing years would account for the lowering of the life expectancy of women (Stone 1981, 59; Hanawalt 1981; French 1986; Goubert 1987, 47–9; cf. R. M. Smith 1984).

Infant Mortality

"The single most important variable affecting the mean size of *all* types of households is the infant mortality rate" (Wheaton 1975, 606). The precise infant mortality rate from antiquity is unrecoverable. At best we can only give a rough approximation based on the meager evidence available in conjunction with some insights from comparative material. The only work done to date on this is by Angel, and it should be used with caution. On the basis of the number of scars, pits, grooves and distortions on the posterior and visceral surfaces of the pubic symphysis from two small samples from the Classical (ten specimens) and the Hellenistic (five specimens), he determined that on average women gave birth to, respectively, 4.3 and 3.6 children (Angel 1975, 176, Table). Of these, Angel calculated that 1.6 and 2.0 died in infancy, thus producing an infant survival rate of 2.7 and 1.6 per female and a death ratio of 500 and 700 infants per 1000 adults (Angel 1975, 176–7, Table).

These rates again are somewhat higher than those reported from many other pre-industrial cultures (Laslett 1984b, 111; Burch 1970, 61–9; De Vries 1976, 11; Stone 1981, 59; Hopkins and Burton 1983, 225; Kriedte 1983, 20). According to Ring, medieval Italian peasant families witnessed infant and child mortality of 50–60 percent (Ring 1979, 14–15). Knodel's much more sophisticated analyses of data from Germany demonstrate that infant mortality rates could vary from place to place and by class, but, on the whole, the figures cited above from Greece are not wildly out of line with his results (Knodel 1988, 35–101).

The question of infanticide and the 'anti-natalist' disposition of ancient Greek society has been much discussed of late (Patterson 1985; Eyben 1980/81; Pomeroy 1975; 1983; 1984; Engels 1980; and 1984; Raep-saet 1971; W. V. Harris 1982; Golden 1981; Oldenziel 1987; M. Harris and Ross 1987a, 79–84). In particular, the debate has focused on the selective removal of female infants from the household. Patterson's sensible article properly warns us against oversimplification by emphasizing the complexity of the issue. Yet, when hard choices had to be made about the gender of children to be raised, there was probably a bias in favor of males. For this reason, in the model constructed below, I have opted for two sons and one daughter.

Residence Pattern

The dominant resident pattern, at least in the early years of marriage, was not necessarily neolocal. There are examples of both patrilocal and patrivirilocal. I attempted to quantify this as best I could using the evidence in the forensic speeches and found that in 74.3 percent of the cases known (N – 52) from ancient Greece continued residence with parents is indicated or implied. It seems to have been expected that at least one of the household's offspring would have continued to reside in the natal household after marriage.

The fourth-century textual data from Athens find support in the archaeological record. The classical town site of Olynthos in northern Greece contained roughly the same number of houses over a period of 120 years. There does not seem to have been constant building of houses for newly-weds. Instead we see in a number of cases that the paternal household was physically divided into smaller units (Robinson and Graham 1938, 84). Such is the case in an earlier period as well as Zagora on Andros and Koukounaries on Paros (Ian Morris, pers. comm.). This is paralleled by the findings of Behar in her work on the Spanish village of

Santa Maria del Monte (Behar 1986, 55–60) and by Benedict's study on the domestic cycle in a Turkish provincial town (Benedict 1976, 228; see also, Abu-Zahra 1976, 160–1; Kramer 1982b, 670–1; Horne 1982; 677–8). In both cases they found that the extended family unit was common at some point in the development cycle, and that the residence pattern was patrilocal or patrivirilocal. It was only in cases where heirs squabbled over the house that it was physically divided.

What is the resultant development cycle in other cultures manifesting structural and demographic characteristics similar to those outlined above for Greece? Demographic studies of early modern and modern Greece (Panayiotopoulos 1985; Couroucli 1985; Allen 1976; Aschenbrenner 1976; Bialor 1976) and on medieval and early modern Italy (Ring 1979; Zanetti 1977; Herlihy and Klapisch-Zuber 1985; Kertzer 1984; 1985), all suggest that there will be a high number of widows, a considerable number of families will be composite, that is where one or more conjugal units are compelled to join through the loss of a spouse, and that at some point in the development cycle extended and/or multiple domestic units will result. This conclusion is supported by computer simulations conducted by Kenneth Wachter and others (Wachter, Hammel, and Laslett 1978). The comparative material shows us the relationship between a given set of variables and a certain pattern of household morphology. By analogy, then, we should expect to find something similar in the case of the ancient Greek household.

Coresident Kin: Some Examples

Before we can model the life cylce, we must first propose an answer to the question of the number of coresident kin, or the Mean Household Size (MHS).

I have employed the categories first systematically defined by Laslett (1972; 1983, Table 17.5; 1984a, 360–1) and then subsequently adopted by many working in the field (Mendels 1986). These are:

1 Simply family households: this refers to one containing a married couple alone, married couples with child(ren), widows or widowers with child(ren).
2 Extended family household: it consists of a conjugal family unit and one or more relatives other than offspring. Such relatives include either spouse's parents, siblings, or cousins.
3 Multiple family unit: it is composed of two or more conjugal families connected by kinship or marriage and coresiding. Also known as a "joint" family. These categories have provided the basis for a great deal of cross-cultural research.

The following statement from Humphreys encapsulates the dominant view on the MHS in antiquity: "Athenian familes were always relatively small" (1983, 76). The evidence for this conclusion originates in the forensic speeches and the prescriptive works of the philosophers. It is very much the consensus among ancient historians that the simple, conjugal or nuclear family was the overwhelmingly predominant form. Indeed in the only book-length study in modern times devoted solely to the ancient family, Lacey could spare only one footnote on the question of the size and structure of the entity he was studying. When larger domestic units are detected in the evidence, they are summarily dismissed (Lacey 1968, 307 n. 79); as in this by Humphreys: "The extended households of Priam and Nestor in the *Iliad* and the *Odyssey* appear to be exceptional" (Humphreys 1983, 76 n. 5; she is in fact referring to a joint rather than an extended household). The "normal" Greek household, then, contained a nuclear family and the residence pattern was neolocal; that is upon marriage the newly-weds would set up a separate and autonomous household. This is the orthodox view and it is acceptable only up to a certain point.

It is common to use the forensic speeches as the source for genealogies, and to tabulate the number of children mentioned for each family group. Thus, for example, Raepsaet (1973) tabulated the total number of individuals by age set in the speeches of Isaios, Demosthenes, and Lysias, then divided it by the number of families and produced a figure of 2.14 children per family. This gives a mean household size of 4.14.

If one were to count the minimum number of children per household, one would reach the result that 67 percent of the families in Athens numbered between 2 and 4 individuals, 29 percent had 4–6 members, and 4 percent were greater than 6. I repeated the exercise utilizing the much larger body of genealogical data contained in Davies's monumental prosopography of Athenian propertied families (1971) and found that, even though they refer solely to the elite, the results were very similar to those derived from Isaios: 0–2 children – 62.5 percent; 3–4 – 32.2 percent; >4–5.3 percent.

These figures compare quite favorably with those produced by, for example, Peter Laslett (1972, Table 1.3), who shows that all of the 35 groups drawn from many parts of the world had mean household sizes of between 4 and 5. Numerous studies since then have shown that mean household size of this magnitude was common in many parts of the world during the pre-industrial period.

The orthodox view of the ancient Greek household, then, would seem to be essentially accurate. Yet we can go further. For a start, the figures presented above can be seen as representing only the minimum number of individuals per household. We often cannot be sure that all the members of the household were mentioned in the court-room proceedings. Women are certainly under-represented in our sources: in the forensic speeches 67 percent of the total number of people mentioned are men; in the genealogical files created by Davies, men constitute 68.6 percent of the total. Is this gender imbalance real? I think not. In the 19 cases presented in the speeches of Isaios, for example, where we can be sure that all the members of the household are mentioned, daughters outnumber sons by 54 percent to 46 percent (23 to 19), a more acceptable gender ration (Wevers 1969; Isager 1981–2; Gould 1980). If we paint these "missing women" into the picture, then the average number of coresident kin in Greek households starts to approach the upper end of Laslett's scale.

An extended example illustrates the type of situation that was probably quite common and highlights some of the features we have been discussing.

Mantitheos, son of Mantias of Thorikos, Attika, brought two suits against his two step-brothers. The speeches written for him by the orator Demosthenes survive and contained in them is a vivid portrayal of household composition (Demosthenes 39 and 40). Mantitheos' mother was the daughter of Polyaratus and the sister of Menoxenos, Bathyllos, and Periander. She was given in marriage first to Kleon, the son of Kleomedon, and bore him three daughters and one son. When Kleon died, she returned to her paternal household, leaving her children to be reared by her husband's kinsmen.

While she was married, her father died. Thus it fell upon Menoxenos and Bathyllos, as Periander was still a minor at this time, to provide her with her dowry for her marriage to Mantias. She bore him two sons, one of whom died in infancy.

This was his second marriage, as he had been wed previously to an Athenian woman, Plangon, whom he had divorced. With Plangon he had one son. After the divorce, she and her son returned to her paternal household, consisting of at least her father and mother and three brothers; shortly after her return, her father died.

When his second wife died, Mantias refused to receive Plangon or her children into his house formally, although he did continue to have sex with her and together they had another son. Eventually after considerable litigation, he agreed to recognize paternity of the two boys. Before he did so, however, he had Mantitheos take a bride in spite of his age – he was only 18. Mantitheos, his wife, and their daughter resided in his father's house until his death. At that time, Mantitheos received into the house both of his two step-brothers and agreed to share the inheritance with them. This fascinating tale goes on but for our purposes its utility ends here.

None of the households described above conform to the pattern one would expect based on the orthodox view of the Greek household.

1   Household of Mantitheos' mother. When the father died, he left a

household consisting of two adults sons (married or unmarried), one adolescent son, and presumably a widow. After her remarriage to Mantias, the four small children from her first marriage remained in this household, raising the total number of its members to at least eight and spanning three generations. Note also the absence of a single conjugal pair.

2 Household of Plangon's family. The reason for Mantias' divorcing Plangon focused on her father's political disgrace and financial collapse. After the divorce, her father's household consisted of himself and his wife, Plangon and her eldest son, and her three brothers. Little is known of these men and so it it uncertain whether or not they were married at this time. Plangon was in her late 20s at the time and so unless she was considerably older than her brothers, they would either have reached or be nearing maturity (Davies 1971, 365–6).

3 The household of Mantitheos. In its early stages, this unit conformed to the norm: Mantitheos, his younger brother, and their parents. It quickly changed. First, his brother and then his mother died, leaving only father, son, and domestic slaves. At a later stage, a bride and then a child were introduced into the picture. This configuration is the classic vertically extended domestic unit: conjugal pair, offspring, plus widowed parent. Its appearance, however, was fleeting. Within a few years of Mantitheos' marriage, his father died. At that point, Mantitheos allowed his two step-brothers to move into the house and to become full participants in its life. The elder of them Boiotios, was slightly older than Mantitheos and unmarried and the other was still an adolescent. Step four in the development of this household saw it containing a conjugal pair with child, an adult, and an adolescent male. This produced a household with a total of three adults and two children, and an unspecified number of domestic slaves.

None of the three households discussed above fits the picture of the "normal" Greek family. Instead what we see are households containing complex mixtures of close and distant kin, of families fractured by divorce or death residing in single households, creating composite family units. While households of the type discussed above may not have been the numerical norm in ancient Greece, and it is probably the case that the simple conjugal family was the most prevalent, the evidence cited above shows how mutable even that unit was over time – a point which becomes even more evident when we adopt an approach based on the life cycle.

Both historical studies and computer simulations have show that, with the type of demographic constraints outlined above, even if every family was consciously seeking to produce an extended or multiple household, only about 30 percent would ever be able to do it (Ruggles 1987, 120, building on and critiquing Wachter and Laslett 1978; Le Bras and

Wachter 1978; Benedict 1976, 221–2; Whitaker 1976). Recently Kertzer has raised questions about the "demographic limitation" theory of the formation of joint households, pointing out that these types do occur in well-documented historical cases. As he indicates, however, they appear primarily in areas where share-cropping is the dominant form of peasant land tenure (Kertzer 1984, 337–45; 1989, 1–16). The main point concerning the potential vertical extension remains intact: few grandparents would have survived for long after their children had reached adulthood and so the possible period for extension would have been short.

Some confirmation that this was the case in antiquity comes from an Athenian inscription (*IG* 2^2 2344). It contains a list of the members enrolled in the phratry (an association discussed later in Chapter 7) of Paiania, a region of Athens. Boys began the process of becoming fully integrated into their community by being introduced and enrolled in the phratry, an event which occurred when they reached puberty. In none of the eight households recorded on the roll were grandfathers alive when their eldest grandsons reached their early teens (Hedrick 1989, 131).

If we return to the figures for the mean family size derived from the ancient sources and add on the missing girls and factor in the development cycle, then it appears that ancient Greek society comes close to the mathematical maximum for the percentage of extended families at any single point in time. The numerous simple, nuclear households, so prominent in the historical record, represent then households on their way toward extension or demographic failures.

Widows

In many of the groups cited above which had demographic profiles and marriage patterns similar to ancient Greece, widows seem to be prominent. Given the ages at marriage and the ages at death for both men and women, even though men lived slightly longer than women, it was inevitable that if a woman survived the rigors of childbirth that there was a high probability that she would become a widow. Recent research on the subject has demonstrated that widows were numerous in the past and that their position in society was complex: if they were rich, then widows could have wielded considerable power; if they were poor, then widows were among the society's most vulnerable members (Chaytor 1980, 43–4; A. Wolf 1981; Holderness 1984; Brodsky 1986; Franklin 1986; Laslett 1988, 154–5; Chabot 1988).

In ancient Greece as well, widows appear prominently. Of the married women mentioned in the orations of Isaios, for example, 35 percent were at one point widows. For the large sample derived from Davies, the figure rises to closer to 40 percent; if we add on divorced women, then the figure increases to near 50 percent. Overwhelmingly as well it seems that widows were expected to live with their sons (Lysias 12.9–11; Lysias 24.6; Demosthenes 55.23; Demosthenes 57.31). It was, after all, the primary duty of children to care for an "aged" parent (Pseudo-Aristotle 1343b5; Isaios 2.10; Isaios 7.30). And for Theophrastos at least, the failure to care for one's widowed mother was the surest indication of complete moral bankruptcy (Theophrastos *Char* 6).

Amongst the widows whose life courses I was able to chart in the forensic speeches 65 percent remained unwed – a rather typical figure from the pre-industrial world (Livvi-Bacci 1981; J. E. Smith 1981; Schofield and Wrigley 1981; Corsini 1981). Only if there were no children or only infants would there be strong pressure on the woman to remarry (cf. W. E. Thompson 1972). Hunter's perceptive examination of the life of Kleoboule, the mother of Demosthenes, shows that widows could remain so if they desired and that they could exhibit considerable authority inside the household (V. Hunter 1989; on the position of old women in general see, Bremmer 1987).

Because of the large number of widows and their tendency to coreside with one of their children – a son if possible – there would, therefore, have been a considerable number of vertically extended families in ancient Greece. Given the rules concerning the obligation to see to the marriage arrangements of one's siblings, horizontally extended and multiple domestic units would have been fairly common as well.

The Life Cycle of the Ancient Household

Based on the evidence presented so far I propose the following reconstruction of the "average" ancient Greek household life cylce (figures 2.1 and 2.2). I have postulated a life cycle of 24 years. Given the demographic parameters, it seems to provide the best fit. Parenthetically, it should be pointed out that the final phase of the sequence set forth here seamlessly merges into Phase 1 of the next cycle and does not really have a separate existence on its own. It has been kept here for demonstrative purposes only. The 24-year life cycle of the household has been divided into eight three-year periods or *triennia*.

The new *oikos* was formed when the eldest son married and brought his bride into his natal household. The asummption here is that because of his age, patrivirilocal or, given that his father was probably deceased at this point, virilocal residence would have occurred. At this point, his age would have been somewhere in the middle to late 20s. Also resident in the household would have been his widowed mother, enjoying the later years of her fourth decade, and a teenage younger sibling (Figure 2, Phase 1).

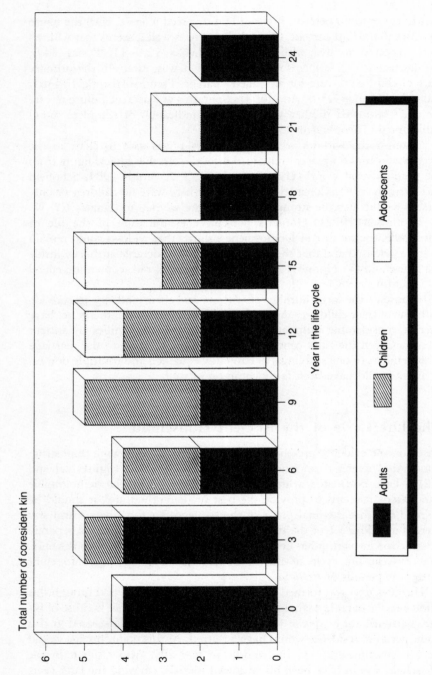

Fig. 2.1 Model of Ancient Household Life Cycle.

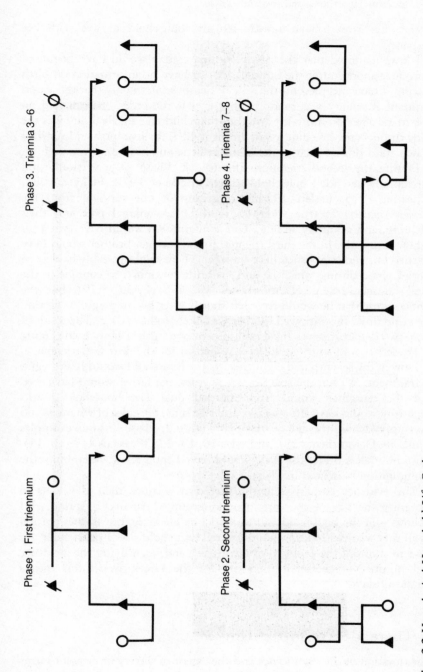

Fig. 2.2 Hypothetical Household Life Cycle.

Their sister would have already left the household to live with her husband.

I have assumed that the newly formed couple would have begun to reproduce shortly after the nuptials. As we have no information on birth spacing, I have accepted for the sake of demonstration only that the action of infant mortality was random, that is that the order of birth had no systematic effect on mortality and thus that children's survivability was the same through the breeding years. In the model, the live birth and survival of one child during each of the first three triennia has been proposed.

During the second triennium (figure 2.2, Phase 2), a vertically and horizontally extended household existed (Berkner 1972; Plakans 1984; Wheaton 1975; Laslett 1984a), consisting of one survivor from the parents' generation (the widowed mother), a conjugal pair and their offspring, and a solitary sibling. This configuration would have lasted for a short time only. In the third triennium, the younger brother would have married out and established his own *oikos*. There might possibly have been a brief phase during which he and his bride continued to coreside in the natal household (e.g., Demosthenes 39.24–5; Lysias 3.29), but the chances were that he would have left shortly after his marriage. At around the same time, the widowed mother was likely to have died. The result of these two departures was the establishment of a nuclear household (Figure 2, Phase 3). And so it would have remained for the next five triennia.

During the seventh and eight triennia the household would have begun to fragment. Within the space of a few years, the father would have died and the daughter would have married out. The household head's departure would have left a widow and two sons, the elder of whom would have approaching the age of majority (Figure 2, Phase 4; some examples of this are Demosthenes 29, 38; Lysias 10, 19, 32, 39; Isaios 1, 7, 10, 11). Once he took a bride, the cycle would have begun anew, resembling the configuration presented in Phase 1.

The evidence employed in the preceding sections then allows us to recognize the size of the coresident kingroup – parents, offspring, and siblings – in the household and to model its life cycle, but it does not tell us all that we need to know about overall household size. In particular, we have to confront the problem of identifying and quantifying the incidence and number of coresident non-kin: for the Greek world this means primarily slaves.

Is There a Slave in the House?

The question of the significance and the extent of slavery on peasant farms has been the subject of much debate recently among ancient historians. Geographically, the primary participants in the argument have chosen to focus on ancient Athens. One side argues that "the addition of some slave help to the farmer's own capacity was essential for all but the richest and the poorest" (Jameson 1977/78, 125). The farms of the richest were worked exclusively by slaves and other forms of dependent or hired labor and so slaves did represent an addition to the owner's labor because he himself did not work. The poorest held parcels of land so small as to obviate the need for additional labor. But for the majority of Athenian households, some slaves were desired and required. The opposing view contends that "most properties would [have been] worked by peasants and their families" (Wood 1983, 31; 1988). The modal household labor force, on the latter view then, consisted only of coresident kin with occasional assistance from non-resident kin, friends, and neighbors. My own view falls between the two. I argue that all but the poorest peasant households sought to own slaves, but that at all times it was difficult for most to do so and that slave ownership fluctuated in response to variations in the household life cycle. I begin by discussing the essential arguments of each side.

Jameson correctly eschews the "numbers game,"[3] preferring instead to focus on the structural factors which made slavery necessary for most households. His argument hinges on three interrelated hypotheses.

1   During the Classical period because of population growth, Athenian farmers needed to increase agricultural production, and this could only be accomplished through intensification, which in turn required higher levels of labor input (Jameson 1977/78, 129).

2   The Athenian political system (in the widest sense of the term) placed certain demands on its citizens which necessitated their absence from their farms frequently. Their ability to carry out their duties as citizens could have been compromised by the need to work longer hours on their farms. Therefore, in order to be a "model Athenian Citizen" (Jameson 1977/78, 124), a slave was required to supplant the citizen's labor.

3   Slaves were relatively cheap, at least when compared to the price of mules (150–200 drachmai for a slave as opposed to 225–400 for a mule (Jameson 1977/78, 139). Thus the social benefit of owning a slave outweighed the economic costs of purchasing one.

In addition to these more concrete arguments, there is the impressionistic evidence garnered from Greek literature which depicts slaves as being ubiquitous in ancient Athens. And for these reasons, the majority of Athenian peasant households owned slaves alongside whom they toiled in the fields when not called upon to participate in the affairs of state.

Wood concentrated her comments on the question of the linkage between intensification, labor, and political participation (Wood 1983, 6–15). While granting with unnecessary qualifications that intensification took place, she queried the presumed need for slaves in order to increase production. First, many peasant societies underwent a similar process of intensification and yet did not develop slavery (Wood 1983, 7–8). She supports this observation with the results of comparative studies (Boserup 1981, 8–28). As to proposed impact of citizenship, she observes "far from explaining why the ordinary Attic farmer might have been compelled to transfer some of the "intensified" labor to slaves, the citizenship of the Attic peasant actually *reduced* the need for labor intensification, in a sense off-setting demographic pressures, by limiting the need for surplus production in ways unknown in any other documented 'peasant' society" (Wood 1983, 8). The remainder of her critique of Jameson's work dwells on the comparatively low level of surplus extraction imposed by the Athenian state on its own citizens. This last observation concerning the role of the state is certainly correct, and it is a point I shall return to in a later chapter. Furthermore, she notes that peasants everywhere have to divide their time between productive and non-productive pursuits and that most are able to establish a balance without recourse to slavery (Wood 1983, 25). After a detailed discussion of De Ste Croix's work (1982), and a superficial review of the ancient sources for specifically agricultural slaves, she reaches the conclusion that most Athenian households did not possess slaves.

In support of this contention she cites works by Finley (1960, 56; 1980, 82). And, indeed, he did argue that most farms in the ancient world were operated by a peasant and his family. Nevertheless, what she fails to credit were Finley's observations concerning the deeply felt desire at all levels of ancient society to own slaves (Finley 1960).

Some aspects of her argument can be taken further. Wood never addressed the question of just how much time Athenians needed to devote to public life in order to fulfill their role as citizens. Recent assessments indicate that citizen participation in the political process at both the local and the statewide levels could easily have been infrequent and sporadic if so desired (M. H. Hansen 1983; L. B. Carter 1986; Whitehead 1986, 90–2). Even the inclusion of jury duty and the holding of political office do not change the picture very much. Military service and rowing were much more time consuming, but the latter called mainly on the very poor who may have been landless and on young men who had not yet established their own household and were perhaps expendable labor from their natal household. Other military services could readily have integrated into the agricultural cycle and therefore not have required that farmers be absent during periods of peak labor demand.

Some additional points support the argument of the non-viability of slave ownership for households of modest means. First, while a slave may have been cheaper than a mule, the purchase of either represented a considerable capital investment on the part of a four- to six-hectare farm, as a comparison of the price of a slave with other commodities demon-strates. For example, at the level of household caloric consumption used in this study (discussed in full in Chapter 4), the cost of a slave represented the same level of expenditure for the household as the purchase of wheat sufficient to feed it for 19 months.[4] A similar picture appears if we compare the price of a slave with livestock prices: sheep:slave, 16–20:1 goats:slave, 16:1; cattle:slave, 2:1 (livestock prices taken from Jameson 1988, 91; see also Osborne, 1985, 143). Finally, for 200 drachmai a man could have rented a functioning farm, including farm buildings (*IG* 2^2 2499). Slaves were not cheap.

The computer simulation models presented later on (in Chapter 4) indicate that a four- to six-, and perhaps even larger, hectare farm would have frequently been hard-pressed to produce enough to feed a household consisting of a coresident kingroup and slaves, let alone generate a surplus above subsistence large enough to permit the accumulation of sufficient expendable cash to purchase a slave. But the simulations also indicated that at certain phases of the household labor may have been in short supply and so the addition of a slave would have been economically feasible as well as socially desirable. These additional points might seem to tilt the balance in favor of Wood's position, but this is not necessarily so. By posing the problem in terms of a bipolar opposition between ownership and non-ownership and then concentrating on determining the relative ratio of one to the other, she oversimplifies a more complex reality and sets up an unanswerable question. Many of the arguments presented above concern the feasibility of slave ownership and tell us little about actual ownership. Ancient households clearly aspired to own slaves. Wealthy households owned slaves as a matter of course; poor households never had them; but in the middle, there was the majority of households which endeavored to invest in slaves when they could (a decision contingent on factors such as the stage of the household's life cycle, the labor supply available from resident kin, the size of the farm, the amount of investable capital at hand, and the extent of peer pressure to own slaves) and which were compelled occasionally to divest themselves of slaves by necessity. Therefore, the actual percentage of households possessing slaves at any one time was constantly changing in rhythm with the fortunes of individual households, and accordingly, attempting to specify a static figure for ownership is fruitless as well as misleading.

3   Adaptive Measures in the Agricultural System

The rain, the sun, the frost, they could all destroy me. I fight with lies. I fool myself into thinking I will survive.

Andreas Balokas

Agricultural Systems and Risk Minimization

Agricultural systems must contain mechanisms which allow for survival during periods of crop failure and recovery afterwards.

Anthony H. Galt

I argued in Chapter 1 that, in general, peasant agricultural production aimed primarily to minimize the risk of subsistence failure and to maximize the opportunities for survival (Lipton 1968, 330–4). In this chapter I analyze the various adaptive measures found in peasant agricultural systems generically and the ancient Greek agricultural systems specifically, which enable peasants to respond to ever-changing environmental and economic conditions. Throughout the emphasis is on options and on how, depending upon a variety of factors, Greek peasants could have chosen to employ certain ones which minimized risk. They constantly had to make critical decisions. In Barlett's words "Decision making involves evaluation of different options, usually followed by an assessment that one option is preferable. To understand agricultural decisions, the approach used to measure how farmers balance the costs and benefits of alternative strategies is crucial. The allocation of resources to alternative ends is seen in all aspects of agricultural production . . ." (Barlett 1980b, 137). Agricultural decision making should be viewed as a protracted "series of separate but linked sequential choices" (Ortiz 1980, 178; 1983) made by peasants from a range of alternatives on the basis of their knowledge of past events (yields), their "best guesses" as to probable outcome of the current event, and the constraints influencing their production aims, for example, size of farm, the worker:consumer ratio, and the size of externally generated exactions (Cancian 1980, 162–4; Barlett 1980a, 7–9; Gladwin 1980, 48; Bennett and Kanel 1983; De Vries 1980, 626).

Unlike anthropologists or development economists we cannot ask our subjects to rationalize their decisions nor can we peer into their households and observe them over time. Nowhere are the deficiencies of our sources for the domestic economy more frustratingly apparent than on this vital point. Consequently, we have to proceed with great caution. Armed with insights from the literature on agricultural decision making and empirical evidence from other peasant cultures, we can, nonetheless, attempt to elucidate the key options available in the agricultural systems of ancient Greece and indicate the ways that peasants employed them as adaptations to a hazard-fraught environment.

All across the Greek world the yields of the major subsistence crops varied greatly from year to year (Gallant 1982b, 23–36; Garnsey, Gallant and Rathbone 1984, 31–5; Garnsey 1988a, 10–17; Gallant 1989; 395–8; Garnsey and Gallant in progress; also, see below, table 4.10). Farmers ancient and modern, have had to gear their agricultural practices to this crucial fact. Failure to do so would have resulted in chronic malnutrition, deprivation, or even starvation. All agricultural systems represent a set of adaptations to certain specific, enduring environmental conditions (Gallant 1982a, 21–4; Gallant 1989, 396), and to other, more transient socio-political ones as well (Snaydon and Elston 1976; Barlett 1980a; Lees 1983, 187; Bennett and Kanel 1983, 233–6). There is a constant interplay between these extraneous factors and the household's production strategies. As Ellen puts it, "in an environment which is constantly changing, and where there is, therefore, continuous change in the constraints acting on the system, feedback operates between the subsystems to cause mutually adaptive changes within them" (Ellen 1982, 180). Most of the works devoted to ancient farming focus almost exclusively on technology to the detriment of a more dynamic economic analysis (e.g., Heitland 1921; K. D. White 1974; Spurr 1986). So rather than present yet another description of the technology of ancient farming, I follow the general line of approach set forth by Chayanov and others and view it as a series of articulated production strategies chosen by individual households on the basis of their perceived subsistence needs, their labor product, and the demands of extra-household claimants who had to be accommodated from the household's resources.

An agricultural system consists of all aspects of agrarian production, important among which are the selection of the species of crops grown, the timing of planting and harvesting, the fallow arrangements, and the post-harvest treatment of crops (Spencer and Stewart 1973; Duckham and Masefield 1970; Grigg 1974). I purposely have spoken of *agricultural systems* because at different times in various places and amongst different groups in ancient Greece several productive strategies were in use simultaneously. Given the nature of our evidence, it is difficult for us to pinpoint this variation across time and space in as detailed a fashion as we might wish. Instead what I propose is to define the full range of possible strategies available and then determine which configurations seem to have been the most consistently chosen. We can thereby elucidate those core adaptations of the ancient agricultural systems, ehance our understanding of the domestic economy, and erect the framework for the creation of a simulated "model" peasant household economy.

Adaptive Measures in Action

Embedded deep in the ancient agrarian systems was a coherent and integrated set of adaptive measures which allowed peasants the flexibility to alter their productive strategies so as to take account of the prevailing environmental conditions. Too frequently ancient historians have imposed a strait-jacket of uniformity and rigidity of practice on ancient farmers (as Halstead (1987a, 83–7) clearly demonstrates). The paucity of the sources is partly to blame, but a lack of familiarity with peasant agriculture has contributed as well. In breaking with these views, I align myself with recent work on Greek agriculture by, among others, Garnsey (1988a), Halstead (1981a; 1981b; 1987a; 1987b), and G. Jones (1987) in emphasizing the diversity of possible strategies and envisioning agricultural practices as the results of specific decisions made by ancient farmers.

Crop Diversification

I begin with crop diversification. This refers to the growing of a wide variety of crops, each possessing slightly different nutritional requirements and growth cycles. "Crop diversification," Liebenow states, "provides protection against plant diseases as well as against drought and other vagaries of weather, since each crop has it own specific susceptibilities" (Liebenow 1987, 383). It is an effective, and thus widely employed, risk-buffering mechanism. In terms of productivity, diversification sacrifices output per crop for output reliability of all the crops. For this reason colonial empires in the recent past compelled peasants to monocrop, the opposite of diversification, in order to increase the production of certain, often export-bound crops (Scott 1976, 200–1; Goodman and Redclift 1981, 68–99; Greenough 1982; 62–9, Watts 1983, 20, 148–86; McCann 1987a, 149; Cummings 1987, 112–17; Liebenow 1987, 382).

Peasants in southeast Asia integrate maize and cassava into their agrarian system because both of them have growth cycles and nutritional requirements different from rice, the dominant crop in the region (Scott 1977, 17; Seavoy 1986, 131). Indian farmers likewise cultivate a wide range of cereals, pulses, and fruit crops as a means of spreading risk (Seavoy 1986, 248). In pre-industrial Europe, certain cereals, such as hard wheats and rye, were sown as complementary pairs; in addition, peasants also grew numerous other crops (Halpern 1958, 76; Sutherland 1981, 447; post 1985, 101–4). Crop diversification amongst African and Middle Eastern cultures is very well documented (in addition to the works cited above, see, Wisner, and Mbithi 1974, 93; Hill 1982, 57; de Garine and Koppert 1988, 231) and is especially prevalent in semi-arid regions (A. Cohen 1965, 20; I. Singh and Subramanian 1986, 96). Crop diversification is thus a very widespread practice.

In the Mediterranean regions, peasants consistently cultivate in combination wheat, barley, a wide range of pulses including chickpeas, broad beans, lentils, kidney beans, and peas, maize, millet, vines, olves, and fruits (Diamond 1947, 13; Allbaugh 1953, 266–7; de Vooys and Piket 1958, 52; de Vooys 1959, 32; Aschenbrenner 1976, 210; Bialor 1976, 227; R. M. Bell 1979, 18; Forbes 1976b, 5–11; 1982, 312–23). A detailed statistical examination of recent agronomic data from Greece shows how the major subsistence crops can be meshed into a coherent production system (see Appendix 1). Based on this material, we can infer the following.

First, wheat and barley yields are strongly correlated, as we should expect given that both occupy the same environmental niche (Gallant 1989, 399–400). Broad beans as well co-vary with both wheat and barley in most places. They too are autumn-sown. Because of the need for considerable quantities of moisture and their low resistance to drought, their growth cycle more closely than the other legumes approximates that of wheat and barley (Arnon 1972, 235–7; Garnsey, Gallant, and Rathbone 1984, 33). Indeed, only at Athens, Samos, and Larisa (in the region of Thessaly) is there no statistically significant correlation between them and at least one of the primary cereal crops.

Second, lentils and chickpeas are sown in late winter and early spring; both are drought resistant once established but need considerable quantities of moisture early in their growth cycle (Arnon 1972, 237–40; Saxena 1982, 111). Moreover, since they can be planted either in late fall–early winter or at different times during the winter, they can give the farmer a degree of flexibility not possible with some of the other species. Thus, because they can occupy a number of different environmental niches, statistically we see no clear pattern of co-variance with the main autumn-sown crops. In some regions, Achaia, Aitholia, Herakleion, Ioannina, Kalmata, Kozani, and Phthiotis, they are correlated with all the other crops. In the Argolid, Athens, Kavala, Larisa, Lesbos, Samos, and Thessaloniki, they clearly complement those species. Lentils and chickpeas can thus be integrated into a unified cropping strategy in such a way so as to spread the risk of failure.

Third, the figures in Appendix 1 indicate that in some regions the species analyzed co-vary completely. It is for this reason that farmers grow a number of other crops as well; in modern Greence for example, peas, vetch, millet, maize, kidney beans, rye, and oats are all commonly grown.

Further analyses are required in order to strengthen my argument, but nonetheless the very fact that they are grown is evidence for crop diversification.

From the material presented so far, we can conclude that crop diversification is a production strategy commonly employed by peasants in diverse parts of the world, including the Mediterranean. Furthermore, quantitative analyses indicate that they can be integrated into a coherent system. We can now examine the evidence for crop diversification from antiquity.

Our best source on ancient Greek agriculture is Theophrastos. This pupil of Aristotle was a polymath of prodigious dimensions whose interests extended to include plant biology and agronomy. It was never his intention to describe peasant agriculture, but scattered throughout his works are specific references to actual practices and recommendations concerning others. From his texts we can conclude that he knew of certain practices and occasionally we can infer that that knowledge was common. Theophrastos clearly envisages a cropping sequence much like the one outlined above. Begin with barley, wheats, and broad beans in the autumn, he states, and follow them with lentils, chickpeas, and peas in the spring (Theophrastos *HP* 8.1.1–4). Save the millets, sesame, celery, and hedge-mustard for summer (Theophrastos *HP* 8.1.4). Theophrastos recommends that farmers should grow a very wide variety of crops whose growing seasons complement one another (Theophrastos *HP* 8.1.2). His views find support in other sources.

Writers as diverse in their topics and interests as Athenaios, the comedian Aristophanes (Ehereberg 1951),and Galen (Fidanze 1979, 81) provide ample testimony to the fact that ancient farmers produced and consumed a very diverse variety of crops. Analyses of archaeological deposits tell the same tale (Kroll 1984; G. Jones 1987; Halstead 1987b).

Crop diversification was one of the primary adaptive mechanisms available to ancient farmers for minimizing risk. But, as I noted above in regard to the impact of colonial empires in the modern world, the viability of diversification was contingent on the household being able to decide for itself which crops to plant – a situation unlikely to occur if it was compelled to produce larger quantities of a single crop.

Intercropping

At its simplest intercropping refers to the cultivation of two different plant species on the same piece of land. As a production strategy it is predicted upon the existence of crop diversity. Agronomists have identified three variant, though not mutually exclusive, categories of intercropping – mixed cultivation, row intercropping, and relay cropping (Isom and Worker 1979, 206–8; Okigbo 1980, 234).

Mixed cropping refes to the cultivation of two crops together with no arrangement as to the spacing or distribution of the crops. Isom and Worker list a number of advantages and disadvantages to mixed cropping. Among the disadvantages are:

1 Crop care and cultivation require more labor, especially if the crops are slightly out of the phase. In this case weeding and harvesting, for example, would have to be done at different times.
2 Crop management requires a greater investment of time.
3 The crops have to be chosen very carefully otherwise through competition one might destroy the other.
4 The yield per crop is usually lower. (Wylie 1989, 169)

The advantages clearly show how mixed cropping can act as a risk-buffer and help to explain why it, in conjunction with row intercropping and relay cropping, are practiced in so many areas of the world. Of particular importance for us is the intercropping of cereals and legumes (*India*: McAlpin 1979, 47; 1983, 12; Seavoy 1986, 248; *Mexico*: Kirby 1974, 125; *Africa*: Isom and Worker 1979, 207; Okigbo 1980, 235; van Apeldoorn 1981, 92; Hill 1982, 179–80; I. Singh and Subramanian 1986, 96; *Syria*: Saxena 1982, 114; *Italy*: Delano Smith 1979, 176; *Greece*: Allbaugh 1953, 258; Myrick and Witucki 1971, 11; Forbes 1976a; 1982, 312–23). If the plants selected are compatible, then we find:

1 Greater overall yields per hectare;
2 better control of weeds through plant competition and the elimination of pests;
3 the elimination of lodging, in the case of cereals;
4 a lessening of soil erosion because of the more extensive plant canopy;
5 the maintenance of soil fertility – provided that the farmer mixes certain legumes and cereals; and
6 greater assurance of at least some return because of the diminished likelihood of all the crops failing simultaneously. (Isom and Worker 1979, 206; Snaydon and Elston 1976, 50; Spitters 1980, 221–3; Okigbo 1980, 239–42)

All told, Isom and Worker conclude that "*mixed cropping is a method of crop insurance against failure to produce food*" 1979, 206 (my italics).

Intercropping and relay cropping are simply variant forms of mixed cropping. With intercropping, the plants are planted in rows, particularly if cereals and legumes or cereals and vines are involved. Since vines and olives are usually planted in rows or with wide spaces between them, they are ideally suited for intercropping with either cereals or legumes (Gavrielides 1976, 148; Okigbo 1980, 239). If the latter two are to be cultivated together, then they must be sown by "dibbling" (the planting of seeds individually often with a drill stick) rather than by broadcasting (Isom and

Worker 1979, 207). This would increase the amount of labor required to plant the crop. Compared to the benefits derived from intercropping, for many peasant households apparently, that is a small price to pay.

Relay cropping refers to the planting of two different crops successively on the same piece of land during a single growth season (Ison and Worker 1979, 207; Spitters 1980, 226–7; Okigbo 1980, 234). This last aspect distinguishes relay cropping from continuous cropping. The requirements of relay cropping in semi-arid climates such as Greece are fourfold:

1   The paired crops must have short growing seasons so that both obtain sufficient moisture and time to mature.
2   The character of the first crop must be such that it can be harvested during the rainy season.
3   The first crop must not leave harmful residues which may impair the growth of the second crop or provide a habitat for pests or disease.
4   A large pool of labor must be available to harvest the first crop, to prepare the seedbed, and to plant the second over a relatively short time span. (Isom and Worker 1979, 207)

Combinations known to be cultivated in this manner are three-month wheat or barley and lentils, wheat or barley and cowpeas, wheat or barley and millet, wheat and vetch, sorghum and millet (Isom and Worker 1979, 207; Okigbo 1980, 239; G. Jones 1987, 118). The primary advantages of relay cropping are (1) a greater increase in yield per hectare; (2) minimal disruption to the overall annual crop sequence; and (3) greater flexibility because the farmer does not have to decide about the second crop until the disposition of the first becomes evident. In addition, the only prerequisites for the implementation of the strategy are sufficient labor-power and the right seeds.

All three versions of intercropping were known and presumably employed in ancient Greece. Theophrastos provides possible testimony to relay cropping in his discussion of quick-ripening barley species. In Chalkeia on Rhodes, he states, they sow wheat and barley together in the autumn, then they harvest the barley early and sow some more which they reap "with the remaining crops" (Theophrastos HP 8.2.9). His intention here is to demonstrate the exceptional fertility of the soils at Chalkeia; nevertheless, the passage indicates an awareness of the possible application of intercropping. Moreover, from his discussion of the various pulses it appears that he considers the relay cropping of pulses, particularly chickpeas, a viable possibility (Theophrastos HP 8.5.6).

In references to row intercropping, Theophrastos notes that wheat, barley, and certain pulses can be planted at various times during the growing season and can be integrated with vines and olives. Although he does not specifically state that they should be interspersed with another crop, it is implied (in particular, HP 8.3.5, 8.6.1; CP 3.6.1). I would tentatively suggest then that integrating cereals, pulses, and tree crops was a characteristic feature of the ancient Greek countryside just as it is in many regions of the modern.

In regard to the mixing of seeds from two species with similar growth cycles and sowing them together on the same plot, the textual sources are mute. It is very common in modern Greece for wheat and barley to be mixed (called *smigo*) and sown (Jardé [1925] 1979, 9, 77, 204–5; M. Clark 1977, 54; Kondomihis 1985, 52) and I suspect that it went on in antiquity as well. At present, some archaeological deposits from Makedonia may be indicative of the mixing of emmer wheat and spelt, but it is unclear whether the seeds came from the threshing floor that way or were mixed later in the storeroom (G. Jones 1987, 120–1). More research needs to be done on this subject before the argument can be conclusively proven.

Intercropping in its variant forms was available to ancient peasants and it provided them with additional options for coping with climatic variability by reducing the risk that all their food crops would have been affected by a single trauma. Successful implementation of intercropping required that the household have the ability to muster its labor resources at critical times of the year and have to hand the requisite seeds. Therefore, any external developments which impaired their capacity to do either of these things would have rendered intercropping irrelevant.

Fragmentation of Land Holdings

One of the most common characteristics of peasant agriculture is the fragmentation of land holdings (Chayanov [1966] 1986, 174–9). The practice has been repeatedly observed and frequently bemoaned in regions scattered across the globe (*African*: Hankins 1974, 103; McCann 1987a, 147; Vaughan 1985, 183; van Apeldoorn 1981, 92; Hill 1982, 53–54; *India and Asia*: Scott 1976, 14; Popkin 1979, 49–50; C. A. Gregory 1982, 98; McAlpin 1979, 147; 1983, 12; *Europe*: Seavoy 1986, 85; Banfield 1958, 50; Cole and Wolf 1974, 8; Fenoaltea 1975; 1976, 129; 1977; Galt 1975, 1, 3, 4–8; 1979; McCloskey 1972, 19; 1976, 126, 131; 1977; J. Schneider 1969, 114; B. M. S. Campbell 1984, 90; R. M. Smith 1984, 140). To many development economists, the seemingly excessive division of land holdings into numerous widely scattered plots epitomizes the "irrationality" and "inefficiency" of peasant agriculture (e.g. K. Thompson 1963, 170–2; Damaskenides 1965, 25–8); in the view of one pair of physical geographers, it is simply "a well-know evil" (de Vooys and Piket 1958, 38). McCloskey summarizes concisely the gist of the most common objection to land fragmentation: "This is a most peculiar way to hold land, or at any rate so it has seemed to most observers of the system . . . because it appears to *reduce output*, a strange burden for a community near starvation to assume" (1976, 124, my italics). And yet the practice is ubiquitous and enduring. A more in-depth examination will help us to understand the underlying logic behind it.

The strategy of land fragmentation has a long pedigree in modern Greece. A statistical study of an eighteenth-century land cadaster for the Baron Duodo's estate on the island of Kerkyra shows that his 2,085 hectare estate was divided into 625 plots located in 21 villages scattered all across the island (Gallant 1986b, 526).

Assessments of land holdings among peasant families in more recent times shows much the same thing only on a smaller scale. In Messenia, Sauerwein found that on average households owned 2.5 hectares of land divided into 5.4 plots, but occasionally holdings were divided into 18 and 19 plots (1968, 227, 229). In the Argolid, he observed that the average was 3.7 hectares separated into 6.7 plots, figures which he found to be comparable with those from the Peloponnesos as a whole (3.5 hectares in 6.4 plots) (Sauerwein 1971, 33). On Crete, Allbaugh reported that 52 percent of all farms were divided into between 5 and 15 plots (1953, 538), and Panayiotou and Papachristodoulou discovered that in Cyprus the average peasant held 2.3 hectares in 8.5 plots (1983, 3). Figures of similar magnitude are reported from Boiotia (Slaughter and Kasimis 1986, 130–1), Thessaly (de Vooys 1959, 38), Arkadia (de Vooys and Piket 1958, 38), Methana (Forbes 1982, 330–4), and the island of Melos (Wagstaff and Augustson 1982, 108).

Country-wide, Damaskenides reported that the average number of plots per household varied between 7.5 and 12.5 and that they ranged in size from .48 to .78 of a hectare (1965, 28), and his figures are in line with those produced by Kenneth Thompson's survey of 210 farms scattered across Greece (1963, 43–199). Clearly land fragmentation is an integral part of the agrarian systems of modern Greece.

The traditions of devolving property through pure partible inheritance (that is the division of the household estate into equal shares for each heir) and the dowering of daughters with land are often held responsible for land fragmentation (Seavoy 1986, 67; Damaskenides 1965, 28; Slaughter and Kasimis 1986, 130; de Vooys 1959, 38; McNall 1974, 52; Galt 1975, 3; Kenna 1976b, 27; Forbes 1982, 131–57). And indeed they are very effective mechanisms for this purpose. Unfortunately, much of the literature critical to land fragmentation seems to envisage these customs as operating with a will of their own, independent of the peasants themselves. "Economists, government planners and the representative of international agencies have generally viewed [land fragmentation] as a valueless result of egalitarian inheritance systems, of irrational attachments to particular parcels, or of general hunger for land; as, in short, a pointless obstacle to agricultural progress on a par with scared cows and excessive numbers of feast days, to be cleared away, if necessary by force, as soon as possible" (McCloskey 1976, 126).

The argument goes that land is divided into tiny parcels because of inheritance and dowry, and households then have to deal with these uneconomical bits of land. Land fragmentation is, therefore, externally imposed on the household. In fact, the opposite is the case. Rather than being maladaptive, pure partible inheritance and dowering in land have continued precisely because they provide the means to desirable ends. First, dowry and partible inheritance work together to provide the newly formed household with sufficient land to survive (Schlegal and Eloul 1988, 301–2; de Vooys 1959, 38; Douglass 1980, 344), and second, they ensure that the new household possesses land drawn from various areas (that is some from the territory of the wife's natal household and some from the groom's), thereby allowing them to exploit different micro-environments. Consequently, fragmentation of land holdings provides the household with a way of reducing subsistence risk by ensuring that it will take more than a small, localized trauma to wipe out all of the household's crops. Microspatial environmental diversity is in this way made to work to the farmer's benefit, a point peasants make clear when asked about it.

"Why should the plots be all together? We are more secure this way; fire, bad weather, and other things won't get all our crops." So Kenneth Thompson was told by a Greek farmer when conducting his survey (1963, 170–1). Thompson, nevertheless, went on to upbraid him for the practice. McNall was told the same thing when he asked Andreas Balokas, a peasant from Attica, about fragmentation. "'Why aren't [the field] all together, Andreas? You work even harder [with them spilt up].' 'Yes,' he replied, 'but who can tell what will happen? Maybe the hail will fall on my wheat fields here. If it does, I will still have my other plot. *I will have something to eat*" (McNall 1974, 58; my italics). When asked, peasants repeatedly stated that risk minimization was their intention with land fragmentation; like Andreas Balokas, they aim to ensure that at least some food would be available from some of their fields (Banfield 1958, 60; Seavoy 1986, 248; C. A. Gregory 1982, 98).

More rigorous support for the correctness of the peasants' justification of land fragmentation comes from McCloskey's work on medieval England. He compared the amount of variation of income on scattered and consolidated holdings and concluded that

> The results are strong. With scattered holdings peasants faced disaster – disaster not meaning, of course, starvation for everyone in the community, but misery for most that was worthy of memory, prayer and fear – about one year in thirteen. With consolidated holdings, forsaking the advantages of [crop] diversificaiton, they would have faced it about one year in nine. To put the case another way, scattering doubles the probability of surviving twenty years and triples the probability of surviving thirty years without disaster. (McCloseky 1976, 132)[5]

Similar analyses conducted by Forbes on data from Methana produced analogous results (Forbes 1982, 328–50). Cultivating scattered plots of land effectively reduces the probability of a total production failure.

Turning to ancient Greece, there is no direct discussion of farm fragmentation. Instead we have to look to sources which provide us with indirect confirmation of the practice of holding land in scattered plots and the existence of cultural traditions. On the basis of analogies drawn from comparative evidence we can infer fragmented farms.

Occasionally we gain insights into the geographical distribution of an individual's property because of some special occurrence in their lives. Such is the case with the men whose property was auctioned in Athens in 415/4 BC. Many of them owned land located in different parts of Attica as well as outside of it (Pritchett 1953; 1956, 275–6; Osborne 1985, 51). These were, of course, exceptional men who owned larger amounts of land scattered over greater distances than was possible for a peasant. I would suggest, however, that their exceptionality lay in the scale at which their estates were fragmented rather than in the practice itself. In the forensic speeches from fourth-century Athens, there are 21 instances where an individual's property holdings are made known; in 16 of these more than one plot of land was owned (Osborne 1985, 48). Osborne also discusses a group of Athenian inscriptions from the fourth century which record sales of land confiscated from condemned debtors by representatives of the state (1985, 52). He found that 6 (out of 19) men owned land in the deme, or county, adjacent to their own and 13 held land in distant demes. These men clearly were spreading their holdings widely across Attica. Moreover, it seems highly unlikely that Theophrastos was alone in appreciating that the agroclimate varied across Attica (*HP* 8.2.11). Thus the acquisition of land scattered in different regions could well have been intentional.

In his will, Kossos of Dodona in Epiros specificed how his four different plots of land were to be disposed (Dareste, Haussoullier, and Reinach [1895] 1965, 61). Unfortunately this is the only extant will in which the property of the deceased is explicitly catalogued. In most of the others, some variant of the formula "the house and all properties" with no further qualification is employed (Dareste, Haussoullier, and Reinach [1895] 1965, 59).

If the linkage between the practices of devolving land by pure partible inheritance and dowering with property and land fragmentation is accepted, then after a generation or two ancient Greek peasants would have work farms consisting of numerous, scattered plots of land.

Pure partible inheritance was the legal norm in ancient Greece (Willetts 1967, 19–20, Gortyn Law Code col. 4, 35–40; A. R. W. Harrison 1968, 130–2; Lane Fox 1983, 211–16). Hesiod's poem *Works and Days* has as its centerpiece the squabbling between the poet and his brother over the division of their partimony. From at least 700, it would seem that siblings quarreling over an inheritance was a literary *topos* comprehensible to ancient Greeks (Lamberton 1988). And it seems to have remained a practical problem as well, thus the custom of drawing lots for apportioning patrimones ([Demosthenes] 48.12; Lysias 16.12; Lane Fox 1983, 212–13; Levy 1959).

Lane Fox correctly reminds us that the legal prescription of pure partible inheritance did not guarantee its universal application. As he points out, households in other cultures find ingenious ways to circumvent the law (1983, 210, 219–20). Two points need clarification however. First, he implicitly assumes that land fragmentation was undesirable and thus to be avoided. But as we have seen, that was probably not the case. Second, the comparative evidence he cites for noncompliance refers primarily to the wealthier members of society. They sought to keep together their very large estates as an economic unit, something affluent households could do because they produced enough to ensure an income for all of the children. And because of their access to education and the other privileges of wealth, siblings could find alternative livelihoods (Martinez-Alier 1971, 28; J. P. Cooper 1976, 268–76; Douglass 1980, 348; Pedlow 1982; Bonfield 1986). None of these factors hold true for peasant families (Douglass 1980, 344). Ancient peasants then probably adhered more strictly to the norm of pure partible inheritance than their wealthier compatriots.

Dowry and indirect dowry were customary all across the Greek world (Wolff 1944; Schaps 1979, 74–88; Schlegal and Eloul 1988, 293–303; Cox 1988, 382–4; Foxhall 1989, 11–13). Obviously this did not preclude a woman from marrying without a dowry, but certainly there were strong social pressures on her family to provide her with one, and the gossip would have been malicious if they failed to do so (Cox 1988, 384; Foxhall 1989, 12). Whether or not land was included in the dowry varied from place to place. Foxhall argues that land was probably included in dowries among the poor at Athens (Foxhall 1989, 12 n. 58), and certainly at Gortyn on Crete (Willetts 1967, 20–2, Gortyn Law Code col. 6), at Mykonos (Dareste, Haussoullier, and Reinach [1895] 1965, 51, cl. 7 and 8; *SIG*[3] 1215), and Tinos (Dareste, Haussoullier, and Reinach [1895] 1965, 64–106) this was the case. Guiraud has marshalled additional evidence and arugued the case for the inclusion of land in dowries ([1893] 1979, 242–3; Schaps 1979).

Thus, in ancient Greece, as in many other peasant societies, farmers sought to minimize the risk of losing all their food crops by obtaining land, often in very small plots, widely scattered around their abode. In doing so they exploited localized microenvironments but at the cost of increased labor expenditure in travel time.

Cropping Strategies

The three adaptive mechanisms discussed so far were the primary ones peasants utilized to minimize risk. They had access to other, more minor ones as well. At every stage of production, the farmer had options which enabled him to adjust his strategy to suit the prevailing climatic conditions. While these gave him flexibility in responding to conditions, their efficacy was limited to only minor short-term fluctuations. Here again, each of these options required that the household have the capacity to employ its resources with impunity.

Sowing Rates   One of the first decisions a farmer had to make concerned the sowing rate. His choice determined the level of output. Ancient historians, in their search for an answer to the question of the "productivity" of ancient agriculture, have occasionally imposed a rigid strait-jacket on peasants (e.g., White 1965; J. K. Evans 1981, 429), as Halstead wittily observes (1987a, 85). For the peasant farmer, there was no "normal" seed:yield ratio. Instead, his sowing rate each year was determined by considerations like the amount of precipitation which had already fallen, the types of soil on his land, the life-cyle stage of his household, the number of consumers in his household, the available labor product, the amount of seed in storage, and the level of the previous year's harvest. Depending upon these, he could alter the sowing rate to suit both the prevailing conditions and his immediate production goals. A more detailed examination of the agronomic literature and some examples drawn from peasant farms demonstrate how varying the sowing rate operates as a flexible adaptive measure for minimizing risk.

"One of the main factors determining the optimum sowing rate is available moisture" (Peterson 1965, 228), and "the main factor determining the rate of seeding usually adopted in dry regions is the amount of moisture expected to be available to the crop: The drier the conditions, the more sparse the stand sown" (Arnon 1972, 48). These are representative of sentiments expressed by agronomists. By varying the sowing rate, the farmer exerts control over the amount of competition between plants for moisture in the soil. Dry conditions require a light sowing because this optimizes the quantity of water available to each plant and thus increases the probability of a successful growth cycle (Isom and Worker 1979, 213; Fredrick 1965, 149). Two points need to be stressed. First, both authors indicate that moisture is the key factor in determining the sowing rate, and second, that the decision about the precise rate is based on the farmer's expectations, which are based on climatic variability over the previous few years. As Halstead puts it "the farmer is aiming at a moving target with a weapon of gradually shifting calibre" (1987a, 85).

After moisture, soil type is the most important environmental consideration. With heavy, clay-rich soils the farmer needs to sow more profusely in order to ensure successful establishment of the crop and tillering (Peterson 1965, 228–9; Arnon 1972, 48).[6] Figure 3.1 depicts the hypothetical relationship between moisture, soil type, and sowing rates.

In addition to these purely environmental considerations, the farmer must also decide upon which production goals best serve the interests of his household in any given year: does he need to maximize the yield per unit area (i.e. total output in kilograms:hectare) or the yield per quantity of seed (i.e. the ratio between kilograms of seed sown:kilograms of seeds produced) (Bland 1971, 27).

Table 3.1 portrays the relationship between sowing rate, total output, and seed:yield ratio based on data from the eastern Mediterranean. Experiments on a farm in Cyprus showed that both wheat and barley when sown more lightly by drilling rather than more heavily with broadcasting produced, respectively, 23 percent and 37 percent higher yields (Payiatas and Papachristodoulou 1973, 6). The reason for this is that heavier sowing leads to a higher density of plants per square meter but lessens the number of tillers each plant sends out. Thus the larger number of plants produces on aggregate more grain, but because of the reduction in the number of tillers, each individual plant produces less. With lighter sowing, the opposite occurs. Each plant sends out more tillers, thus increasing the

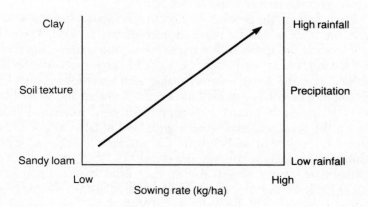

Fig. 3.1 Relationship between Soil Texture, Precipitation, and Sowing Rates.

Table 3.1   Relationship between sowing rates, total output, and seed:yield ratio

| Sowing rate (kg/ha) | Wheat | |
	Yield (kgs)	Return
60	1,460	1:24.3
100	1,520	1:15.2
140	1,560	1:11.1
Sowing rate (kg/ha)	Lentils	
	Yield (kgs)	Return
80	865	1:10.8
120	948	1:7.9
160	1,008	1:6.3
200	1,029	1:5.2

Sources: Worcellow 1969, 505; Saxena 1982, 116.

return per seed but lowering the total output per unit of land (Snaydon and Elston 1976, 49; Sinha 1977, 58–9).

The figures in table 3.1 demonstrate clearly that if a farmer desires to produce the maximum amount, all environmental variables being equal, he should sow as heavily as possible. If, however, he needs to conserve seeds, then the best strategy is to sow more lightly. Some examples show how this gives the farmer response flexibility.

A poor crop from the previous year could necessitate a lower sowing rate because the seeds would be required immediately as food. Lower than normal levels of precipitation during the pre-sowing season could dictate a lighter sowing because seed might be needed in case a second crop has to be planted. But, the saving a farmer makes with lower sowing rates comes at the cost of greater labor input. Lower rates of sowing and wider spacing between plants create greater opportunity for weed infestation. Success hinges on the household expending a great deal of labor at just the right moment. L. S. Jordan and Shaner, for example, emphasize that the scheduling of weeding is critically important (1979, 267).

Furthermore, results of tests run on data from Portugal suggest that output at lower sowing rates may be more stable. Cutileiro recorded figures on sowing rates and yields from the area of Villa Nova over a period of 44 years. He categorized seeding rates as either high (approximately 90 kg/ha) or low (approximately 70 kg/ha) (Cutileiro 1971, 300–1). I calculated coefficients of variation for total output at both the high and low sowing rates and they indicate that at the low rate output varied by 31.4 percent per year, whereas at the higher rate the figure was 38.3 percent.

These results are suggestive rather than conclusive. More research needs to be done on this problem before we can be sure of this observation. What we can conclude at this point though is that variable sowing rates provide the household with an adaptation to both environmental conditions and economic-demographic circumstances.

Theophrastos was knowledgeable in the ways that variable sowing rates could be used, and I do not think that we stretch the bounds of credibility to suppose that others appreciated them as well. He emphasizes the giving of careful consideration to soil type when deciding on the sowing rate, and advises sowing heavy stands on clay-rich soils and light stands on sandy soils (*HP* 8.6.2). As do modern agronomists, he also appreciated the vital role of climate (*HP* 8.7.6). It seems to me quite likely that peasants in the past tailored their sowing rates in the manner described above.

Weeding   Another adaptive mechanism related to the last is weeding. I argued earlier that in order for the manipulation of lower sowing rates to work effectively, the household would have needed to expend much more effort weeding to diminish competition between the desired domesticates and their unwanted rivals for vital soil moisture. Accordingly the household could buffer itself from crop yield fluctuations by intensifying weeding as needed.

Some comparative figures demonstrate just how important the removal of weeds can be (see table 3.2). Jordan and Shaner report results in line with Basler's work (1979). They found that the yields of most cereals are reduced by approximately 70 percent if no steps are taken to destroy weeds (Jordan and Shaner 1979, 267). Sinha reports that on average legume yields are reduced by 50–60 percent and in extreme circumstances, yields may be lowered by up to 85 percent unless some weeding is done (1977, 91–2; see also Skerman 1977, 161). According to Smartt, after the agroclimate, weeding has the greatest impact on crop yields (1976, 176–7).

Weeds create problems because they adapt well to local conditions and so they will be intense, successful competitors unless humans intervene. Before the advent of chemical weed-killers, the only ways to remove weeds

Table 3.2 Impact of weeding on the yield of lentils

Sowing rate (kg/ha)	Clean weeded (kg)	Unweeded (kg)
100	642.3	59.8
150	546.8	89.9
200	440.5	61.9

Source: Basler 1982, 145.

were to pull them up by hand, to uproot them with a hoe, to cut them with a sickle, or to plow them under. All are extremely time-consuming, labor intensive tasks. Estimates of the amount of time involved vary, but all point to the the same conclusion. Jordan and Shaner found that one half the total labor input on some farms was for weeding. Lewis noted that peasants often spent three times more effort weeding than plowing (1949). Moreover, crops need to be cleaned of weeds more at certain junctures in their growth cycle than others (Jordan and Shaner 1979, 267). Basler found that on average 56 man-days per hectare were expended weeding lentils (1982, 147). But the potential reduction in yield required it.

Theophrastos once again provides much valuable information. He is acutely aware of the importance of weeding, and spends a considerable amount of space discussing which species are the most troublesome and the ways of dealing with them. For example he warns that if the farmer does not take action against the dreaded bedstraw, then he can easily lose his entire lentil crop to it (*HP* 8.8.4). Wheat and barley could be overcome by darnel. Some believed that wheat "could be transformed" into darnel if the farmer was not careful (*HP* 8.7.1). Weeding provided ancient farmers with a means of conserving soil moisture and yields, if labor was available in the household and could be disposed of freely.

Seedbed Preparation and Plowing   Another management decision peasants have to make involves the preparation of the seedbeds for their crops. They can vary the timing, frequency, and equipment involved in seedbed preparation (or tillage) according to the prevailing, and predicted, conditions, and their production goals. Two methods predominated – hoeing and plowing. Often these two techniques are set in an evolutionary sequence with hoeing representing the more "primitive" technology. This is misguided. One technique never totally supplanted the other. In antiquity, for example, the plow and the hoe were used side by side; a preference for one or the other depended on factors like the size of the holding and the abundance of labor (Goody 1976). While the bulk of the literary sources focus on plowing (Theophrastos *HP* 8.1; Xenophon *Oik* *16.14–15*), the discovery of hoes at ancient Greek habitation sites shows that they were widely employed as well (*Olynthos*: Robinson 1941, 343–4). Which of those two techniques a farmer opted for represented a decision made repeatedly in response to numerous variables, and by varying his selection he could adapt his production strategies to changing conditions.

The two aims of tillage are the conservation of soil moisture and the creation of a layer of topsoil which is loose, open, and composed of fairly uniformly sized particles. Both allow seeds to establish themselves easily and to obtain moisture and nutrients more efficiently. The second of these is accomplished by "slacking," a "process by which the larger clods and aggregates formed by tillage are reduced to smaller particles, perhaps even to individual soil grains, upon wetting. The destruciton of the larger particles decreases void sizes and porosity and increases interparticle cohesion by bringing particles into closer contact" (Henderson 1979, 225). Because of the effect of slacking, the peasant farmer can exert some control over the movement of moisture in the soil. Frequent but shallow working of the land can help to conserve water, an aspect of critical importance in semi-arid regions. Khan reports that in India fields tilled with a wooden plowshare at a depth of five inches yielded more than those prepared to a greater depth with an iron-shod plow. The shallower plowing produced a friable layer of top-soil but prevented extensive soil moisture loss (Khan 1963, 68–9; see also Blok 1969, 97; Forbes 1976b, 5–11). Clarke and Russell as well present clear evidence of a strong correlation between the attention given to seedbed preparation and the level of productivity (1979, 296). Careful tillage was very much to the farmer's advantage.

The essential differences between tilling the land with an animal-drawn plow and working it with a hand-held hoe are labor-time and capital investment. Tillage with a hoe is extremely labor intensive but low in capital costs. All the farmer needs is a strong back, a stick, and a metal hoe-head. With a plow, the opposite is the case. Labor time is lessened – according to Oscar Lewis three times less time is spent by Mexican peasants on field preparation if a plow is employed (1949, 121) – but capital costs are high. Plow oxen, in particular, tend to be very expensive to acquire and to maintain, requiring large quantities of feed and massive amounts of water (Wagstaff and Gamble 1982, 100). Farmers could seek access to oxen by sharing with kinsmen or neighbors or temporarily borrowing one; they could also use donkeys or mules. Nevertheless, the relative costs of plowing would still be higher than with a hoe.

Moreover, there is some evidence that productivity might higher with hoe tillage. In Mexicon, Lewis noted that the average yields with hoes were equal to the best yields from plowed fields and that the best yields from hoed fields were three times higher than the average on plowed plots (1949, 124). I find these figures suggestive of a more widespread pattern but not conclusive on their own. Further research, it seems to me, is needed before we can generalize validly on the comparative productivity of the hoe versus the plow. Nonetheless, Lewis' data are suggestive.

All things being equal, plowing is the preferred technique. The faster work rates, the manure produced by the animals, the prestige of livestock ownership, and their potential as a source of food or income in a crisis all enhance the attraction of having large quadrupeds (Gibbs and Nielson 1976). But all things are seldom equal, and so the possession and utilization of large traction animals varied from household to household based on wealth, household size, size of land-holdings, and the like. If the household possessed a large pool of labor and little land, tillage by hoe would have been preferred. If drier than normal conditions were occurring or were predicted on the basis of weather signs, then the need to conserve soil moisture might have led to the use of hoes. The practice of intercropping on small plots of land where the intrusion of large animals would do more harm than good might also make the hoe the tool of choice. Simply put, the farmer decided the method of tillage employed on a regular basis with due regard to his household's economic and demographic circumstance at the time. Here again, the key to to successful peasant farming lay in flexibility of response.

Fallow   I draw the same conclusion for the practice of fallowing as well. Halstead has convincingly demonstrated that the propensity of some ancient historians to assume that bare fallowing was *de rigueur* in antiquity is misguided (1987a, 81–3; Garnsey 1988a, 93–4). As he points out, "traditional bare fallowing is integrally related to a specific historical context and should not be extrapolated back into the distant past uncritically." But old views die hard (Skydsgaard 1988,78). I stated some time ago that "it is quite likely that a combination of fallow systems would have been used" (1982a, 114) in antiquity, and I see no reason to alter that view. Instead of rehashing old arguments, I refer the reader to Halstead's article.

Esther Boserup has led the way in categorizing the various fallow arrangements. Building on her earlier work (1965, 15–16), she recently presented a five-part scheme (Boserup 1981, 19; see also Chayanov [1966] 1986, 139–59):

1   Forest-fallow: one or two consecutive crops followed by a period of 15 to 20 years fallow.
2   Bush-fallow: two or more consecutive crops followed by a period of 8 to 10 years fallow.
3   Short-fallow: one or two consecutive crops followed by 1 or 2 years fallow.
4   Annual cropping: One crop is cultivated each year and the land allowed to remain fallow only a few months.
5   Multicropping: Two or more crops are grown successively on the same plot of land each year without any fallow.

The order of the various schemes reflects the ratio of capital investment to land; forest-fallow, for example, requires a great deal of land but only a small investment of labor and capital. Just the opposite is the case with multicropping. At each level there is an intensification of production as greater output per unit area is achieved at the cost of greater input. Boserup asserted that population density was the critical factor in initiating the shift from one system to the next (1981, 20–8), and further studies have established the general correctness of her argument (Gallant 1982a, 115–17; Brookfield 1972; Wharton 1965, 13; Datoo 1976, 112; Brown and Podolefsky 1967; Grigg 1974; 1976; 1980; Jameson 1977/78,

126–7). Her work was scaled to a macrolevel, and while it is clear that on the whole there is a positive correlation between fallow arrangements and population density, nevertheless at a microlevel individual households adopt different practices depending upon numerous factors.

Inside the household, the decision as to which fallow system to employ was based on factors such as:

1   The labor product: if few hands were available, then the fallow period might have to be extended.
2   The amount of land a household possessed: smallholders do not have the option of leaving portions of their land idle for long.
3   The location of their plots: land close to their residence could be worked more intensively than more distant plots.
4   Livestock holdings: manure and the capacity to prepare the seedbeds quickly are critical to the success of the more intensive methods.
5   The household's tenurial arrangements: sharecroppers and tenants often do not make the decision concerning fallow.

Not surprisingly, then, we find groups employing a number of different schemes simultaneously (Banfield 1958, 49; R. M. Bell 1979, 18; Blok 1969, 97; Lawless 1977, 393; de Vooys and Piket 1958, 39–40, 59). Moreover, in most of these studies, fallow, if practiced at all, was integrated into a coherent crop-rotation scheme. At Megalopolis, for example, a modified form of annual cropping with a rotation of winter wheat (sown in October–November and harvested in June), fallow (June–March), and then sorghum (March–September) was practiced by a number of households (de Vooys and Piket 1958, 59). Chapman noted that most of the households in the village he studied employed an annual cropping scheme of winter legumes–summer fallow–winter wheat–summer fallow–winter barley–summer fallow–winter legumes (1971, 18). The presence of millet and sorghum in their storerooms also opens up the possibility that either of them could be substituted for summer fallow if required.

The random surveys of Thessalian farms conducted by de Vooys and Piket demonstrated many of the points made earlier. They recorded information on household size and composition, land holdings, livestock, and the distribution of crops (de Vooys and Piket 1958). I focus here on the last two in particular. Figure 3.2 depicts the distribution of crops in farms from 12 randomly selected villages from across the region. Four categories of land use were defined: fallow, fodder, cash crops, and wheat. It should be noted that many of the supposed cash crops were consumed by the household as well. Diversity of cropping strategies is immediately apparent. As a means of exploring further the rationale behind the practice of fallowing, Pearson correlation coefficients were employed. The results of the test are presented in table 3.3. The importance of the household's

Table 3.3 Pearson correlation coefficients of crops, fallow and livestock holdings on Thessalian farms

	Holdings	Wheat	Fallow	Fodder	Sheep	Cattle
Holdings	———	.864*	.962*	.963*	.891*	.544
Wheat		———	.756*	.752*	.661*	.284
Fallow			———	.998*	.936*	.635
Fodder				———	.959*	.631
Sheep					———	.667*
Cattle						———

* indicates that the coefficient is statistically significant at the 0.01 level.

wealth, as measured by the amount of land it owned (but not its size as there was no correlation between household size and any of the other factors anlyzed here), seems clear. Those with the most land were able to support a larger livestock population, which in turn led to their devoting more land to fallow and to fodder crops. Smaller households did not have land to spare for fallow or fodder and so could not support many animals. Thus, while the average number of sheep per household was, 31.7 the standard deviation was 55.3, and the mode was 0, indicating the very unequal distribution of livestock holdings.[7] In general, we should expect to find a number of different land use schemes and fallow rotations in use simultaneously in the same community, and if the Thessalian evidence can act as an accurate guide, then wealth clearly played a vital role in determining which of these was selected.

Moreover, fallow had few advantages except on farms with large livestock holdings. The result of cropping experiments on Cyprus and in Australia showing that bare fallowing is much less productive than either manured annual cropping or legume–cereal rotation (reported by Halstead (1987a, 82)) receive confirmation from work carried out by the Waite Institute. Their experiments indicated that the steepest decline in wheat yields occurred with a bare fallow–wheat arrangement. Even annual cropping of wheat performed better than a combination of bare fallow and wheat, primarily because the latter accelerated the rate at which nitrogen was removed from the soil (Clarke and Russell 1979, 291). For these reasons, bare fallow is attractive in only certain situations none of which were pertinent to the needs of peasant farmers in ancient Greece.

Ancient Greek farmers produced and consumed a wide variety of crops, including a number of different cereals and pulses. Given the arguments made above concerning bare fallow, we might anticipate that ancient farmers also integrated those different species into various cropping schedules.

Hesiod describes either short-fallow or multicropping, land under grain cultivation, fallow, and a fodder crop (though the last two might

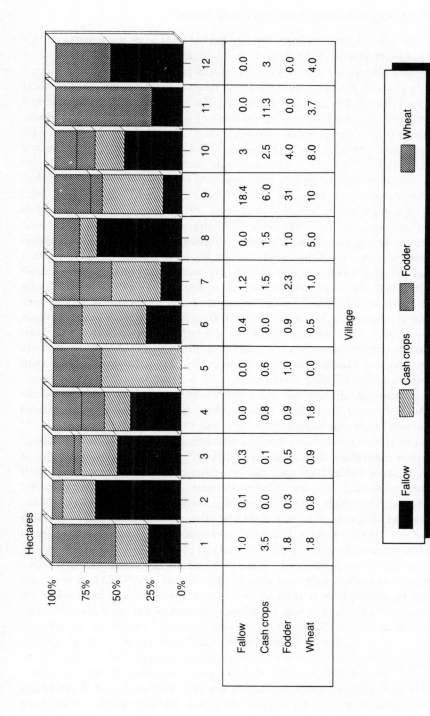

Fig. 3.2 Distribution of Crops in Thessalian Villages.

be the same) are mentioned, but the precise timing of the different crops is unclear (Hesiod *WD* 573–5, 596–600, 607; Gallant 1982a, 114 contains a more detailed discussion on this point). Short-fallow or annual cropping are the systems Xenophon recommends on his slave-worked estate (*Oik* 16.14–15), and by stating that at times slaves gangs armed with hoes should till the land, he shows his awareness that even greater intensification was a viable possibility. It is Theophrastos, however, who once again provides our best evidence. In his account he demonstrates a knowledge of how the various cereals and numerous pulses could be integrated into rotation schemes, and in particular, of how some pulses help restore fertility to the soil (*HP* 8.2.9, 8.7.2, 9.1; *CP* 4.8.1–3; Hodkinson 1988, 42–3; cf. Skydsgaard 1988, 83 where a misreading of the text seems to have occurred). Furthermore, two passages suggest that multicropping as well was known. In speaking of Chalkeia on Rhodes, he states that they plant consecutive barley crops during the same season, thus leaving open the possibility of near continuous cropping (*HP* 8.2.9). Of the Black Sea region, he observes "two sowings apparently are made of all cereals, one in winter and one in spring, at which time they also sow their legumes" (*HP* 8.4.6). The Black Sea is an area where year-round cultivation is possible and where true spring sown–late summer harvested cereals are cultivated (Gallant 1982c). If the practice described by Theophrastos was occurring on the same plot of land, then multicropping is being described.

Additional support for the existence of a range of fallow/rotation schemes comes from land leases. Many of these have recently been discussed by Hodkinson (1988, 43) and Osborne (1988). Some clearly specify the rotation of legumes and cereals (e.g. *IG* 2^2.1241; 2493); others require that fallow must be set aside (*IG* 2^2.2498; *SIG* ^{3}963); implying, of course, that left to their own devices, tenants might not have done so. If bare fallow was customary, why the need to demand it contractually? Granted, the renter may be attempting to forestall abuses by tenants out to get a quick return. In any event, the leases still support the position that ancient Greek farmers knew of and applied a number of different fallow/rotation mixes.

In sum, as with the other cropping strategies, the peasant decided which of the various schemes he would implement, on which plots of land, and how frequently he would do so, in response to a number of factors. Having these options enabled him to adapt to a variable climate and changing conditions.

Irrigation

One last adaptive mechanism requires comment and that is irrigation. The potential utility of irrigation for Greek peasant agriculture need not delay us long. With the exception of certain areas, usually upland karstic basins like Mantineia (Hodkinson and Hodkinson 1981) or remnant lake beds like parts of Thessaly and Makedonia (Garnsey, Gallant, and Rathbone 1984, 30), Greece is not a land well-suited to irrigation. There are few large rivers and hence most surface runoff occurs in sheets or in steep torrents. Therefore until the advent of deep wells and electric pumps, irrigation played only a very minor role in Greek peasant agriculture (Allbaugh 1953, 258–9; Damaskenides 1965, 30; Bialor 1976, 227; Lawless 1977, 520; Metochis 1980, 247–52).

Knapp has collected the references by ancient Greek authors concerning irrigation, and they are not plentiful (1919, 74). Some attempts were occasionally made at artificially controlling water flow; the fourth-third century *BC* dam at Mytikas in Akarnania (Murray 1984) and the numerous attempts at hydromanagement around Lake Kopais in Boiotia (Kalcyk 1988, 5–14) provide examples. But such structures were not common, and while Murray's effort to pinpoint the construction of the Mytikas dam to a specific drought seems forced, the broader implication he draws that it was constructed as part of a more general move toward intensification of agricultural production has merit (Murray 1984, 202–3). Nevertheless, the generalization that irrigation played an extremely marginal role in ancient Greek agriculture seems sound.

Alternative Production Strategies

All of the strategies discussed so far concerned decisions about production, but another crucial set of options confronted the household after the harvest. They needed to decide how the various crops would be processed for domestic consumption. Here again the household has to make a critical decisions based on their knowledge of the amount of food they had currently available, their best guess as to what the yields for the crops still growing would be, and their estimates as to their food needs later in the year. Certain foodstuffs gave the household some flexibility because they could either be consumed immediately, stored for later, or invested in the production of secondary products like livestock. A few examples make this proposition clearer.

Peasants could eat fruits and vines without delay after the harvest if food stocks were low or dry and store them for later. The latter would probably have been preferred because it enabled them to budget their dietary intake more efficiently and dried fruits have much more calories by weight than fresh. 100 grams of fresh apricots, for example, have 48 kilocalories whereas the same weight dried has 260; fresh grapes have 67 kilocalories/ 100 grams as opposed to 289 when dried (Hirschmann 1979, 212–17). The same is true of other fruits as well.

With other tree products, nuts for example, the household had the option of either keeping them for human consumption or feeding them to livestock.

They also had flexibility with their field crops. All of the pulses grown in antiquity could have been consumed fresh or dried depending on the circumstances. Some crops, such as vetch, millet, and mustard greens, could serve as food for humans when other crops failed, or as fodder for animals or as green manure when times were good (Ghatak and Ingersent 1984, 6). Indeed most of the species grown by ancient Greek peasants could have been processed in a number of different ways. The viability of these alternative strategies was directly related to the degree to which the household was able to decide which crops were grown and how the final product was disposed of.

Conclusions

Farmers were constantly confronted with the need to make decisions. In a sense, they entered into a game with the natural environment, pitting their knowledge of past events (yields), their technology, and their domestic resources against a range of natural hazards (Shubik 1987). The parameters of the game were constantly shifting on all sides. The array of hazards and their occurrence probability were alway in flux. The productive capacity of the household shifted in response to its life cycle, since this affected both the consumption needs and the productive capabilities of the household. The game was complicated further by the demands of those outside of the household seeking a share of its produce in the form of taxes, tithes, and the demands of kinsmen and community. Enmeshed in this web of risks and uncertainties, the farmer regularly had to make critical decisions concerning the types of crops he grew, where he grew them, and the production strategies he would employ with them.

I argued at the beginning of this chapter that ancient farmers had as their primary goal the attaining of a secure subsistence for their household and thus household self-reproduction. If the household produced enough to meet its internal demands and satisfied the claims of the extra-household agencies, then it won the game. If it failed to match its goals, then alternative strategies had to be set in motion.

In this chapter, I examined the range of production decisions farmers had to make and the variant forms of them they could have called upon. These gave agriculturalists a high degree of flexibility in responding to uncertainty and were primarily prophylactic in intent, but they entailed a loss in overall productivity in exchange for output stability. Given the choice, it is a trade-off peasant cultivators in general are quite willing to make.

All of the adaptive mechanisms discussed in this chapter had one critical aspect in common: they all required higher levels of labor input and were, therefore, contingent upon the household having a free hand in determining the disposition of its resources and the scheduling of its labor. Any erosion of their capacity to do so would have lessened the efficacy of these measures and rendered the household more vulnerable to subsistence risk. There were two broad sources of such constraints. One was generated internally by the household itself through the functioning of the life cycle, the size of the farm, the location of its fields, and the like. The other was imposed by forces outside the household's control in the form increasingly exploitative demands on the household's production. In the next chapter I turn to the structural demands generated internally by the household itself.

4   Structural Constraints and the Household Vulnerability Cycle

Peasants, one of the most longed-lived forms of human organization known to recorded history, seem always to walk a razor-thin line between survival and extinction.

David Arnold

Structural Constraints and the Domestic Economy

My aim in this chapter is to define that "razor-thin" line through a detailed analysis of the domestic economy.

The heart of the domestic economy is the production, distribution, and consumption of food. Chayanov was the first person to develop fully a model of the peasant farm which gave pride of place to the balance between producers and consumers (Chayanov [1966] 1986, 53–69; Durrenburger 1984, 7–9). He argued that there was an equilibrium between labor intensity and the drudgery of labor. By this Chayanov meant that peasants would increase their labor to boost output in order to meet rising domestic food demands, but that they would not raise it beyond the point at which the benefits of labor were surpassed by drudgery (81–2). His work has sparked both emulation and debate (Sahlins 1972; Barlett 1982b, 137–60; Durrenberger 1984; R.M. Smith 1984, 22–5; Birdwell-Pheasant 1984, 263–6; B.R.M. Harrison 1974; 1976). I focus primarily on the issue of the producer:consumer ratio and its relation to the household life cycle.

In addition to the producer: consumer ratio, there are a number of other critically important factors which shape the production strategies of peasant farmers and affect both the potentiality and efficacy of those adaptive measures analyzed in the previous chapter. They act as constraints upon the potential and actual economic behavior of the household (see figure 4.1). Many of these constraints are enduring, and, because they are built into the infrastructure and structure of society, out of the household's control (Chayanov [1966] 1986, 50–1; Copping 1976; O. Harris 1982; Lees 1983).While they persist, these constraints are mutable, varying over time in response to both internal and external factors, and thus the domestic economy must be constantly adapting to these shifts (Binswanger 1978; Ellen 1982; Gross 1983; Lees 1983; Bennett and Kannel 1983;

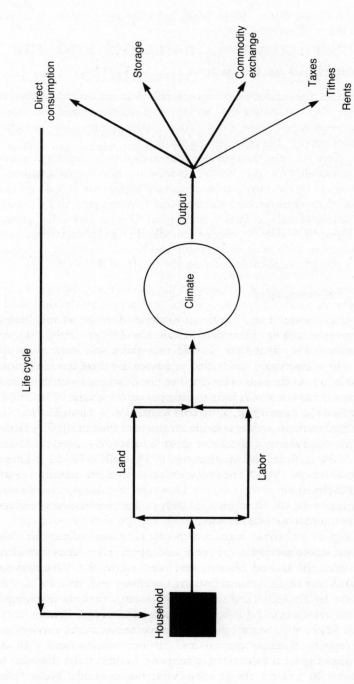

Fig. 4.1 Household Input and Output.

R.M. Smith 1984; Bates 1983; Wall 1983, 263–6; E.P. Scott 1984a; Watts 1988).

The Household as Consumer

Nowhere does the underlying logic of the domestic economy become clearer than when we analyze the two key elements of demand and supply. In Chayanovian terms, these are the food supply needs of the household and its labor supply. I begin with the former.

As is so often the case, the evidence from antiquity is insufficient in both quantity and quality for us to be able to draw any firm conclusions, and so our estimates as to the most probable dietary regime are based on (a) an assessment of modern recommended caloric requirements and (b) actual observed levels of caloric intake from rural Greece and other peasant cultures. From these data, I propose a model diet and then test it against material remains, such as organic residue and human bones, as a means of estimating the goodness-of-fit between the model and reality.

Calories as Recommended

The answer to the question "How many calories does the average human need to consume each day in order to sustain a healthy existence?" is not as straightforward as it might seem. The definition of what constitutes proper nutrition and malnutrition has varied as advances in scientific techniques have occurred and as the issue of diet has become politicized with the increasing incidence of famine and its links to financial aid (Copping 1976, 272–5; Ferro-Luzzi and Spadoni 1978, 515–16; Dennell 1979, 124). The problem of protein malnutrition and its possible incidence in spite of the ingestion of the recommended amount of calories spurred further controversy (Tremolieres 1963; Ferro-Luzzi and Spadoni 1978; Dennell 1979, 124; Diener, Moore, and Muttow 1980). The problems posed by these questions cannot be given here the attention they deserve. However, they do raise one dilemma for us: the figures on the recommended daily caloric requirements produced by different international bodies vary.

In figure 4.2 I present a diagram depicting the ranges of recommended daily caloric intake categorized by age and gender. The data have been compiled from the United Nations Food and Agriculture Organization, the US Food and Drug Administration (Goodhart and Shils 1973, 263; Hirschmann 1979, 247–8), the National Research Council (Pennington and Church 1985, xix), and independent researchers (e.g., Bender 1979). In all cases, I have selected the figures for individuals of average weight and moderate activity. For some age groups, girls between the ages of 10 and 12 for example, there is substantial agreement. In other cases, like that for men between 20 and 39, the estimates differ substantially. Nonetheless, the figures provided here will act as a guide for the construction of a model

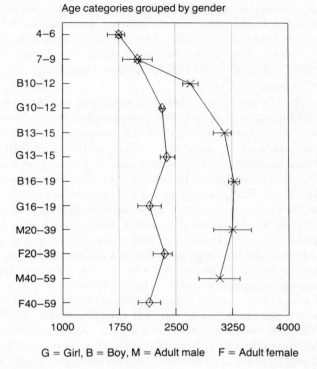

Fig. 4.2 Recommended Daily Caloric Intake.

diet once they have been tempered with information on actual consumption rates.

Calories as Observed

Two questions interest us at this juncture. First, how does the empirical data compare to the recommended rates described above: do they provide an accurate guide as to actual peasant behavior? And second, what foodstuffs and in which proportions do modern Mediterranean peasants consume in order to achieve those levels? Ethnographies and reports prepared by governmental or aid-agency officials constitute our primary sources.

The work by Allbaugh on the island of Crete in 1948 is often cited by students of the ancient diet as a source for the ('typical') Greek peasant diet (van Wersch 1972; Wagstaff and Gamble, 1982; Sanders 1985). There has been a tendency to use his results without due concern for their typicality. In 1948, after all, Crete had just emerged from the travails of World War II, a period of dearth which to this day is enshrined in popular consciousness as the "time of hunger" (Herzfeld 1985, 19–20). Moreover

Allbaugh's work was associated with the United States' aid programs for southern Europe and thus had a political purpose. In addition, he conducted his fieldwork at a time when dietary patterns were changing in the face of external intrusion (Allbaugh 1953, 100–1; see also, Sweet-Escott 1954; McNeill 1957). Bearing these factors in mind, we can examine his results.

Allbaugh conducted two random sampling surveys, one of 128 households for a period of one week and the other of 765 households for one year. For the latter, members of the household themselves filled in forms with estimates of their diet (Allbaugh 1953, 98). Based on an extrapolation from the one-week survey data, he projected an average daily intake of 2,547 kilocalories (107, table 9, 112). Two additional points should be noted. First, this figure is much lower than the 3,362 figure arrived at on the basis of Cretans' own estimates of their diet (107, table 9) and second, 39 percent of the calories were derived from cereals and cereal products (114). He did not analyze the data in any greater detail except to present the full range of results and the percentiles. So, we do not know how caloric intake breaks down by gender or by age, and thus we cannot test the estimates produced in the previous section. Given, however, that the range of consumption extended from 829 to 5,707 kilocalories and that 25 percent of those sampled consumed over 3,473, we can assume that there was a great deal of variation. Age and gender probably had something to do with it, but Allbaugh's results do not resolve the issue (507, table 50). It seems to me that based on the biases in his data that he admits to and the uncertainties about whom the results apply to, Allbaugh's results need additional support if they are to uphold the edifice often erected upon them.

There are, fortunately, a number of studies from the period just before and immediately after the Second World War which can be set alongside Allbaugh's work. Diamond, for example, produced a report for the United Nations Refugee operation and, as well as chronicling the horrors of the wartime famine, he presented the findings of a pre-war survey (Diamond 1947, 22).[8] In similar fashion, the Greek Office of Information published in 1941 the results of a nationwide survey conducted toward the end of the Metaxas regime as a prelude to a land reform act (*Greece Basic Statistics* 1941, 31). Finally, May compiled data from Greece as part of her global survey of malnutrition; she produced data for the years 1948–50 (inclusive), 1952–3 and 1959 (May 1963, 268). As the source of her data she cites the UNFAO report for 1961 with no further qualification.

While these studies can help to put the Cretan data into perspective, they suffer from the same drawback: the results are never broken down further than a simple average per person per day. Furthermore, we are given no details about the methodological basis of the surveys upon which they are based.

Table 4.1 presents a compilation of these various surveys. The divergences in the data are disturbing but in some cases, at least, explicable. For example, the variation in the amount of potatoes consumed in Crete as opposed to other parts of Greece reflects the fact that in many other areas maize rather than potatoes is the primary supplemental crop. Other figures, such as the very high estimate for wine consumption on Crete, are explicable by the biases of the researcher. In this case, Allbaugh inflated the estimate because he believed that the Cretans were not being truthful about the amount of wine they drank (Allbaugh 1953, 106).

The range for the average amount of kilocalories consumed per day, however, is not as easily explained. Without more information on the sampling methodology employed by the different surveys we have no way of assessing the possible impact of sample size, geographical distribution, and recording techniques as potential sources of distortion. Nor can we come to grips with other possible causes of bias, such as a tendency to paint as bleak a picture as possible in order to enhance the possibilities of obtaining foreign aid.

Furthermore, we are unable to test the validity of the recommended figures because none of these surveys breaks the data down by age or by gender. That all of the estimates on the "average" daily caloric intake fall within the recommended ranges should not surprise us but that alone does not get us very far.

Table 4.1 Diet by type of food (kg)

| | Allbaugh | | Diamond | Metaxas | May | |
	Week	Year			1952/3	1959
Cereals	128	166	175	188	146	164
Potatoes	59	63	15	17	40	40
Sugar	5	NA	10	10	9	12
Pulses	20	27	35	9	16	17
Olives/vegetables	176	124	NA	79	90	116
Meat/Eggs	29	20	16	22	22	35
Oils	25	45	15	NA	15	18
Wine	10	52	39	NA	NA	NA
Kilocalories/day/person	2,547	3,362	2,450	2,163	2,460	2,900

One conclusion, however, stands out clearly: the results of Allbaugh's work, or any of the others for that matter, should be employed cautiously (cf. Wagstaff and Auguston 1982, 124–30; Wagstaff, Augustson, and Gamble 1982, 174–80, for example).

If we turn to the ethnographic literature from modern Greece, we get some assistance, but not much. For the most part, anthropologists in Greece have not been interested in the more material aspects of life, and thus have not devoted much attention to diet. The few surveys attempted were frequently by ethnographers attached to one of the multidisciplinary, historical-archaeological-anthropological projects which have been conducted in Greece over the last 20 years. As part of the Minnesota Messenia project, Aschenbrenner conducted ethnographical fieldwork in the region. He concluded that 50 percent of the total calories were derived from cereals, especially in the form of wheat bread which was consumed at a rate of 0.31 kilograms per day (or 113 kg/year). Cereals were prepared in other ways and thus the total quantity of cereals consumed was probably higher (Aschenbrenner 1972, 59). In the peninsula of Methana during the 1970s peasants were found to consume between 150 and 200 kg/person/ year and to have derived from that source 30–45 percent of the total calories (Clark 1976a, 127; Foxhall and Forbes 1982, 68). Since in none of these cases are the data broken down into more detailed categories, we can do little more than conclude that cereals constituted a major element in the modern Greek peasant diet.

Some comparative figures put the modern Greek material into perspective. Surridge found that Cypriots during the 1920s consumed on average 0.625 kilograms of bread per day (equivalent to 2,250 kcals/day/person); on our estimates, this would account for anywhere from 85 and 90 percent of the total calories ingested (Surridge 1930, 32). Counihan cites figures from the 1930s which show that Sardinian peasants obtained 78 percent of their daily calories from cereal products (Counihan 1984, 49). Bermus found that the Fulani consumed 160 kg/person/year and the Tuarge 204 kg/person/year, and that these quantities amounted to 69–70 percent of their total calories (1988, 33). Casimir noted that eastern Turkish peasants ate close to 300 kg/person/year (1988, 349). This is quite a high figure but one not out of line with Hillman's 320 kg/person/year recorded in the Anatolian village of Asvan (Hillman 1973b, 229). On the basis of their surveys in rural India, Malhotra and Gadgil estimated a cereal consumption rate of 185 kg/person/year (1988, 384). Table 4.2 contains information from a selection of Middle Eastern countries. The general range resembles the figures cited above, and the total caloric consumption is not too dissimilar from the data in table 4.1.

The comparative data generally support the picture of the peasant diet based on the Greek evidence alone. So we can conclude that it is presenting

Table 4.2 Cereal consumption and total calories in the Middle East

	Cereals (kg/person/ year)	Total (kcals)
Egypt	168.2	2,940
Israel	117.2	2,830
Lebanon	121.6	2,630
Jordan	135.9	2,540
Syria	157.6	2,330
Iraq	129.6	2,100

Source: Clawson *et al.*, 1971, 101, 156–7.

us with the means to assess the probable dietary regime from antiquity, but only in the most general of terms. The lack of further specification of the variation in caloric consumption according to age and gender prevents us from determining the accuracy of the recommended levels as a reflection of actual practices.

A Working Estimate

Some estimates of the ancient diet need to be made. Undoubtedly the best work on the subject to date is that by Foxhall and Forbes (1982). They systematically collected all the ancient references on cereal consumption, converted these into modern form, and then compared them to the salient figures on modern Greek peasants, drawing in particular on some of the works discussed above. After a perusal of the ancient sources they found that a *choinix* of wheat per man per day was considered a "rule of thumb" approximation. The *choinix* amounted to 0.84 kilograms or 2,803 kilocalories. Taken at face value, these figures imply that anywhere from 90 percent to 120 percent of the daily recommended diet was supplied by wheat—a most unlikely situation. As they point out, what we are probably dealing with is a tendency by the ancients to round their estimates upward, so that a figure such as a *choinix* probably represented to them what a man ought to eat, not what he necessarily required to subsist.

On the basis of the modern Greek data, they lower the figure for grain consumption to 212 kg/person/year, citing the supposed greater consumption of olives by modern Greek peasants as their reason,[9] and based on their estimate of a daily intake of 2,583 kilocalories, this amounted to 70–75 percent of the total diet (Foxhall and Forbes 1982, 71). Other attempts at reconstructing the ancient diet have for the most part utilized these results (Garnsey 1984; 1988a; Garnsey, Gallant, and Rathbone 1984; Figueira 1984).

Following the lead of the comparative material, we might assume that the remaining bulk of the daily calories was probably derived from vegetables, fresh fruit, and legumes. Confirmation for this view is forthcoming from the literary sources (Fidanza 1979, 81). The passage cited at the beginning of this chapter vividly portrays the importance of vegetables in the diet of the very poor. In his voluminous work, Athenaios makes frequent mention of a wide variety of fruits and vegetables. Galen discusses at great length the various vegetables and fruits eaten by all classes of society. Thus, while we cannot put a precise figure to it, it seems clear that vegetables and fruits made up an important part of the ancient diet. Combining the results of the last two sections, then, we can postulate a dietary regime for the ancient peasant consisting of approximately 65–70 percent cereal products, 20–25 percent fruits, pulses, and vegetables, 5–15 percent oils, meat, and wine.

Old Bones and the Diet

The data presented so far have reflected modern recommendations of how much people should eat, observations on what modern peasants in the circum-Mediterranean region do eat, and ancient estimations of what they ought to have eaten. One body of evidence preserved from the ancient world which may permit some occasional glimpses of what peasants actually did eat is their bones.

Recent works on osteology and paleopathology have shed valuable light on past foodways (Wells 1975; Wing and Brown 1979; Huss-Ashmore, Goodman, and Armelagos 1982; Martin, Goodman, and Armelagos 1985; Stini 1985; Buikstra and Miekle 1985; Powell 1985). Detailed metrical, visual, and chemical analyses of human bones have enabled anthropologists to draw inferences about past nutritional standards and periodic food stress (see Huss-Ashmore, Goodman and Armelagos 1982, 397 for a definition of food stress). In addition to the study of human bones, advances have been made in the analysis of other organic matter, such as fecal material, plants, seeds, and animal bones, as a means of elucidating dietary patterns in the past (Frey 1985; Parmalee 1985; C. E. Smith 1985). There will always be difficulties in the interpretation of these studies, but when integrated with ethnographic data, the possibility of addressing major issues concerning diet and nutrition in human communities in a long-term evolutionary perspective becomes more viable (Freedman 1977; Wilson 1977; Carbon and Keel 1985; Keene 1985; Leone and Palkovicj 1985; M. Harris and Ross 1987a; Roosevelt 1987; M. N. Cohen 1987).

We encounter an obstacle when we turn to ancient Greece: until recently few archaeologists working in Greece have taken much interest in human bones. Consequently, the number of studies at our disposal are few. For the most part, the works of Angel and Bisel provide our only sources. Based on them, I draw some tentative inferences about the general nutritional status of Greeks during the Classical and Hellenistic periods as a means of assessing the validity of the diet proposed earlier.

I begin with stature (table 4.3). While not without its interpretive difficulties (Wells 1975, 767–8), stature can provide valuable clues as to an individual's overall nutritional status and the adequacy of the diet (Angel 1975, 178). On the basis of samples drawn from various parts of Greece, Angel and Bisel calculated the mean stature of adult men and women (Angel 1972, table 2, 62, table 5, 72; Angel 1975, table; Bisel 1980, 66) I present their data and compare them to figures from Crete in the 1940s, Greece in 1963, and Cyprus in 1972.

The results show a remarkable degree of uniformity. With the exception of Bisel's figure on women at Athens during the Classical period, the mean stature from antiquity to the present is within one standard deviation. The explanation for the one exception probably lies with the tiny sample of two cases employed by Bisel. Her figure for men at classical Athens is based on

Table 4.3 Mean stature of men and women during the Classical, Hellenistic and Modern periods (cm)

	Men		Women	
	Mean	SD	Mean	SD
CLASSICAL (N–57)				
Greece	169.8	NA	156.3	NA
Athens	174.6	3.9	149.5	3.8
Akanthos	169.2	3.0	157.1	2.5
HELLENISTIC (N–60)				
Greece	171.8	NA	156.6	NA
Athens	171.1	6.0	155.5	6.0
MODERN (N–3000 +)				
Crete	164.0	NA	156.3	NA
Cyprus (Island)	165.1	NA	NA	NA
Cyprus (North coast)	168.0	NA	NA	NA
Greece (1963)	170.5	NA	NA	NA

SD – standard deviation; NA – data not available.

Source: Angel 1972, Table 2, 62.

only ten examples and so must be suspect as well. All the remaining figures fall well within the sampling error and thus could easily have been drawn from the same population. Given the similarities between the various samples, about the only inference we can draw from the figures is that if the contemporary peasant diet allowed for the attainment of these statures, then, given the close similarity between the levels of stature, the ancient diet was probably on the same order of magnitude. This observation, however, does not get us very far. If we want to inquire more deeply into the actual break-down of the diet, then clearly we need other measures.

The study of dentition has the potential to provide information on the composition of the diet. Dental lesions, for example, can tell us about the relative levels of protein in the diet (Angel 1975, 178) and "few diseases have so direct a relationship with nutrition as dental caries" (Wells 1975, 730). The number of caries can provide some indications about the relative proportions of sugar and protein consumed. Dental wear patterns have the potential to inform us about the composition of the diet, and in particular, about the cereal content and role of meat (Wells 1975, 741–4; S. Powell 1985; Rose, Condon, and Goodman 1985). Here again, interpretation of the data is neither straightforward nor unequivocal.

The rates of caries per mouth during the Classical and Hellenistic periods were lower than in either the preceding or the succeeding periods (Angel 1975, Table), but they were still higher than in other areas of western Europe. Wells suggested that greater consumption of honey and dried fruits in Greece provided the explanation for this (733), implying that perhaps we should adjust our hypothetical diet to include more of these and less cereals. But before we do so, it should be pointed out that while the percentage of carious teeth in ancient Greek mouths was greater than among their western European counterparts, that figure pales in comparison with modern Greeks (Classical 4.0, Hellenistic 5.5, and modern 15.9 caries per mouth (Angel 1975, Table; Wells 1975, 734)). Since the diets of modern Greeks, as presented earlier, did not contain large quantities of honey or dried fruits and were overwhelmingly cereal-based, it is difficult to see any justification for shifting the ratio of the latter for the former based on the rate of dental carries. If any adjustment is called for it may be to increase the amount of meat or legumes in the diet because the greater quantities of protein they could have provided may account for the lower rate of carious teeth. Following Jameson's convincing confirmation of the paucity of meat in the diet in Classical Athens (1988, 105–6), we might perhaps consider altering the ratio of cereals to pulses consumed in antiquity. Until more evidence is available, however, we must leave this merely as a suggestion for future enquiry.

The analytic technique with the greatest potential for reconstructing past diets is trace elements analysis (Gilbert 1985). The only trace elements analyses available are those by Bisel. As we have seen, the size of her samples was such as to preclude our drawing any but the most tentative of inferences from her results. None the less, since they are the only figures available, we need to examine them. I present the data on zinc and strontium in table 4.4. These two elements were selected because of their sensitivity to the relative amounts of meat and plant matter consumed. Zinc is provided primarily by meat and fish and its absorption can be impaired by an overabundance of fiber in the diet (Bisel 1980, 20; Huss-Ashmore, Goodman, and Armelagos 1982, 451). Strontium, on the other hand, is a good indicator of vegetable consumption. Animals actively discriminate against strontium and remove it through renal excretion. Plants accumulate strontium and store it in their leaves and stalks (Huss-Ashmore, Goodman and Armelagos 1982, 451). Accordingly the ratio of strontium to zinc can provide a measure of the relative balance between meat and plant matter consumed.

As table 4.4 indicates, in both periods women seem to have lower Sr/Zn ratios than men, and men during the Classical period seem to have eaten the least amount of meat. Given the relative barrenness of the Mediterranean as a fishing ground (Gallant 1985a), I have placed more emphasis on the role of meat. Both these observation go against the bulk of our other evidence. Jameson, for example, provides solid evidence that meat was probably more readily available and distributed to Athenians,

Table 4.4 Zinc and strontium content of skeletal remains from Athens

	Male	Female
CLASSICAL		
N	5	1
Zinc (mg/g)	128.3	162.2
SD	13.8	—
Strontium (mg/g)	145.4	120.2
SD	27.7	—
Sr/Zn ratio	1.13	0.74
HELLENISTIC		
N	5	12
Zinc (mg/g)	186.6	145.6
SD	84.6	28.2
Strontium (mg/g)	156.6	113.5
SD	68.6	25.7
Sr/Zn ratio	0.83	0.78

SD – standard deviation.
Source: Bisel 1980, 71, 73.

and in particular Athenian men, during the Classical period than in other epochs (Jameson 1988). If anything, we should expect the St/Zn ratios to be the exact opposite of those presented in table 4.4.

Two arguments can be made for not changing our estimate of the ancient diet. First, the small samples Bisel analyzed (for example only one female from the Classical period was examined) make the results suspect. Second, the very high levels of standard deviation indicate that the quantities measured varied considerably, and this, in conjunction with the previous point, means that until much more work of this type is conducted Bisel's results should not be accepted at face value.

To sum up the evidence from the bones. First, on average, the ancient diet provided sufficient calories for growth and the relative parity of stature between ancient and modern Greeks means that our use of the modern data as a guide, albeit a crude one, to the past is valid. Second, the relatively lower levels of dental lesions and caries in antiquity may indicate that the consumption of pulses was higher than now and that we should adjust our hypothetical diet accordingly. Third, the results of trace elements analysis were based on such small samples that no meaningful inferences can be drawn from then.

Diet and the Life Cycle

It remains now to propose some hypothetical scheme for the total number of kilocalories consumed per day by men and women of different ages. Guided by the range of recommendations recorded in figure 4.2 and the qualifications and adjustments suggested in the other sections of this chapter, I have employed the following scheme (table 4.5). The recommended kilocalories per day have been broken down by age and gender.

If we combine these figures with the household life cycle set forth earlier, then we can model the aggregate caloric demand of the household as it develops over time. The results are portrayed in figure 4.3.

The household in its initial formation required roughly 3,500,000 kilocalories per year. This figure would rise to its zenith during the first triennium and then fall as the younger sibling married out and the widowed mother died. The next peak level would be attained sometime during the fifth and sixth triennia, a time when the children started to consume around the same quantities as adults. Decline would set in as the household fissured through death and out-marriage until it reached a nadir of approximately 2,000,000 kilocalories.

If we use the figures presented above concerning the composition of the diet, that is 65 percent of the kilocalories in cereals, 25 percent in vegetables and pulses, and 10 percent in olive oil and wine, then we can discern the total quantity of kilocalories required from each of these food groups. Figure 4.3 and table 4.6 contain these data. They will provide the

Table 4.5 Caloric consumption per day by gender and age

Age	Kcal
Children	
4–6	1,830
7–9	2,190
Male Adolescents	
10–12	2,600
13–15	2,900
16–19	3,070
Female Adolescents	
10–12	2,350
13–15	2,490
16–19	2,310
Adult Male	
20–39	3,000
Adult Female	
20–39	2,200
Adult Female	
Pregnant	2,500

Table 4.6 Dietary and land-holding needs over the life cycle

Life cycle	Cereals		Pulse/ vegetables		Oil/ wine	
	(kcals)	(ha)	(kcals)	(ha)	(kcals)	(ha)
0	2,354,250	1.32	1,177,125	1.89	392,375	0.15
3	2,586,390	0.44	1,293,195	2.08	431,065	0.10
6	1,914,060	1.06	957,030	1.54	319,010	0.13
9	2,417,760	1.35	1,208,880	1.94	402,960	0.16
12	2,689,320	1.50	1,344,660	2.16	448,220	0.18
15	2,888,610	1.61	1,444,350	2.32	481,435	0.19
18	2,229,420	1.17	1,114,710	1.79	371,570	0.15
21	1,773,900	0.98	886,950	1.42	295,650	0.06
24	1,154,130	0.64	577,065	0.93	144,500	0.04

basis for all the later simulations of the domestic economy. I would stress again that the quantities of kilocalories cited here refer only to the subsistence needs of the households. Other variable will be incorporated into the model shortly.

Figure 4.3 presents in summary fashion the most basic production goal of the household. When confronted with various options and choices, a major factor guiding the farmer's decision would have been the attainment of production sufficient to provide those quantities of kilocalories. Bearing

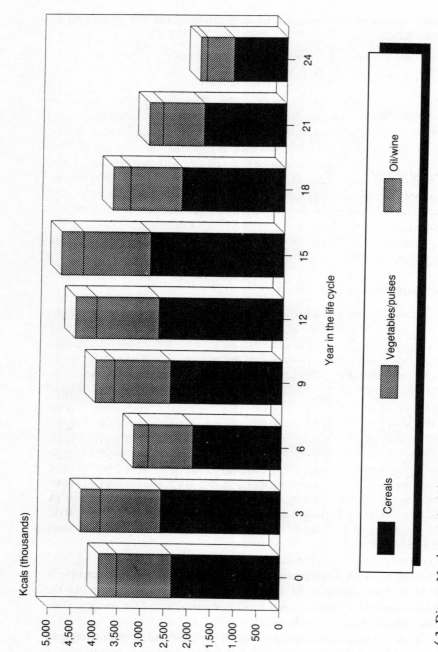

Fig. 4.3 Dietary Needs over the Life Cycle.

these figures in mind, we can turn to an examination of the household as a unit of production.

The Household as Producer

At the heart of Chayanov's theory of peasant economy lay the consumer: worker ratio. And so, having defined the output target at which the model household had to aim, that is the consumer side of the equation, we can turn to a discussion of the labor product. For Chayanov, "the amount of the labor product is mainly determined by the size and composition of the working family, the number of its members capable of work, then by the productivity of the labor unit, and – this is especially important – by the degree of labor effort – the degree of self-exploitation through which the working members effect a certain number of labor units in the course of the year" (Chayanov [1966] 1986, 5–6). We shall be less concerned with "self-exploitation" than with the more useful concept of the labor product.

Labor Requirements and Yields of the Main Crops

Before modelling the labor product of the household over its life cycle we need to examine the amount of man-power required to produce the crops most commonly grown in the Mediterranean. And for this we must turn to comparative data once again. When examining this evidence we must bear in mind that the recorded labor inputs reflect the operation of a specific agricultural system rather than universal biological requirements. The amount of labor the household expends on the production of a certain crop is a decision made each year, and so the figures on labor inputs can change markedly. The data presented here are meant to act only as a guide.

Pepelasis and Yotopoulos found that their sample of farmers from around Greece invested 26 man-days/hectare/year (hereafter, md/ha/year) in the production of wheat and 20 in barley (62, 100–2). Davis recorded a rate of 21 md/ha/year for cereals at Pisticci in Italy (Davis 1973, App. 6). Both these sets of figures seem low compared to elsewhere. On Melos, for example, households spent 48 md/ha/year on wheat and 45 md/ha/year on barley (Wagstaff and Augustson 1982, 117). These are much more in line with results reported from Mexico (47.8 md/ha/year; O. Lewis 1949, 121), Spain (32–5 md/ha/year), Lombardy (55–70 md/ha/year) and Ferrara (49 md/ha/year) in Italy (K.D. White 1965, 103, 105, with adjustments to account for the time spent harvesting). The Roman agronomist Columella recommended 42 md/ha/year (2.12.17; K.D. White 1965, 103; Duncan-Jones 1972, 327–33). For analytical purposes, a figure of 48 md/ha/year for cereals has been adopted.

For the remaining two groups of crops, olives and vines and vegetables and legumes, I have chosen to calculate composite figures. Recorded rates of 125 md/ha/year for olives, 108 md/ha/year for peas, and 147 md/ha/year for vines (Davis 1973, App. 6). Pepelasis and Yotopoulos reported labor inputs by adult males to be approximately 100 md/ha/year (Pepelasis and Yotopoulos 1962, 102). The inclusion of supplementary labor increases this figure somewhat and is more in line with evidence from other sources. Melian households expend 175 md/ha/year (Wagstaff and Augustson 1982, 177). Both legumes and vegetables require more labor than cereals. It takes on the order of 150 md/ha/year to grow lentils with traditional technology (Khayrallah 1982, 135). Similar labor inputs are reported for the other pulses as well. The average for vegetables and legumes is raised considerably by the inclusion of labor-intensive plants such as celery, chicory, cauliflower, and leeks. Anywhere from 175 to 200 md/ha/year may be needed to grow these crops. Thus I employ 175 md/ha/year for this group.

The next question we face is how to calculate labor input per household member. I have employed the following scale of labor coefficients: adult male 1.0, adolescent male 0.9, adult and adolescent females, 0.7, elderly adults and children 0.5 (based in part on Pepelasis and Yotopoulos 1962, 109; Wagstaff and Auguston 1982, 113–14; C. Clark and Haswell 1971, 120–21; Hesiod WD 441–7). In some cultures children begin working in the fields and around the house, particularly in poorer households from age six onward (e.g. Mexico, see Schumann 1985, 283–5).

In order to assess the relationship between the labor product and the household's needs, we need to know about output and productivity as well (Sicular 1986). The methodological justification for applying modern crop yield data to the past cannot be discussed in detail here (Garnsey and Gallant, in progress). Nonetheless, a few comments are in order.

An obvious point is that comparative data should be drawn only from areas practicing a similar type of agriculture, though this alone is insufficient. The lack of mechanization does not necessarily define "traditional" agriculture nor should we accept uncritically yields produced in the recent past as inherently retrodictable because of age alone. Sensitivity should be shown to the social, political, and economic context whence the data are derived. To take an obvious example, it would be a mistake to assume that crop yields from Greece during the late nineteenth and early twentieth centuries are applicable directly to the past just because they were produced with "pre-modern" technology. Consideration must be given to the possible impact on crop yields of the massive outmigration of man-power, a factor which would have directly affected the labor product and limited the potential for labor-intensive cropping strategies.

Finally, because of the high levels of interannual variability in Greece, it should go without saying that reliance on a short time series or, as some have done, one year alone (Jardé 1979 [1925], 53) simply invites distortion. The representativeness of any given year by itself will always be open to question.

With these caveats in mind, I present in Table 4.7 the means for crop yields from various regions of Greece and for the country as a whole over the period from 1911 until 1950 with some gaps and omissions caused by the various wars and civil disruptions.[10] As well as presenting figures on output in kilograms per hectare, I have included the same in kilocalories as well, using a conversion rate of 3,100 kcal/kg for wheat, 2,650 kcal/kg for barley, 1,200 kcal/kg for broad beans, 1,750 kcal/kg for lentils, and 1,440 kcal/kg for chickpeas (Paul and South-gate 1979; P. Fisher and Bender 1979; Hirschmann 1979; Abu-Shakra and Tannous 1982, 191–202; Foxhall and Forbes 1982, 57, 72). For

Table 4.7 Yields of the major crops, 1911–1950 (kg/ha)

	Wheat	Barley	Broad beans	Lentils
REGION				
Achaia	642.7	695.5	743.5	594.5
Aitolia	666.4	666.9	650.9	537.2
Argolid	624.5	733.4	542.7	498.1
Arkadia	470.0	598.7	657.2	410.9
Athens	629.1	793.7	630.9	539.9
Evros	871.9	990.3	638.4	611.2
Evvoia	540.0	552.7	602.7	444.5
Crete	748.1	902.6	624.7	578.8
Epiros	536.4	563.6	478.7	589.1
Kalamata	571.8	650.9	659.1	482.7
Kavala	903.2	907.0	976.0	608.1
Kefalonia	754.8	698.1	876.4	718.8
Kerkyra	581.0	529.1	521.9	547.7
Korinth	611.0	708.8	537.2	484.6
Kozani	720.0	899.0	691.4	449.4
Lakonia	646.4	627.7	621.8	453.6
Lesbos	662.6	689.2	539.6	465.1
Phthiotis	668.2	650.0	460.9	370.0
Thessaly	889.5	1,097.1	886.9	504.0
Zakynthos	733.6	689.1	1098.2	924.6
Mean	673.56	732.17	671.955	540.64
SD	114.85	149.33	163.95	118.73
Max	903.2	1,097.1	1,098.2	924.6
Min	470.0	529.1	460.9	370.0
Kcals (Mean)	2,088,036	1,903,642	806,346	946,120

each crop, a wide range of mean yields was recorded; in the case of wheat, for example, the difference between the highest average yield and the lowest was 423 kg/ha. The areas with consistently low yields, like Arkadia and Evvoia, were places which had suffered greatly from population loss and thus a diminution of manpower (Houliarakis 1975, 50–8); consequently we should be wary of generalizing on the basis of these figures. The general level of output depicted here is in line with data from other Mediterranean countries (discussed in full by Garnsey and Gallant, in progress), and while I suspect that ancient yields might well have been higher, we shall use these as baselines for the remainder of the chapter bearing in mind that they probably tend toward the low side.

The Labor Supply over the Life Cycle

On the basis of the data presented in the last section, we can estimate the development of the labor product and the labor requirement of the household over its life cycle. The first step is to calculate the total labor supply using the coefficients for age and gender.

The number of days per year an individual works can vary greatly depending on a range of factors, such as Chayanov's "drudgery index," the number and duration made on the peasant's time by familial and communal obligations, the social ideology of labor and leisure, and illness. Consistently in the comparative literature, averages in the area of 175 to 200 days per year occur and are applied here. Figure 4.4 depicts the development of the labor supply over the life cycle. A modified "s-curve" is the result when the data are smoothed with a fitted polynomial curve.[11] During the first two triennia, labor seems plentiful because of the presence of an adult male, a late adolescent male, and two adult females. The supply drops in the third triennium as the widowed mother dies and the younger brother establishes his own *oikos*. It then begins to increase as children are born and grow, attaining its zenith after about 15 years. Diminution commences as the father dies and siblings depart from their natal household, and it continues until the last phase – when, of course, the cycle begins again.

These figures take on much more meaning when we compare them with the household's labor requirements over the same span of time. I calculated the latter as follows (see table 4.8):

1   Based on the ratio of 65:25:10, I determined the total quantity of kilocalories needed from the three food groups in the diet during each triennium;

2   in line with the output levels described earlier, the amount of land necessary to produce it was calculated;

Table 4.8 Required and available labor over the life cycle

Life cycle	Cereals		Pulse/ vegetables		Oil/ wine	
	(kcals)	(ha)	(kcals)	(ha)	(kcals)	(ha)
0	2,354,250	1.3	1,177,125	1.9	382,375	0.15
3	2,586,390	1.4	1,293,195	2.1	431,065	0.17
6	1,914,060	1.1	957,030	1.5	319,065	0.13
9	2,417,760	1.4	1,208,880	1.9	402,960	0.16
12	2,689,320	1.5	1,344,660	2.2	448,220	0.18
15	2,888,610	1.6	1,444,350	2.3	481,435	0.19
18	2,229,420	1.2	1,114,710	1.8	371,570	0.15
21	1,773,900	0.9	886,950	1.4	295,650	0.06
24	1,154,130	0.6	577,065	0.9	144,500	0.04

Labor

Required	Available	
	175	200
md/year	md/year	md/year
420	560	640
462	560	640
343	385	440
432	473	540
481	630	720
516	665	760
395	577	660
296	455	520
200	262	300

3   then, by applying labor input estimates, the total labor requirement of the household was computed. In figure 4.5 the results are plotted against the labor product at 175 md/year and 200 md/year.

Two tendencies are evident. First, during both the early and middle stages of the life cycle, the household possessed more labor than it needed to produce its minimum subsistence. Second, in contrast, during the third and the sixth triennia, labor was in short supply. In other words, with the parameters we have imposed on the model to this point, it seems that there were cyclical phases when labor was either in surplus or in deficit. This observation has far-reaching implications in light of the discussion presented in Chapter 4 on the relationship between the effectiveness of agricultural adaptive measures and manpower. But before we can most fully explore this issue, we need to incorporate farm size into the simulation.

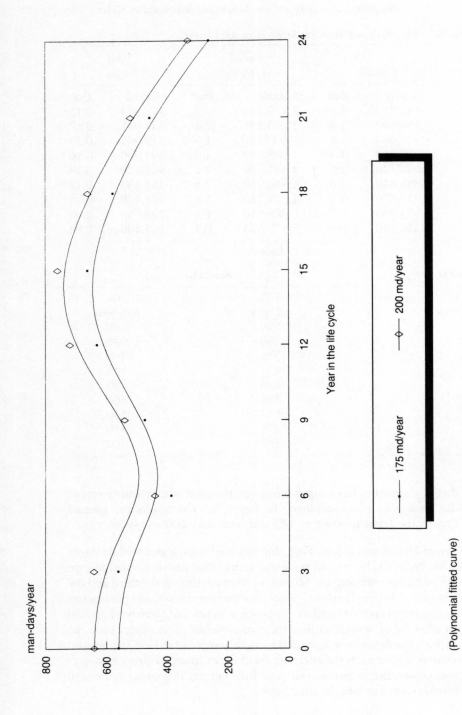

man-days/year

Year in the life cycle

—•— 175 md/year   —◇— 200 md/year

(Polynomial fitted curve)

Fig. 4.4 Labor Available in Model Household.

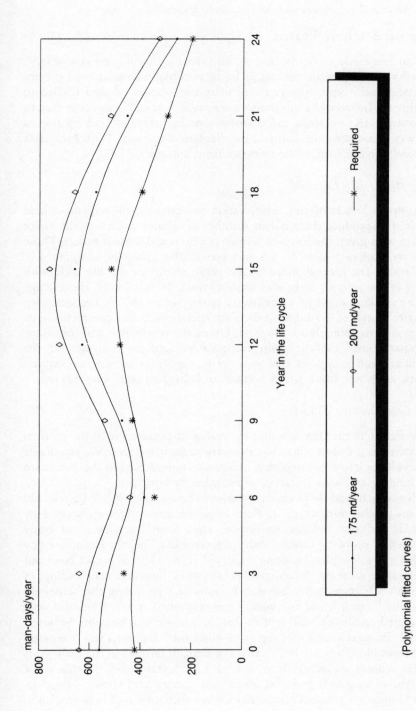

Fig. 4.5 Labor Available against Labor Required to Produce Subsistence Minimum.

Size of Ancient Farms

The ancient evidence on the size of the "average" farm is meager at best. In order to compensate for this as far as possible, we can use the dietary estimates and output figures to calculate the amount of land needed to provide the household's subsistence over the life cycle. We can next turn to the comparative evidence and examine actual patterns of land-holding as one way of assessing the utility of the diet-based estimate. With these data in mind, we can turn to the evidence from antiquity.

How Big is Big Enough?

One approach to answering this question is to calculate the amount of land required to produce the requisite number of calories in each of the major food groups given the levels of output per hectare discussed earlier. Those data are provided in table 4.6 and presented graphically in figure 4.6. Predictably the general shape of the curve resembles the life cycle with peaks in the second, fifth, and sixth triennia. In real terms, the average quantity of land required varies from a starting point of 3.36 hectares, then rising to a high of 4.12 during the sixth triennium before commencing its decrease as the household dissolved. Given the production and consumption parameters derived from comparative sources from around the Mediterranean it appears that in order to supply its subsistence requirements, anywhere from 3 to 4 hectares of cultivated land were needed.

The Comparative Evidence

How well does that figure reflect the reality of peasant life in the modern Mediterranean and in other contemporary peasant societies? We can divide this evidence into two categories: indigenous estimates as to the minimum size holding and actual practice as recorded by outsiders.

How much land do peasants consider to be enough? While they would put no precise number to it, Portuguese peasants when questioned by O'Neill did not hesitate to impose their own assessment on other households' property, usually with statements like "he/she has only a tiny garden and a few plots—nothing" (O'Neill 1987, 76). When O'Neill put quantitative values to the indigenous categories, he found that holdings of less than 3 hectares were considered "nothing," providing the household with only "a little bread and wine," and that farms of 3 to 6 hectares were considered small (O'Neill 1987, 76–7). Among the peasants he interviewed, Brögger found that the "rule of thumb" for them was 5 hectares per household (Brögger 1971, 38). For Bengali farmers in the early years of this century, anywhere from 2.5 to 3.25 hectares was thought to be enough, so long as it included some high quality land (Bose 1986, 51). And Hungarian peasants considered anyone with a farm of between 2.8 to

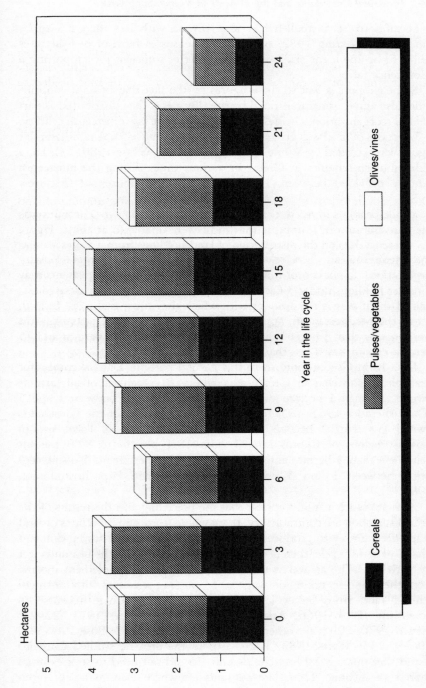

Fig. 4.6 Land Required to Produce Subsistence Minimum.

5 hectares to be a small-holder and anyone with less than 2.8 to be "indigent" (Netting 1982, 644). By consensus, a farm of 3–6 hectares seems to be about the size peasants consider to sufficient for supporting a subsistence farm.

Some support is lent to these figures by the fact that peasant communities also agree, as demonstrated by the allotments they distributed as part of land reorganization schemes. In Sicily during the late nineteenth century, 4.5 hectares of land was given to peasants (Blok 1966, 9). A not dissimilar figure was recorded by White for central Italy (C. White 1980, 13). Land redistribution schemes in Greece at various times during the nineteenth century provided between 5 and 7 hectares per household (McGrew 1985).

While peasants in recent times may have agreed that 3 to 5 hectares was the bare minimum, it appears that most were unable to attain it. Figure 4.7 presents data on the distribution of land-holdings from 15 sites around the Mediterranean.[12] A relatively consistent picture emerges. Peasant expectations do not conform to reality. O'Neill's Portuguese peasants may consider holdings under 3 hectares to be barely viable but for close to one half of them that is the amount with which they must make do. Indeed, across the Mediterranean, approximately 50 percent of the peasant farms were smaller than 3 hectares and cumulatively between 65 percent and 75 percent encompassed less than 5 hectares.

Data from Greece conform to this general pattern. Damaskenides, for example, found that in Greece as a whole 28.5 percent of all farmers owned less than 1 hectare and 56.6 percent possessed between 1 and 5 (Damaskenides 1965, 27). In Messenia 63.6 percent of the households owned less than 2 hectares (Sauerwein 1968, 234–5). Farm size in various regions of Cyprus ranged from 18.1 percent to 87.3 percent being less than 1 hectare and an additional 12.7 percent to 55.4 percent being between 1 and 5 hectares (Panayiotou and Papachristodoulou 1983, 2).

At first glance it might appear that the preceding and the results of the previous section are contradictory. If anywhere from 1 to 3 hectares of land is required simply to produce enough food for the family during different phases of its life cycle, then how can such a large sector of the peasantry get by with less? The answer is that they do not. They supplement income from their land by taking on wage labor, pooling resources with kinsmen, renting land from larger land owners, and by frequent recourse to borrowing (Blok 1966; Arlacchi 1983; Martinez-Alier 1971, 22–23; Hirsch 1970, 22–3; for other areas, see Hill 1982, 142; Bose 1986, 29, 106–9, 135; Watts 1983, 122–139). In the area he studied Cutileiro found that out of 480 households only 26 did not need to seek external sources of income. They, like peasants elsewhere, had to accept often unpalatable solutions to the problem of ensuring their subsistence. This

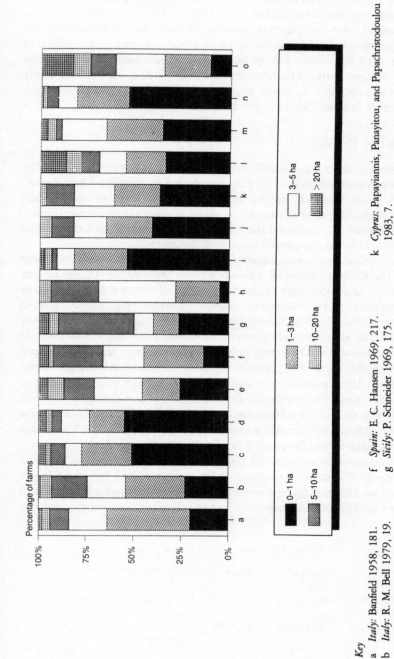

Percentage of farms

Fig. 4.7 Comparative Data on Farm Size.

Key

a *Italy:* Banfield 1958, 181.
b *Italy:* R. M. Bell 1979, 19.
c *Italy:* Brögger 1971, 37.
d *Italy:* J. Davis 1973, 76.
e *Turkey:* Hale 1981, 184.
f *Spain:* E. C. Hansen 1969, 217.
g *Sicily:* P. Schneider 1969, 175.
h *Italy:* Silverman 1975, 51
i *Italy:* White 1980, 85.
j *Greece:* Just 1981, unpublished
   field notes.
k *Cyprus:* Papayiannis, Panayitou, and Papachristodoulou
   1983, 7.
l *Portugal:* Cutileiro 1971, 41.
m *Jordan:* Clawson, Landsberg and Alexander 1971, 225.
n *Lebanon:* Clawson, Landsberg and Alexander 1971, 225.
o *Portugal:* O'Neill 1987, 89.

dilemma could be exacerbated when we consider the possible impact of interannual crop yield variability.

In general, the comparative sources support the estimation of the minimum farm size being on the order of 3 hectares, and that holdings of between 4 to 6 hectares can be considered as normative figures for an average peasant farm. The comparative indicate that all too frequently peasants are not able to attain even the minimum-sized holding. With these figures in mind, we can turn to the ancient material.

The Ancient Evidence

The ancient sources are divisible into two groups (Cooper 1977–8). The first refers to cases where land is being distributed to individual households, and the second consists of the occasional allusion to an individual's land-holdings. The former can tell us about consensual, "rule of thumb" notions as to what constituted the "average" farm, while the latter tells us more about what some people actually possessed.

For a culture which established roughly 200 colonies over a 300 year period, the Greeks produced remarkably few documents concerning the distribution and allotment of land. A series of decrees from Larisa in Thessaly during the Hellenistic period provides our largest sample (Habicht 1976, 151–74; Salviat and Vatin 1974, 247–62; SEG 26 nos 672–76). The allotments are given in the Greek plethra, I follow Burford Cooper in using an 11:1 ratio of plethra per hectare (Burford Cooper 1977–8, 169). Table 4.9 presents the relevent statistics from the Larisa documents. Allotments average slightly over 5 hectares, and this seems to have the amount which they considered normative (as witnessed by a mode of 4.5). The size of the allotments varied greatly. Why one person was given only .09 of a hectare while another received 23 we do not know. But the importance of the figure of 5 hectares seems clear.

Five and one half hectares (60 plethra) seems to have been the standard allotment at Pharsalos during the third century (DGI 567). Andreyev produced an identical figure for the plots given to Athenians on the island of Lesbos in 427 BC (Andreyev 1974, 14). Four to six hectares seems to

Table 4.9 Land distribution at Larisa

Sample size	Mean	Median	Mode
44	5.1	4.5	4.5

Minimum	Maximum	Standard deviation
.09	23	5

have been the amount of land ancient communities considered sufficient for the average household.

Evidence for actual holdings is very scarce and its interpretation ambiguous. For example, when a speaker in a forensic speech states that he has 4.5 hectares of land we have no way of discerning whether or not this represents all of his land or only that portion relevant to the litigation (see, for example, Isaios 5.22). Yet what there is of it does support the figures cited above.

Archaeological remains can provide us with some insights. Pečirka surmised on the basis of field walls and house remains on the Chersonesos that the average holdings there were between 3.3 and 5 hectares, although some were as large as 25 hectares (Pečirka 1973, 142–3). Archaeological surface survey has the potential to shed valuable light on this problem, but at present those surveys employing methodologies capable of doing so are either incomplete or have not yet published their results. Thus, the preliminary report from the Canadian-Karystia Project that some farm-steads, based on the area encompassed by their field walls, averaged 9 hectares should be seen as suggestive and no more (Keller and Wallace 1988, 154).[12]

Taken together, the ancient evidence closely resembles the comparative material. In both cases, a household was thought to need between 4 and 6 hectares in order to be viable. Accordingly these two figures will be employed as the baselines for the simulation of the domestic economy which follow.

Land and Labor over Time

Simply to state that the average farm was on the order of 4 to 6 hectares does not go far enough because it omits the fact that land-holdings, like the household itself, do not remain static over time (McInnis 1977). In order to model the variation in farm size diachronically two initial assumptions have to be made: that pure partible inheritance was enforced; and that peasant women received land in their dowry equal to or only slightly smaller than the shares awarded to their brothers. The basis for these two statements was presented in the previous chapter. By incorporating these two assumptions into the model, the pattern of land-holding depicted in figure 4.8 is produced.

A 6 hectare farm begins the life cycle with 8 hectares composed of the two brothers' patrimony and the dowry of the elder brother's wife. When the younger sibling marries during the second or third triennium, the portfolio is reduced to 6 hectares. It maintains this size until the daughter leaves, taking her dowry land with her. The shape of the distribution pattern remains the same with a 4 hectare farm. In sum, because of the action of the life cycle, the household has the most land early in its career.

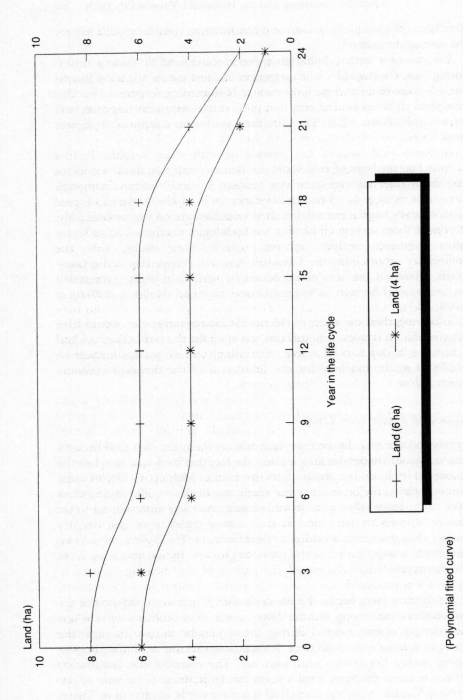

Fig. 4.8 Farm Size over the Life Cycle.

There follows in sequence phases of fragmentation, consolidation, and then fragmentation again.

We can next examine the labor product required to work a 4-to-6 hectare estate using the labor coefficients defined earlier (figure 4.9) and then compare that figure with the cycle of land-holdings (figure 4.10). One important assumption must be borne in mind. The labor input figures were based on the notion that all the land was under cultivation with field crops. If fallow is included, then we have to increase the total size of the estate.

Two far-reaching inferences can be drawn. First, the supposed labor surplus in the early phases of the household's development disappears. While it is the case that there is a labor surplus in relation to the subsistence needs of the group, if the household intended to work all of its land fully, then there is barely enough labor to work a 4 hectare farm at 175 md/year and not enough to work a 6 hectare unit even at 200 md/year. The discrepancy could be increased as well because it was exactly at this phase of the life cycle when the younger brother would be undergoing the rituals and duties associated with the transition to manhood – military training as an ephebe for example (Golden 1979) – and when the wife would have been bearing children much of the time. Consequently, they would have been unable to devote their full time to work on the farm. During these phases, it is highly likely that some particularly well-off peasant households would have required supplemental labor in the form of bought (slaves), borrowed, or hired labor at peak periods.

Second, during the middle stages of its career, the household would have possessed a considerable labor surplus. A shortage of labor persisted until the third triennium when the household split and children started to become workers. During the fourth triennium, the household's labor product would have outstripped its labor requirements, a trend which would have continued until near the end of the cycle, after having attained its zenith at the 15-year mark when almost 200 md/year or 400 md/year of surplus labor was present. As Chayanov showed in the case of Russian peasants, it was at this stage in the life cycle that the consumer: producer ratio shifted significantly (1986 [1966] 54–63; see also R.M. Smith 1984, 70). Clearly, the middle period was a vital one for the household.

This is not to argue that underemployment of this magnitude regularly occurred on ancient farms. I have deliberately kept all of the production parameters of the model constant. But in light of the conclusions drawn in the previous chapter, it is clear that many households could have significantly *intensified* their production during the middle phases of the life cycle.

All of the calculations to this point have been based on the household's subsistence requirements. This is a gross simplification. There were always additional needs to be met and other claimants to the farm's fruits. Two of

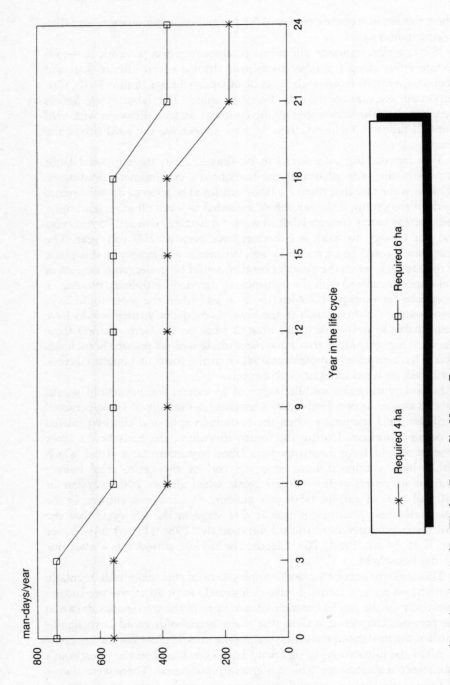

Fig. 4.9 Labor Required to Work a Four or Six Hectare Farm.

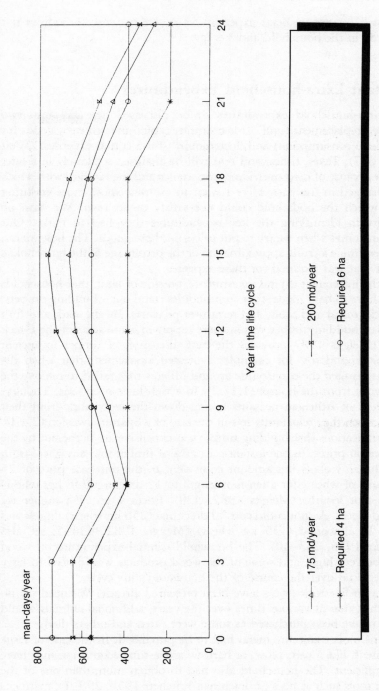

Fig. 4.10 Labor Required to Work a Four or Six Hectare Farm against Labor Available over the Life Cycle.

these will occupy us next: expenditures necessary for commodities not produced in the household and storage.

Constant Extra-household Expenditures

The extra-household expenditures to be discussed here fall into two groups: "replacement fund" (for example, capital investments, goods for immediate consumption) and "ceremonial" fund (ritual expenses) (Wolf 1966, 6–7). Taxes, tithes, and rent will be analyzed separately in a later chapter because of their overriding importance and the rapidity with which they changed in the past. Here I want to examine those more enduring needs which the household could not satisfy on its own. We have no difficulty in identifying the key expenditures they had to make. Our problem comes when we try to put prices on those goods. The best we can do is determine a crude approximation of the percentage of the household's budget that was required for these expenses.

Of the infrequent capital investments, outside of land, that households would have to have made, four commodities stand out – building timbers, livestock, metal and tools, and terracotta products. By the sixth and fifth centuries, building timber was in short supply in some areas of the Greek world (Meiggs 1982 provides the best discussion of timber in ancient Greece). Herodotos, for example, expressed amazement that when the Lydians ravaged the countryside around Miletos they failed to remove the woodwork from the houses (1.17.2). In a well-known episode, Thoukydides tells of Athenian peasants taking down the woodwork from their homes when they reluctantly left in the face of a Spartan invasion (2.4.1). These indications that building timber was expensive are borne out by the evidence on prices. In one instance, lengths of timber sold anywhere from 3 drachmai 3 obols (an amount equivalent to the purchase price of 25 kilograms of wheat) for a ten-foot length to 12 drachmai (48 kgs wheat) for 24-foot lengths (Meiggs 1982, 428). Prices were even higher for finished pieces. A door could cost 70 drachmai (256 kg wheat), lintels and jambs 17 drachmai (135 kg wheat) (Meggis 1982, 434–5; see also Pritchett 1956, 233–40). The household's initial expenditure on wood could be very high, and some of the wood products would need to have been replaced over the course of the household's life cycle.

Data on livestock prices have been presented already. We need say no more than that at various times over the years, additional animals would have to have been purchased as some were eaten and others died.

Farms tools using any metal had to be purchased. In the case of large equipment, like a cart, plow, or harrow, a one-time acquisition may have been sufficient. The household also had to obtain more than one of the smaller tools such as hoes (2 drachmai: Pritchett 1956, 290–1), mattocks

(3 drachmai, one obol: Pritchett 1956, 302–3), pruning knives, and sickles (Robinson 1941, 335–46). These would also have to have been replaced as they wore out or were lost over the course of the life cycle.

The skills of a specialist were needed to make the storage jars used on Greek farms. At Olynthos, the price of storage pithoi ranged from 31 drachmai (248 kg wheat) to 53 drachmai (424 kg wheat) (Robinson and Graham 1938, 314–316). Since on average a farm required three or more such jars, a sum close to the equivalent to one year's wheat supply would have been required to purchase storage jars. Roof tiles, bricks, and ceramic vessels were all needed and had to be purchased on an irregular basis. While inexpensive singly, the aggregate costs would have placed an additional strain on the household budget (Pritchett 1956, 281–7).

Moreover, other commodities like salt, charcoal and wood, and honey would have to have been obtained on a fairly regular basis. I focus on wood and charcoal. The importance of fuel for cooking, warmth, and light needs no comment. Over the course of a year, an average peasant household in the modern Argolid consumed approximately 2,000 kilograms of wood and charcoal (Forbes and Koster 1976, 122). In the past, some of it may have been supplied from cuttings and prunings accumulated on the farm, and some gathered from uncultivated macchia and woodlands – providing, of course, that people could obtain access to those areas and the rights to remove wood from them. When these two sources fell short of the household's requirements, peasants would have to have turned to the charcoal dealer. Even if we assume that only one quarter to one fifth of the fuel used was in the form of charcoal, at a price of 1 drachma and 3 obols per talent (1 talent equals 25.6 kg (Meiggs 1982, 479); for prices, see Glotz 1913; 1916; Pritchett 1956, 296–7), expenditures could have mounted quickly to either 30 drachmai *per annum*, if one quarter was purchased, or, if it was one fifth, 24 drachmai *per annum*.

Finally, over the course of the year and at various times during the life cycle, the household incurred certain costs for both annual ritual celebrations, such as those of the Zeus Ktesios and Zeus Herkeios (Isaios 8.15–16; Antiphon 1.16–20; Mikalson 1983, 83) among others, and periodic *rite de passage* and life-cycle ceremonies, such as weddings, births, male and female initiation ceremonies, and funerals (Mikalson 1983, 84–5). In addition to these primarily household affairs, people were supposed to participate in festivals and ceremonies celebrated by the associations they belonged to, their villages, their demes, and their state. As I argue later, in the case of last few, peasants expected their "betters" to bear the brunt of the costs. But, the *oikos* economy had to bear the burden of ceremonies conducted inside of it either directly through the removal of produce from the larder or indirectly through borrowing.

In this section I have given some rough approximations of the range and extent of expenditures which the household had to make over its life cycle.

Putting precise figures to them is difficult but clearly, in aggregate, they were not inconsiderable. Not all the expenditures cited here were irreducible: they could have been foregone if resources were in short supply. Some belt-tightening and improvisation could have put off expenditures until times improved. Nevertheless, taken together it seems to me that a figure of 10 percent for the household's replacement fund and ceremonial fund would, if anything, be a conservative estimate.

Storage as Strategy

The storage strategies adopted by ancient peasants can tell us a great deal about the ways they attempted to cope with fluctuations in their food supply and the degree to which the market had intruded into the household. I turn first to some comparative evidence which indicates that, if they are free to dispose of their produce as they wish, peasants on the whole aim at having anywhere from a year to a year and a half's supply of food in storage. An examination of both the ancient literary sources and the remains of ancient houses suggests that they also aimed at stockpiling similar amounts. Finally, I assess the drawbacks of relying on storage alone as a risk-buffering mechanism, placing especial emphasis on the problem of storability and potential losses in storage.

Indian peasants try to have anywhere from 10 to 14 months' worth of grain in storage at any one time (McAlpin 1979, 148; 1983, 13). A similar figure was reported by one study of African farmers (De Garine and Koppert 1988, 233). According to one survey of subsistence farmers in Guatemala, they aim at accumulating at least one year's food supply (Gladwin 1980, 80). Detailed analyses of medieval English household inventories indicate that they aimed at having approximately one year's food supply on hand, and if possible they tried to accumulate 18 months' worth of food (Fenoaltea 1976, 137–9). A fairly consistent pattern then seems to be evident indicating that peasants sought to store food for 12–18 months.

Forbes's work with households on the Greek peninsula of Methana indicated that they sought to have in their storerooms two full years' worth of wheat and four years' worth of olive oil (Forbes 1982, 234–5). These figures are somewhat higher than those reported above. When it is borne in mind that these quantities represent what the farmer wants to have on hand, not what he necessarily has, then they seem more in line with the comparative evidence. In any case, it is clear that modern Greek peasants aim to store quantities of food stuffs in their houses.

Xenophon relates that when Agesipolis, one of the Spartan Kings, endeavored to invade the state of Mantineia the first thing he did was to have his men ravage the land, but because the previous year's grain crop had been so good, he was told that it would take a considerable amount of time before it could be starved into submission. The passage clearly implies that the Mantineians had enough grain in their houses to feed themselves for at least one campaign season if not more. Agesipolis worried that his allies would desert him for their homes before the siege compelled the Mantineians to surrender because of the need to return to their farms (Xenophon *Hell* 5.2.4). I grant that this incident occurred during a war and so might be indicative only of war-time stockpiling, but the fact that only two years previously the people of Argos had received grain from the Mantineians suggests that they did not have much prior warning and that the grain on hand was perhaps representative of "normal" storage (Xenophon *Hell* 5.2.2).

A law at Selymbria stated that "private persons should hand over their grain to the state at a fixed price, keeping for themselves only one year's supply" (Pseudo-Aristotle 1348b1–1349a3). The second clause clearly implies that left on their own people would have kept more than one year's supply of grain on hand.

A courtroom drama from Athens gives yet another glimpse into an ancient storeroom. A heavy shower turned a streambed into a small torrent which, because part of the watercourse had been walled off, flooded another farmer's house. Consequently, the two households found themselves in court. It appears that 120 kilograms of barley and 20 kilograms of wheat were soaked by the flood. This seems to have been a household in the early stages of its development as a widowed mother is attested, and so using a figure based on the second or third triennium of the life cycle, this was enough grain to feed the household for approximately 40 days. Since the storm probably took place in winter, the rainy season at Athens, this represented part of the previous year's harvest. Moreover, given the defendant's comments concerning the amount, it is clear that much more than this was expected to be in storage (Demosthenes 55.24–6).

The occurrence of periodic markets for armies on the march and garrisons also suggests that peasants tried to hold on to as much of their crop yields as possible. Repeatedly we hear of an army traversing through friendly territory sending out advance scouts to arrange for the local peasants to mobilize and to make foodstuffs available for sale (e.g., Xenophon *Hell* 6.4.9; Xenophon *An* 2.3.24, 2.4.5; Pseudo-Aristotle 1350a24–37). Often very little forewarning was given and so the goods that the peasants had to sell were those which they had kept in storage for their own consumption.

The study of Thessaly by Garnsey, Gallant and Rathbone (1984) based on epigraphical evidence indicated that approximately 30 percent to 50 percent of the previous season's bumper wheat crop was still in the hands, or storage bins, of the primary producers the following spring, the time of year that is typically associated with scarcity. This amount would have been sufficient to feed the population of Thessaly for 14 to 16 months. Security through storage was clearly in the Thessalian peasants' minds. An examination of the archaeological evidence suggests that these figures are not unreasonable. One difficulty we face with this material is that all we have available are permanent storage facilities, and in particular storage jars. Grains could have been stored in baskets and in sunken pits (Weinstein 1973, 272; Kramer 1982a, 100–5). The former are lost to us and the latter are not always reported in sufficient detail by the excavators. For example at the site of Olynthos, the archaeologists identified all rooms with plastered walls as bathrooms, even though most of them were located adjacent to cooking areas (as evidenced by the discovery of ovens and other equipment associated with food preparation). It is highly likely that rooms like the ones found in houses A9, Avi2, Avi9, and Aviil (Robinson and Graham 1938, 78, 114,117) were grain stores. Thus, because we can quantify only the amount of storage available in jars, we underestimate the total area used. This is counterbalanced, however, by the fact that liquids were most likely kept in these jars, and so by using figures for storage based on grain we can compensate for this. The figures produced below, therefore, can provide a fairly accurate guide.

The following calculations are based on remains from Olynthos. At house Axi10 (Robinson and Graham 1938, 312–16), for example, four sunken pithoi were found, three intact. Depending on how they are reconstructed the total storage capacity was either 810 or 900 liters, equalling either 625 kg or 695 kg (Foxhall and Forbes 1982, 44: 0.772 kg/liter). At conversion rate of 3,100 kilocalories per kilogram, we obtain figures of 1,937,500 with the low estimate and 2,154,500 with the higher one. Combining this information with the life cycle data and a dietary figure of 65 percent of the total caloric intake in cereals produced earlier, we can conclude that the household had in storage grain sufficient for anywhere from 10 to 12 months (low estimate) or 11 to 13 months (high estimate) depending upon the life cycle phase.[13] This house is representative of the town as a whole (Robinson and Graham 1938, 61–128, 207–8). In fact, such emphasis was placed by them on storage facilities that, in at least one case, a man bought additional storerooms in addition to a house (Robinson 1934, 127–9; we find this practice elsewhere as well, e.g., Tinos (Dareste, Haussoullier, and Reinach 1965 {1895}, 74)).

Archaeological deposits from other sites support this picture. For example, even in Athens, where we might expect less reliance on physical storage and more on the market, some households devoted considerable space to food storage. One of the houses from the north slope of the Areopagus hill had one storeroom with five sunken pithoi and an adjacent room with a cement floor which was probably used for grain storage (J.E. Jones 1975, 82–3).

Together the comparative, documentary, and archaeological data present a coherent picture. Ancient peasants, it appears, aimed at having anywhere from 10 to 16 months' worth of food in their storerooms. This would have given them some cushion in case of reduced yields in the next growing season. But, on its own, physical storage of argricultural produce could not provide either a reliable or an extensive buffer against crop yield variability, primarily because of losses due to deterioration while in storage.

The critical problem with the storage of cereals and legumes centers on three primary factors: (a) the temperature and moisture of the seed grains when stored; (b) the temperature and moisture content of the intergranular air in the storage environment; and (c) the relation of the stored bulk to the external environment (Smith 1969, xv, 10; M.C. Rhodes 1980, 11–15).

With both grains and pulses, careful drying and sieving of the seeds is imperative in order to remove pests and to establish the correct moisture levels (Arnon 1972, 233). As Smartt (1976, 91) notes "provided that the moisture level is sufficiently low (10% or less), storage temperature is not excessively high and infestation by storage pests avoided, the nutritive value [of the seeds] can be maintained for several years." His figure for moisture content is slightly low; most authorities opt for 14–15 percent (Smith 1969, 2; Bland 1971, 38; M.C. Rhodes 1980, 15). If the moisture content rises much above 15 percent, then fungal growth commences (Smith 1969, 2–3). Fungal mycelia are always present on grain seeds, but they flourish better on weeds. Thus, conscientious removal of weeds can diminish fungal growth but cannot stop it. Insect infestation and fungal growth go hand-in-hand. The metabolism of the insects causes the temperature and the moisture content of the intergranular air to rise, thereby initiating fungal reproduction (Hall, Haswell, and Oxley 1956; M.C. Rhodes 1980, 13; Hunter 1980, 84). Mites especially can destroy a storeroom where the "economic loss is caused not so much by what the mites eat, as by the damage that results from changes in the moisture content of the medium which they initiate and the resultant mould growth and taint" (Smith 1969, 9; see also Hunter 1980, 84). The parasite then creates an ideal environment for the growth of its favorite food, and both destroy the stored grains. In addition to these pests, other threats to the storeroom are weevils, grain borers, rodents, snakes, and other assorted insects and animals (Hunter 1980, 79–90). Therefore, unless great care is given to the storage environment, losses can amount to anywhere from 50 percent to 80 percent (Hall, Haswell, and Oxley 1956; Smith 1969, ii; Smartt 1976, 124; Singer 1980, 7; Barreveld 1980, 43; Payne and Dowler 1980, 125; Parrack 1981, 44; d'Altroy and Earle 1985, 191–3; de Garine and Koppert 1988, 233; Huss-Ashmore and Thomas 1988, 464–5).

With the storage technology available in antiquity losses of similar magnitude would have been likely. Storage in pithoi, baskets, or even plaster-lined pits would not have enabled ancient farmers to control the moisture content of the intergranular environment closely enough to prevent the growth of fungi and insect infestations. And, if the numerous reptilian and small mamal remains found in a pithos at Nichoria (Messenia) are representative, then crop losses in storage would have been extremely high (Sloan and Duncan 1978, 75–6).

Theophrastos discusses some of the measures taken to reduce moisture in storage areas. In particular he recommends mixing certain types of clay-rich soils with the grains at a rate of 48 parts grain to one part soil (Theophrastos *HP* 8.11.7). Philo of Byzantium makes the same recommendation (B25–26, cited in Garlan 1974, 303) A late third-century inscription from the island of Evvoia indicates that this was probably a regular practice (Welles 1938, 252–3). The document sets out the duties of the civilian overseer of the food stores for a military garrison. Among his duties, he is to see "that they take in wheat, dried, from the last harvest and immediately order that it be mixed with Chalkidian earth" (Welles 1938, 252). The document also shows how acutely aware they were of the potential problems posed by moisture in the grain stores. "They are to inspect the wheat granaries as follows: during the six months of summer, after each rainstorm; during the winter months, every ten days. And if there has been any seepage of water into the wheat stores, then they are to make repairs immediately" (Welles 1938, 252).

While we cannot quantify the magnitude of food losses in storage, we can assume that they would have been sizeable, and that for this reason, reliance on storage alone would have greatly increased the household's risk of suffering a subsistence crisis. Other, alternative coping mechanisms had, therefore, to be developed. Some of the most important of these are discussed in the next chapter. But first, building on the implications of discussions above, we can examine the role of the market in ancient Greek peasants' lives, focusing in particular on the extent of their involvement in it.

Ancient Peasants, Surplus, and the Market

A thorough examination of the relationship between ancient peasants and the market would take us well beyond the scope of this work.[14] It is a topic of immense importance and one in need of serious attention.[15] My intention in this section is more modest. The argument presented here is that in general peasants in ancient Greece did not regularly mobilize their surplus production through the mechanism of the market. They chose instead to store it physically at the levels discussed earlier, invest it in the production of secondary commodities like livestock, or use it to create bonds of obligation through participation in reciprocal feasting with co-villagers. The discussion here sets up the argument to be made later (in Chapter 7) that when peasants were compelled to participate more fully in market transactions either because of diminished food supplies inside the household—necessitating their entrance into the market as buyers on unfavorable terms – or because of the imposition of increasingly high levels of taxes which had to be paid in cash – necessitating their entrance into the market as sellers on unfavorable terms. The end result of the first was chronic indebtedness, and in conjunction with the second, it led to a diminution of the effectiveness of many of their adaptive measures and response strategies for coping with crop yield variability (Arnold 1988, 51).

An orientation toward production for direct consumption, or subsistence, does not mean that peasants intentionally aimed not to produce a "surplus" or that they never became involved in market transactions. The following from Ghatak and Ingersent captures well the distinction: "whereas a purely subsistence farmer is not necessarily fully self-sufficient, a fully self-sufficient farmer may also produce a marketable surplus. However, if no market exists, or if the farmer does not desire a cash income, the surplus may be reabsorbed by the farm family which consequently increases its consumption to match the larger-sized crop" (Ghatak and Ingersent 1984, 6).

The type of economic activity envisaged here can be categorized best as *simple commodity production*, the salient characteristics of which are: (a) an emphasis on production for direct use by the producers; (b) an emphasis on exchange for use value (schematized as "use value – exchange value – use value"); (c) reliance on domestic labor supplemented by non-commoditized labor obtained through social relations (Chevalier 1983; G. Smith 1985; O. Harris 1982, 145). Ideally, economic transactions are inseparable from social transactions. The emphasis here is on the ideal: when dealing with patrons, landlords, tax collectors, and merchant middlemen, for example, only a thin veneer of sociability may cover a hard core of economic reality. The end result of simple commodity production is to make peasants averse to being more than only marginal participants in markets (Goodman and Redclift 1981, 68–127; Russell 1987, 147; Wylie 1989, 169; Bose 1986, 70; C.A. Gregory 1982, 29; Seavoy 1986, 387–91; J.C. Scott 1976, 13–15; van Apeldoorn 1981, 96; McCann 1987a, 69–70; Watts 1988, 276–83; 1983, 187–206; Vaughan 1987, 77–8).

The kind of exchange described by simple commodity production resembles closely Aristotle's description of exchange (*NE* 1133a5–b40; Aristotle *Pol* 1257al). While the interpretation of these passages and their implications for our understanding of Greek economic thought are not without controversy (Polanyi 1957b; Finley 1974; Meikle 1979; Lowry 1987, 192–212), the general proposition that Aristotle placed primary importance on use value and exchange for use value is generally accepted. For him, exchange of goods should occur only as the need arose and then only for the goods one needed (Aristotle *Pol* 125715–16).

The regularity of markets can tell us about their importance. If they were infrequent affairs, then we may legitimately infer that they did not play a major role in peoples' lives. Obviously, wherever there were large, relatively stable groups of non-primary producing consumers, as at large towns like Athens and ceremonial centers like Delphi and Olympia, daily markets were required to service the demand for food. Yet, even in these cases we need to be aware of the likelihood that much of the produce made available for those markets came from large estates rather than peasant holdings (e.g., Phainippos (Demosthenes 23.166–7)), that only peasants living in the immediate area might have participated directly, if only occasionally, in the market, and that merchant middlemen provided a sizeable percentage of the supply having acquired it from peasants who had a disposable surplus and a need for cash, for example the Platean cheese-merchants who on the last day of the month came to Athens to sell cheese they had obtained in the countryside (Lysias 23.6) or the grain dealers about whom so much has been written (Garnsey 1984; Garnsey 1988a, 137–49; Montgomery 1986; Marianne V. Hansen 1984; Figueira 1986).[16] The anecdote concerning the Athenian Perikles' whole-hearted integration into the market was meant to distinguish him from other wealthy men, who presumably were more reluctant participants (Plutarch *Per* 16.3–5; Campbell 1983). And the well-known passage from Aristophanes' *Ach* (33–6) about the absence of market exchange in Attic village has lost none of its poignancy through repeated citation.

In Greek communities generally, markets were periodic. Recently, de Ligt and de Neeve have discussed the evidence for one type – the periodic market with long intervals – and they found it usually to be associated with religious festivals (de Ligt and de Neeve 1988). As well as providing an occasion for venerating the deities, religious festivals were ideal for socializing and trade.

Most of these festivals took place during a hiatus in the agricultural year, after the harvest when households would have had a fair idea about the state of their food supply for the coming year and thus would have known what their surplus was. Sellers and buyers were provided with an ideal venue. "For traders periodic markets are a means to make a living on products for which insufficient demand exists to make a permanent establishment in one place viable. Or they may be a means for them to buy up surpluses which are available only periodically" (de Ligt and de Neeve 1988, 401). We should not, however, lose sight of the social dimension to these affairs. They also provided an ideal opportunity for the household to accumulate social capital by expending its surplus on a feast for kin and friends. The two actions were not mutually exclusive, but simply different options open to the household for mobilizing its surplus at festival markets.

Other indications for the lack of regular markets come from descriptions of military campaigns. We hear repeatedly of episodes where armies on the march through friendly territory had to send representatives ahead in order to organize a market for the army (e.g. Xenophon *Hell* 6.4.9; 2.3.24, 2.4.5; Pseudo-Aristotle 1349b24–29, 1350a1–15). If markets were normal and peasant participation regular, such a measure would have been unnecessary. Possibly another intimation of this is provided by a passage by Aineias Taktikos (23.4) where he recommends that, in addition to being paid in cash, mercenaries should be billeted and fed in the houses of wealthy men (see also Xenophon *Ana* 7.2.6; Polyainos 2.30.1, 22.29). In this case, the lack of markets made imposing hired warriors on the domestic economy of the wealthy the simplest way of supplying them with food. It is also cheaper to live off the rich.

Finally, I concluded in the last section that ancient peasants in general aimed at storing anywhere from 10 to 16 months' worth of food. Even the lure of high prices failed to move the Selymbrians and the Thessalians to dip into their pithoi and remove grain for sale. Food in a jar was preferred to coins in a pouch. For, as Aristotle noted, "a man rich in currency will often be at a loss to procure his basic subsistence; and surely it is absurd that that thing should be counted as wealth which a man may possess in abundance and yet nonetheless die of starvation" (Aristotle *Pol* 1257b13–15).

In sum, the market seems to have played only a minor, peripheral role in the domestic economy of most Greek peasants. As with other groups practicing simple commodity production, they opted for alternative strategies of surplus mobilization which better enabled them to buffer themselves against subsistence risk. Thus, in the model household to be discussed in the next section, we will omit from discussion the possible impact of the market and the "commoditization" of agricultural production. Later on, however, we shall return to it.

The Vulnerability Cycle and Adaptive Measures

We can now bring together the results of the previous sections and construct a dynamic model of the peasant farm. The model demonstrates the precariousness of the domestic economy and distinguishes certain phases of the household life cycle when the household was most vulnerable to risk, a pattern we shall call the "vulnerability cycle." In some respects, the vulnerability cycle resembles the "nuclear-hardship principle" (Laslett 1988, 153–6; R.M. Smith 1984, 73; Wales 1984, 359), particularly as it was employed by Smith. The essential difference is that nuclear hardship is seen as stemming from the strict application of the rules of nuclear houshold formation and the impact it has on those who become bereft of their nuclear unit – widows, widowers, and orphans for example. The vulnerability cycle refers more specifically to those periods during the household life cycle when it experiences heightened susceptibility to subsistence risk. The two concepts are complementary; they simply place the emphasis on different aspects.

Before we can construct a dynamic model of the domestic economy, we need to arrive at an estimate of crop yield variability for each of the major food groups. I present in table 4.10 the Coefficients of Variation of the

Table 4.10 Crop yield variability in various regions of Greece

	Wheat	Barley	Kidney beans	Broad beans	Lentils	Chickpeas
Achaia	36	38	29	44	37	28
Aitolia	47	46	39	37	34	45
Argolid	34	30	53	43	37	55
Arkadia	44	35	47	44	32	37
Athens	31	23	32	23	28	72
Attika	30	29	40	58	24	38
Evros	42	40	36	41	29	25
Evvoia	44	49	42	37	36	43
Herakleion	30	30	46	44	29	30
Ioannina	28	54	30	44	30	36
Kalamata	38	33	43	70	41	43
Karditsa	36	35	35	48	22	22
Kavala	47	40	43	32	41	41
Kephalenia	28	29	59	43	35	39
Kerkyra	40	40	44	34	31	52
Korinth	40	36	39	40	41	45
Kozani	46	45	46	53	35	37
Lakonia	36	37	45	43	45	31
Larisa	49	49	52	47	51	49
Lefkas	29	29	27	37	81	41
Lesbos	36	37	46	45	26	37
Magnesia	26	30	39	37	35	15
Phthiotis	50	51	56	50	40	35
Thessaloniki	39	36	43	34	32	36
Trikala	53	47	52	58	34	36
Zakynthos	21	36	56	40	29	35

major subsistence crops from across the Greek world (in additon, see Gallant, 1989, 397). Based on these results, a calculation was made of the minimum and the maximum amount of land needed to produce these crops. These figures were then plotted against the development cycle of land on a 4 and a 6 hectare farm and against the household's subsistence requirement – again expressed in land. The results are presented in figure 4.11.

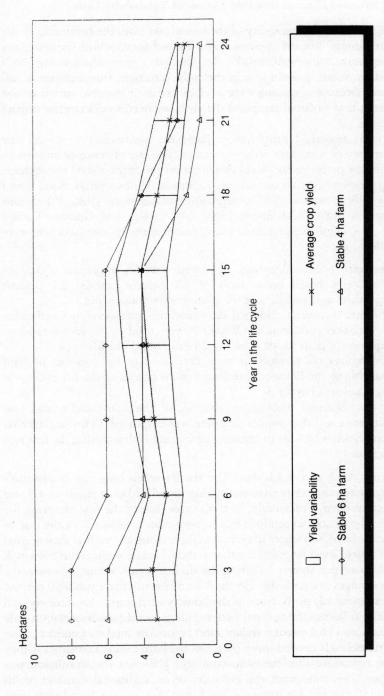

Fig. 4.11 Amount of Land Required to Produce Subsistence Minimum when Variability is Included.

The increasing vulnerability of the household from the beginning of the third triennium onward appears again. Indeed for much of the time, a 4 hectare farm falls well inside the shaded region designating high variability. While pointing us in the right direction, this measure is still too crude because it measures the average range of possible variation and thus lacks that essential temporal dynamic we need to discern the impact of climate.

For this reason, I employed a computer simulation to model the performance of a peasant farm over time. The use of machine models to simulate the performance of subsistence level production is on the increase among development economists (e.g., Strauss 1986a; Singh, Squire, and Strauss 1986a; Strauss 1986b; Singh and Subramanian 1986; V.E. Smith and Strauss 1986; R.M. Smith 1984, 68–72; Roe and Graham-Tomasi 1986). The inital steps taken in the creation of the model used here were the following:

1   The rate of consumption employed was an aggregate figure in kilocalories based on a ratio of 65 percent cereals, 25 percent vegetables and pulses, and 10 percent olives and vines.
2   The data on output discussed above and the corresponding Coefficients of Variation presented in Chapter 3 were used to produce a random sequence of crop yields over the 24-year houshold life cycle.
3   The figures on production were correlated to the amount of land available to the household during various phases of the life cycle – as discussed in Chapter 3.
4   It was assumed throughout that all of the household's land was cultivated and that annual cropping was employed. (This implies that households were able to obtain supplemental labor during the first two triennia.)

Figures 4.12 and 4.13 show the results when only the household's subsistence requirements were run against simulated crop yields on a 4 and a 6 hectare farm. Predictably, in both cases during the first six years the household was able to produce much more than it required: in the case of a 4 hectare farm, anywhere from two to three times as much as they needed and, of course, even larger quantities on the 6 hectare estate. (But more will be said about this shortly.) During the middle four triennia, however, the picture changes dramatically. On the 4 hectare farm, there was a 30 percent (4 years out of 12) probability of the household failing to produce enough food. The 6 hectare farm fared better, failing to attain sufficiency on only two occasions (16.7 percent failure rate) before the final triennium.

All households needed more than just the bare caloric necessities if they were to reproduce themselves successfully. Therefore the simulation was run again, this time with the inclusion of an additional demand of 40 percent (30 percent for storage – the figure that we concluded they were

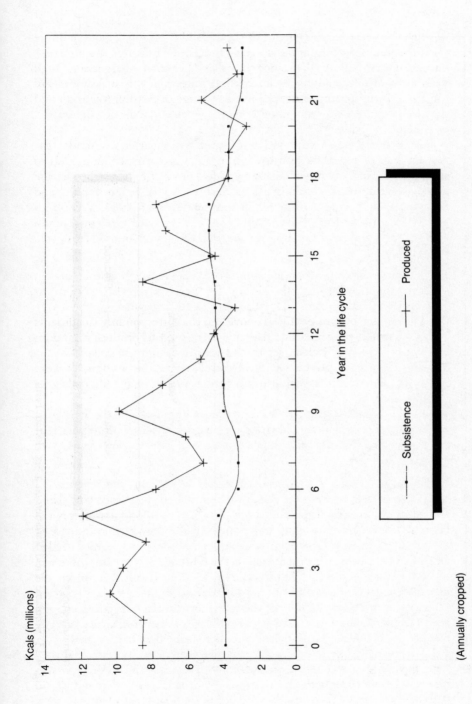

Kcals (millions)

Year in the life cycle

(Annually cropped)

Fig. 4.12 Simulated Yield Variation on a Four Hectare Farm.

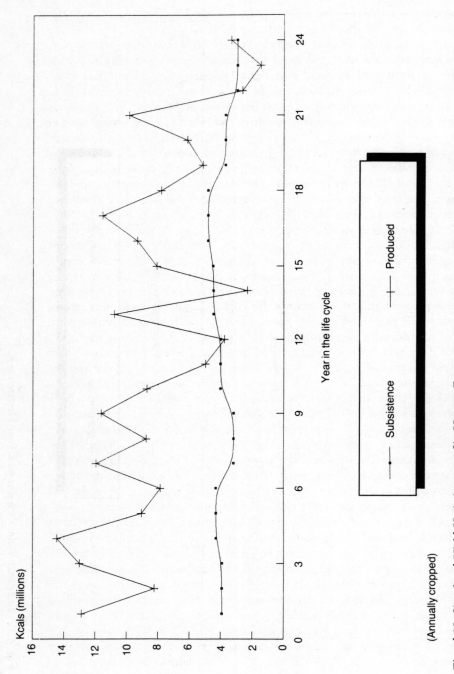

Kcals (millions)

(Annually cropped)

Fig. 4.13 Simulated Yield Variation on a Six Hectare Farm.

aiming at – and 10 percent for constant extra-household expenditures). The results are provided in figures 4.14 and 4.15.

Once again it appears that during the first two triennia peasant households could have produced significantly more than they required. But we must bear in mind that the additional labor supply had to be accounted for, probably with a share of the crop given to the workers as a "gift," and that during these phases of the life cycle greater demands were made on the household's resources. For example, the capital needed to establish the younger sibling in his own *oikos* had to be accumulated. In addition, resources had to be mobilized to underwrite the costs of his wedding, the funeral of their mother, and the birth festivals of at least three children. On each occasion the household was expected to hold feasts, the lavishness of which would have been the subject of gossip for weeks afterward (Hesiod *WD* 335–72; Theophrastos *Char* 9.2, 20.7, 22.4). Nevertheless, we should be aware of the possibility that they might not have cultivated all of their land. The results of the simulations also demonstrate conclusively the vulnerability of the household during the middle four triennia. A 4 hectare farm would have failed to match its production goals fully two-thirds of the time (8 out of 12 years or 66.7 percent) and, if we include the remainder of the cycle, this figures rises to 72 percent. Even a 6 hectare unit would have been unsuccessful one third of the time during the middle period of the life cycle and up to half if we take into account the final six years. There appears, then, to be a marked cyclical pattern of vulnerability during which times the average ancient household found itself in a very precarious economic position.

Greek peasants were not powerless in the face of their fickle environment. As we saw vividly in the last chapter, embedded in their agricultural system was a range of adaptive mechanisms for coping with variability. For example, they could have (a) tilled their fields with hoes rather than plowing them, (b) increased the amount of time spent weeding, (c) drill sown rather than broadcast seeds, (d) rearranged the spatial distribution of crops with a greater regard for labor input in order to reduce travel, and (e) spent more energy gathering and spreading manure and compost.

All of these measures required more intensive application of labor, labor which households had available during the period of maximum vulnerability. This raises the problem of the utility of additional consumption, the marginal utility of labor, and the drudgery associated with the additional labor (Chayanov 1986 [1966], 50–3). Recently, Calavan discussed this question in relation to risk and uncertainly; the two flowcharts he produced to represent the decision-making sequence on peasant farms were used to structure parts of the simulation presented next (Calavan 1984, 61–5).

The simulation was run again, this time with output levels raised in order to account for intensificaiton. The problem I faced here was in determining the rate at which to increase output. In light of the

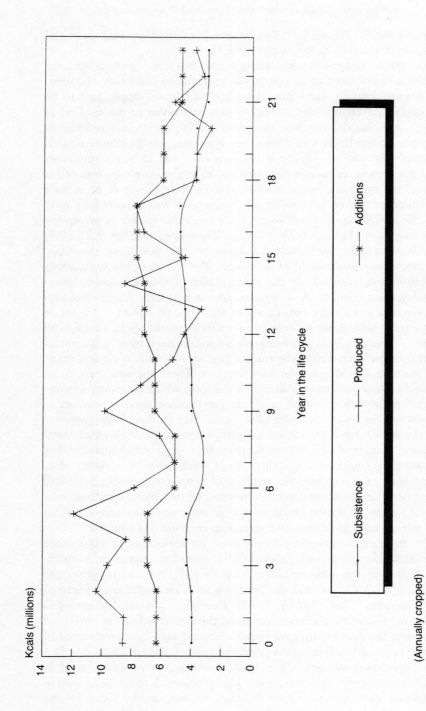

Kcals (millions)

Year in the life cycle

— Subsistence   —+— Produced   —*— Additions

(Annually cropped)

Fig. 4.14 Simulated Yield Variation on a Four Hectare Farm, including Storage and Expenditures.

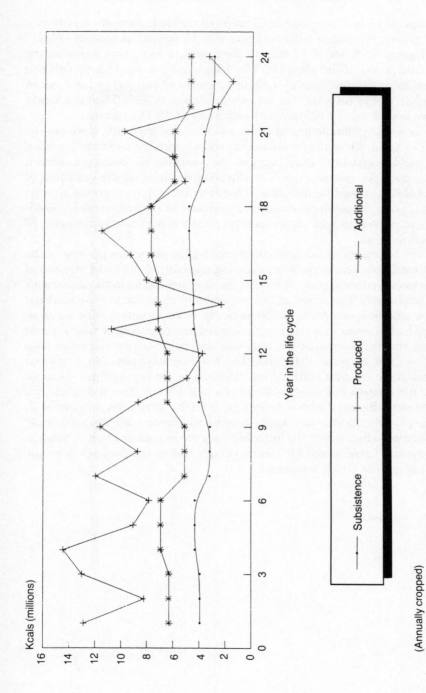

Kcals (millions)

Year in the life cycle

— Subsistence   — Produced   — Additional

(Annually cropped)

Fig. 4.15 Simulated Yield Variation on a Six Hectare Farm, including Storage and Expenditures.

comparative data presented in Chapter 3 I decided to employ a ratio of a 40 percent increase in labor resulting in a 33 percent increase in yields.

Figures 4.16 and 4.17 display the results. I focus once again on the middle period of the life cycle. The 4 hectare farm would have failed to meet its production goals in 4 out of 12 years (33 percent) and in 7 out of the last 18 (39 percent). The corresponding figures with 6 hectares would have been 3 out 12 (25 percent) and 6 out of 18 (33 percent).

As with any simulation based on a randomized sequence, if we ran the model again, we would be unlikely to end up with the same configuration of yield variability. But, because the variation is based on known sequences, the general pattern of distribution, and thus the estimated of probability, would be the same. Therefore, the output from the simulations, given the assumptions and the quantitative parameters we imposed, should provide us with an accurate gauge of the economic performance of peasant farms.

The results presented demonstrate the highly precarious position of the ancient Greek peasantry. With alarming regularity they would have found themselves running short of food in the face climatically induced shortfalls in production. The action of the vulnerability cycle would have rendered their situation even more problematic. In order to ensure their survival, they had to resort to a range of stratagems, the operation of which would have enabled them to cope with one and possibly two successive crop failures but no more than that. The response strategies they employed when those traumas occurred are discussed in the next chapter. I cannot end this discussion, though, without pointing out that taxes and tithes were systematically and deliberately omitted from the simulation. In Chapter 7, I employ the model once again in order to demonstrate the profoundly deleterious effect which the imposition of ever-increasing levels of taxation in the late Classical and Hellenistic periods had on the domestic economy of the ancient Greek household.

Kcals (millions)

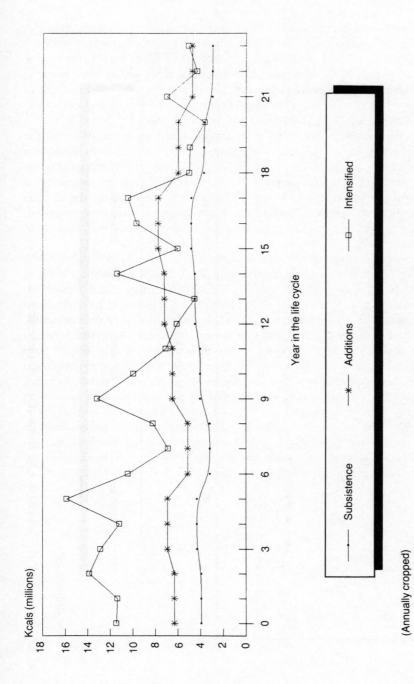

(Annually cropped)

Fig. 4.16 Simulated Yield Variation on a Four Hectare Farm, after Intensification.

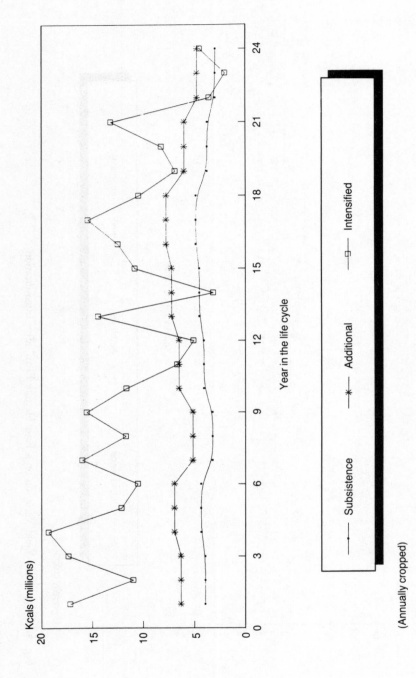

Kcals (millions)

Year in the life cycle

Subsistence ——•——   Additional ——*——   Intensified ——□——

(Annually cropped)

Fig. 4.17 Simulated Yield Variation on a Six Hectare Farm, after Intensification.

5 Response Strategies to Food Shortage: Household "Self-Help" Systems

> My husband is a poor man and I am his aged wife with a daughter, a son, and this sweet young girl, five in all are we. If three of us get dinner, then the other two must share a tiny barley cake. We make sounds of wretched wailing when we have nothing to eat, and our pallor grows pale from the lack of food. The sum total of our subsistence comes from these – broad beans, lupines, a turnip, greens, various legumes, vetch, beech-nuts, iris bulbs, a cicada or two, chickpeas, wild pears, and those god-given blessings from mother earth, darlings of my heart, dried figs.
>
> Alexis of Thourioi

The adaptive measures discussed in an earlier chapter were prophylactic in intent. Operating together as a coherent agrarian system, they enabled ancient farmers to minimize the risk of a total production failure. Nevertheless, the frequency and the magnitude of crop yield fluctuations were such that, unless further actions were taken, the household's food resources would often have been insufficient to meet its needs. Examinations of other cultures indicate that they employ a hierarchically ordered set of response strategies as a means of coping with food shortages. In this chapter I analyze in a comparative framework the response strategies available to and employed by Greek households.

Cropping Strategies in a Crisis

Ancient farmers had at their disposal a wealth of agro-environmental information about the plants they cultivated. Often this knowledge was encoded in the form of parables or sayings. Theophrastos recorded over 200 such sayings about the weather; some of them, moreover, contained very accurate means for predicting the weather over both the long and the short term. Farmers used this information to structure their cropping strategies. Obviously, numerous other factors as well helped to shape their thinking, such as the size and location, of their land-holdings, the amount of labor available in the household, and the extra-household demands they had to satisfy. Within the bounds set by these demands, farmers had considerable flexibility in deciding how to manipulate their crops (Wilmsen and Durham 1988). Peasant farmers were constant sky-watchers, obsessed with the climate (Gallant 1982b, 21). And when they perceived that environmental conditions were posing a threat to the yields of their crops, they could act to mitigate the impact of the trauma or to compensate for any losses it might cause. Such *response strategies* provided the first tier in a hierarchically ordered sequence of actions peasants could take to forestall or prevent a subsistence crisis. The best way to observe these strategies in operation is to examine how ancient peasants could have responded to varying climatic conditions as the agricultural year progressed.

The timing and the extent of the winter rains were the first threats posed by the climate. If too much precipitation fell, germination could be delayed. This would extend the growing season and render the crop more vulnerable to spring drought; in addition, it could cause the seeds to rot in the ground. A farmer could prevent this by hoeing his fields, thereby aerating the soil (Xenophon *Oik* 17.12–13), if sufficient labor was available. A drought during November and December as well could easily destroy the seeds (Arnon 1972, 14; Briggs 1978, 248–9). In the event of either occurring, by the end of December a critical farm management decision had to be made concerning the viability of the crops. Winter wheats, barleys, and legumes planted much after the end of December would have been unlikely to complete their growth cycle before the summer drought began; if that happened, the probability of a total crop failure was high (Fisher 1973).

Once a farm decided that his winter crops were in jeopardy, then, assuming he had sufficient seeds, labor power, and access to traction animals, he could plant a second crop. But, as Theophrastos warned, the yield would be lower regardless of the weather during the remainder of the growth season (*HP* 8.6.1). None the less, by planting a second crop in this way, at least some food would be assured – if, that is, no other event ruined it. Sowing a second crop was a commonly observed response (Hankins 1974, 103; Wisner and Mbithi 1974, 88; Post 1985, 95).

The next crucial decision came at the end of February. Depending on the state of the autumn-sown crops, a farmer would have to determine the locations and the quantity of the spring crops he would plant. Both spring wheats and barleys were available, and many of the legumes consumed in Greece were spring crops. We can assume that many farmers would have been producing them as a matter of course, but that the extent to which they cultivated such crops would have been determined by the propects of the winter crops. In this way they represented a potential response strategy.

If the yields of both the autumn and the spring-sown crops proved deficient, farmers could endeavor to produce some food by planting a quick-ripening summer crop. Theophrastos discussed three such crops: sesame, millet, and Italian millet (*HP* 8.1.4). These species were known and grown in the Greek world since the Late Bronze Age (Kroll 1984,

243–6; Jones 1987, 118, 122). They are all hardy, drought-resistant, and fast-growing. Like spring-sown cereals and legumes, they complement the growth cycle of the winter cereals well and so could have easily been integrated into a continuous cropping strategy, but I suspect, and have argued elsewhere, that their main function was as a secondary, crisis-response crop (Gallant 1985b; see also, Spurr 1983; Arnon 1972, 381–7). Their long-term storability also enhance their role as an emergency crop. Both millet and sesame seeds retain their potency over long periods of time (Theophrastos *HP* 8.11.2) and so they could be kept in storage until needed.

Three features limited the viability and the utility of the measures discussed so far. First, each of them required labor at times which directly competed with other agricultural activities. Planting a crop in December, for example, would have necessitated shifting labor away from the olive harvest. In order for these measures to work, the household needed to be able to allocate its members' labor power. If extra-household agencies could control the disposition of labor, these strategies simply would not have been viable options. Second, each of them required the investment of household resources, in particular traction animals. The key to planting a second crop successfully was the speed with which it could be sown. Access to traction animals would have been essential. Third, these response strategies were predicated on the assumption that peasant households would have had in storage the needed seeds, and that they could have afforded the luxury of planting rather than eating them (Gallant 1989, 402; Forbes 1982, 44, 356–77).

Wild Thing(s)

When food stores began to dwindle, ancient Greeks, like peasants elsewhere, could exploit a wide variety of wild resources in order to supplement or to replace their normal dietary regime (*Africa*: Corkhill 1949, 1–12; van Apeldoorn 1981, 82; Vaughan 1985, 187; Wisner and Mbithi 1974, 90; Colson 1979, 21, 22, 25; de Garine and Koppert 1988, 236; Bratton 1987, 224; Watts 1983, 333; 1988, 273; Richards 1986, 123–4; *India*: Bhandari 1974, 73–81; *Bangladesh*: Currey 1981, 128–9, Fig. 11; *China*: Chang 1977, 6–21; Dando 1980, 80–7; *North America*: Wilkens 1970, 286–95; Handy and Handy 1972, 274–6; Minnis 1985, 36: *Europe*: Curtis and Gilbey 1944; Dando 1980, 145; Goure 1962; Sutherland 1981, 441; Parry 1978, 89; Blok 1974, 19). The list of wild foodstuffs found in Greece and the Mediterranean is impressively long (see, for example, the extensive but not exhaustive catalogues provided by Rackham (1983, 347–9) and Evans (1980b, 165–7)), but an analysis of the total amount of calories *per capita* that these alternative foodstuffs could have provided leads us to the sobering conclusion that wild, gathered plants, animals, and fish would have been unable to act as anything more than a short-term response to food shortages.

Gathering Wild Flora

The most comprehensive studies on the utilization of wild, gathered plants by Greek agriculturalists are by Mari Clark (1976a; 1976b; 1976c; 1977). She found that the peasants of Methana, a small peninsula in the Peloponnesos, consume on a regular basis 38 wild plant species, divided into three major groups: leafy plants, nuts, and berries. Leafy plants predominate. Among those gathered are dock, dandelion, chicory, sow thistle, and red poppy. Valonia oak acorns and holm oak acorns are the most commonly eaten nuts, and pears, blackberries, prickly pear cactus, and strawberry tree were the favored fruits (1977, 58). Turning to the ancient world, the long and detailed accounts of the natural flora of Greece by Theophrastos (see, in particular, *HP* 3, 7; *CP* 1–2), Athenaios, (2, 3) and Galen (6.38–9) conclusively demonstrate that all these species, as well as numerous others, were utilized by the human communities there (see also, Frayn 1979, 57–72; Evans 1980a, 138–9).

In the course of a "normal" year modern Greek peasants use wild leaves, berries, and nuts to add flavor and texture to their otherwise dull cereal–legumes–olive based diet. In addition, because many of these plants have different growth cycles from the cultivated plants, they can fill in the seasonal gaps. For example, Clark noted a bimodal consumption pattern with the peaks occurring in October–December and April–June (1976b, 260–3; Clark 1977, 57; see also, Wagstaff and Gamble 1982, 103). During these periods, wild resources contribute anywhere from 8 percent to 20 percent of the total calories consumed by peasant households (1977, 52). While Clark did not directly observe the following progression in operation, the wealth of comparative material cited earlier would suggest that the amount of emphasis placed upon wild resources increases commensurately with the decrease in the yields of the major food crops. As households begin to realize that the crops are failing, they start to expend more time and labor gathering wild plants, fruits, and nuts which they eat either fresh or, in the case of nuts and fruits, processed and stored for consumption later. Acorns, for example, are readily storable as whole nuts in pithoi (storage jars); later, if conditions improve, the acorns are fed to pigs or, if the subsistence crisis deepens, the nuts are roasted and eaten by humans; they are also ground into flour and stored in jars or in baskets, and eaten later as porridge mixed with honey and milk or baked into bread (Xenophon *Ana* 5.4.27; Galen 6.38, 620; E. Anderson 1924; Coon 1974, 26, 141–2;

Garbarino 1976, 169–70). If conditions continue to deteriorate, the household turns increasingly to gathered foodstuffs.

The best discussion of the use of gathered "famine foods" in the ancient world is provided by Galen. He observed that when the major cereal crops failed, peasants turned first to other cultivated cereals, often planting such a crop as in the strategies outlined earlier in this chapter. He mentions specifically millet being used in this capacity (6.15). Peasants looked next to wild, gathered cereals, legumes, and weeds such as wild oats (6.14), wild chickling, bird's pease, calavance, and fenugreek (6.15). Along with these, they consumed acorns, wild plums, wild pears, bramble, dog-thorn, and the like (6.38). Moreover, "when forced by hunger people eat *pyrethium, sia, alexander,* fennel, wild chervil, chicory, gum soccory, gingidium, will carrot and the shoots of a great many shrubs and trees" (6.39). Finally, when starvation was imminent, people consumed such unpalatable plants as darnel, dodder, and even bitter vetch (6.32).

Scattered throughout his compilation of anecdotes and stories on food and dining, Athenaios referred to a wide variety of wild, gathered vegetables, fruits, and nuts. In his second book, for example, he recorded long descriptions of the various types of nuts available in the eastern Mediterranean and the manifold ways in which they were prepared for human consumption (Athenaios 2.50–8;). It appears that there were even treatises describing the best way to prepare wild plants; Athenaios (2.68) cited passages from a lost work by Diokles of Karystos "On Health" which detailed the best ways to cook, among others, wild lettuce, watercress, coriander, mustard greens, garlic, and poppy. And an account of the importance of wild plants to the diet of the poor more vivid than the one cited at the start of this chapter would be hard to find. Clearly, wild, gathered plants were utilized by the poor regularly and by the rest of the peasantry frequently when crop yields fell.

Analyses of organic remains from the Late Bronze Age–Early Iron Age (c.1200–800 BC) site of Kastanas in Makedonia indicate that acorns, danewort, bladder cherry, strawberry, and celery were gathered and consumed presumably on a regular basis (Kroll 1984, 244–6).

It is clear from both written sources and the archaeological evidence that ancient Greek peasants consumed a very wide array of wild plants in their efforts to respond to a reduction in their food supply. Nevertheless, for three reasons, these resources could have acted only as a temporary response to food shortage.

The first shortcoming pertains to the reliability of wild plant species in the face of a climatic crisis (Allen W. Johnson and Earle 1987, 30). They grow in two broad zones – cultivated fields and non-cultivated areas like macchia, gariga, and woodlands (Rackham 1983). The plants found in cultivated fields are usually those whose growth cycle and nutritional requirements directly compete with domesticated crops. Thus, the wild species would suffer from the selfsame climatic trauma which threatened the primary crop. Wild plants growing on fallow fields would most likely fare better, but the amount of land allowed to go fallow probably varied considerably from place to place and from time to time; and, if it was only the large land-holders who were permitted the luxury of practicing any type of systematic fallowing, peasants would need to obtain permission before being able to gather the plants growing there. It would seem then that the availability of wild plants growing in cultivated areas would fluctuate considerably from year to year.

Macchia, gariga, and woodland are separate and distinct plant communities, and each is susceptible to further subdivision internally. Rackham describes six series of macchia found in modern Boiotia (1983, 301–3). These plant communities contained a wide variety of species with growth cycles slightly different from each other and certainly different from the major cultivated species. For this reason, they produced edible matter at times when the cultivated areas did not. Theophrastos, for example, noted that the fruit of wild trees often ripened later than that of cultivated trees (*HP* 3.4.1). Density per unit area is the major drawback to the plants located in these ecological zones: they are usually found in small communities scattered over a wide area. Even in aggregate, the total calories available from the edible biomass of macchia, gariga, and woodland plant communities was relatively small.

Second, because of the low calorific content of many wild plant species, ancient Greeks would have had to consume prodigious quantities in order for them fully to supplant cereals and legumes in the diet. Some examples demonstrate this graphically. In order to obtain the same amount of kilocalories contained in 1 kilogram of wheat bread, a person needs to eat 12.8 kilograms of dock or 8 kilograms of dandelion greens, 8.5 kilograms of prickly pears, or just 5.8 kilograms of regular pears (all figures are taken from Clark 1976a, 139 and Hirschmann 1979). It is doubtful whether many people had either the time to collect or the stomach to eat the 12.6 kilograms of mushrooms needed to replace 1 kilogram of wheat bread. Nuts and dried seeds provided a more concentrated source of calories – both pine nuts and sesame seeds, for example, have nearly twice the kilocalories per weight of wheat bread but nonetheless it would be a very time-consuming task to collect even these quantities.

Third, the potential role of wild gathered plants in the diet was severely limited by population density (Colson 1979, 25; Allen W. Johnson and Earle 1987, 60–1; Halstead 1987b, 81). Comparative studies of hunter-gatherer groups in different parts of the globe indicate that, depending on the natural abundance of their territory, such cultures require between 1.4 and 40 square miles of terrain per person in order to ensure their subsistence (Johnson and Earle 1987, 32, 45; Winterhalter 1986; 1987). Uncultivated land tracts of these dimensions were simply not available in most parts of ancient Greece and, if anything, their size diminished over time because, even through there were very few "urban" settlements in ancient Greece, the size and number of the many towns and villages in general increased during the periods under examination. This growth in numbers would have altered the man:land ratio. Simply put, the larger the population, the smaller the role that wild resources could have played in the diet on a *per capita* basis. Furthermore, the expansion of settlement into the countryside, particularly during the fourth century, regardless of whether it is indicative of an overall increase in population or merely evidence of more intensive exploitation of the landscape, would have reduced the amount of uncultivated land, thereby further diminishing the quantity of wild resources. Morveover, even if large tracts of uncultivated land existed, there is still the question of its accessibility. Davies cites nine cases from Athens where we can discern the land-holdings of members of the elite; in three of them, sizeable areas of scrub land were recorded. Access to these areas for gathering, hunting, and pasturage would have depended upon the goodwill of the owners (1984a, 53–4). Based on these observations, it is apparent that wild plants could have provided only a minor, temporary response to a subsistence crisis (Johnson and Bakash 1987). The basic correctness of this observation is altered little if we include in the discussion terrestrial fauna and marine resources as well.

Hunting for a Meal

That ancient Greeks hunted and consumed wild animals on a fairly regular basis is not in doubt. The bones of prey such as red deer, roe deer, ray (a type of deer), rabbit, boar, bear, partridge, pigeon, and duck, for example, have been found in the rubbish dumps of the Classical–Hellenistic town of Kassope (H. Friedl 1984; Boessneck 1986). Likewise at Thorikos in Attica (Gautier 1965, 73), Lokris Epizephere in Italy (Errico and Moigne 1985), Didyma in Asia Minor (von den Driesch and Boessneck 1983, 620; Boessneck and Schaeffer 1986, 196–8), Thebes in Boiotia (Boessneck and Schaffer 1973), and Korinth in the Peloponnesos, (Reese 1987, 258, 260) the bones of wild animals have been found, and according to Xenophon wild game was often served in the Spartan common mess (Xenophon L. P. 5.3; Hodkinson 1983, 254). Scenes of the pursuit or the capture of wild game figure in Greek iconography as well (see J.K. Anderson 1975, 50, 54). Hunting was often portrayed as the sport of gentlemen; thus, that quintessential aristocrat, Xenophon of Athens, penned a lengthy pamphlet on the proper way to hunt and to raise hunting hounds (*Kyn*; see also Anderson 1975, 30–56; Hull 1964). Our concern is less with the equestrian nobleman chasing after the lion or the boar than with the humble peasant setting a simple trap for an unsuspecting hare. While we have no direct testimony, it seem highly probable that, in response to a reduction in crop yields, ancient peasants would increase the amount of time they spent hunting, but, given the elusiveness of their prey and the diminishing ratio of wild to cultivated land, the labor input:caloric output ratio would have been low. According to one study, the labor cost in kilocalories per kilogram with hunting and gathering was 1,151 compared to only 80 with gardening (Johnson 1980, 26). Furthermore, the frequency of failure would have been high (Johnson and Bakash 1987, 403). As a means of supplementing the diet and of producing some high protein meat during times of crisis, hunting could play an important, but necessarily secondary role (Richards 1986, 124; Johnson and Earle 1987, 30; Halstead 1987b, 81; Johnson and Bakash 1987, 394–5).

Fish in a Pickle

The same is true with fish and other marine resources. One of the advantages which in-shore maritime species offers is reliability. Crustaceans, mollusks, and the like can be found perennially in the same areas. Thus peasants in modern Greece and elsewhere utilize these species as a dietary supplement, providing themselves with a source of much-needed protein (Clark 1976a, 264; 1977, 50; Starke and Voorhies 1978). This gives them the important value of being available on a predictable basis (Yesner 1987, 287–8, 294). And, indeed, shells are very commonly found at ancient Greece habitation sites (*Korinth*: Reese 1987, 258; *Kassope*: Boessneck 1986; Friedl 1984; *Thorikos*: Gautier 1965, 73–5). Demersal, in-shore species of fish also tend to be far more predictable than either pelagic or anadromous species (Gallant 1985a, 25; Yesner 1987, 292–293). Pelagic species, such as mackerel, tunny, and bonito, are potentially a much abundant source of sustenance (Gallant 1985a, 27–8; Yesner 1987, 294); for a start, they travel in shoals which can attain a size numbering in the thousands of fish, and, within limits, they travel along predictable routes. Thus, they should have played an important role in the diet, and for some time modern scholars assumed that such was the case.

A recent quantitative study of the potential productivity of ancient fishing, however, has demonstrated that this image can mislead. While both mollusk and demersal species of fish occur in the same areas year after year, they have a very low labor input:calorific output ratio (Gallant 1985a, 25; Yesner 1987, 288; Johnson 1980, 26). Far too often the solitary fisherman with his reed pole would return home with an empty creel. Pelagic species, it appears, are not as reliable as was once assumed. The migration can vary considerably from year to year, and, given the technology available to ancient fishermen, it was likely that their expeditions onto the briny deep would have come up empty (Gallant 1985a,

31–6; Yesner 1987, 294). Unquestionably, maritime resources provided a vitally important supplement to the ancient diet, and indeed it is highly probable that their role increased during a subsistence crisis (Gallant 1985a, 40–4), but nevertheless, as with wild gathered plants and animals, they could never have provided anything more than a short-term solution to the problem of periodic dearth.

Once it became clear that crop yields were going to be diminished, ancient peasants turned to their natural habitat as a valuable source of food. They had available a wide range of resources from which to choose and an extensive body of folk knowledge about how to use them. Nevertheless, such sources were of limited utility and could only have played a marginal, supplementary role. In the face of a deepening subsistence crisis, peasants had to make difficult choices: they could either reduce the number of consumers in the household or they could begin the painful process of stripping the household of valued assets. In either case, they might be taking the first step down a slippery slope which could leave them permanently in a state of dependence.

Asset Stripping

The choices confronting a peasant household became harder as the range of feasible response strategies narrowed. It was noted earlier that whenever possible, peasants endeavored to minimize the frequency of dealings with outsiders. Long experience had shown that such interaction could easily end with their becoming dependent on these alien forces. Thus, before turning to them, households endeavored to manipulate their own resources. In the face of dwindling domestic food supplies and the failure of alternatve production schemes to compensate for them, one of the next, but hardest, choices a household had to make was to begin the process of selectively removing assets. The capital required to ensure the perpetuation of the household as a unit of production/reproduction had to be exchanged for consumable foodstuffs in order for it to meet its immediate caloric needs. Short-term survival took precedence over long-term viability. But once a household began to decapitalize, it severely reduced its ability to respond once the crisis had passed. In Timmerman's terminology, it had become less *resilient* and, in the long term, more *vulnerable* (Timmerman 1981, 20–3).

Slaughtering and Selling Livestock

"Rural capital accumulated in the form of livestock – especially oxen – disappeared virtually overnight." Thus James McCann begins his account of decapitalization in Nigeria during the subsistence crises and famine of 1889–92 (1987a, 30). The removal of livestock from the household either by slaughter or sale is a response strategy encountered in numerous peasant cultures (Vaughan 1985, 188; van Apeldoorn 1981, 69; Hankins 1974, 103; Parry 1978, 89; Colson 1979, 26; Wisner and Mbithi 1974, 94; de Garine and Koppert 1988, 231; Pingle 1988, 414; Dirks 1980, 27; Alamgir 1981, 21; Currey 1981, 128–9; den Hartog 1981, 157; Watts 1983, 432–5; 1988, 278;). Moreover, the devastation to the lievstock population could be truly awesome. In England during the subsistence crises of the 1740s it is estimated that one-half of the sheep population perished (Post 1985, 92). In more recent times, 80 percent of cattle, 50 percent of sheep, and 30 percent of goats were killed during the droughts in Tigrai and Wallo, Ethiopia, during the 1970s (Degefu 1987, 31), and, according to Watts, loss rates of 70–90 percent in East African livestock herds were not uncommon (1983, 387–9; Watts 1987, 192).

The justification for slaughtering or selling livestock is clear and unambiguous. As human food selection descended the ladder of preferences, increasingly people came into competition with animals. Since in determining their preferences, humans came first, with livestock it quickly became a case of "use them or lose them" (Bratton 1987, 225). When the primary subsistence cereals ran low, if possible peasants turned to other grains, like oats and alfalfa; since these were normally consumed by livestock, alternative, wild plants and vegetation had to be found for them. But within a short time the human community would have needed to resort to exploiting these as well. Furthermore, because of the loss of pasturage and the impact of malnutrition, animals began to produce diminishing quantities of secondary products, like milk and cheese. Figures produced by Dahl and Hjort for sheep indicate that a household of 5–6 persons would require 115 to 130 sheep if they were to live off the meat alone (1976, 220) which, in turn would require a flock size of 360–400 animals (Halstead 1981a, 314). Keeping such flocks would have been difficult for peasant households at any time and it was clearly an impossibility during a drought. At this point, few choices remained: peasants could attempt to transport their animals to another region in the hope of finding pasturage there; they could slaughter the animals and process the meat both for immediate consumption and for storage; they could sell the animal and use the cash to purchase subsistence cereals from the marketplace.

Undoubtedly, the first option listed above was preferable, but very few households found themselves in a position to utilize it. There were too many risks. The attrition rate among the already weakened animals was high, and so only large flocks and herds had any chance of survival. There were often no guarantees that pasturage was available in neighboring regions or that, even if it existed, one could get access to it. Both men and animals could easily perish on the road. It seems clear that transporting animals away from a stricken area was an option open only to wealthy individuals because they were the ones possessing large herds, they had the contacts in other regions which were needed to ensure access to pasturage, and, since they were not doing the actual moving, the risk to them was lower.

Slaughtering livestock was certainly a common practice. The meat from the animal provided immediate sustenance and the foods which the beasts would have needed became available for human consumption (Halstead 1987a, 81, 83); nevertheless, empirical data from actual subsistence crises suggests that households eventually had to sell some of their livestock. According to Watts, in the village of Kaita, Nigeria, during the 1970s nearly 50 percent of the households had to resort to selling livestock (1983, 432); support for this observation is found in the empirical studies cited at the beginning of this section. The rationale for selling rather than eating livestock lay with a dietary preference for cereals over meat and the sound calculation that the equivalent *value* in grain would provide more calories over a longer period of time than meat.

The sale of livestock, nevertheless, usually ended with the peasant losing out. Empirical studies of price fluctuations during subsistence crises indicate that after an initial rise, the value of livestock plummeted while the price of grain skyrocketed (Hankins 1974, 103; Sen 1981, 105–11, especially Tables 7.6 and 7.7; van Apeldoorn 1981, 46, 69; Minnis 1985, 29, 31; McCann 1987a, 77; Watts 1988, 278; De Souza 1987, 42). In Nigeria, for example, Watts found that the exchange ratio of livestock to cereals shifted from a pre-crisis level of 1:41 to a low of 1:13 during the crisis (1983, 386). At another place, cereal prices rose by 300 percent while the price for livestock fell by 75 percent (Watts 1983, 385). It appears then that once the calculation had been made to sell animals, the relative prices of the commodities mattered little. The survival of the household dictated that, even at the very imbalanced exchange rates cited above, livestock had to be traded for cereals because of the caloric content of the latter. Thus, in many cases, there was a rush by peasant families to sell, and this drove the price down. A seller's market in grain co-existed with a buyer's market in livestock, and those with the resources to take advantage of the situation did so.

Watts recorded by class the responses to a food shortage taken by farmers in the village of Kaita. He divided the community into three strata. He found that 62.8 percent of those in the lowest wealth group and 38.6 percent from the middle group sold livestock, while only 7 percent of those in the wealthiest class did so. Conversely, while no one from the lowest group and only 2 percent from the middle group bought any animals, 37.5 percent of upper-class households did so. Furthermore, the cash obtained from these sales was used by 91 percent of the poorest households to buy grain, often from the 46 percent of the upper class who were selling it (Watts 1988, 278). Based on these figures, he concluded

that "during a subsistence crisis epicycles of accumulation and capitaliza-
tion can occur simultaneously within a single community, intensifying
extant patterns of differentiation and immiseration" (1988 278). Simply
put, the highly imbalanced exchange rate of livestock for cereals during a
subsistence crisis led to the rich getting richer and the poor getting poorer.

We can infer from the available evidence that the situation described
above pertained in ancient Greece as well. For a start, ownership of
livestock extended far down the social scale (Hodkinson 1988, 37). Even
the poorest farmer would endeavor to keep a few sheep, goats, pigs, a
donkey or two, and a yoke of plow oxen if he could. All of these were
certainly consumed by Greek households as shown by the bone remains
found in most ancient settlements (*Thorikos*: Gautier 1965, 72–5; *Kassope*:
Friedl 1984; Boessneck 1986; *Lokris Epizephere*: Errico and Moigne 1985;
Didyma: Von den Driesch and Boessneck 1983, 620; Boessneck and
Schaeffer 1986, 196–198; *Thebes*: Boessneck and Schaffer 1973, *Korinth*:
Reese 1987, 258, 260).

Oxen, in particular, would have been highly prized because of their high
purchase price and up-keep costs. While many small-holders would have
made do with donkeys or hoes, comparative figures provided by McCann
suggest that they would have to have worked about one-third longer on
seed-bed preparation with hoes. Moreover, fruitful cultivation of some
areas, especially those characterized by clay-rich soils, would only have
been feasible if plow oxen were used. For these reasons, Aristotle concluded
that "oxen serve the poor in place of a slave" (*Pol* 1252b5). I suspect that
this passage reflects more the high price of slaves than it does the ubiquity
of cattle ownership. Depending on the fertility of the region and the
density of population, wealthy and even middling peasants may have
possessed oxen. The following story suggests this was so for one place. The
Sicilian tyrant Dionysios imposed so severe a tax on plow oxen that
numerous peasants were unable to pay the imposts. As a response to this,
Dionysios repealed the tax. Everyone went out in search of oxen. After a
short time, when many had acquired beasts, Dionysios reimposed the tax
and ruthlessly collected it; many however, preferred to slaughter their
animals rather than pay the tax (Pseudo-Aristotle 1349b6–14).

Other evidence suggesting that most households owned some livestock
include the statement by Thoukydides that when Attica was threatened
with invasion by the Spartans during the late 430s the people sent their
sheep and cattle to Evvoia for safety, a step they were able to take because
the island was under Athenian political control (2.14). As a means of
increasing his revenues, Kondalus, the governor of the province of Karia
(in modern Turkey) during the fourth century did the following. As he
passed through peasant villages, the locals would give him gifts of
livestock; he would refuse to accept them at the time, telling the peasants
that they should enjoy the use of their animals and that he would ask for

the beasts later. When that day arrived, in addition to confiscating the animals, he charged the peasants taxes back-dated to the time they had given him the animals (Pseudo-Aristotle 1348a19–23). It would appear, then, that livestock holding, particularly of sheep, goats, and pigs, probably extended well down the socio-economic ladder.

Moreover, livestock were vitally important to the household economy. In addition to their value as traction animals, oxen provided manure, meat, and hides. Sheep and goats produced milk, cheese, wool, and the like. For some households the secondary products of these animals afforded one of the few means of obtaining cash; Ailian (NA 16.32) records a description from an earlier author of the practice on the island of Kea of intensive sheep-rearing for the production of fine cheese earmarked for the market-place. Livestock rearing was an integral component in the agricultural systems of ancient Greece.

Turning next to the possible response strategies open to ancient peasants in the face of drought-induced subsistence crise, the slaughtering and/or selling of livestock appear to have been about the only viable options. Transporting their animals to another region was simply not possible for most people for two reasons. First, the small size of their holdings made it simply uneconomical, given the attendant risks involved, for example death on the road or bandits, to attempt to transport their animals elsewhere; this suggestion is reinforced by the fact that, even during normal times, only wealthy men with large herds practiced systematic, large-scale transhumance, and even then it was not a common practice (Halstead 1987a, 79; Cherry 1988, 8–9; Hodkinson 1988, 55; Garnsey 1988b; cf. Georgoudi 1974; Skydsgaard 1988). Second, because of the small size of ancient Greek states, geographical mobility was severely restricted. Unless some type of bilateral agreement existed between states which permitted the movement to or through each other's territory, like those known between Myania and Hypania in Lokris (Bousquet 1965) and between Aigai and Olympos in Aiolis (Moretti 1966), or unless a purely personal arrangement had been concluded between an individual and a state (for citations see Hodkinson 1988, 52–3), a person would have been unable to transport his animals through the territory of another state. Here again, the extant evidence indicates that those obtaining such special privileges in another state were wealthy men, who were frequently being rewarded for the services they had rendered during a subsistence crisis.

Since removing livestock seems to have been extremely difficult, only slaughtering or selling remained feasible possibilities. While the amount of evidence for the emergency killing of livestock is not abundant, it is suggestive of a more widespread practice. In the 390s when the state of Korinth was under threat of attack from Sparta, the Korinthians moved their livestock into the town and, we are told, lived off their animals for some time (Xenophon Hell 4.5.1). Well 97/362 from the Athenian

Agora contained a deposit dated to the first century BC, and perhaps to the siege of the town by the Roman general Sulla, filled with numerous bones from "larger domestic animals" and the remains of at least 100 dogs, indicating that in addition to more normal farm animals even creatures which Greeks did not normally eat were killed and consumed during a crisis (Angel 1945, 311, 330; Day 1984; Reese 1987, 263).

There is admittedly little direct ancient evidence for the widespread selling of livestock during a crisis, but, in the light of the comparative material presented above, we can reasonably infer from what does survive that the practice occurred. For a start, the small numbers of animals held by most households, the lack of geographical mobility, and the dearth of alternative foodstuffs left few other options. In addition, there are hints of crisis selling scattered in the ancient sources. Pseudo-Aristotle relates the story of how during a subsistence crisis Sosipolis of Antissa confiscated all the animals earmarked for sacrifice to Dionysios and sold them on the open market; the proceeds from the sale were kept by the state (1347a25–31). While not directly attesting the activity of peasants, this passage does suggest that the selling of livestock during a crisis occurred, and that there were potential buyers for them: the state, religious cults, and wealthy private citizens.

There are a number of examples of individuals who were granted pasturage rights by a state because of some service they had rendered to it. That communities placed such great emphasis on the control of pasture indicates the importance they gave to livestock rearing. In some cases, they were men from neighboring states and thus could easily have shifted their animals (e.g., the case of Eubolos of Elateia who was awarded pasturage rights in nearby Orchomenos (Migeotte 1984, 48–53) and, in others, like the cases of Kallon of Akraiphia (*SEG* 3.356; Migeotte 1984, 74–8) and Kleuedra and Olioympicha of Kopais (*SEG* 22.432; Migeotte 1984, 72–4) they were locals whose animals gained tax-exempt status. In yet other cases, it is clear the individuals being honored did not reside close to the communtiy which was honoring them (e.g., *IG* 9.2.62 and 63 form Lamia in Thessaly). All of these people were given these privileges because of their actions during a crisis; the state owed them debts. It would not be stretching the imagination too much to suggest that the animals these people pastured had been acquired locally, probably as a result of crisis selling.

Unlike many contemporary situations, in antiquity there was another major buyer in addition to members of the elite: religious cults. That animal sacrifice played a critical role in Greek religion and that each year thousands of beasts were slaughtered are facts too well known to require comment here (Jameson 1988; see also, Burkert 1979; 1983; Detienne and Vernant 1979). Not only did the sacrificing of animals continue during a crisis, but it probably increased (Burkert 1983, 264–8). Many Greeks believed that natural phenomena, such as drought, were caused by the gods out of anger at the actions of men and that only by appeasing their divinities through animal sacrifice, prayer, and the punishment of a scapegoat could the crisis be resolved (Burkert 1983, 264). A fragment of the sixth-century BC poet Hipponax relates that when a climatic trauma occurred, the community of Kolophon selected a scapegoat. The man was initially fattened up with figs, barley cakes, and cheese; after that he was beaten about the genitals with squill and twigs from wild olive trees and then finally burned at the stake (5–11). The practice of scapegoating during times of trouble was common in Greece and represents an extreme form of action (Herodotos 5.82; 7.171; 9.91–4; Bremmer 1983; Parker 1983, 258–60; Hughes 1986, 217–317). More common was simple animal sacrifice. Thus, as in many other cases (in general, Arnold 1988, 76–7 and, in particular, Hankins 1974, 102 (Africa); Sutherland 1981, 434–449 (Brittany)), magico-religious activities would have increased during a subsistence crisis, and in Greece this would have had the added effect of generating a greater demand for sacrificial animals. While some cults had their own flocks (Tegea for example (*IG* 5.10, 11, and 17)), most purchased the needed animals from private individuals.

Two factors lead me to suggest that it was members of the elite who were best able to capitalize on this demand for meat. First, sacrificial animals were selected carefully and had to be in good health (Jameson 1988, 87); only those men who possessed considerable resources would have been able to keep their animals healthy during a crisis. Second, because those choosing the animals for sacrifice on behalf of cults were usually themselves members of the elite, it seems highly likely that they would have purchased them whenever possible from kinsmen or friends. To conclude, those with large livestock holdings and other agricultural resources could have profited during a subsistence crisis by purchasing at low prices animals from peasants and then selling them or their own animals to religious cults at inflated prices.[17] In any case, a large sector of the peasantry would find itself bereft of livestock.

Selling Slaves

There were only two other categories of assets which households could liquidate in response to crop failures: slaves and land. It was argued earlier that while slave holding was common in ancient Greece, on the whole most peasants did not own slaves. Those who did, however, could soon find themselves in the position of having to make a crucial decision as to who ate and who did not. For many, it seems likely that, just as with livestock, the point would have come when sale or loss were the only options left. The only direct evidence for the selling of slaves during an emergency refers to the northern Greek town of Mende. We are told that, during an unspecified crisis, the state passed a measure declaring that every citizen with slaves had to sell all of them save one male and one female; the money generated by the sale was to be lent to the state (Pseudo-Aristotle 1350a12–15). What is unclear is who was actually buying the slaves. Presumably, given the terms of the decree, they had to be non-citizens, but I suspect that wealthy citizens would have found ways to circumvent the letter of the law. In any case, it seems likely that in most places, if a family commanded a large enough resource base, then they could count on being able to purchase slaves at reduced prices during a crisis.

Selling or Mortgaging Land

As in most agrarian societies, ancient Greeks were extremely reluctant to part with their land. Direct ownership of land was the only sure way of establishing entitlement to food and most peasants owned some land. Moreover, the maintenance of the ancestral *oikos* or household was a key cog in the psychological and social structure of the ancient world. Materially, it found its best expression in the concept of *autarkeia* or self-sufficiency, the notion that the household should produce all of what it consumed. However impossible an ideal it may have been it remained a prominent component in Greek ideology (Finley 1985, 97, 109–112; Springboard 1986). As Achilles movingly told Odysseus when they met in Hades, nothing in life could be worse than being a landless man doomed to wander without any property of his own (Homer *OD* 11.488–91). Land was dearly sought and held on to tenaciously. Thus, to mortgage or to sell it was a last-ditch measure.

Unfortunately many households frequently found themselves in a position where selling some or all of their land was the only option open to them. Watts noted that in Kaita nearly one-quarter of the members of the lowest wealth group had either to sell or pledge their land during the food shortage of 1973–4; conversely, at the same time, 10 percent of the wealthiest group took the opportunity to buy land (1988, 278). In fourteenth-century Norfolk, there was a very strong correlation between the cereal harvest and the market in land. Based on a quantitative study of the land market, Campbell concluded that "the inference to be drawn from this would appear to be that consecutive years of harvest failure reduced the peasantry to such a state that they were obligated to sell land in order to buy food and that only a fortuitous run of good harvests put them in a position to recoup their loses" (B.M.S. Campbell 1984, 113). The same pattern of *inter-vivos* land transfers increasing precipitously after a poor harvest was detected at Suffolk as well (R.M. Smith 1984, 153, 159). The pattern was clearly widespread (see also, van Apeldoorn 1981, 94; McCann 1987a, 81–3; Parry 1981, 327; Wisner and Mbithi 1974, 94; Currey 1981, 128–30). Direct ancient testimony of the selling of land during a subsistence crisis is scarce, but we can infer that it occurred for the following reasons.

First, there is copious evidence for the pledging of land as security. As Finley has shown, the preserved Athenian *horoi*, or encumbrance markers, refer to wealthy men borrowing large sums of money (1951; Finley 1981a; Gernet 1981a); nevertheless, it is highly likely that the practice of pledging land against a debt extended far down the socio-economic ladder, it was only the practice of recording the transaction on stone that did not. Furthermore, that land could be lost or sold because of debt is certain, and there is a great deal of evidence concerning debt, particularly debt incurred during food shortages. This topic will be discussed in much more detail in Chapter 7. At this point all we need do is to note that peasants might have to mortgage or sell their land in order to obtain a loan, to buy food, and that it might then be confiscated in lieu of a debt (Gallant 1989, 247).

Second, the results of expropriation either by sale or for debt are widely documented, especially from the fourth century onwards. Isokrates, for example, paints a vivid picture of large bands of men and their families roving across the Greek countryside in search of land. He talks of peasants who had lost their land and had been forced to wander the road as vagabonds, resulting frequently in their taking up a life of violence (Isokrates *Pan* 68; see below pp. 138–9). Either that, or find themselves in the ugly grip of debt bondage (De Ste Croix 1982, 162–5). Thus, repeatedly from that time onwards, the cry of "redistribution of land and cancellation of debts" echoed across the Greek world (Fuks 1972; 1974; 1979; 1984; Gehrke 1985). While not everyone who was compelled to sell their land did so out of debt incurred during a food shortage or crisis selling, it is likely that many did so. With the sale of land, the household was on the verge of liquidating itself out of existence. Before such a drastic step, measures would have been taken to reduce the size of the household by selectively removing members on either a short-term or long-term basis.

Households in Fragments

When the specter of food shortage appeared, households had the options of stripping assets to acquire food or reducing the number of mouths they had to feed. A parallel strategy to decapitalization involved the selective removal of household members as a means of maximizing the chances of the remaining members coping with the crisis (Colson 1979, 26; Greenough 1982, 11, 221–2).

Removing Dependents from the Household

Repeatedly in the comparative literature we find examples of households divesting themselves of members during a subsistence crisis and after some of the strategies discussed above had proved inadequate. In particular, attention is often focussed on the youngest and, for two reasons, the most vulnerable members of the household. First, because of their special nutritional requirements, children begin to feel the effects of food shortage first, and are therefore often the first victims. Second, because of the belief that childern may die no matter what, households often resolves to optimize the survival opportunities of other members. Thus, when deciding how the food supply is portioned out, preference is usually given to the older, more productive members of the household because it is their capacity to labor and to remain active, hunting or gathering for example, which is most needed for the survival of the entire unit (Corkhill 1949, 1–12; Aykroyd 1974, 13–16; Greenough 1982, 221–2; Bharati and Basu 1988; Wheeler and Abdullah 1988, 439–40). Moreover, in the case of infants, their continued rearing jeopardizes the life of the mother, and this forces a decision as to which of these will live (Aykroyd 1974, 13–16; Alamgir 1981, 30; Wheeler and Abdullah 1988, 444). Children can be separated from the household in two ways: those actions which remove the child on a temporary basis and those which lead to a permanent fragmentation of the household.

As difficult as if often was for ancient households to give up some of their younger members, and particularly among poorer households, it had to be done in order to enhance the life chances of the remaining children (Garnsey 1988a, 64; Golden 1988; cf. with qualifications, Finley 1981b, 159).

Probably the most common strategy for removing children temporarily was to send them to live with relatives or friends until the crisis had passed. There are certainly ancient testimonies to the practice of households taking in kin during a crisis; for example, in one case a man and his family took in his sister and her children after her husband had died (Lysias 3.6), and in another, sisters, nieces, and cousins set adrift because of war moved into the household of a kinsmen (Xenophon *Mem* 2.7.2). While neither of these cases refers to action taken during a subsistence crisis and both relate to a permanent or semi-permanent move, nonetheless they demonstrate a general propensity toward accepting kin during times of trouble into one's own household. By extension, it would seem likely that the same sort of behavior would have been manifested during periods of scarcity.

The major drawback to sending children to live with nearby relatives or friends is that those households would probably be suffering from the same problems with food shortages. Many regions of Greece are marked by synchronous variability and so in order for the removal of children to ensure their survival they would have to have been sent to households located in another state away from the affected area. Here once again, the small size and tight restrictions on membership in Greek city-states acted as an impediment to inter-regional movement. Most of one's kin probably resided in the territory of the same state. The exceptions to this would be those households which had already sent out members to help found or reside in a colony and individuals who had contracted dyadic interpersonal bonds with "friends" in other states.

The first option would have unavailable to most people. While it was incumbent upon a *xenos* to aid and succor his counterpart and his family in times of trouble – see, for example, the story recounted by Lysias (6) – such ties were restricted to members of the elite (Herman 1987, 24–6).

Jackson describes the practice among the Akamba of Kenya of "pawning" their children during a crisis. As he describes it, "pawnship involved persons being left in another family's keeping during the season of famine. Additionally, that family was granted control over the pawn's labor, if the pawn was of sufficient age to labor. Ultimate power over the legal person of the pawn remained vested in the pawn's original family" (Jackson 1985, 205). In some ways, then, it is very similar to the practice envisaged above. Pawnship, however, could become permanent, with the pawn being left permanently in the care of the recipient household.

Other possible strategies available for removing children permanently were the following. Households which did not have an heir would often adopt a child (A.R.W. Harrison 1969, 82–96). And while most of the known cases of adoption did not involve peasants or occur during times of food shortage, the possibility that children could shift between households through adoption was a real one.

Parents could render a child to a craftsman or artisan as an apprentice, often at around the age of 14 or 15 (Finley 1981b, 160). Entailed in this would be the signing of a contract between the two parties in which the terms of the transaction, including the specification of the child's legal guardian, would be set out (Burford 1972, 87–91). Such "pauper apprenticeships" commonly occurred at the lowest levels of seventeenth-century English society (Wales 1984, 376), and this may be what Isokrates is referring to when he states that because of debt and poverty many children had been compelled to work for wages (Isokrates *Pan* 68). Since craftsmen were often itinerant, such a move could have led to the child being effectively removed from danger.

Giving daughters away in marriage was a possibility, but an unlikely one. For the rich, such a measure was probably unnecessary, and for the poor it was ineffective becase the spouse pool would have been geographically restricted and detecting eligible and willing mates during a time of food shortage would usually have been a fruitless task.

The giving away or selling of children, unpalatable as it may have been, was an option employed recurrently. In the tale of the wicked courtesan Neaira, we are told that she was given over as a small child to a madame who reared and trained her in her craft (Pseudo-Demosthenes

59). Slave traders may have been despised as such (see, for example, the exchange between the Khremylos and "Poverty" in Aristophanes' *Pl* 510–26) but in times of dire need they could be a source of cash in exchange for a child which may not have been able to survive a severe shortage in any case. Herodotos informs us that among the Thrakians the selling of children was not uncommon (5.6.2–3). It could be argued that because they were non-Greeks the passage is not germane to our discussion, but there is evidence which implies that Greeks as well on occasion had to sell their children.

An aura of harsh reality surrounds the dialogue between the Megarian "bumpkin" and his two daughters in Aristophanes' *Ach* (729–35) when he asks them "would you rather be sold as slaves or starve to death?" and they reply "Be sold" (De Ste Croix 1982, 163). We cannot rule out the possibility, as well, that the "attractive young boys" purchased by the unscrupulous Panionios from the island of Chios were sold by poor families out of necessity (Herodotos 8.104–6). In the same passage from Isokrates cited above, he says that because of debt many children have been reduced to slavery (Isokrates *Pan* 68).

When the Athenian orator Demosthenes wanted to cast aspersions upon the character of Meidias, he told the jury that "His true (natal) mother was the smartest of all humans; this reputed mother who adopted him was the silliest woman in the world: the reason being the former sold him as soon as he was born and the latter bought him when she might have gotten a better bargain at the same price" (21.149). Whether or not the story was literally true is irrelevant for our purposes; that Demosthenes was employing one of the most damning accusations he could make seems clear.

In like manner, when Demosthenes wanted to demonstrate the reprehensible character of Timokrates, he tells the jury that Timokrates sold his sister to a man from Kerkyra (24.202–3). Probably, what he had done was to give her in marriage to a foreigner. But, by referring to the deal as a "sale," Demosthenes was attempting to strike a sensitive chord in his audience. The sting to both these stories lay in their verisimilitude: unless the possibility of selling children was real and the practice known to a jury of Athenian men, the passages make no sense.

In at least one Greek community, the selling of newborns was institutionalized: "There is a particularly just and humane law at Thebes that no Theban may expose his child or condemn it to death by abandoning it in a deserted place. If the child's father really is in dire poverty, then whether the child is male or female he must bring it in its swaddling bands to the magistrates as soon as the mother's labor has ended, and they must take the baby and give it to whoever will pay them the least amount of money for it. An agreement must be made with this person stipulating that it should look after the baby and is to have it as his

male or female slave when it is grown up, and to use its labor in return for
having to look after it" (Ailian *VH* 2.7; transl. Wiedemann 1984, 117–18;
see also, Garlan 1988, 45). While this piece of legislation refers specifically
to newborns, it is quite likely that children up to the age of majority could
have been sold off in a similar manner (De Ste Croix 1982, 170).

For a slightly later period (first century AD) there is good evidence for
the selling of children explicity for the purpose of obtaining food to feed
other members of the household (De Ste Croix 1982, 170) and it seems
likely, given the evidence cited above, that it was practiced in earlier times
as well.

The Theban decree leads us to the final and least reversible option for
removing children on a permanent basis: exposure. Much of the literature
on exposure (often confusing it with infanticide) focuses on the question of
female infanticide and its prevalence (Eyben 1980/81; Engels 1980;
1984; W.V. Harris 1982; Pomeroy 1975; 1983; 1984; Golden 1981;
Oldenziel 1987). In a penetrating examination of the problem, Patterson
demonstrates the complexity of the issue and the need to be aware of the
great variability of the practice from place to place and from time to time
(1985). Echoing the views of Plutarch (*Mor* 497e), she notes that exposure
by reason of poverty did occur as a means of improving the life chances of
the remaining children (Patterson 1985, 114, 117). I would go further
and argue that the selective exposure or neglect of infants, and not just
newborns, would have occurred during a subsistence crisis. While as yet
unparalleled from ancient Greece, the 175 fetuses, newborns, and infants
found in the Athenian Agora well 97/362 stand as mute testimony to the
high rate of mortality, arguably human-induced or enhanced by selective
neglect, among young children during times of food shortage (Angel
1945, 311, 330).

Adults Only

Another way that households could reduce the number of mouths that had
to be fed was by encouraging late adolescent and adult members to leave
on either a temporary or a permanent basis. During certain phases of the
life cycle the household was more vulnerable to subsistence risk. Coinci-
dentally, these are also the times when sons were nearing adulthood but
still residing in their natal household. One of the primary ways that
households could most successfully cope was for younger members,
particularly men, to take on forms of wage labor which would remove
them from their home territory (Colson 1979, 26; McAlpin 1979, 148;
Vaughan 1985, 186; de Garine and Koppert1988, 241).

I focus on three in particular: shepherding, rowing, and mercenary
service. All of them enabled individuals to flee from a region suffering from
dearth, but each had its drawbacks.

The impression created by the sources is that shepherds were often slaves (see, for example, Isaios 6.33). But as Hodkinson notes "there is sufficient evidence for the employment of hired labor as an alternative to slave herdsmen" to suggest that they were a viable alternative to slave labor (1988, 55). Such free shepherds were usually extremely poor and landless. We saw earlier how during a subsistence crisis wealthy owners of large flocks might have attempted to diminish their losses by moving the animals to another region. For this reason, it is likely that the demand for hired shepherds increased. Nevertheless, proportionally, so few of them would have been needed that taking on wage labor as a shepherd would not have been a viable possibility for many.

With rowing and other mercenary service, lack of opportunity for large number was not the case. I begin with rowing. In any given year, perhaps as many as one-half to three-quarters of a million rowers were needed by states and private individuals.[18] Obviously the precise number of rowers would have fluctuated from year to year, but these figures are sufficient to give an idea of the numbers involved. As a response strategy, becoming a rower had the advantages of temporarily removing hungry mouths from the household and of providing a source of income. In one instance that we know of, for example, an Athenian ship's captain found himself short of cash while sailing in the Black Sea and was confronted with angry rowers, demanding their wages because they needed the money "to feed their families" (Demosthenes 50.11). Men could enlist for the duration of a campaign or for one voyage, and at the end of that time they could return to the family.

Furthermore, the opportunities to gain labor as rowers were to be found all across the Greek world. While states may have sought to hire their poorer citizens, in many cases this was not feasible. When, for example, the people of Herakleia Pontike (a small state in the Black Sea region) needed 6,800 rowers to man their ships, they were unlikely to find them all among their own numbers (Pseudo-Aristotle 1347b3–15). Even Athens, undoubtedly the largest employer of rowers for much of the period we are dealing with, hired both its own citizens and foreigners (B.Jordan 1975, 211, 250–1; Morrison and Coates 1986, 115). We can envision, then, a rather large and amorphous labor market constantly fluctuating in size and varying from place to place; yet, in aggregate, it produced a rather constant demand. If one desired wage labor as rower, one could find it. The following example is indicative. In the episode cited above about the discontented rowers, we are told that they *en masse* jumped ship, leaving the Athenian captain without any rowers. After soliciting a loan from his family's *xenos*, he hired a crew on the spot (Demosthenes 50.18). There had to have been men seeking work around the docks in the town where he was stranded in order for this to have happened. Moreover, the decision by the previous rowers to desert had to be predicated on the assumption that work on another ship would get them back to Athens. There had, therefore, to be a fairly active labor market in rowers. In response to a short-fall in crops, then, one or more male members of a household could temporarily remove themselves and generate cash with which to purchase foodstuffs by taking on wage labor as rowers on a ship.

Mercenary service as a warrior could act as a response mechanism to risk in two ways. First, it provided an opportunity for households to rid themselves of excess male mouths on a temporary basis (as did boarding a ship as a rower). Second, in face of dire poverty and imminent loss of land or life, a man could move his entire household with him when he enlisted as a mercenary (Aineias Taktikos 24.7). In this section, I want to focus only on the first point; the second will be covered below.

"Having thus found matches for our sisters, men of the jury, and being ourselves of military age, we enlisted with [the mercenary Captain] Iphikrates and went off to Thrake to fight. After a short time, having proved our worth there, we had saved some cash and so returned home" (Isaios 2.6). Thus one of the sons of Eponymos testified before an Athenian jury. Annually would-be tyrants, states in conflict, and kings on the make sought men like the sons of Eponymos for their armies. When Cyrus wished to contest the Persian throne with his brother, he assembled an army that included 13,000 Greek mercenaries (Roy 1967, 301–2 compiled from Xenophon's *Ana*). Mercenaries had been a feature of the Greek world from the seventh century (Snodgrass 1980, 110), but beginning in the bellicose fourth century and steadily growing thereafter, mercenaries were increasingly in demand (Griffith 1935; Parke 1933; Marinovich 1962, 57; H.F. Miller 1984). In any given year, a man in search of mercenary service could usually find a job. He might have to take to the road and go to well-known mercenary haunts, like Aspendos or Tainaron (Griffith 1935, 299), but there would be work, wages, and food waiting for him there.

This type of mercenary service was seen by the families involved as a means of temporarily removing young men either because of poverty or because of short-term shortage (Griffith 1935, 238–9; Parke 1933, 228–31; Roy 1967, 317–18). Often these men had families of their own to which they hoped to return (Xenophon *Ana* 6.4.8; Marinovich 1962, 64; Miller 1984, 154–5) – that is if they survived the fighting and were not captured and sold as slaves (Xenophon *Ana* 7.1.36; 7.2.6; Diodoros Sikeliotes 16.63.5). Many of them did not make the return trip (Roy 1967, 317–18). Moreover, others may not have found a welcome reception when they did. Lewis recounts an incident in which a father attempted to obtain divorces for his two daughters while their husbands were away (N. Lewis 1982, 170). The decree issued by Alexander the Great in 324 on behalf of the "Tegean" exiles, many of whom may have been mercenaries (for evidence on mercenaries being exiled from their community see, Marinovich 1962, 64), amply demonstrates the potential difficulties facing men after their service abroad had ended (Heisserer 1980, 228–9). In sum then, mercenary service could alleviate stress on the household economy in the short term, but in the long run it may have left many families permanently ruptured.

Two other types of activity, brigandage and piracy, were related to mercenary service and acted in a similar manner as response strategies. When a man left his household to seek out military action, he could become a member of a bandit gang. In antiquity, as in other periods, the line separating legitimate from illegitimate men of action was a fine one (see, for example, Gallant 1988, 269–90); as Gabbert, echoing a long held view, puts it: "it is clear from some of our sources that the role of pirate and mercenary could be interchangeable" (Gabbert 1986, 156). Moreover, according to Aristotle, poverty and want were the twin evils driving men to become bandits (*Pol* 1267a1–5). Other sources as well reinforce this point that an increasingly impoverished and risk-prone peasantry was proving to be a fertile breeding ground for brigands and pirates (Ormerod 1924, 69–70; Garlan 1978, 9–10; Gabbert 1986, 158) and that peasants in some areas more than others, like Crete (Brulé 1978) and the Cyclades (Ducrey 1983), were lured by poverty to a life outside the law. Just as with mercenary service, men faced with dearth and shortages could opt to flee a stricken area temporarily and seek an income as brigands or pirates, but for the overwhelming majority this supposed short-term separation from their household could end in permanent dislocation.

There was one other means by which households could divest themselves permanently of members: colonization. The practice of colonization by the Greeks is usually associated with the eighth, seventh, and sixth centuries BC (Snodgrass 1980, 40–2; Boardman 1980), but it continued through the classical period (Van Soesbergen 1983) and, if anything, accelerated during the Hellenistic period (G.M. Cohen 1978). Aristotle, in one of his few explicit discussions of famine, envisaged a situation where deteriorating climatic conditions could lead to the slow and piecemeal disintegration of a community, as some people left singly and others by household (*Mete* 1.14.13–28).

While entire households could uproot and relocate, it was also possible for them to give up just one member. The best-known example comes from the Archaic period and concerns the island of Thera, which, we are told, when faced with dearth after a number of consecutive crop failures required each family on pain of death to hand over one son for colonization (Meiggs and Lewis 1969, No. 5). Two purposes would be served by this. First, colonization lessened some of the strain on the household's food supplies, and second, it created a potential refuge for one or more members of the natal household during the next crisis. The drawback, of course, was that there was no way of knowing in advance whether or not the colonists would find land to settle on, and even if they did, that the colony would be successful.

Households on the Move

An all too familiar picture from parts of the world in the recent past is that of refugee families fleeing their homes and seeking shelter in camps often far away from their famine-ravaged homeland (Seavoy 1986, 73; Alamgir 1981, 21; Currey 1981, 130; den Hartog 1981, 157; Colson 1979, 26). Some are compelled to leave because their grain bins have run dry, others, because of debt and expropriation, have lost their entitlement to food supplies, but in either case they face the prospect of imminent starvation. In the ancient Greek world there seem to have been two schemes by which communities could remove entire households from among their number: colonization and mercenary service. From the point of view of the household, these were ways of escaping poverty, immiseration, debt, and possible death.

The following passage presents the rationale given by men for uprooting their families and going off to Sicily in order to join a military campaign against Carthage in 307: "not a few of the other Greeks too were eager to share the enterprise, hoping to divide up between them the finest parts of Africa and to plunder the wealth of Carthage. For owing to the continuous wars and the struggles of the rulers against each other Greece had become poor and miserable; consequently, many believed that they should not merely gain benefits but would escape from the misfortunes of the times" by seeking service as mercenaries (Diodoros Sikeliotes 20.40.6–7). Two points require comment. First, we should note that poverty was a major factor in driving these men to become mercenaries; second, that in addition to wages and booty these men were seeking land on which to settle with their families. Both of these points require further examination.

"Many [Greeks]," proclaimed the Athenian Isokrates, "because of the lack of basic subsistence are compelled to enlist in foreign armies and are being killed fighting for their enemies against their friends" (*Pan* 168). The link between peasant impoverishment and the growing number of mercenaries was a theme Isokrates referred to often (Isokrates *Phil* 97; Isokrates *Arch* 15.57–8; Fuks 1972; 1974; 1979). And he was not alone in drawing this connection (for a fuller discussion on this point, see Parke 1933, 228–31; Griffith 1935, 283; Marinovich 1962, 73; Garlan 1978, 97; H.F. Miller 1984, 158). Clearly, from the fourth century onward, an increasing number of Greek families found themselves in the untenable position where after employing all the adaptive measures and resorting to many of the response strategies discussed so far, they were still either so deeply in debt that they were on the verge of losing their land (see Chapter

7) or else on the brink of going under in the face of crops losses. For many, flight was one of the few options left to them.

Increasingly, men accompanied by their entire family took to the road in search of mercenary service. The fortunate ones were able to find employment. Having done so, they would have ensured for themselves and their families a temporary source of cash income and access to food supplies at reasonable prices (Griffith 1935, 271). Depending on the state of the mercenary market and the character of the paymaster, additional benefits may have been provided.

Eumenes I of Pergamon, for example, set out in a contract dated to 260 the following terms of employment for his men: (a) the prices for wine and wheat were fixed, thus buffering them from the vagaries of the capricious and fickle marketplace; (b) the campaigning season would last for only ten months; (c) they were granted dispensation from certain taxes; (d) benefits would be provided to those who were unable to find employment after their contracts had expired; (e) the orphans and widows of any man killed in battle were to be provided for (*OGIS* I. 266). Other employers held out the most prized prospect of all – land.

During the period 228–220, the state of Miletos hired mercenaries from around the Aegean. After a time, these men and their families were enrolled as citizens of Miletos and settled in the town of Myous (Kawerau and Rehm 1914, 34–93). Indeed, many of the colonies established during the Hellenistic period consisted of mercenaries and their families (Cohen 1978).

The unfortunate ones did not find steady employment and so ended up joining the burgeoning "dangerous class" in late Classical–Hellenistic Greece. Isokrates vented his ire most fully against those who failed to perceive the growing dangers in a situation where "some [Greeks] are being put to death contrary to the law in their own states [and] others are wandering with their women and children in foreign lands [i.e. outside their own *polis*]" (*Pan* 168–9). He urged that states take measures "to settle those who now, for lack of the daily necessities of life, are wandering about and causing damage to whomsoever they encounter," prophesying that "if we do not stop these men from banding together by providing them with sufficient livelihood, they will grow before we notice it into such a great mass that they will be no less terrifying to the Greeks than to the barbarians" (*Pan* 168–9).

Life on the road must have been arduous. The third-century traveler Herakleides Kretikos describes with a sense of awe the people of Tanagara who "know how to respect justice, good faith and hospitality. To their indigent citizens and to the wandering poor they give from what they have and allow them to share freely, for they [the Tanagrans] are a people far removed from unjust greed" (Herakleides Kretikos 9.20–4; Pfister 1951, 76). If the Tanagrans were exceptional, then obviously the broader implication is that most communities were not as hospitable to the wandering poor. Indeed, more often than not these destitute wayfarers were perceived by communities as a threat. Thus, the advice of the ever-practical Aineias Taktikos was for communities on a war footing to monitor carefully such vagabonds and to expel them from time to time (10.10). Furthermore, disconnected from their networks of kin and friends, vagabonds were left bereft of support and on their own. Recent works on other historical periods provide sound comparative evidence for the incidence of vagrancy and vagabonds in circumstances similar to those existing in the ancient world and they support the argument that the indigent were unlikely to find consistent support from communities outside of their own (Pound 1971; Hufton 1972; 1974; Slack 1974; Beier 1985; Pullan 1988; McIntosh 1988; Adler 1989). To many Greek families such a fate may have been at times inescapable.

Selling Labor

The solicitation of daily wage labor is another common response strategy (Gregory 1982, 4; Seavoy 1986, 201; Hankins 1974, 103; Sutherland 1981, 448; Wisner and Mbithi 1974, 88; Colson 1979, 26). In Watts's survey, for example, 93 percent of the men in the lowest wealth class sought wage labor (1983, 440; 1987, 178). Sen, as well, comments on the rush of men to hire themselves out, often at greatly reduced *per diem* wages (1981, 64–7). [19] This, in turn, creates a labor glut which limits the efficacy of this strategy.

For antiquity this deficiency is compounded by the fact that wage labor for free citizens was never very highly developed anyway (Finley 1985, 65–9, 107–8; Finley 1983, 41). Undoubtedly there were always men who had no land or other source of livelihood and so they took on labor as construction workers or porters (Hopper 1979, 136–46; Garlan 1980; Kreissig 1980; Lepore 1980; Welskopf 1980). For others, seasonal work as agricultural laborers on the estates of large landowners provided a way to earn some extra food, if they were paid in kind, or cash. Nevertheless, the number of opportunities for such labor were never great, and they diminished sharply during a subsistence crisis when, in addition to landless men, numerous small-holders sought work and wealthy owners of slaves tried to hire them out. Moreover, since the single largest category of jobs were as agricultural workers and since the crisis was probably precipitated by adverse climatic conditions, any type of work would have been scarce. Hired labor, then, was unlikely to prove of much value to families having to cope with marked reductions in their food supplies.

Short-term Salvation, Long-term Deterioration: the Loss of Resilience

The response strategies discussed in this chapter can be divided into two main groups: those which entailed alterations to the way household resources were manipulated and the exploitation of alternative foodstuffs, and those which required that the household divest itself of both animate and inanimate assets. My argument is that while these response strategies may have proved effective in alleviating food shortages in the short-term, in the long-term they acted to reduce considerably the household's *resiliency* or ability to respond and recover once the crisis had passed. This, in conjunction with the limitations inherent in each of the response strategies, meant that households had to turn to outsiders for assistance, and that by so doing they opened the door to becoming dependent on those individuals.

The following factors impaired the utility of the first set of strategies. First, the ability to produce alternative food crops was contingent on the farmer having the necessary seeds, and his being able to plant, rather than eat, them (Gallant 1989, 402). Second, the farmer had no assurance that the precipitating cause of the initial crop failure would not destroy the second crop as well. As a risk-buffering mechanism, planting a second crop was an option not available to all households and was, moreover, unreliable. Third, many households undoubtedly exploited wild, gathered resources, but historically specific circumstances such as the pattern of land-holdings, population density, and the prevailing microenvironmental conditions controlled both the number of people who could be supported by them and the duration of that support. Peasants had to employ other means for coping with dearth.

The second set of strategies had the potential to alleviate short-term shortages but at great cost. The concept of resiliency helps us to understand why. Resiliency refers to the ability of a system to respond and to maintain one or more forms of equilibrium after suffering a trauma. In Timmerman's words "*Resilience* [is] the measure of a system's, or part of a system's capacity to absorb and recover from the occurrence of a hazardous event" (1981, 21). In terms of the household economy, some of the key factors in determining resiliency were the availability of seeds, traction animals, man-power, and the continued access to the means of production, land. Many of the response strategies diminished the household's resilience, thereby impairing its ability to respond once the crisis had passed and rendering it in the long term more vulnerable to subsistence risk.

Figure 5.1 depicts the relationship between response strategies and resiliency. The left vertical axis represents the amount of resources a household expends by opting for a certain response strategy. For example, a greater quantity of resources is laid out by splitting the household

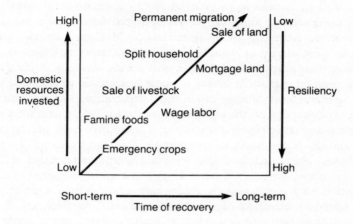

Fig. 5.1 Response Strategies and Resiliency.

membership than by gathering famine foods. The right vertical axis depicts the degree of resiliency of the various actions. Taking on wage labor has a higher resiliency than selling land because the latter could permanently impair the household's ability to recover after a crisis had passed. The horizontal axis measures the recovery time associated with the different strategies; that is, it will take a household longer to recover if it had to sell land than simply resort to emergency crops. Combined, the three axes allow us to assess the impact of the response strategies. Gathering famine foods, for example, requires a rather low investment of household resources, primarily labor and time, has a rather high resiliency, and the household can recover from its implementation quickly.

An examination of Figure 5.1 clearly demonstrates that as the hierarchy of options is ascended, the total amount of resources a household invests also increases. In turn, this decapitalization has an inverse, negative impact on the household's resiliency. This is seen most explicitly with the loss of livestock. Without traction animals, certain soils could not have been as effectively cultivated, or if they could, yields would probably be lower; without the secondary products derived from animals, some households would have lost their means of obtaining a cash income with which to purchase necessary commodities not produced in the household itself;

without manure, crop yields would be lower (Lawton and Wilkie 1979; Gallant 1985b, 415; Halstead 1987a, 81; Hodkinson 1988, 49–50). The outcome of all of these would have been a reduction in the household's income and an increase in its vulnerability to environmental stress.

An examination of some comparative material demonstrates this process in operation. Referring to decapitalization, McCann observed that in Ethiopia "The ability of households to survive depends largely on their success at minimizing risk, a difficult task during drought. A corollary to this proposition is that the ability of some households to resist the effects of drought and food shortage can in those circumstances transmogrify into a process of enrichment, through the use of existing social institutions. The ownership and labor power of oxen play a major role in the process, where rural capital (i.e., oxen) is concentrated in the hands of particular households which therefore have a strong relative advantage" (1987b, 259). He notes, furthermore, that when households attempted to resume production after the famine they were able to do so only after assistance from wealthier members of their communities: "Farmers who had no surplus had to purchase new stock at highly inflated prices, trade labor obligations for use of their richer neighbor's oxen, or migrate out in the hope of attaching themselves to relatives or an influential landowner" (McCann 1987a, 30). The end results of crisis decapitalization, in particular because of the loss of livestock and land, were an increasing polarization in wealth and the creation of many more vulnerable households. Watts captures this problem well: "Crudely put, while the poor resorted to the sale of livestock, pledged farms, incurred debts, sold their labor power, and borrowed grain at usurious rates, their wealthy counterparts bought stock at deflated prices in conditions of oversupply, sold or lent grain to needy families, purchased wage labor at depressed prices, and purchased the scarcest resource of all on their own terms, namely land" (Watts 1983, 440). In short, the rich could get richer and the poor very much poorer through crisis decapitalization.

When confronted with the inherent limitations of their response strategies and the loss of resiliency caused by them, peasant households turned increasingly to outsiders for assistance in coping with crop yield losses and subsistence crises. Reliance on interpersonal relationships, however, exposed them to the risk of becoming caught in a nexus of debt and dependency from which they might never escape. In order to peceive and comprehend the interplay between the classes in the ancient world over risk and survival, we have to examine both the moral underpinnings and active working of ancient interpersonal relations and their bases in kinship, "friendship," associations, and patronage.

6 "With a Little Help from My Friends": Interpersonal Risk-buffering Behavior

Since he lives in an environment of scarcity, competition for wealth and power is seen as a zero-sum contest in which his losses are another's gain and vice-versa. His very survival is constantly threatened by the caprice of nature and by social forces beyond his control. In such an environment, where subsistence needs are paramount and physical security uncertain, a modicum of protection and insurance can often be gained only by depending on a superior who undertakes personally to provide for his clients.

James C. Scott

Introduction

No household is an island unto itself. The resources to which members of a household could claim entitlement were limited and could greatly vary from year to year. So, while peasants in the past demonstrated a high degree of ingenuity in manipulating their resources, they would often have to call on the assistance of individuals from outside the household in times of crisis, particularly if the crisis extended past one growing season or if it was especially severe. Four broad categories of people constituted an individual's support network: kinsmen, neighbors and "friends," associations, and patrons. Together, these formed a household's third-order defense against food shortages, dearth, and famine.

The Obligation to Give, and to Receive

All societies create a centralized matrix of rules which structure the generalized exchange of resources and services. These rules establish a set of expectations regarding what kinds of assistance individuals could anticipate from kinsmen, friends, or patrons. Granted, those expectations may not always have been met, but nonetheless individuals *per force* had to base their decisions on them. Two key propositions guide our discussion of the rules of exchange and interpersonal relations in ancient Greece. First, I contend that there was an ideology of interpersonal relations firmly grounded in an ethos of obligation, and second, that the extent and the assurance of assistance in times of trouble were directly proportional to the degree and to the intimacy of the connection between individuals.

Broadly speaking there are two general spheres of exchange relations: one strictly between individuals and another between an individual and a corporate entity. Both share the same ideology based on the dual concepts of *obligation* and *reciprocity*. Gouldner defines what he termed a "norm of reciprocity", and he argues that in its minimal form, it is universal (1977). The minimum requirements of reciprocity are: "(1) people should help those who have helped them, and (2) people should not injure those who have helped them" (Gouldner 1977, 35). Orenstein, as well, argues for a "pan-human" moral disposition to reciprocity; one is always obligated to reciprocate (1980, 69; Duby 1974, 48–53; Arlacchi 1983, 50; Cashdan 1985; Weiner 1985). Their conclusions are indisputable, but not particularly useful analytically. We need to examine in more concrete terms the ways cultures construct and legitimize the forms that reciprocity and obligation take in specific societies in order to elucidate further the Greek case.

The belief that reciprocity both signifies and creates (and recreates) a bond between equals is a recurring ideological feature of interpersonal relations (Eisenstadt and Roniger 1981; 1984; Hutson 1971; Goode 1978; Schwimmer 1979; MacCormack 1976). Thus, in popular discourse such relationships are described in terms connotating trust and intimacy: "These aspects [trust and intimacy] were seen as manifest in the close links between patron–client bonds, pseudo–kinship, ritual kinship or friendship relations on the one hand, and such concepts as 'honour' or spiritual dimensions of interpersonal links on the other" (Eisenstadt and Roniger 1984, 27; see also Litwak and Szelwmyi 1969). This has been observed in numerous, diverse cultures (*Italy and Sicily*: Silverman 1968; 1977; Blok 1969; Galt 1974; Graziano 1977; Arlacchi 1983, 47–57; *Latin America*: Schmidt 1977; G.M. Foster 1977; *Asia*: Price 1978; Kiefer, 1968; Landé 1977). But this image of equality can mislead.

A second, seemingly incompatible ideological construct has been identified as prevalent. George Foster, after an examination of numerous peasant societies, concluded that most of them had an ideational structure which included a concept of "limited good".

> By "Image of Limited Good" I mean that broad areas of peasant behavior are patterned in such a fashion as to suggest that peasants view their social, economic and natural universe – their total environment – as one in which all desired things in life, such as land, wealth, health, friendship and love, manliness and honor, respect and status, power and influence, security and safety, *exist in finite quantity and are always in short supply, as far as the peasant is concerned.*   (Foster 1965, 296)

His model has been subjected to heated debate at both the theoretical and the empirical levels (Bennett 1966; Kaplan and Saler 1966; Piker

1966; Foster 1972; J.R. Gregory 1975). Nonetheless, as with the kindred concept of "amoral familism" (Banfield 1958; Wichers 1964; Silverman 1968; R.A. Miller 1974; Berkowitz 1984), an ideology approximating to the "Limited Good" is found in most peasant societies, including modern Greece (McNall 1974; J.K. Campbell 1964, 38; Bialor 1968; Kenna 1976a, 350; cf. du Boulay and Williams 1987).

At first glance, the ideology of "Limited Good" appears incompatible with the need to maintain the facade of equality in interpersoanl relations, but they two are variant manifestation of the same behavioral mode. According to the "Limited Good" notion, each individual, or individual household, is locked into a continual struggle with every other person for access to those resources required for life. Simultaneously, however, individual actors appreciate that their chances of success in the game depend upon their ablity to construct and manipulate alliances with those who have resources which they desire. The ideology of equality permits the construction of such networks without the need arising for either side to claim an advantage over the other, even though both are struggling for such an advantage. The two notions, then, of the "Limited Good" and of the essential "equality" between partners involved in an exchange based on reciprocity are merely two manifestations of the same ideology and moral order.

McCann captures well the interplay of the two: "The moral order itself has two expressions. One concerns basic political and religious symbols that gave legal society a place within the greater cultural system and rational-ized the domination of the state and its local representatives; the other is expressed in the rhythms of day-to-day life and concerns the pattern of behavior which reconciled the need for social harmony amid competition for scarce resources between individuals and households" (1987a, 90). Eisenstadt and Roniger have highlighted three such inherent contradic-tions: "First, a peculiar combination of inequality and asymmetry in power with seeming mutual solidarity expressed in terms of personal identity and interpersonal sentiments and obligations; second, a combination of poten-tial coercion and exploitation with voluntary relations and compelling mutual obligations; third, a combination of the emphasis on these obligations and solidarity with the somewhat illegal or semi-legal aspect of these relations" (1981, 277; see also Adams 1971; Hutson 1971).

The social image of equality often masks a social praxis of inequality (E.P. Thompson 1975, 258–69; Lemarchand 1981, 10). This is partic-ularly true of the form of interpersonal relationship referred to under the broad rubric of patron–client ties, or simply clientism. This is a type of interpersonal relationship noted for its asymmetry in terms of the wealth, power, and prestige of the partners (Boissevain 1974 26; Blok 1969, 156; Eisenstadt and Roniger 1981, 272; 1980, 51–2; 1984; Gellner 1977, 1; Lemarchand 1981, 15; J.C. Scott 1976, 125; 1977a, 23–4; Silverman

1977, 10; Weingrod 1977). Many cultures then accept that all interpersonal bonds in their idealized form are based on an ideology of equality, but they also have a marked tendency toward clientism.

We can now turn to evidence from ancient Greece armed with the insight that in cultures where an ideology of social equality, an ethos of reciprocity and obligation, and the concept of the "Limited Good" exist, we should also expect to find well-developed systems of clientism (Eisenstadt and Roniger 1984, 204–19). The burden of the rest of this section is to demonstrate that both the ideology of social equality and the notion of the "Limited Good" were present in the Greek world after 500 BC, and, thus by analogy, we can infer the existence of vertical patron–client connections, even though they are not prominent in the sources. Our sources from antiquity focus almost exclusively on the ideational aspects of obligation and reciprocity, stressing in particular the aspect of equality.

That an ideology of obligation and reciprocity flourished during the "Dark Age" (c. 1000–750 BC) and the Archaic period (c. 750–500 BC) is unquestioned. In the poems of Homer, reciprocity and gift-giving formed a central social institution (Finley 1977; Qviller 1981; Donlan 1981; 1985; Morris 1986a). The works of Hesiod and Theognis demonstrate the continued importance of obligation and reciprocity into the sixth century BC (Walcot 1970; Gallant 1982a, Millett 1984; Figueira 1985; Perisynakis 1986; Morris 1986b).

A recent examination of the institution of ritualized friendship in the Classical and Hellenistic periods, moreover, indicates that reciprocity was still a potent ingredient in Greek interpersonal relationships: "To understand such sustained, complex, and long-term efforts [to maintain friendship], the operation of a further feature of ritualized friendship must be assumed: the confidence it inspired that the other side would be *morally committed to reciprocate*. This confidence acted as a kind of primitive insurance system, increasing the likelihood that engagements would be kept and obligations honored" (Herman 1987, 92; my italics). Futher analysis of the ancient sources merely reinforces this conclusion.

Aristotle in his ethical works provides the most articulate and explicit discussion of the norm of reciprocity in Greece. His analysis of interpersonal relations is couched in the language of friendship, a trait shared by many of our other sources as well. But, as we have seen, such terminology is quite flexible and is found in numerous cultures; we should, thus, follow Goldhill's advice and not allow our conceptualization of "friendship" to cloud our analysis of it in the past (1986, 78–9).

In the *Nicomachean Ethics*, Aristotle begins by defining three calibers of friendship: one based on pleasure or carnal desire, another based on utilitarian needs or mutual benefit, and the last, and best, the pure friendship of disinterested equals based on moral goodness. His last was the "ideal type" but all were commonly found and could shade into one another (*NE* 1,161–5; John M. Cooper 1980; S.R.L. Clark 1975). More will be said about Aristotle on friendship later. For the moment I want to focus on his attitude toward reciprocity and obligation.

Clearly Aristotle conceived all interpersonal relations as being based on the notion of reciprocity: "For friendship is said to be *reciprocated* goodwill. But perhaps we should add that friends are aware of the reciprocated goodwill" (*NE* 1155b34). Aristotle reiterates this view (*NE* 1162b9–11, 1162b18, 1163a1–10). On Cooper's interpretation, Aristotelian friendship cannot exist without reciprocity: "A fully-fledged friendship will exist, then, when such intentions [of each other's well-being] are recognized by both parties as existing reciprocally" (1980, 311). Even where the partners are unequal, there is always the obligation to reciprocate: "the benefactor supplies him with aid on the assumption that he will get an equal return" (*NE* 1163a19). Finally, Aristotle also assumes that the obligation to reciprocate took on greater compulsion in times of crisis: "Conversely, it is presumably appropriate to go eagerly, without having to be called, to friends in misfortune. For it is proper to a friend to benefit, especially to benefit a friend in need who has not demanded it, since this is finer and pleasanter to both friends" (*NE* 1171b21–4). For Aristotle reciprocity and obligation were the two key concepts in shaping the form and content of interpersonal relations. Nor was he alone in this.

Xenophon clearly espouses a similar view. "And if you wanted to induce one of your friends to watch your property when you were away, what would you do? Obviously, I would first try to take care of his while he was away" (*Mem* 2.3.11). Much of his discussion demonstrates the extent to which cold calculation of an individual's wealth, power, and status played a role in the process of selecting "friends" (*Mem* 2.5), indicating a behavioral mode based on an ideology of obligation and reciprocity.

In the same vein, Isokrates recommends "Make no man your friend before you know he treated his former friends" (*Demon*. 24). This was to ensure that the prospective friend conformed to the norm of reciprocity (*Demon*. 26). The moral imperative evinced by this ideology underlay numerous passages in the forensic speeches of the fourth century BC. For example, "He acted this way because he conceived it to be the duty of a 'good' man to *assist his friends* . . ." (Lysias 17.59). Numerous passages similar to this one could be cited, but the general point is sufficiently made already (see, Chroust 1956; Pearson 1962, 136–79; Adkins 1963; Connor 1971, 11; Fraisse 1974, 107–22; Donlan 1980, 137–53; Goldhill 1986, 78–106). An examination of the ancient sources leads to the conclusion that during the Classical and Hellenistic periods, the two concepts of obligation and reciprocity lay at the heart of the ideology of interpersonal relations.

Having thus firmly established the existence of one of the two key institutions we were seeking, we can turn to an examination of the second. Did ancient Greeks have an ideational structure approximate to Foster's "Limited Good"? Walcot has conducted the most detailed examination of this question and he concludes that indeed such as attitude flourished in ancient Greece (Walcot 1977). In the sources from Hesiod onward, he found that the notions of envy and jealousy were prevalent at all levels of Greek society, that Greeks felt themselves to be locked into ceaseless competition with other members of their community for material possessions, status, and power. "The Greeks were acutely aware of the problem [of endemic competition], and they at least faced up to it fearlessly, acknowledging that man was envious and making no attempt to suppress the unpalatable fact that envy was manifest everywhere" (1977, 10). We need not share Walcot's view on the moral courage of ancient Greeks in order to accept the broader conclusion that embedded in the dominant ideology of the past was a notion highly reminiscent of Foster's "Limited Good."

To this point, the discussion has focussed solely on the ideological basis of strictly interpersonal relations. Before continuing, we must briefly examine how the conclusions drawn above affect the structure of relations between certain individuals and the communities they inhabit.

Generally, cultures which manifest a well-developed ideology of interpersonal relations based on obligation and reciprocity, also practice variant forms of "communal patronage" (see, Goodell 1986, 252–3 for the distinctions between communal patronage and patronage and "paternalism"). The belief that those with greater access to and control of vital resources have a moral obligation to employ them on the community's behalf is built into the ideational system. In her study of an Italian town, for example, Silverman found that there were "certain members of the elite who were defined, and defined themselves, as protectors and benefactors of the community. According to the ideology, these persons bestowed material benefits, political advantages, and glory upon the community as a whole; they in turn were entitled to obedience, respect, and the loyalty of the community" (1977, 12). The pattern is indeed widespread (Eisenstadt and Roniger 1981, 279; 1984, 48–165; Greenough 1982, 20; Adams 1971; Hutson 1971; Codd 1971; Colclough 1971; Bailey 1971a; Graves 1983; Littlewood 1981; McCann 1987a, 62; Lemarchand 1981; Roeder 1984; Wade 1971; Sarti 1985, 56).

An inherent tension perpetually exists between the ideology and the reality of communal patronage. At an ideological level, "the position of the well-off villagers is legitimized only to the extent that their resources are employed in ways which meet broadly defined welfare needs of the village" (Scott 1976, 157–92; J.C. Scott 1977a, 25). So long as the mask of equality remained in place and elites could be held accountable to a normative standard of behavior, a certain amount of exploitation was acceptable. But, as La Lone points out, the ideological façade was critically important: "As ideology [reciprocity and obligation] permits political elites to make what appears – in material terms – to be extremely asymmetrical exchanges with subordinates and to portray such exchanges as *generosity*" (1982, 296; Goodell 1986, 247).

The evidence from ancient Greece that reciprocity and obligation were central concepts structuring peasant expectations toward the elite is plentiful. The following aptly capture this. "When the well-to-do prevail upon themselves to lend to the have-nots and help them and benefit them, herein at last is pity and an end to isolation and [the beginning of] friendship and *homonia* (social harmony) and other blessings such as no man could enumerate" (Demokritos frag. 255 [fifth century BC]). "It is [Proper Reasoning] that brings us to terms over mutual obligations and through this the poor receive from the men of wealth and the rich give to the needy, both trusting that by means of this that they will be treated fairly" (Archytas frag. 437 [fourth century BC]). Both of these passages forcefully articulate the position that it was the moral duty of the elite to aid the needy in a crisis.

Occasionally the expectation that the elite would redistribute resources to the community became more than a strictly moral duty (Thompson 1971). At Athens, for example, it became an institutionalized obligation. Through the practice of the *liturgy*, men possessing wealth over a specified amount were legally required to undertake certain activities on behalf of the state: funding public festivals and feasts, underwriting the costs of maintaining a warship, and the like. Some of these burdens were voluntary; others required that men be drafted (Finley 1983, 32–5; N.R.E. Fisher 1976, 25–30; Davies 1967; 1984a, 15–23; P.J. Rhodes 1982; Roberts 1986; Veyne 1976, 186–208; Ruschenbusch 1985, 237–40; Knox 1985; Gabrielsen 1987a; 1987b; Gauthier 1985, 118). Nevertheless, even in Athens, the expectation that wealthy men should be munificent on the community's behalf rested on an ideology of obligation and reciprocity. Men redistributed private goods and personal services to the community at large, and, in return, the community reciprocated by bestowing upon them honors, rank, privileges, and power (Whitehead 1983). The anticipation of elite assistance during a crisis was based on a norm of reciprocity and the moral duty that it imposed, but the actual fulfillment of those duties was firmly connected to the ability of the community to hold its elites accountable for their actions.

Obligation and reciprocity were the two key concepts underlying the ideational structure of interpersonal relations in ancient Greece. But before we can examine how interpersonal relations were employed as a risk-management strategy in Greek communities, one final topic requires analysis.

What factors determined the strength of the bond of reciprocity and obligation between two individuals or between two households? Obviously the answer to this question is critically important. When constructing a support network, people had to predicate their decisions on some commonly accepted and shared beliefs concerning the extent and the reliability of the assistance they could expect from certain categories of individuals (brothers, kinsmen, neighbors, patrons, etc.) and the social and material costs they would have to pay in order to obtain them. An examination of models derived from ethnographic studies indicates that the degree of intimacy, trust, and affection between two individuals has a direct bearing on the level of obligation and the assurance of assistance a person may expect.

Sahlins developed the following model of interpersonal exchange. He defined three categories of reciprocity, each of which has its own chrono-logical, spatial, and social dimension. He labels the first type "generalized reciprocity." It refers to transactions not necessarily involving goods and services of equal value. Temporally, the exchange need not be simulta-neous. Geographically, this type of reciprocity involves individuals residing close to one another. Socially, it occurs between people closely bound by ties of kinship or affection. An example of it would be the constant giving and taking between individual members of the same household. His second category is "balanced reciprocity." This is a form of direct exchange of goods and services which are notionally equal. Reciprocity should occur simultaneously. The partners may reside in close proximity, but that is not a necessary element in the exchange. Socially, it usually involves people from the same or from neighboring villages. Examples of it would be bridal prestations or inter-household feasting. His last group he calls "negative reciprocity." It is conducted for net utilitarian advantage. Each partner attempts to extract as much as possible from the other. The exchange usually occurs between people who do not reside near each other and who may be connected only through this transaction (Sahlins 1972, 191–6; see also Gouldner 1977, 36). While useful as a guide to the types of reciprocity that occur, Sahlins's model is incomplete (MacCormack 1976, 89–104).

Two other models can help us to understand the problem of obligation more thoroughly. The first is adapted from Scott's work on southeast Asia (see table 6.1 J.C. Scott 1977b, 137)). The second model relies on the work by Eisenstadt and Roniger (1984, 7; see table 6.2).

All three models tell much the same story, but each places the emphasis on different aspects of interpersonal relationships. The endpoints on Scott's scale and Eisenstadt and Roniger's categories of "exclusive" and "casual" friendships approximate Sahlins's generalized and negative reciprocity. At one end of the spectrum, the bond between partners is persistent, lasting long after any single transaction has been completed: indeed, it is presumed

Table 6.1 Spectrum of interpersonal bonds based on the quality of the exchange

Quality	Spectrum	
Duration of bond	more persistent	less persistent
Extent of relations	multiplex	simplex
Structural/ class differentiation between partners	little or no differentiation	some or high levels of differentiation
Resource base	local, personal	external
Affective/ instrumental balance	higher ratio of affective to instrumental ties	lower ratio of affective to instrumental ties
Local resource control	more local monopoly	less local monopoly
Density of coverage	greater density	less density

Table 6.2 Dimensions and types of friendship

Type	Dimensions		
	Exclusive	Close	Casual
Expressive/ instrumental	primarily expressive	expressive/ instrumental	largely instrumental
Dyadic/polyadic	dyadic/ exclusive	multiple dyads	polyadic
Intimacy	inclusive	selective	incidental
Mutability	assumed permanent	hoped durable	not stressed

Note: Based on Eisenstadt and Roniger 1984.

to be permanent. Most often exchanges at this level are between people who consider themselves to be equal and who are bound to one another by a wide range of ties, prominent among which is affection. Transactions will be frequent but of a limited character because each person controls few resources. At the other end of the scale are transactions which involve individuals who are patently not equals in terms of wealth and power. One is always dominant over the other. The relationship between them may be restricted to one transaction and is based on mutual need. Each seeks to obtain the maximum gain from the other. Exchanges occur less frequently but more wealth is involved because one party, the dominant member, controls a much wider range of resources.

These models indicate that the strength of the obligation between individuals is directly related to the way they conceive the social bond between them. If there are multiple ties between them, then the degree of moral obligation to provide assistance increases: the so-called multiplex relationship. Correspondingly, the expectation of assistance decreases proportionally to the number and the complexity of the social bonds (Boissevain 1974; 1977; Bloch 1973, 77; A.C. Mayer 1977; Landé 1977). We would expect, therefore, that when constructing a network of interpersonal relations as part of a risk-management strategy, people would seek to establish as many ties in as many different contexts as possible.

We can draw four conclusions from this section. First, there flourished in ancient Greece an ideational structure based on a norm of reciprocity and a deeply entrenched notion of obligation. Second, these two concepts shaped the form and content of interpersonal relations and communal patronage. Third, a strong sense of moral duty underlay communal patronage. Fourth, the extent and assurance of assistance from individuals was related to the number and types of personal bonds connecting two people (multiplex versus simplex), and that armed with this, men created hierarchically differentiated support networks. Structurally this network resembled a series of concentric spheres (see fig. 6.1). At the heart of the network was the household; next came kinsmen, then friends (ritual and institutional), neighbors, quasi-associations, and finally patrons. The re-

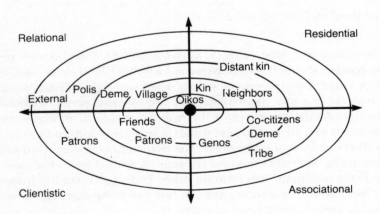

Fig. 6.1 Model of the Social Universe of Ancient Greeks.

mainder of this chapter analyses each of these, focusing in particular on their strengths and limitations as risk-managements tools.

Kinsmen in Crises

Kinsmen are ideally an individual's first line of defense in a subsistence crisis. In most cultures, kinsmen expect aid from relations in a crisis (Boissevain 1977, 283–4; Eisenstadt and Roniger 1981, 278–9; G.M. Foster 1977, 21; E.R. Wolf 1977, 170; Bloch 1973, 75–87; J.K. Campbell 1964, 19–20, 38; Abu-Zahra 1976; Kenny 1977; Faber 1981, 157; Du Bouley 1984; Woolf 1986, 16; Laslett 1988, 156–61). But in reality there is always an interplay between altruistic, corporate responsibility and self-interest (Hamer 1982, 304). Pitt-Rivers captures this sentiment well: "The axiom of prescriptive altruism is called into existence by the initial assumption that every man, individually or in solidarity with a collectivley with which he identifies himself, seeks his own interest and advancement, be it directly or through the medium of reciprocity, immediate or deferred, direct or by some system of exchange" (1973, 89; in following this line of approach, Pitt-Rivers took his lead from Fortes 1969. See also, Faber 1981, 157–8). Recently Laslett has discussed the question of kinship and mutual assistance and related it the "nucelar hardship" principle (Laslett 1988, 160). Kinship alone merely describes the form of the connection between two individuals; the dialogue presented above provides its behavioral dynamic (D. Freeman 1973; Chaytor 1980, 27; O.Harris 1982, 146). The question broached in this section is how did ancient Greeks use their kin in a crisis? What expectations did they have? How did they mediate a course between corporate responsibility and self-interest? We begin with the center of the "kinship region": the household (Wolf 1977, 170).

The structure and life cycle of the ancient Greek *oikos* was discussed at length in Chapter 2. It was noted there that the household was defined as a collectivity of individuals who were usually, but not necessarily, related to one another and who formed the central unit of production/consumption and reproduction. Generalized exchange was the norm inside the household. Self-interest was sublimated to the common good of the group and each member equally partook of the household's resources. Commensality was critically important. According to Back, "the demarcation of self is quickly and best established by maintaining and exhibiting some contrast between oneself and others," and the acting of eating together provides a readily visible means of achieving this end (Back 1977, 31; see also Counihan 1984, 47–57). As we have seen, first and foremost in the minds of ancient Greeks was the preservation of this unit during a crisis. Since the members of a household shared the same resource base, their fortunes during times of trouble were inextricably linked and shared. They had to turn to kinsmen for aid.

The positive aspects of kinship for risk-management are the following. First, because the bonds between kinsmen were multiplex, the moral obligation to provide assistance was strong. In the dialogue between self-interest and corporate responsibility, so long as one's own household was not at threat, then the good of the kingroup came next. Second, the bonds between kinsmen were perpetual. Households were connected by kinship until their extinction (Firth 1969).

The idea that both consanguineous and affinal kinsmen were morally obligated to assist each other pervades Greek literature. Sokrates, for example, tells Chairekrates that he should patch up his differences with his brother because nothing is to be desired more than harmony between kinsmen (Xenophon *Mem* 2.3). Moreover, our sources are unequivocal in their judgement that during a crisis, kin come first (Isokrates *Demon.* 10; Isaios 8.33; Aristotle *NE* 1160a6, 1165a25). Demosthenes in a forensic speech summarizes this attitude well. In questioning a man's motives for lending money, he states: "Yet none of these men is your kinsmen or a member of your household or has *any natural call upon you*" (24.196). The obvious conclusion to be drawn from this is that kinsmen did have a powerful natural and moral obligation to help their relatives.

The speaker of Lysias *Oration* 3 tells of how he took in his sister and her children after her husband had died (3.6). Aristarchos bemoans his economic fate to Sokrates after he had to provide support for large numbers of sisters, nieces, and female cousins who had been deserted because of war (Xenophon *Mem* 2.7.2). Men were to give gifts, not loans, to their relations (Theophrastos *Char* 18.7) and they should never cheat them (Demosthenes 21.130).

When physical rather than material support was needed, men once again would took to kin. On two documented occasions when street fights broke out, kin stood toe-to-toe against a common foe (Lysias, 3.33; Demosthenes, 54.10). If a dispute occurred between kinsmen, the disputants often selected another kinsman to arbitrate (Isaios 2.30; for comparative evidence, see Brögger 1968; 1971; Bialor 1968; Noland 1980). If a case did go to court, then kinsmen were expected to testify on each other's behalf (Humphreys 1986). In one well-known case, a man needed to establish his claim to citizenship. He called on first his brothers, then his paternal uncles and cousins, and finally, all his agnatic male kinsmen to testify on his behalf (Demosthenes 57.19–24). The evidence is clear: in times of crisis, kinsmen should provide succor and assistance.

In this regard, affinal kinship had one major advantage over consanguineous relations. Individual households had little control over the distribution of blood kin, whereas they did over affines. One of the ways in which peasant households could use kinship as a risk-buffering mechanism would be to form alliances through marriages with groups in other locales. Given the rather limited residential mobility found in most pre-industrial societies, consanguineous kin would probably live nearby. By making affines out of people in another area, a source of aid would be created which could be called on in case of a localized trauma. This is not to argue that risk-buffering was foremost in the minds of Greek men when selecting mates for their children, but that along with wealth, prestige, status, and power, location did play a role in their thinking (Lysias 19.14–17; Xenophon *Oik* 7.11; Osborne 1985, 130–31; Schlegal and Eloul (1988) present persuasive arguments along this line based on an extensive examination of the ethnographic literature).

There are, however, three serious shortcomings which restricted the utility of kinsmen as sources of aid during subsistence crises. First, simple demographics limited the size of the kingroup. Second, because they came from the same class and wealth group, the amount of assistance kin could provide was restricted. Third, the spatial distribution of kinsmen would set narrow parameters for effective assistance. If kinsmen lived nearby, then they would be liable to suffer from the same perturbations causing the subsistence crisis. If, however, they lived some distance away, then the degree of affective ties between kin would be diminished. Empirical studies indicate that kinship bonds suffer a type of "distance decay" – relatives feel less obligated to aid one another the further apart they reside (Martinez-Alier 1971, 128; Landé 1977, 78; Bloch 1973; Woolf 1986, 16; Laslett 1988, 160). Households can compensate for these deficiencies by cementing ties with, on the one hand, non-kin who live in close proximity – neighbors – and, on the other, non-kin who reside some distance away but who are bound by ties of friendship.

Friends and Neighbors

> Invite your friend, but not your enemy,
> To dine; especially, be cordial to
> Your neighbor, for if trouble comes at home,
> A neighbor's there, at hand; while in-laws take
> Some time to arm themselves. It is a curse
> To have a worthless neighbor; equally,
> A good one is a blessing; he who is
> So blest possesses something of great worth.
> No cow of yours will stray away if you
> Have watchful neighbours. Measure carefully
> When you must borrow from your neighbor, then,
> Pay back the same, or more, if possible,
> And you will have a friend in time of need.
>
> Hesiod *WD* 342–53

In response to the limitations of kinship as a risk-buffering mechanism, peasants turned to non-kinsmen: friends and neighbors (Georges-Roegen 1970, 68; Foster 1977, 23; S.T. Freeman 1970). The above passage from the poet Hesiod captures well both the advantages and the disadvantages of relying on friends as a form of risk-management, and these are analyzed in this section.

The axion that one can choose one's friends but not one's relatives is precisely correct. An ancient Greek chose his friends on the basis of a wide range of criteria, prominent among which was the other person's track record of assisting his friends in times of need, as the following passage makes clear: " 'But tell me, Sokrates, what sort of person should we make as our friend?' 'Presumably one who has the opposite qualities {to those cited earlier] – who is self-controlled with regard to physical pleasures, and who proves to be good at managing his own affairs, reliable in his dealings with others, and eager to come to the aid of his friends.' " When asked how one could tell if a man would make a good friend, Sokrates led his companion in the dialogue to conclude "that anyone who has evidently treated his past friends well will obviously do good to his subsequent friends too" (Xenophon *Men* 2.6.3–7; see also, Isokrated *Demon*. 24). Men selected their friends with care and nurtured the relationship by taking heed of the moral dictates of reciprocity. Isokrates goes so far as to state that one should prize wealth only to the extent that it allowed one to bear a heavy loss (by which Xenophon means the prevention of the household's extinction) and it enabled one to help a worthy friend in need (*Demon*. 28; Xenophon *Oik* 1.14).

Julian Pitt-Rivers's essay "The Kith and the Kin" provides an excellent introduction to this topic (1973). He argues that there is a spectrum of interpersonal relationships bounded, on the one side, by "real" kinship and on the other, by unritualized friendship (1973, 95–6). Structurally his system is based on the notion of simplex versus multiplex bonds. Individuals attempt to solidify the relationships by making their friends more like kin. This is accomplished by institutionalizing friendship through ritual. From the evidence contained in the ancient sources it is clear that they are describing bonds of amity which go beyond casual acquaintance and which resemble closely institutional friendship.

In a recent work, Gabriel Herman discusses one type of institutional friendship, *xenia* or guest friendship with men from outside one's own state, and more will be said about this later (1987). Ancient Greeks attempted to strengthen their relationships with men from outside their own households by ritually transforming these nominal outsiders into fictive insiders through pseudo-kinship.

Generically, one of the most important categories of outsiders was neighbors. On account of their geographical propinquity, neighbors were an ideal source of material assistance. As Aristotle noted "the members of the village separated in different households had at their disposal a number of different things which they had to exchange with one another, *as needs arose*, by way of exchange in kind . . ." (*Pol* 1257a5–6). It was commonly accepted in Greece that neighbors would lend items such as food, tools, and animals to each other as required (Hesiod *WD* 352–3, 335, 398–400, 409, 452–5; Theophrastos *Char* 9.7). This is true of many preindustrial cultures as well (*Mexico*: Foster 1977, 224; *France*: Segalen 1984, 172–97; *England*: Fenoaltea 1976, 131–2; O.Harris 1982, 147; *Asia*: Hanks 1975; *Sicily*: Chapman 1971, 140; *Turkey*: Benedict 1976, 233).

In many cultures, commensality was a critically important component in defining "friendship" and "neighborliness": "The offering of food and drink is the quintessence of this reaffirmation, and if someone professes friendship but fails in this informal exchange he is said to be a 'friend with his lips on the outside,' that is, not a genuine friend" (Foster 1977, 24). Theophratsos was clearly aware that reciprocal feasting between neighbors was a means of redistributing foodstuffs and of reinforcing the bond of amity between men (Theophrastos *Char* 10.11; see below pages 171–2). Kirby describes in detail this pratice in Oaxaca, Mexico. A single household heavily borrows from kinsmen and friends foodstuffs with which they hold a feast for their neighbors and friends. Over a period of time, the loan is paid back, but in the meantime, the feast-givers are fêted by fellow members of their village (Kirby 1974, 127). Neighbors were also expected to lend a helping hand in the fields (Lysias 7.18; see also Bloch 1973), to watch over another man's fields and property if he had to be away from them (Demosthenes 53.4), and to provide some muscle in case of a fight (Lysias 1.23, 41).

Many of the same types of actions were anticipated from friends. They should unstintingly come forward and lend a fist in a fight (Demosthenes 54.7; Lysias 1.23; 3.23; Diodoros Sikeliotes 19.6.4). When confronted with litigation, worthy friends would either offer to testify on a man's behalf or to remain silent if that be expedient (Demosthenes 53.1; Isaios 9.16). Most important friends were expected to provide willingly economic support in a crisis. Ideally, this aid should be given freely as a gift, for, as Aristotle phrased it, "Where a loan is involved, there is no friendship; for if a man is a friend, he gives, not lends" (*Problems* 29.2). Few, however, reached this lofty perch of moral rectitude, and most frequently friends provided aid in the form of interest-free loans (Demosthenes 50.56; 53.7; Lysias 19.22; Theophrastos *Char* 17.9; see also for comparative evidence on this point, Macfarlane 1970, 55–6; Appleby 1978, 48).

But herein lay a critical disadvantage to their reliability. Recurrently the call of kinsmen and friends on a household's resources could coincide. "Thus the crux of the paradoxical and ambivalent relations between friendship and kinship lies in their sharing many characteristics while, symbolically and organizationally, friendship appears distinct from kinship and even potentially opposed it" (Eisenstadt and Roniger 1984, 17; see also Kenna 1976a; Bialor 1968; Faber 1981, 158; Herzfeld 1984, 656–7). Unless bound to one another by trust and amity, neighbors could be powerfully malevolent foes. For example, because of their close proximity, neighbors could gain knowledge about the affairs of others and this knowledge could be used in the form of gossip to destroy a household's reputation (Lysias 17.12; Demosthenes 21.104; Bialor 1968; McNall 1974, 89; Bailey 1971a, 2; Blaxter 1971; Boissevain 1974, 76; Du Boulay 1976; Haviland 1977; Gilmore 1987, 53–76). They could also surreptitiously rustle animals or, even worse, destroy crops (Hesiod *WD* 343; Demosthenes 53.15–16; 55.1; Lysias 7.18; Bialor 1968). Consequently, most cultures devise strategies for enhancing and increasing the number of linkages between individuals and households in an attempt to reduce the magnitude of the distinction between kin and non-kin. Nevertheless there was the potential for neighbors to become nasty and friends to become foes.

Friends and neighbors formed an indispensable set of sources of aid and assistance during a crisis. The advantage of friends and neighbors over kinsmen when constructing a subsistence crisis support network were that the group was readily expandable, the individuals included were specifically selected, and they resided near enough to be available when needed. Furthermore, by institutionalizing friendship, the bond between two households was strengthened and perpetuated. Nonetheless, three critical shortcomings limited the utility of friends and neighbors as risk-buffers in all but very minor subsistence crises.

First, there was always a latent tension between the interests of a man's own household, his duty to his kin, and his obligations to his friends. And it is clear that the interests of the household came first.

Second, because friends were ideally economic equals, each would have access to roughly the same resource base.

Third, the fact of geography which made neighbors a ready source of aid also meant that, given the high degree of synchronized, regional variability of crop yield fluctuations, they would also suffer similar magnitudes of crop losses.

Clearly Greek peasants could not rely solely on kinsmen, friends, and neighbors for their subsistence insurance. Instead they had to expand their support networks outward in space and upward in the social hierarchy. Links had to be forged with men who controlled greater quantities of food supplies and whose economic reach extended beyond the realm of the village. One way to accomplish this was through the creation of interpersonal relationships with men of wealth and power, relationships best described by the term clientism.

Friends of Friends: Patrons, Clients, and Communities

If friends give gifts, make friends.
Anonymous Italian peasant cited in Arlacchi 1983

The phrase patron–client refers to a particular type of interpersonal relationship found in most pre-industrial, agrarian societies. The following from Eisenstadt and Roniger presents the salient characteristics of patronage: "first, a rather peculiar combination of inequality and asymmetry in power with seeming mutual solidarity expressed in terms of personal identity and interpersonal sentiments and obligations; second, a combination of potential coercion and exploitation with voluntary relations and mutual obligations; third, a combination of emphasis on such mutual obligations and solidarity or reciprocity between patrons and clients with the somewhat illegal or semi-legal aspect of these relations" (1984, 49). Patronage is thus particularistic and dyadic, that is it links two individuals into a relationship peculiar to them at a specific point in time, and invariably the two partners come from divergent social and economic postions; furthermore, the flow of goods and services between them is unequal (Gallant 1982a; 1989; Boissevain 1974; 1977; Cashdan 1985; Colclough 1971; Eisenstadt and Roniger 1980; 1981; Gellner 1977; Lemarchand 1981; J.C. Scott 1976; 1977a; 1977b; Silverman 1977; Weingrod 1977; Foster 1977; Landé 1977; Littlewood 1981; J.D. Powell 1977; Bailey 1971a; 1971b; 1971c; Galt 1974). The patron gathers in far more than he gives out. Yet, because of the ideology of reciprocity and obligation which underlay this form of social relation, technically, the client could exert a strong moral claim to assistance from the patron (an aspect of the relationship discussed in more detail below) (J.C. Scott 1976; Gallant 1989, 404–5). Indeed when assessing the value of a patron, the client was acutely aware of this as Wylie shows: "the poor man would need to determine judiciously when to switch patrons if the old one showed signs of becoming less generous" (Wylie 1989, 163). Patrons were *expected* to provide assistance when called on.

Patronage appears as a prominent feature in a wide range of socio-political settings. Nevertheless, we can draw some generalizations about the types of systems in which it occurs most regularly and frequently. Patron–client relations flourish where:

1   Politically, a very weak central authority is unable to assert effective control throughout its territory, thereby providing and opportunity for sub-groups to exert their own power and influence locally (Schneider, Schenider, and Hansen 1977).
2   There is a differential access to vital resources, such as land and capital, markets, and political power.

3   Positions providing accessibility to the above are ascriptive and based on qualifications such as wealth, juridical status, or ethnicity.
4   There flourishes an ideational system which emphasizes social equality and reciprocity in interpersonal relationships.

All these features are found in ancient Greece. Number one, as we shall see in Chapter 7, characterized the period after the formation of the empires in the Hellenistic period. Numbers two and three existed at all times during antiquity; the latter in particular was a prominent feature of the Greek *polis*. We concluded earlier that an ideational system similar to the one described in number four constituted a central element in ancient Greek society.

On the spectra of interpersonal bonds, patron–client relations fall firmly in Sahlins's category of "negative" reciprocity, Scott's simplex bond, and Eisenstadt and Roniger's casual friendship. As in many other cultures, clientistic bonds in ancient Greece were masked as "friendship," for example in Aristotle's typology it is called "utilitarian friendship" (*NE* 1162a2–5). The following aptly summarizes the patron–client bond from a client's eye view: "But the needy person, the inferior in the [utilitarian] friendship, takes the opposite view [to that of the patron] saying that it is proper that a 'virtuous' man come to his [the client's] aid when necessary. For what use is it, as the saying goes, to be the friend of an excellent or powerful man if you are not going to gain anything by it?" (*NE* 1163a33–5). What peasants hoped to gain by it, I would argue, was subsistence insurance at the lowest premium possible. Patronage, as defined above, constituted a critically important element in the social and economic systems of ancient Greece.

We noticed earlier that one of the defining aspects of patron–client dyads was that they were particularistic and face-to-face. These facts of clientism raised two problems for peasants, as Aristotle clearly saw (*NE* 1157a4; Langholm 1984).

First, if patronage was to provide a secure form of subsistence insurance, then the bond between patron and client had to be perpetuated. Thus, while any single exchange transaction between them was particularistic, the actual exchange entitlement was generalized and open-ended. In short, the client had to be able to rely in the future on material assistance from his patron when necessary.

Second, since patrons came from a very different social class and economic stratum from peasant clients, the venues which permitted their two worlds to intersect were limited. Unless they created a social context which enabled clients to increase the number of ties between themselves and a patron, that is to move from simplex to more multiplex interpersonal bonds, the two problems cited above would have loomed large.

We have seen that friends and neighbors were more fully integrated into an individual's interpersonal network through the use of institutionalized friendship and fictive kinship. In the case of patronage, however, neither of these would have been particularly effective because of the cultural and economic gulf between elites and peasants. One of the few exceptions to this statement was the institution of godparenthood (Du Boulay 1974, 162–8; 1984; Gallant 1988, 280–2; Kenna 1976a, esp. 351; Mintz and Wolf 1971; Pitt- Rivers 1976, J.K. Campbell 1964, 222; Hammel 1968, 81–7; Nunti and Bell 1980; Lynch 1986). Through marriage or baptismal sponsorship a peasant household could create a powerful connection with a wealthy patron. Indeed, it is clear that in many cultures godparents were selected precisely because of the economic resources they possessed. Furthermore, the moral obligation of a godfather to provide assistance in times of need was very strong. Ancient Greeks, however, had no equivalent institution and so instead had to rely primarily on the second type of mechanism for enhancing patron–client ties found in peasant societies: co-membership in a corporate entity or "association."

By association we refer to an "enduring, presumably perpetual group with determinate boundaries and membership, having an internal organization and a unitary set of external relations, and self-regulating" (Goodell 1986, 247). They were self-identifying sub-groups enclosed in a larger socio-political system, providing, in some contexts, a buffer between their members and the wider system of which they were a part (Eisenstadt and Roniger 1984, 35). Associations were usually supra-village and always sub-state level organizations. Furthermore, their membership crosscut economic strata and class boundaries. And it was this aspect in particular which made such organizations ideal settings for elite–peasant interaction. Such groups were found in a wide range of cultures. Often they had as their focus religion or cultic rituals, they practiced commensality, and, like ritualized friendship, they mimicked kinship (Webster 1968; Boissevain 1974; 1977; Sweetman 1978). Numerous associations underlay ancient Greek society.

Some combination of residence, descent, and ascription provided the basis for membership in associations in ancient Greece. Social organizations such as *gene, phratriai, orgeones,* and *thiasoi* featured prominently in every Greek state (Andrewes 1957; Cairns 1986; Charneux 1984; Foucart 1873; G.Jones 1987; Roussel 1976; Stanton 1986). As with so many other topics, however, our best evidence comes form Athens. Two groupings in particular require comment. The first is the *demos* or deme: the territorially based unit out of which the Athenian state was constructed. Membership in the state was established through attachment to a deme and this, in turn, was based on descent and residence (Whitehead 1986; Osborne 1985; Davies 1977/78). Co-membership in a deme reinforced the bonds of residential solidarity. In addition, since geographically disparate demes were grouped into clusters known as *trittyes,* bonds of solidarity and group allegiance became extended across Attica (Osborne

1985, 90–1). Furthermore, individuals of widely differing social rank and wealth belonged to the same demes. Thus, the deme provided an ideal venue for elite–peasant contact and for the display of beneficence and patronage by the former not only to the deme as a corporate entity but to individual members as well (Whitehead 1986, 126, 128, 152–60, 175, 246–7; Osborne, 1985, 1–5, 56, 87). As Whitehead concludes, amongst demesmen there should be "contact, familiarity and help" and they should consider themselves to be "friends" (1985, 232–3).

Organizations like the *phratry, orgeones,* and *thiasoi* were associations based on fictive kinship bonds. There was some overlap in membership between them and admission was contingent on descent and ascription (Calhoun 1913; Andrewes 1961; Ferguson 1910; 1938; 1944; Fisher 1976; Hedrick 1983; 1988; 1989; Roussel 1976; Tod 1932). Analogously to demes, men of widely divergent rank and wealth belonged. The ceremonies performed by them provided opportunities for ritualized encounters between elite and non-elite, and the kinship-like bonds which co-membership established increased the moral obligation to furnish assistance in times of need (Lysias 8.1–20; Demosthenes 21.156; 57.22–4; Connor 1971; 22–3; Pusey 1940; for examples from elsewhere, see Silverman 1981, 164; W.C. Jordan 1988, 33).

As Osborne puts it "the phratry looks after its own" (1985, 91). Furthermore, because members of these solidarities came from all across Attica, individuals could diminish risk by having access to potential patrons from other areas (Osborne 1985, 73).

Co-membership in associations established a controlled, ritualized context in which elites and non-elites could interact. Accordingly, it is highly likely that when crises arose, peasants would seek their patrons from men of wealth and power in these groups. Nevertheless, although the bond between them was mediated by their associational bonds, the essential economic tie between them was based on inequality and asymmetrical obligations. In short, associations helped foster the formation of patron–client bonds, but the precise nature of that tie was molded less by associational affinity than by socio-political accountability. For that reason, latent in the nature of patronage was the potential for exploitation.

The evidence from ancient Greece on the exact rules, structures, and expectations involved in patron–client dyads requires qualification. First, because of the elitist bias of the literary sources, evidence for elite–peasant dyads is notably scarce. We hear much more about political factions than about village patrons. The same is true of much of the evidence from the forensic speeches of the fourth century. Second, public documents such as inscriptions refer mainly to communal rather than private patronage. Nevertheless, a careful examination of this material in conjunction with analogies drawn from comparative sources reveals that elite–peasant dyads were a critical cog in ancient Greek risk-buffering strategies.

We can identify five types of actions which clients expect of their patrons. Three occur in normative contexts and result in the clients obtaining access to basic subsistence. The other two become operative during and after a subsistence crisis, and they act to prevent a client's household from suffering famine or to enable it to rebound when the crisis has passed. These are not, however, discrete categories of action but parts of an interactive feedback system, the operation of which results in the enrichment of the patron and the degradation of the client into an often permanent state of dependency.

(1) On a day-to-day basis, a good patron should act to ensure that his clients have access to the means of production–land. The way in which he does so is to take on as tenants or as share croppers individuals who are attached to him through clientage. The exact terms of the tenancy are subject to negotiations and factors affecting the nature of the agreement are the availability of land and population density. If land is scarce or access to it limited or if the ratio of peasants to available land is high, then tenants are at a severe disadvanatge when negotiating tenancy terms. In such cases, the patron is meant to be a more lenient landlord to his clients than to non-clients, providing better terms or allowing them to rent better land (Landé 1977; Lemarchand 1981; Seavoy 1986, 256; Blok 1974; Galt 1974; C.White 1980; Davis 1973; Silverman 1975; Scott 1977a; Schmidt 1977; Gouldner 1977; Hill 1982, 63). The difference these aspects could make to a peasant family is significant. In the case of the terms of the tenancy, for example, the designation of payment in cash or in kind and the timing of the payment could spell the difference between survival and dearth for a poor family (Simoni 1979, 121). If the rent was due in kind and was assessd as a percentage of the crop, then the share-cropper would be in a very disadvantageous position if the yield was low but it would act to their benefit if the yield was high (Scott 1976, 44–52; Huang 1985, 203–14). If the rent was assessed in cash, then the timing of the payment was critical; the worst-case scenario is for rent to be be due immediately after the harvest when the prices are low (Cheung 1969, 64; Duby 1974, 228–9; Scott 1976, 44–52; Pearce 1983, 45–6, 49; Cooper 1984; Currie 1981; Huang 1985, 212; Reid 1987). Significantly, all of these aspects of the landlord–tenant relationship were open to negotiation and the degree to which the parties were linked to one another by social bonds helped to shape the agreement.

The ratio of independent small-holders to tenants to share croppers in ancient Greece varied from place to place and from time to time. For example in Asia Minor during the Hellenistic period, a much higher proportion of the peasantry obtained access to land through tenancy agreements and share cropping than during the Classical period (Rostovtzeff 1941, 278, 465, 509; Atkinson 1968; Finley 1983, 33). Furthermore, none of these statuses need necessarily have been permanent. Depending on its economic circumstances or its life cycle phase, a household could find itself enmeshed in a number of different combinations of tenurial arrangements; although once caught in the vicious cycle of dependency and debt, escape would have proven difficult for many (Pertev 1986, 35; Russell 1987, 153). Accordingly, it seems highly likely that in ancient Greece a sizeable, but not precisely quantifiable, sector of the peasantry obtained access to land by contracting some type of conditional tenure agreement with large land-owners (Finley 1951; 1981b; Fuks 1972, 25; D.M. Lewis 1973; Jameson 1982; Osborne 1987, 41–4; 1988). For that reason, we may justly expect that patronage connections would have been actively sought by households which were either bereft of land or at a stage in their development cycle when extra-land was needed.

(2) Another way that patrons were expected to assist their clients was through seasonal wage labor. Since most patrons in peasant societies were large owners, regardless of whether or not the bulk of their permanent labor force was slave or free, during critical periods of the agricultural cycle they would require additional labor. The process by which individuals were chosen was not disinterested; clients would be preferred to non-clients, and conversely, by forming patronage ties with a large landowner, a peasant enhanced his chances of obtaining seasonal work. In many instances, the cash made through it spelled the difference between a household's surviving through another year (Gellner 1977; Jackson 1985; Maraspini 1968; Seavoy 1986, 256; Blok 1966; 1969; Eisenstadt and Roniger 1981; van Apeldoorn 1981, 57; Heath 1973; Galt 1974; 1979; Davis 1969; 1973; Hill 1982, 63; Huang 1985, 195–9, 214–16; G. Evans 1988, 239).

Seasonal wage labor was required perennially. "The evidence, small though it may be in quantity, is overwhelming in its impact. Free hired labour was casual and seasonal, its place determined by the limits beyond which it would have been absurd to purchase and maintain a slave force, most obviously to meet exceptional short-terms needs of harvesting in agriculture." The men who performed these tasks "were independent peasants and craftsmen happy to be able to add something to their regular, low earnings" (Finley 1985, 73; 1983, 41; see also Zimmermann 1974; De Ste. Croix 1982, 179–97). Whether it be amongst the poor Athenians gathering at the hill of Kolonos during the Classical period (Fuks 1984) or displaced peasants in Asia Minor during the third century BC seeking work on a large landed estate (Kreissig 1980), wage labor on a regular annual basis was critical to the household economy. And, if the work of Bardhan and Rudra can provide a useful guide, interpersonal relations played a critical role in determining who received paid employment and who did not (1986). Their research in India showed that employers sought to hire men whom they knew and with whom they had more than incidental contact, and that peasants accepted work from these men even though they could have gotten higher wages elsewhere because by establishing a one-to-one patronal relationship with a large landowner they ensured a source of "regular credit and emergency help" (Bardhan and Rudra 1986, 91). David Kertzer in his work on day laborers in central Italy during the nineteenth century found that this was the case there as well (Kertzer 1984; see also Huang 1985, 215–16 for evidence from north China).

(3) Patrons were also supposed to divert resources to their clients by providing access to their own supplies and by giving gifts. One of the primary examples of this is "gleaning." This term was derived from Medieval England and describes a practice known from Biblical times (Ruth, 2.1–23) whereby peasants were able to scour their lord's fields after the grain harvest had been completed and to gather any residue which had been left behind (Ault 1961/62; Postan 1966, 165; Hilton 1973, 137–9). Such a custom is found in a wide range of cultures (for examples, see: Martinez-Alier 1971, 72–5; Gouldner 1977; Seavoy 1986, 63). A variant form of gleaning occurred in ancient Greece. In his caricature of a cheapskate, Theophrastos tells of a man so closefisted that he "would not let anybody sample the figs from his trees, or cut across his fields [thus preventing them from sampling the fruits as they went], or pick up a miserable olive or date which has fallen to the ground" (Theophrastos *Char* 10.8). The wealthy Athenian Kimon, we are told, "fed many of his fellow demesmen: any member of his deme could come to him daily and receive adequate supplies; furthermore, none of his estates were enclosed so that anyone who wished could help himself to his crops" (Aristotle *Ath* 27.3; Plutarch *Kim* 10.1–3). A patron worth his salt, then, was to be openhanded or, to employ a metaphor based on kinship, he was to treat his clients as he would his own children. Aristotle (*NE* 1161a15) adopted a pastoral image as his metaphor for patronage: for him, a patron was akin to a watchful shepherd protecting his peasant sheep.

(4) All the measures discussed so far provided needed foodstuffs or access to land on which a farmer could produce food. Once a crisis had struck and all of the coping mechanisms discussed in previous chapters had been exhausted, however, peasants had no choice but to turn to wealthy men in the guise of patrons for assistance.[20] Indeed, one of the primary responsibilities of a patron was to help his clients to stay alive during a subsistence crisis. He was meant to do so in two ways: First, through supplying gifts of food and low or no interest loans (Maraspini 1968, 51; Duby 1974, 51–2; McAlpin 1979, 149; 1983, 13; Orenstein 1980, 75; J.C. Scott 1976, 35–55, 89; 1977a; 1977b; Attalides 1977, 138; G.M. Foster 1977, 24; Seavoy 1986, 72–3, 254; Caiti 1986, 114; Silverman 1966; 1970; 1975; 1977) and, second, by remitting rents and debt repayments (Greenough 1982, 47–8; Seavoy 1986, 256; Caiti 1986, 119; W.C. Jordan 1988, 34; G.Evans 1988, 248–9). The "good" patron

was expected to try and ease the burden on his dependents in times of crisis. When the crisis had passed, because of the action of many of the response strategies, households lost resiliency and were thus unable on their own to return to pre-crisis levels of production. Patrons were expected in this case to provide loans for the restoration of capital, usually in the form of seed-gain, tools, manure, and traction animals (van Apeldoorn 1981, 57; McCann 1987a, 81; Greenough 1982, 48; McAlpin 1979; Watts 1988, 278–9).

All these types of actions are attested in ancient Greece. According to Millett, "loan transactions of one type or another are a pervasive feature at all levels of Athenian private life" (Millett 1983, 42). More generally, it was a feature of the entire ancient Greek world. Greek peasants, like small farmers in every pre-industrial society, depended on loans from their wealthy compatriots for their survival. Furthermore, like them, they strived whenever possible to borrow from men with whom they had already established social relations – through either confraternal bonds, or patronage, or both.[21]

The sources are replete with references to constant borrowing and indebtedness (to cite only a sample of examples: Pseudo-Aristotle 1349a1, 1349b1–5; Aristotle *NE* 1159a15, 1161b4–5; Lysias 8.1–20, 19.22, 17.59; Demosthenes 37; 43.69; 53.7; Isokrates *Pan* 132.3, 168; *Phil* 52, 97, 120; *Arch* 11, 15.57–8). Capital loans are explicity described by Pseudo-Aristotle (1349a3–8): Following a severe crisis at Abydos, peasants were in desperate need of capital in order to begin farming again. The state, therefore, passed a law which stated that anyone who lent money or supplies to poor small-holders was to receive a share of future crop yields. This law made sharecroppers out of borrowers. As with any borrowing, once a debt dependency relationship became established it was nearly impossible for the small farmer to get out of it (Pertev 1986, 35; Russell 1987, 153).

During a subsistence crisis, peasants expected forbearance by their patrons. There was among the ancient Greek peasants a deeply held belief that patrons *should* be lenient during a crisis (Ailian *VH* 14.24). The ability of the peasantry to enforce this behavioral standard was contingent on the degree to which they could meaningfully hold the elite accountable for its actions, and this, in turn, was mediated by the dialectic between the "moral economy" and the "political economy."

Patronage Networks beyond the Community: Social Storage

The grain bins of even the largest land-holders would have been exhausted if there were more than one or two consecutive crop failures or a single one of extreme severity. Accordingly, in order for patronage systems to act as truly effective relief agencies, local patrons had to be able to call on resources from outside their immediate locale; indeed, they would have been compelled to turn to men resident beyond the boundaries of their own state. Halstead and O'Shea have explored in a prehistoric context the way in which individual big-men and entire communities could be interconnected through exchange networks based on, in their terminology, "social storage." Mediated through gift exchange relations communities could provide a measure of subsistence insurance by ensuring that other communities were indebted to them because of previous prestations (Halstead 1981b; O'Shea 1981; Halstead and O'Shea 1982; see also, C.A. Gregory 1982; Graves 1983). In the ancient Greek world, three socio-political institutions performed much the same function: *xenia, proxenia*, and interstate "friendship."

Xenia refers to institutionalized friendship, or guest-friendship as it is often called, contracted between members of the elite in different states. The best discussion of it is presented by Herman (1987). He characterizes its thus:

> Guest-friendship served as a device for the promotion of the material and political interests of the elites engaged in it. Individuals integrated into politically separated communities exchanged *substantial amounts of wealth* and performed service for each other. Power, prestige and resources that could be acquired through one system could be readily transferred to the other, and at times the horizontal ties of solidarity which linked together the elites of separate communities were stronger than the vertical ties which bound them to the inferiors within their own communities.   (1987, 8; my italics)

It was ostensibly a purely interpersonal relationship, but in fact it conjoined in perpetuity two households; *xenia* was passed from father to son. The individual partners would compete in ritualized gift-giving: the winner would hold the loser in a state of dependency. As with friendship and patronage, *xenia* bonds were based on an ideology of reciprocity backed by powerful social pressures for adherence. Accordingly, *xenia* gave wealthy men access to resources from outside their polity in times of crisis: "To understand such sustained, complex, and long-term efforts [to maintain *xenia*], the operation of a further feature of ritualised friendship must be assumed: the confidence it inspired that the other side would be morally committed to reciprocate. This confidence acted as a kind of primitive insurance system, increasing the likelihood that engagements would be kept and obligations honored" (Herman 1987, 92). *Xenia* bonds allowed men of wealth to obtain access to resources outside of their home community and they were ideally meant to channel those resources to their co-citizens through patronage bonds.

Through *proxenia* and simple bilateral agreements, communities acting as corporate entities established "friendship"-like bonds between themselves and either a single wealthy household or another community. *Proxenia* in many ways mimicked the older institution of *xenia*: it was passed on between generations, it involved the continual exchange of gifts and services, and it was intended to create a "kin-like" bond (Herman 1987, 132; Gauthier 1972; Wallace 1970). In numerous crises, a community had to rely on the actions of its foreign *proxenos* for vital subsistence assistance (e.g., *IG* $2^{.2.}$ 141 (Athens, 360 BC)). In return the *proxenos* obtained the right to own land in the other community, exemption from taxes, and the ability to import and export goods without paying duty (e.g., Engelmann and Merkelbach 1972, Nos. 53–6 (Erythrai, 355 BC); *SIG*^{3} 278 (Priene, 334 BC)). By establishing an extensive network of *proxenoi*, a community would enhance its ability to call on outsiders for assistance during a subsistence crisis.

Xenia and the like, then, complemented internal patronage relations, and together these two sets of interpersonal social relations provided the dominant source of subsistence insurance in ancient Greece.

Limitations to Interpersonal Bonds as Risk-buffers

The adaptive measures and response strategies discussed previously demonstrated the multiplicity of ways by which peasants attempted to buffer themselves from the vagaries of crop yield fluctuations. Ingenious as these actions were, their utility was circumscribed by the limited resources available in the peasant household. Even the assests of rich peasants could only have been stretched so far. Consequently, exchange relations with other households had to be established and perpetuated in order to asusre the long-term survival of the household. This was accomplished through the construction of elaborate networks of interpersonal relationships.

This chapter began with a detailed discussion of the ancient Greek ideational structure that underlay their interpersonal relationships; we can draw two conclusions. First, the concept of reciprocity was deeply embedded in their ideology and it created a social ethos in which powerful moral pressures could be brought to bear on those who failed to live up to their obligations. Second, the degree of moral compulsion to reciprocate was directly proportional to the strength of the bond between members in interpersonal dyads. Individuals were locked into hierarchically arranged networks of exchange relations and the assuredness of assistance and the magnitude of the obligation to reciprocate varied as one progressed up this hierarchy.

The primary building block in these subsistence support networks was the household. Next in order of importance came kinsmen, both consanguinal and affinal. The type of reciprocity that defined relations between kin was generalized and it was expected that kinsmen would willingly come to one another's aid when called on, so long as doing so did not jeopardize the survival of their own household. But both the timing and the extent of material aid kinsmen could provide were open to question. Consequently, bonds had to be forged with non-kinsmen. As a means of increasing the amount of moral pressures that could be exerted on these outsiders, it was necessary to transform them into insiders, and this was accomplished through fictive kinship or ritual friendship and co-membership in corporate bodies or associations. While neighbors could be friends and friends helped one another, so long as such individuals came from the same class and economic position the amount of assistance they could provide was limited. In order to surmount this difficulty, a household required "special" friends.

Patronage provided the critical cog in a peasant's risk-management system. Effective subsistence insurance could only be obtained by becoming attached to men of wealth and power because they were the only ones who would have had large, predictable surpluses of foodstuffs and the connections with sources outside of the community (be it the village, the county, or the state) which allowed them access to external supplies. Just as with the other forms of interpersonal dyads, the bond could be strengthened by multiplying the number of connections one had with members of the elite. Peasants interacted with the elite most often in the context of associations. Nevertheless, in the end, the linkage between the elite and the peasants was interpersonal.

The exchange entitlement characteristic of patronage was asymmetrical. The peasant gave often and repeatedly and received sporadically. Yet, for many, access to the resources controlled by patrons was all that separated a household from dearth. Such a system, then, could easily slide from paternalism to exploitation, and the "gifts" of patrons could turn into onerous debts. Accountability held the key to preventing this from happening or at least checking the worst excesses, but accountability could change with alarming rapidity, as I shall demonstrate shortly through an analysis of the long-term dialogue between risk, the vulnerability of the domestic economy, and society's ability to cope with the changing balance between them. But before we can fruitfully undertake such a discussion, we must first analyze the final category of coping mechanisms: actions undertaken ostensibly by communities as corporate entities to minimize risk and to reduce the vulnerability of its members to subsistence crises and famines.

The Domestic Economy and
       the Dialectic of Subsistence
       Risk

BLEPYROS: What sort of society do you intend to establish?
PRAXAGORA: Communal. Share and share alike. I'll knock down the
walls and remodel the *Polis* into one big happy household, where all can
come and go as they please.

Aristophanes, *Ekklesiazousai*

Subsistence, Community, and State in Ancient Greece

The metaphor of the community as merely a household writ large, I
believe, lay at the heart of the ancient Greek notion of the *polis*. As in a
household, social relations between members were meant to be hierarchi-
cal, and just as the head of the household was supposed to succor and
protect its members, along with high rank in the community came the
obligation to look out for the interests of those further down the hierarchy
(Finley 1983, 27–8). The community was meant to be an individual's
primary extra-household group, and analogous to the household, the unity
and allegiance of the group were ideally manifested and reaffirmed through
ritualized commensality and inter-household (and inter-class) food-
sharing. Moreover, in the pristine *polis*, an ideology of "share and share
alike" defined the moral obligation of the elite to provide for the rest of the
community in times of crisis (Finley 1983, 27; Lekas 1988, 77–9).

The real world was quite different. The comic bite to Praxagora's words
lay in the common realization by both author and audience that at the time
of their utterance (early fourth century), even in Athens – let alone the rest
of Greece where conditions were worse – her vision was less a statement of
practical ideology than a utopian yearning. Increasingly from that time
onward and proceeding at an accelerated pace slightly later, an economic
rift of increasing dimensions developed between rich and poor in ancient
Greece.[22] The location of the boundary between the moral economy of the
peasantry and the political economy of the elite underwent a process of
mediation and was redrawn—much to the advantage of the latter group.
The result was a redefinition of the elite's role in providing subsistence
support in a crisis. The erosion of communal accountability over the elite's
actions enabled men of wealth and power to establish greater leeway in

establishing the forms of assistance they would provide and the terms on which it was provided.

The Company You Keep: Quasi-groups and Associations as Sources of Aid

Previously I examined the role of associations and quasi-groups as vehicles for socialization between individuals of different classes and for the construction of multi-stranded patron–client dyads within a socially controlled context. The argument presented there was that co-membership in such groups allowed peasants to obtain access to potential patrons in settings where other, social ties could be forged as well as economic ones. In this way, a greater degree of affinity was established than if they had interacted only in a socially neutral context. In this section I examine the role that informal groups of individuals and formal associations played in the redistribution of resources, in particular food. The main conclusion I draw is that, while these entities served as mechanisms for the redistribution of food, their overall economic impact, though not negligible, was comparatively minor, particularly during times of shortage.

I begin at the level of the household and the neighborhood. That informal commensal groups, often referred to as "clubs," were a feature of ancient Greek society has long been known and appreciated (Calhoun 1913; Dow 1976). Modern historians have tended to focus on the practice among the upper class only. In this, they are merely following the lead of the ancient sources, none of which provides a description of a neighborhood get-together akin to Xenophon's lengthy account of the lavish affair involving "generals, nobles, and ambitious politicians" (Xenophon *Sym* 1.5). Nevertheless, there are indications that the custom extended further down the social ladder.

The best evidence for this comes from Theophrastos' caricatures of typical Athenians. While he never explicity describes a commensal gathering, perhaps more tellingly, they are present, lurking in the background in 13 of the 30 caricatures. They were accepted as a common occurrence in everyday life. He seems to be describing two variant, though not mutually exclusive, types. In the first, the host household provided the food from its own resources. Thus, in his description of the "Cheapskate," he states that this was a man so cheap that "when his turn comes to have his neighbors for a meal, he arranges for the meat to be cut into tiny pieces rather than served as chunks" (Theophrastos *Char* 10.11). These affairs often coincided with a ritual occasion – a wedding or some other *rite de passage* ceremony – celebrated by the host household. The "Greedy Man," for example, will keep the sacrificial meat at home and salt it for later rather than sharing it with his friends (Theophrastos *Char* 9.2). From these two passages it is clear that the host household was expected to provide the food and that meat should be included among it.

The second type of commensal group he describes relied on each of the participants to contribute to a common resource pool. So it is that a "Misanthrope" is a man so unsociable that when "a friend wants him to contribute to a fête where everybody pays a share, first, he refuses but then he turns up with some coins claiming that here goes more money down the drain" (Theophrastos *Char* 15.5). It seems that the duty of colleting the food for and the hosting of a get-together rotated among the members. For Theophrastos, abusing one's role as a host was a sure sign of the "Basely Covetous Man," who when "he has the job of collecting contributions for a 'club dinner' where expenses are shared, he declares that it is just that he should have a double ration – and then goes ahead and takes it regardless!" (Theophrastos *Char* 30.4).

The two types of commensal groups could easily coexist and overlap. In either case, the household conducting the dinner was expected to play the major role. It was in fact placing on display its wealth and putting its collective prestige on the line. Whether it was the "Flatterer" waxing lyrical over the lavishness of the repast (Theophrastos *Char* 2.10), the "Fault-finder" complaining about "the watery bean soup and the third-rate wine" (Theophrastos *Char* 17.2), the "Cheapskate" keeping count of the number of flagons of wine consumed (Theophrastos *Char* 10.3), or the "Basely Covetous Man" trying to skimp on the amount of bread he served (Theophrastos *Char* 30.2), it is clear that all aspects of the affair were the subject of gossip and communal assessment as to the wealth and propriety of the host household.

We do not know how many men belonged to these groups, how membership was determined, how often they met, or whether or not members were permitted to take left-overs home for the other members of their households. The impression created is that the group was relatively small, restricted to only a few households. I suspect that geographical propinquity was most important, particularly in villages, and that kinship probably played a role as well. There is simply no indication whether or not the food provided was solely for immediate consumption by the male participants or whether some was earmarked for removal. It is quite possible that while the men dined in the "andron" or men's dining room, the women and children of the participating households were eating together in another part of the host's house. We simply have no evidence on this point.

Among some communities on the island of Crete, a more formalized version of inter-household food sharing developed. Plato contrasts it with the arrangements found at Sparta and concludes that "in Crete the system is more communal, for out of the crops and cattle produced from public lands and the tribute paid by the bondsmen, one part is assigned for the worship of the gods and the maintenance of the public services and the other for the public food sharing. Thus all citizens are maintained from the common funds, women and children as well as men" (Plato *Lg* 847; see also Aristotle *Pol* 1272a17). Slightly later there was a shift in the distribution of the burden of supplying the food more on to the storerooms of the participating households (Garnsey 1988a, 80).

An inscription from the island of Samos exemplifies another type of inter-household food sharing system (*SIG*[3] 976; for a discussion of the document see Shipley 1987, 219–21; Garnsey 1988a, 81; Gallant 1989, 409). This one was based on subscription by a few and distribution to all. The legislation, enacted around the turn of the third century, called for the members of the community to give money. It was to be lent and the interest from these loans was to be used for the establishment of a cash fund; the fund was earmarked for the purchase of grain, in the first instance, from the tithe given to the cult of Hera, and then if more was needed, from other sources as well. Every month for as long as supplies lasted, each resident citizen of Samos was given freely a ration of grain. The size of these portions was such that they could have only acted as a supplement to the household's food supply and no more. How long or how well the system functioned is unknown. Somewhat analogous schemes were implemented elsewhere, but exceptionally little is known about them (see Gallant 1989, 409n. 30 for citations).

The practices described above, but especially the more common informal ones, provided low-level mechanisms for the redistribution and sharing of food between households. Reciprocity and corporatism provided its ideological basis: "those who give now, will get back later" and "all those who give get to share" were the sentiments underlying them (J.C. Scott 1976, 26–9; Watts 1983, 124–6). But there was a hidden edge. Reputations were at stake. As Scott noted "ritual feasts of this kind are the traditional means by which the well-to-do validate their status by conspicuous consumption in which their friends, neighbors, relatives, and often the entire village are invited to share" (Scott 1985, 173). The practice then could easily have taken on a competitive aspect, as households vied with one another to put on the most lavish, meat-laden meal. For some households, they furnished a coping mechanism which helped them to obtain some food, particularly meat, during periods of heightened stress associated with their life cycle development of their particular economic circumstance at a given time. If their co-members showed forbearance, then they might be able to postpone reciprocating until their situation had improved. In "normal" times, commensal groups helped to redistribute relatively small amounts of food between households.

As a crisis response, the utility of such commensal groups was questionable. Many of the response strategies described in Chapter 5 initiated or intensified competition between households for increasingly scarce resources. There was, after all, a finite quantity of wild greens or acorns available, a limited number of potential buyers for livestock and household assets, and only a handful of possible patrons. The ideology of the "limited good" obtained its sharpest definition when vital goods became severely limited. The bonds of obligation and sociability with non-kin and even kin outside of the household could have easily eroded. Not surprisingly, a great deal of comparative evidence indicates that such inter-household cooperation is often one of the first casualties of food shortages (Sahlins 1972; Dirks 1980).

Dirks has assembled data from a wide variety of cultures and demonstrates that repeatedly when resources start to diminish, households begin to look inward. "Under continued stress, individuals drop friends and extended kin from food-sharing networks, restricting generalized reciprocity to close relatives" (Dirks 1980, 28). It is highly likely then that the inter-household food sharing groups in Greek communities would also have ceased to function effectively once individual households' resources began to run out. Clearly, other mechanisms were required.

I argued in the last chapter that individuals were enmeshed in a network of ritual and communal associations, such as *gene, phratrai, orgeones*, and *thiasoi*. One aspect common to all of them was commensality. Periodically throughout the year, the members of these groups would gather together to pay homage to their patron god with sacrifices and feasting (Tod 1932; Ferguson 1944). On these occasions the association would provide the beasts with revenue generated by the leasing of jointly held land (*SIG*[3] 1097) or flocks. In any case, the association acted as an agent of redistribution. Occasionally, when new members were being introduced, individual members supplied the sacrificial animals for group consumption.

Supplemental to these were the local-level political assoiations which conjoined the villagers to the state as a whole. In the case of Athens, this entitiy was the *deme*. Two questions need to be asked: how much food did the *deme* as a collectivity provide for its members and whence came the resources it redistributed? Fortunately, answers to both can be found in two recent studies.

On the basis of some preserved deme sacrificial calendars Jameson has ingeniously calculated the amount of meat which a deme distributed to its members, and he found the amount to be rather small – 1.71 kilograms per peson per year (Jameson 1988, 105). Other foodstuffs were served as well, thus increasing the importance of deme celebrations as a redistributive device.

Whitehead provides the answer to the second question. His discussion indicates that the deme as a collectivity provided the wherewithal for communal feasts. Athenian demes owned certain assets in land and property which were leased and lent, ideally to fellow demesmen (Whitehead 1986, 125, 128, 152–60). The deme as a corporate entity was meant to provide for its members both in good times and in bad. As he puts it, the deme was supposed to be a source of "collective aid" (Whitehead 1986, 158). However, over time this capacity was eroded, and increasingly Athenian demes came to rely on certain individuals of wealth and power; thus Whitehead notes: "Having been formerly responsible only for the jam, one might say, such men were now the providers of much of the bread-and-butter besides" (Whitehead 1986, 175). A similar transition occurred more widely as well.

At the state-wide level, religious cults could function as redistributing mechanisms in two ways: either through the direct distribution at public feasts of foodstuffs derived from resources controlled by the cult or through the selling of basic products at subsidized prices. In both cases, what we need to know is whence the resources were derived, and how and in what quantities they were distributed.

Periodically every month, members of an ancient state met as a collectivity and ritually worshiped their gods with prayers and animal sacrifices. These were occasions for celebrations and for feasts, the costs of which were ideally borne by the state or the cult. This was certainly the case at Athens during its period of pre-eminence. Jameson has calculated that state-sponsored religious festivals at Athens provided two kilograms of beef per year for each citizen (Jameson 1988, 105). The addition of sheep, goats, and pigs raises the estimate of the quantity of meat provided but not significantly. Other foods were consumed as well, for example various breads, leguminous stews, fruits, vegetables, wine, fish, and fowl (Ferguson 1972; Brumfield 1981; Simon 1983; Mikalson 1983), and so all together, Athenian households received not inconsequential quantities of food from the state. More importantly the resources were in theory drawn from sources other than the storerooms of the peasants participants who were to receive more than they gave in tithes or contributions. In this manner, public festivals were expected to supplement the domestic economy. As one jaundiced aristocratic Athenian writer put it "the community, knowing that it is impossible for poor men to make sacrifices and to hold feasts . . . has devised the means to accomplish it. That is why the community makes public sacrifice of numerous victims, but it is the people who are feasted and who obtain an allotment of the victim" (Pseudo-Xenophon, 2.9).

While this ideal was widely accepted, few communities had direct access to resources anywhere near those of Athens, so alternative means of supply had to be found. Some of the large cults, like that dedicated to Apollo on the island of Delos, generated revenue through the leasing of land (Kent 1948) and the lending of money (e.g., *Inscriptiones Delos* 442; *IG* 11.2.161). Other states earmarked the revenue from special taxes for the acquisition of sacrificial animals. A good example of this is the tax on fishing charged by the state of Mykonos for the express purpose of purchasing a white uncastrated sheep for the festival to Poseidon Phykios (SIG^3 1024; see also Andros, IG 12.5.721). At other places the religious organization itself owned the flocks from which sacrificial victims were taken, Tegea for example (IG 5.2. 10, 11, and 17). Most often the state was supposed to supply the resources for such festivities (e.g., Stiris and Phokis, SIG^3 647.18–30), but with increasing frequency from the fourth century onward, states collectively were unable to do so and consequently they had to rely on wealthy individuals to underwrite the costs of communal feasts. A few examples indicate how they did so.

In some cases wealthy men simply provided from their own resources the animals and other victuals needed for the celebration, as in the case of the brothers Kritolaos and Parmenion from Aigiale on the island of Amorgos (IG 17.7.389) who gave the oxen required for the sacrifice to Apollo and Hera and enough food to fête everyone in the community for two days. Aristagoras of Istropolis provides another example of a private individual supplying the food for a public feast (SIG^3 708).

Elsewhere members of the elite gave or lent money to the community which, in turn, let it out with interest. The interest was to be collected annually and used to purchase the food for festivals. An example from the community of Aigiale on Amorgos exemplifies this arrangement (IG 13[7] .515; see, Gauthier 1985, 210–20). Kritolaos (no relation to the one cited above) gave 2,000 drachmai to the community. Public officials lent it out with interest in small instalments (200 drachmai being the maximum) to local men. From the interest, they were to (a) purchase an oxen, wood, honey, milk, oil, and pork; (b) give to each of the young men of the community 1 *mina* of pork; (c) give to each man 1 *choinix* (0.83 kilogram) and each child 1/2 of a *choinix* (0.42 kilograms) of wheat. In this way, each member of the community received food during the three days of the feast and probably had some left over to take home.

Another scheme entailed the community auctioning to the highest bidder the position of chief priest. A second-century document from Priene affords the best known example (SIG^1 1003). If the highest bidder pledged between 6,000 and 12,000 drachmai, then he was absolved from performing certain liturgies. If he offered more than 12,000, then he received exemption from still others. The priest agreed to provide burnt offerings, incense, barley cakes, an ox, a sheep and a suckling pig. In return, he obtained the tongue, the leg and the hide of every sacrificed animal, a free lunch each day at the public meeting house, and he was accorded pride of place at the theater and in all public processions. The community, in short, agreed to accord to this individual honors and privileges in the ceremonial life of the collectivity in exchange for the cash and the resources needed to support those events.

In this way religious festivals acted as a redistributive mechanism: each member of the community received food in exchange for the public bestowal of honor. But by making it an arena of competition between men of power, the community risked becoming transformed into the source for the wherewithal needed by these men to compete. A case in point would be Jason of Pherai in Thessaly: "Now when the festival of the Pythian Apollo was approaching Jason sent orders to the communities under his power to prepare cattle, sheep, goats, and pigs. And it was said that although he laid upon each community a light burden, they contributed over 1,000 cattle and more than 10,000 of the smaller animals" (Xenophon *Mem* 6.4.29). The weight of the burden would have rested more heavily on some than on others. The balance of the exchange between ruler and ruled had shifted. Thessalian farmers in this case gave much more than they received, and this was a trend that developed in many parts of the Greek world.

The best known example of a religious organization indirectly providing subsidized foodstuffs for the market is the cult of Demeter and Kore at Eleusis in Attika.[23] Some time between 420 and 415 BC, the Athenians instituted a policy whereby all Athenian citizens and members of those states under Athens' dominion would give a tithe of one twelve-hundredth of wheat and one six-hundredth of barley to the ceremonial center at Eleusis (*IG* 1^2.76; Clinton 1974, 15; Meiggs 1972, 303–4). The practice continued through the next century. The grain was collected by local officials and then sent to Eleusis. There the cult officials deducted the amount that the cult would need for the coming year, and the rest was placed in storage (Clinton 1974, 15; Mylonas 1961, 125–7). This grain was made available to officials of the state who transported and sold the grain in the town of Athens (Rhodes 1982, 94–7). We do not know when or where the grain was stored before reshipment to Athens nor can we be sure how the decision was made concerning the timing of its release to the market. I can, however, offer some suggestions as to the possible role of the tithe grain in the food supply of Athens.

The overseer's accounts from Eleusis for the year 329/8 have been preserved (*IG* 2^2 .1672), on which are recorded the tithes for that year. Because 329/8 seems to have been a crisis year, characterized by poor crop yields, the accounts can tell us about the possible impact of grain redistribution in both good and bad times. If we accept, following Garnsey (1988a, 101; see also his Table 5), that crop yields for this year were reduced by approximately three-quarters, then by raising the figures accordingly, we arrive at an approximation of the amount of grain the cult received in a good year. I have assumed that the contributions of the allies in 329/8 were based on an average yield. I have employed the dietary estimates proposed in Chapter 4 – with the exception that I have lowered the grain intake/person/day to 1,500 kcal for the crisis year on the assumption that people probably consumed less-and have set out in Table 7.1 a matrix of possibilities about numbers of people who could have been

Table 7.1 Potential role of Eleusinian Tithe grain

Amount sent to Athens	Normal		Crisis	
		Number of people fed		
	(day)	(month)	(day)	(month)
All	166,345	5,545	81,300	2,710
2/3	110,897	3,697	54,200	1,806
1/2	84,538	2,773	40,650	1,355

fed, depending upon how much grain the cult kept for itself.

The quantities involved are paltry. During a normal year, the cult could have provided grain sufficient for only a few thousand people for a month. The same would apply to the crisis-period figures as well, but to conclude that the grain from Eleusis was not important during lean times might be a mistake. We know from the same inscription (*IG* 2^2.1672.289–90) that the officials were selling tithe grain for six drachmai per *medimnos*, a sum slightly above normal but well below the crisis price. In this case the figure on the number of people who could be fed per day (or per week) basis may be more important. If released at the right moment and in large enough quantities, the Eleusinian grain could have acted to dampen price escalation and could have provided cheaper food for the poorer, more vulnerable members of Athenian society. It still would have represented only a stop-gap measure, but nevertheless it may have been vitally important to many poor Athenian households.

Eleusis provides us with the clearest example of a religious organization acting as an agent for the indirect redistribution of agricultural produce from primary producers to non-primary producing consumers in normal conditions, and to everyone during a crisis. And, in this case, we can conclude that its role was not a major one. It might have been of more importance during a subsistence crisis, but even then its impact would have been short term.

Ancient Greek households were embedded in dense networks of both informal and formal commensal groups, all of which were important elements of the domestic economy. Informal food sharing between households would have occurred regularly. Through the action of delayed reciprocity, it could have allowed those households which were slightly more vulnerable than their neighbors to get by. But as a crisis response, its utility was restricted. Other formal groups based on associational or communal ties provided additional foodstuffs regularly throughout the year through direct distribution. And since many of these called on resources other than those extracted from the household, they were even more important. In yet other cases, such groups made necessary items available or permitted access to vital resources, like land, for their members. As agents of indirect redistribution, religious organizations played only a supplementary role. Consequently, ancient communities needed other institutions if they were to cope with subsistence risk.

Security in a Hole: Communal Storage Strategies

Greek states could have followed the lead of their constituent households by seeking to buffer themselves from subsistence risk through the bulk storage of vital foodstuffs, especially grain. An examination of the available textual and archaeological evidence indicates that they did not do so.

Specially-built food storage facilities are extremely rare in ancient Greece. Even the few examples which I have been able to find are suspect. In an open, civic area at Olynthos, Robinson uncovered more than 60 bell-shaped storage pits (Robinson 1946, 297–300). Dimensions ranged from a depth of 1 to 2.8 meters, a rim diameter of 0.95 to 2.15 meters, and a bottom diameter of 0.69 to 2.8 meters. All of them were dated to the period before the Persian invasion of Greece in 479. They bear a close resemblance to underground grain silos found in Italian villages of the last century (Snowdon 1986, 137). And so their identification as storage pits seems likely; the only aspect which causes suspicion is that, in his lengthy descriptions of the artefacts found in the pits, Robinson never mentions the discovery of any organic remains: an oversight on his part perhaps but a worrisome one from our perspective. Even if we accept the identification, the point remains that after 479 the Olynthians ceased to invest in communal storage as a subsistence security measure.

From the Classical and Hellenistic periods, only a handful of examples are known, and even they are suspect. I have mentioned already the *siroi*, or storerooms, at the ceremonial center at Eleusis. They were quite small and incapable of storing grain for more than a few people. At the south Italian Greek settlement of Morgantina, excavators have uncovered two buildings which they have identified as "granaries" (Sjöqvist 1960, 130–1; M. Bell 1988, 321–4). Both are rectangular buildings, one being 32.9 meters long and 7.5 meters wide. Both date to the third century BC. No material evidence was found which supports their identification as granaries. The earlier excavator, Sjöqvist, argued that they were on the supposition that, since the Romans used Morgantina as a depository during their preparations for the invasion of Carthage in 204, they might have stored grain in it. And, if they did, then this implies that it served the same function earlier (Sjöqvist 1960, 131). This is a tenuous argument at best. As the more recent excavator of the site appreciates: "No material evidence of such a use [as a granary] was recovered in the excavation of either building, and it seems in any case highly unlikely that, given the condition of the local climate, cereals would be preserved on the floors of the buildings unless they had by some chance been carbonized" (Bell 1988, 323). If we reject the identification of these two buildings as granaries, than we must do the same for the other long, narrow buildings found elsewhere (e.g., Miletos (Knakfuss 1924, 156–77), Athens (Pounder 1983), and Pergamon (von Szalay and Boehringer 1937, 25–38)), because in each case their recent designation as granaries hinges on the finds at Morgantina (Bell 1988, 324).

There are occasional references to foodstuffs being allocated from communal sources, as in this from a second century document: "and from the public store they [public officials] allocated provision to everyone for a considerable period of time" (Burstein 1985, no. 71, 95–7; Elateia (Phokis)). But we do not know whether the supplies were taken from permanent storage facilities or simply from food supplies gathered by the state during the crisis. Epigraphical evidence for purpose-built mass storage facilities is exceptionally rare and the few examples which exist are ambiguous.

The only solid evidence we have for extra-household storage facilities refers to military garrisons. An inscription discussed earlier indicates that local communities had the responsibility of storing victuals for garrisons which had been imposed on them (Welles 1938). Philo of Byzantium discusses at length the way in which a granary should be constructed, but the context for his account is exclusively military (Philo of Byzantium B 11–28, in Garlan 1974, 302–3). This type of storage was very much bound up with the rise of large predatory states and the goods were destined for distribution to agents of those states and not the local community except in dire emergency.

Grain and other foodstuffs could have been stored in non-purpose-built structures. Baskets and sacks of agricultural produce could easily have been kept in public buildings meant for other purposes, stoas for example. This could only have been a short-term measure. If they attempted to keep food this way for any length of time, then the losses due to moisture, fungi, and pests would have been extremely high (see e.g. D'Altroy and Earle 1985, 191–3). Without structures designed specifically for keeping agricultural products, public storage would not have been a viable response to subsistence risk.

Therefore the absence of mass storage by Greek communities of the Classical and Hellenistic periods stands in marked contradistinction to the emphasis placed on it by Greek households individually and by many other archaic states collectively. During the Classical period, most Greek states were neither strong enough nor bureaucratized enough to extract sizeable quantities of food from their citizenry, so households could retain control over much of their agricultural output. During the Hellenistic period, more aggressive centralized imperial polities developed and they extracted from their subject communities in the form of taxes, tithes, and tribute extremely large quantities of food. In this case, both the household and its community lost their ability to maintain control of their output as the centralized state removed it and redirected it to other ends – in particular, the victualing of their armies, bureaucracies, and urban populations. In this the Hellenistic kingdoms resembled imperial or colonial states elsewhere, though they did not practice mass storage at a level on par with other imperial states such as the Inka (Anders 1981; D'Altroy and Earle 1985; Earle and D'Altroy 1982; La Lone 1982; Johnson and Earle 1987, 263–9) or the Romans (Rickman 1971; 1980; Garnsey 1988a, 188–268). In both periods, then, there were structural impediments to the implementation of strategies based on mass storage at the communal level.

Social Storage between Communities

As an alternative to the direct storage of food supplies, communities endeavored to ensure at least access to external sources of food during a crisis through the establishment of bilateral exchange agreements with other communities. In essence what the two communities did was to agree that in the event of one of them being struck by a shortage, the other would if possible make food available – or least not enforce an embargo. Some examples make their operation clearer.

1   A document dated to the third century records how during a period of food shortage the people of Kos were granted the right to import grain from the Thessalian *koinon* or alliance (Segre 1934).
2   A treaty between Athens and Klazomenai contained a clause stating that in case of a subsistence crisis, Klazomenai could continue to seek assistance from Smyrna and possibly other states in the area (dated to 387; Engelmann and Merkelbach 1973, 482–5). This implies the existence of some sort of agreement between Klazomenai and Smyrna concerning access to the latter's market in times of need.
3   In a piece of legislation enacted at Athens (dated to 430) regarding one of its subject communities in northern Greek, Methone, there is a clause which states that the Methonians could import a specified amount of grain from Byzantium (*IG* $1^2.57$). Here again the existence of some arrangement between Methone and Byzantium seems implied.
4   Repeatedly during the fourth century, Athens established either directly or indirectly agreements with the Bosporan kingdoms regarding access to grain supplies (*IG* 2^2 212; *IG* 2^3 653; Burstein 1978; Garnsey 1988a, 138).

In all of these examples, communities acting collectively attempted to ensure access to food supplies through the establishment of agreements with other communities. The deficiencies of such ties were many. They did not guarantee that food supplies would be available in the other community – which after all might be suffering from the selfsame trauma – only that if a disposable surplus existed, the corresponding community might bid for it. Moreover, even if such a surplus did exist, the community seeking to acquire it still had to mobilize cash reserves in order to purchase it. In any case, both sides in the transaction had to rely on men of wealth from each group to hammer out the arrangements. Not surprisingly, communities called on men who had pre-existing inter-personal relationships with men of influence in the other communities.

We examined the social institution of *xenia* in the last chapter (pp. 167–8) and mentioned that it shaded into the institution of *proxenia*. We saw there as well how men were supposed to employ their inter-personal relationships with powerful men from elsewhere for the good of their own community. The community of Histiaia on the island of Evvoia in 266 BC had *proxenoi* located in 31 different communities (*SIG*^{3} 492). Through *proxenia*, the communities collectively linked themselves to powerful men residing in other communities. In exchange for honors and privileges, like the right to own land, freedom from import and export duties, and in some cases, even citizenship (Gauthier 1985; Herman 1987), *proxenoi* undertook to assist materially the community honoring them. By so doing, many communities abrogated control of external relations during a crisis to members of the elite, and it is to the action of these men that we turn next.

"Good Men" in Crises

In the final analysis all of the strategies described so far eventually came to depend upon the actions of a few rich and powerful men for their effective functioning. In the parlance of the time, these were *euergetai*, literally "doers of good things," or simply "good men." Our attention is riveted on these men because they figure so prominently in the surviving documents. Their activities during times of crisis were considered exceptional and praiseworthy. Thus communities bestowed honors and privileges upon them " so that all may know that the community of [name of community] knows how to honor its benefactors and so that more people may compete to provide benefits to the community because they see worthy men being honored" (*SIG*^{3} 493; this is the standard formula, taken from a third-century document found on Delos). If their actions were considered laudable and honorable, then, by implication, there had to be men behaving in a less than honorable fashion. For example: if a man is proclaimed "benefactor of the people" because he lent money at 20 percent interest to households so that they could purchase his grain at five times the pre-crisis price, then we may legitimately speculate as to the activities of the rogues and scoundrels. They clearly existed and we get the occasional glimpse of their actions. Though we shall never be in a position to analyze their activities in any detail, we can still comprehend with stark clarity their results: chronic debt, peasant expropriation, and the continued and increasing vulnerability of the domestic economy to subsistence risk.

We can identify five categories of actions undertaken by benefactors on behalf of Greek communities. As we shall see, they are not mutually exclusive. On the contrary, the same person often performed one or more of them during the same crisis. The types of actions are: (1) obtaining supplies of food from external sources; (2) giving or selling grain from the individual's own resources; (3) selling grain and other supplies at below the prevailing market price; (4) giving or lending money for the purchase of food; (5) interceding with external agencies on behalf of a community in order to procure grain and other supplies.

An examination of a sample of 30 benefactor decrees from various parts of the Greek world over the two-hundred-and-fifty-year period, 400–150, enables us to gauge the relative frequencies of some of their actions. I have relied heavily on the list of benefactors found in Herman (1981), to which additions were made. I do not pretend that the data presented here are exhaustively complete– merely that they constitute a representative sample (see table 7.2).

We can drawn two inferences. First, "good men" did not give freely from their purses or their larders; moreover, when they did give either grain or cash it was often in small amounts and their purpose seems to have been to act as an incentive for individuals to borrow and buy from them. Second, most of these men were being honored for either getting grain from external sources or for lending cash. I suspect that more often than not they did not actually lend coined money but rather that they lent grain having a specified monetary value. An examination of a handful of documents shows us more clearly how these benefactors behaved during crisis.

I begin with one of the best-known incidences. A late third or early second-century BC inscription from Olbia on the Black Sea records the actions of Protogenes, a member of one of the wealthiest and most

Table 7.2 Relative frequencies of types of acts performed by benefactors

$N - 30$

	YES	NO
Brings grain	16	14
Gives grain	10	20
Gives grain	4	26
Lends cash	16	14

prestigious families in the land (Migeotte 1984, document no. 44, 133–40). Severely reduced crop yields led to a grain shortage with the result that prices rose to one-fifth of a gold piece per *medimnos*. Protogenes agreed to supply 2,000 *medimnoi* at one-tenth of a gold piece per *medimnos*" and whereas the others collected on the spot he himself showed indulgence for one year and did not charge interest" (ll. 29–31).

The following year also witnessed shortages and prices rose to three-quarters of a gold piece per *medimnos* and even one and three-quarters gold pieces per *medimnos*. Protogenes this time offered to lend the state 1,000 gold pieces, 300 interest free, and he supplied 2,500 *medimnoi* (about enouth to feed 6,000–7,000 people for one month); 500 he sold at one-quarter of a gold piece per *medimnos* and 2000 at one-half of a gold piece.

Soon, Protogenes and his father were owned 6,000 gold pieces, A debt crisis loomed because people were unable to meet their obligations on account of continuing bad harvests. Protogenes took the lead in defusing this crisis by cancelling all debts owed him, both capital and interest. At various times during the crisis, then, he sold grain from his estate, lent the money to both the state and to individuals to buy that grain, sometimes with interest and sometimes without. I would emphasize two points: first, huge profits were there to be made, particularly by those who collected payment in full on the spot; second, this episode shows how one subsistence crisis could have left an entire community deeply in the throes of debt.

A third-century inscription from Erythrai, a state on the west coast of modern Turkey, provides another excellent example (Engelmann and Merkelbach 1972, 106–16). A certain Polykritos was appointed "grain official" when there was a shortage of cereals. He gave provision-money to middlemen as an incentive for them to go out and buy wheat. Furthermore, "he made public pronouncements and advanced money with interest for a reserve fund {to buy grain}" (ll. 6–8). But because of the poor crop, no one was willing to part with any of their grain stocks. Polykritos offered to lend additional sums, and he made available *at this point* the grain from his own storerooms: no doubt at prices to his advantage. I infer this because it is stated in the next paragraph that later prices rose to 60 drachmai per *medimnos* (ll. 24–6). Since the normal price at this time for a *medimnos* of wheat was around 5 drachmai per *medimnos* (Garnsey, Gallant, and Rathbone, 1984, 43 n. 56), it is clear that there were huge profits to be made.

Another example reinforces this last point. Ephesos honored with the full range of titles and privileges Agathokles of Rhodes (*SIG*[3] 354). During a subsistence crisis sometimes around 300, he arrived at the market with 2,333 *medimnoi* of grain and "found that the grain in the marketplace was being sold at more than six drachmai per *medimnos*, he was then persuaded by the market official to do a favor to the community, and so he sold all of his grain more cheaply than it was being sold in the market" (ll. 4–7). He was being honored because he sold all of his grain for less than the prevailing price – in this case, presumably he sold his grain for 6 drachmai/*medimnos* – and this acted as an anti-inflationary measure. Nevertheless, Ephesians households still had to find the cash required to buy his grain.

Boulagoras, the son of Alexis, was honored by the inhabitants of the island of Samos because of his numerous actions on their behalf (*SEG* 1.336). On innumerable occasions he pleaded their cause at the court of the reigning monarch, Antiochos. And during a prolonged subsistence crisis he came forward and assisted the community on three separate occasions.

First, he lent money as a deposit for the purchase of grain by middlemen; second, when more cash was needed to attract grain from outside of the island, he matched the funds accumulated by the community through public subscription; third, after the grain arrived and "since there were no resources available to repay the money [owed to creditors], he himself [promised] to pay back the loan on behalf of the community together with all the interest and all other expenses, and he did this quickly" (ll. 39–46). Here again we have a good example of a community collectively and its members individually fallling deeply into debt.

I do not wish to imply that the actions of the men described above were not worthy of honors or that they were not truly benefactors. The communities themselves settled that issue. It is the actions of those unnamed others who were the yardstick against which the benefactors were measured that interest us here. Protogenes did not collect payment for grain on the spot; others did. Protogenes sold grain at prices lower than others and lent money at reduced interest rates and still accumulated debts owed him totalling 6,000 gold pieces; how much could other men gain who sold for more and lent at higher rates? Polykritos sold grain at better than ten times the pre-crisis levels and this was considered worthy of praise; how much more might others have been selling theirs for? Boulagoras lent the community huge sums and showed forbearance about its repayment: clearly the other creditors who were demanding restitution in full immediately were not so lenient.

Insurance at a Premium: Debt and the Peasantry

> The class struggle in the ancient world took the form mainly of a contest between creditors and debtors.
>
> Karl Marx

What are the implications for the domestic economy of ancient Greek peasant households of this need to depend on the actions of private individuals as the major source of assistance in a subsistence crisis? All the evidence indicates that the primary one was debt.

De Ste Croix concluded that beginning in the fourth century and continuing through the Hellenistic period "there was widespread and serious poverty among the mass of people, at the same time as a few rich were perhaps getting richer" (De Ste Croix 1982, 294). The qualification he introduces is unnecessary. As Wasson noted, "wealth was becoming the property of a smaller and smaller group at a time when the majority of the population was living in ever-deeper misery. . . . Mortgages and debts were widespread, so that the numbers of the poor increased from year to year. The gulf between rich and poor was greater [during the Hellenistic period] than at any previous period of Greek history" (Wasson 1973 [1947], 186). Indeed, the rich were getting richer, and as I argued in Chapter 6, crisis management played a critical role in the immiseration of the peasantry and the enrichment of the elite. We find evidence for debt and its correlate – peasant expropriation – everywhere we look.

"And I shall not initiate a redistribution of the land, of the houses and farmsteads nor a cancellation of debts" (SIG^3 526, Itanos, Crete, third century; see, Finley 1983, 109) became a standard clause in the citizenship oath required by states during the Hellenistic period. In the aftermath of a particularly devastating war, the community of Ephesos found that, because so many of its citizens were in debt and were losing their land, civil insurrection was a real possibility. In order to forestall this happening, they enacted a long and complicated piece of legislation which aimed to appease all of the parties involved. The legislators recognized the right of the creditors "to have recovery from the entire property of the debtor, in any way they can and free from all penalty" (SIG^3 364). Nevertheless, it was precisely this sort of ruthless behavior that they needed to stop, so they set up a rotation of five-man panels consisting of randomly selected citizens empowered for a period of five days to negotiate settlements between creditors and debtors. Most peasants lost some of their land to creditors, but because of the intervention of the state, they got to keep some. The implication, of course, is that in more normal circumstances they could have lost all of it.

We saw in a previous chapter how increasing numbers of landless and rootless peasants were compelled to wander the land as vagabonds cast adrift on an undercurrent of poverty. Commentators at the time had no hesitation in pointing to debt and to peasant expropriation as the primary causes (Isokrates *Phil* 52, 97. 120; 168; Fuks 1972; 1974).

"Theokles and Thrasonides in Korinth and Praxis in Mytilene placed little value in property and instead displayed magnanimity seeing their co-citizens in a state of poverty while they themselves were rich. They also advised others to lighten the burden of poverty for those in need. And, after they did not succeed in convincing others, they themselves remitted the debts owed to them, and thus gained not money but life itself. For those whose debts were not remitted attacked their creditors, and wielding the arms of rage, and proffering the most reasonable claims, that of utter destitution, slew their creditors" (Ailian *VH* 14.24).[24]

Too many wealthy men failed to emulate Theokles, Thrasonides, and Praxis, with the result that riots by indebted peasants became alarmingly frequent occurrences in many parts of Greece from the beginning of the fourth century onward. In the 200-year period from 370 to 170, we know of 70 popular uprisings (list complied from Fuks 1974, 59; Gehrke 1985, 13–199). Presumably these were only the most violent or important ones, and thus they earned a mention in our sources. But even with these, the evidence is so slim as to preclude our delving as deeply into the salient aspects and causes of the rebellions as we would like in order to compare them fruitfully to similar violent outbursts elsewhere (Tilly 1982). Nevertheless, in every case that we know of "cancellation of debts" and "redistribution of the land" were the twin banners around which peasants rallied (Fuks 1974, 77; Lekas 1988, 88).

We saw in the last chapter that deeply embedded in Greek society was an ideology based upon the notions of obligation and reciprocity. Peasants *expected* to be obligated to their patrons. In a way, "debt" in their terms provided a form of subsistence insurance (Scott 1976, 32–4; 1977a; Finley 1983, 32; Watts 1983; 1987; 1988; Seavoy 1987; Greenough 1982). Peasants accepted their role as givers in good times in order to insure lenient, "fair" treatment in bad. There are two linked phenomena which seemed to change and which we need to investigate: how and why did households become increasingly enmeshed in a web of debt and why did debt lead to expropriation more frequently than before? The last in particular appears novel in the Hellenistic period. In order to answer these questions, we have to examine the set of changes which led both to the peasant's domestic economy being rendered much more vulnerable to subsistence risk, as well as their communities losing the ability to hold certain of its members accountable for their actions.

From Community to Empire: the Redefinition of Political Economy

> Every door now trembles before the tax-collectors.
>
> Herodas 6.64

The explanation for both the greater vulnerability of the peasantry and the loss of accountability are to be sought in the same place; the major structural changes wrought by the formation of large, predatory imperial states, the Hellenistic kingdoms (Davies 1984b, 256; Austin 1986, 456). Like other similar polities, they had to generate, accumulate, and redistribute massive quantities of wealth (to cite only a few examples: *Latin America*: D'Altroy and Earle 1985; Earle and D'Altroy 1982; La Lone 1983; Johnson and Earle 1987, 263–9; Gledhill 1988; *Rome*: Hopkins 1980; Garnsey 1988a, 188–268; *modern Europe*: L. Tilly 1974; De Vries 1976, 200–3; Root 1987; *Africa*: Watts 1983; McCann 1987a; F. Cooper 1981; 1984; Bryceson 1980; *Oceania and Asia*: J.C. Scott 1976, 57–8; Bakker 1988). The state needed to realign the structure of economic reproduction so as to enable it to accumulate the resources it required (Lonsdale and Berman 1979, 489). A significant transformation of the political economy occurred with the rise of the Hellenistic kingdoms. While the *polis*-system flourished, "the citizen-poor, and in particular the peasantry, were largely free from taxation: occasional sales taxes, harbour dues, and first-fruits to the gods did not add up to a significant burden" (Finley 1983, 32–3; Wood 1988). As the quote at the beginning of this section indicates, in the Hellenistic period people certainly believed that taxes weighed heavily on them, and the discussion which follows indicates that their belief was well-founded.

"To finance the centralized state with its huge expenses in armies, civil servants and courtiers, as well as public works, heavy taxation and royal monopolies were the rule in the Hellenistic states" (Wasson [1947] 1973, 171).Concomitant with the growth of these predatory states, then, was the need to mobilize the wherewithal to support huge armies (Caulk 1979) and to underwrite the lavish expenditure of the new elite. Kings were expected to be open-fisted. "It is obvious therefore that the ideal of the generous king had a very practical basis in reality: a king was expected to deliver the goods, above all to his followers. Hence the economic rapacity of the kings, consumers of wealth on an unending scale" (Austin 1986, 462–3).

Before we can assess the impact that taxes and tribute had on Greek communities, we need to know the quantities involved, the timing of their collection, and the form they took. Our knowledge of the total tax structure in any of the Hellenistic kingdoms is incomplete. We can, nonetheless, gain some impression of their general character.

There were basically three types of exactions: tithes, tribute, and taxes, both direct and indirect. Some of these were paid directly into the coffers of the royal treasury; others were collected by the local community and then channeled outward to the central administration.

Tithes fell into two categories: those paid by individuals working as share-croppers on "royal land" (Rostovtzeff 1934, 464–5; Kreissig 1977) and those paid by communities to the king. Telmessos, for example, rendered to Ptolemy 3 a percentage of their wheat, legumes, millet, sesame, and lupine crops (Burstein 1985, no. 100, 126–8; dated to

240/239). From elsewhere we hear of a tithe levied on wheat and vines (A.H.M. Jones 1974, 160). The usual amount extracted was one-sixth or one-tenth depending upon the crop (Jones 1974, 156).

Hellenistic dynasts also compelled their subject communities to pay tribute, which was levied on the community as a unit (Jones 1974, 159–60; Rostovtzeff 1941, 466; *IG* 12[7].67; Migeotte 1984, no. 49, 168–77; Gauthier 1985, 197–205: *Arkesine, Amorgos*; Migeotte 1984, no. 96, 299–304: *Miletos*; Burstein 1985, no. 95, 120–1; Welles 1974 [1934], no. 14: *Didyma*, 262 BC: Burstein 1985, #33, 43–5; *Teos*, 204/203 BC).

The royal treasury also levied direct *per caput* taxes, the so-called royal tax and the crown tax (Rostovtzeff 1941, 467). But these were minor compared to those direct and indirect taxes which the local communities had to impose in order to raise the revenues demanded by the dynasts (A.H.M. Jones 1974, 160). Kos, for example, imposed taxes on land, vineyards, cattle, gardens, quarries, fisheries, shops, prostitutes, slaves, rent, and houses; on the sale of wool, wheat, beans, bread, fish, wine, and incense (*SIG*[3] 1000; Rostovtzeff 1941, 241–2; Sherwin-White, 1978, 229–35). At Teos, officials taxed plough oxen, sheep, pigs, pack animals, slaves, timber, charcoal, beehives, gardens, wool, and woolens (*SEG* 2.79).

I have presented elsewhere (Gallant 1989, 411–12) detailed analyses of two cases, Miletos and Arkesine on Amorgos, which graphically indicate the magnitude of the tribute imposed by the Hellenistic dynasts. The results of that work are summarized in table 7.3. At Miletos, for example, if one-third of the land was cultivated then it would have required between 45 percent and 36 percent, depending on yield, of the entire agricultural output to pay for the tribute which the community owed to Lysimachos. By way of comparison, Hellenistic peasants in certain regions paid a greater percentage of their total product than their equivalents in France and other European countries during the Ancienne Régime (Goubert 1987, 204; De Vries 1976, 200–1; Kriedte 1983, 93). Moreover, the salient production parameters would have to be shifted considerably in order to alter the conclusion that tribute payments placed a heavy burden on Hellenistic communities.

By incorporating the figures presented in table 7.3 into the computer simulation model employed earlier (in Chapter 5), we can gauge even more precisely the impact that exactions of the magnitude outlined above had on the peasant domestic economy. Figures 7.1 and 7.2 present the results of this exercise. The following assumptions have been made: (a) the figure for production is scaled to the intensified level; (b) the amount expended on "additional" expenses as defined in Chapter 5 has been kept constant; (c) based on the calculations made above, I have estimated the amount removed from the household in the form of taxes and tithes as one-third of the household's total output. On a 4 hectare farm, for

Table 7.3 Comparison of tribute in two Greek communities

Miletos	Amount of land required to pay tribute (ha)		
	% of total area	% cropped of total area	
		(1/2)	(1/3)
Athenian Empire yield			
800 kg/ha	7	14	21
900 kg/ha	6	12	18
Hellenistic yield			
800 kg/ha	15	30	45
900 kg/ha	12	24	36
Arkesine, Amorgos			
	% of total area	% cropped of total area	
		(1/2)	(1/3)
Athenian Empire yield			
800 kg/ha	1.3	2.6	4
900 kg/ha	1	2	3
Hellenistic yield			
800 kg/ha	13	26	39
900 kg/ha	12	24	36

example, in 14 out of the 24 years of the life cycle production would not have attained the necessary level; for the middle triennia (3–7), that is after the formation of a nuclear household, it appears that this would have occurred close to three-quarters of the time. On a 6 hectare farm, it would have happened in 12 out of 24 years and in 8 out of the middle 15 years. By tightening their belts with regard to non-vital expenditures, peasants could have reduced the frequency of failure, but I suspect not by much. The simulation indicates unequivocally that households were placed at a much higher level of risk by the imposition of taxes.

The timing of tax collection is also of critical importance (Watts 1983, 265). Unfortunately the ancient evidence on this point is extremely scanty. The grain tithe in Ptolemaic Egypt was collected directly from the threshing floor (A.H.M. Jones 1974, 156). This was obviously the optimal time for doing so. If peasants were compelled to pay the other direct taxes and tribute at this time, then they were caught in a bind. Because these exactions were payable in cash, peasants had to convert their agricultural produce into hard currency. And since everyone needed to sell at the same

Kcals (millions)

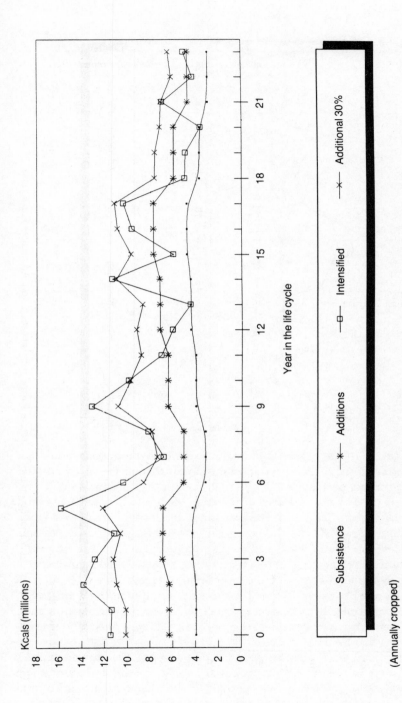

(Annually cropped)

— Subsistence · · · ·   —□— Additions   —*— Intensified   —×— Additional 30%

Fig. 7.1 Simulated Yield Variation on a Four Hectare Farm: Intensification and Additional Extractions.

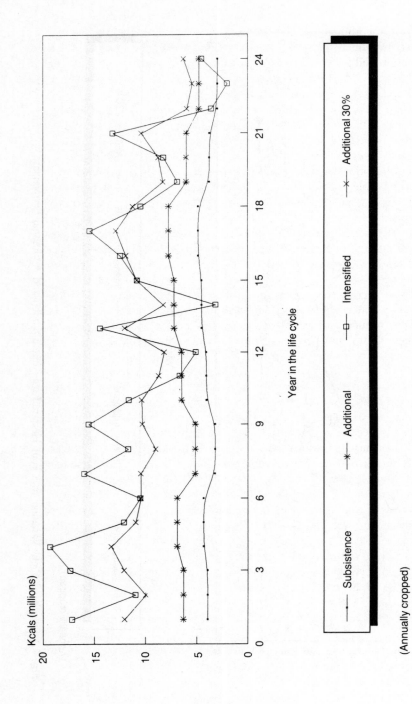

(Annually cropped)

Fig. 7.2 Simulated Yield Variation on a Six Hectare Farm: Intensification and Additional Extractions.

time, prices would have fallen. In short, peasants entered a buyer's market as sellers (Wylie 1989, 172). And the grain which they sold at this time they might well have had to buy back later in the year – at a much higher price (Arnold 1988, 55). Moreover, the various taxes on sales ate even further into their already meager resources.

Ancient households could become trapped in a vicious cycle of dependency. Exactions of the magnitude envisaged here would have rendered inoperable some of the household's adaptive mechanisms and response strategies. Because so much more was removed from the household, options such as planting a second crop or a spring-sown crop were impossible on account of a lack of seeds. Storage strategies would have to have been radically altered, thus removing a key risk-buffering mechanism.

The heightened vulnerability of the household and the far greater susceptibility to production failure, as demonstrated in figures 7.1 and 7.2, would have meant that the effects of crisis decapitalization were exacerbated: once livestock or human capital was lost, because of the greater frequency of crisis, they were unlikely to ever be recovered. The loss of livestock and manpower would have made the peasants even more liable to risk by reducing the number of options open to them. Access to wild resources would have been curtailed when individuals privately owned thousands of hectares of cultivated and uncultivated land (e.g., the huge estates of Laodike (Burstein 1985, no. 23; Welles 1974 [1934], no. 18) and Aristodikides (Burstein 1985, no. 21)). As the range of options narrowed, the efficacy of those which remained diminished as well. The resiliency of the domestic economy was thereby reduced. Increasingly households needed to turn to patrons, middlemen, and money-lenders, and so debt has also to be included in the equation. Given the margin of surplus production depicted in figures 7.1 and 7.2, it is clear that once peasant households fell into debt, they were likely to remain that way. As Walbank makes clear in his summary on the conditions of peasants in many areas of the Hellenistic world: "a low living standard, the absence of any margin to meet lean years or upsets due to mobilization and war will have played a large part in reducing peasants to a condition of dependence from which it was virtually impossible to emerge"(Walbank 1981, 166; a sentiment echoed widely in the comparative literature as well: Wylie 1989, 183–4; Scott 1976, 10; Pertev 1986, 35; W.C. Jordan 1988, 39; Russell 1987, 153).

Debt, then, increased vulnerability and lessened resiliency. More and more, households had to seek assistance from wealthy members of their community, and this led to a confrontation between the moral economy based on the ideology discussed in the previous chapter and the new political economy analyzed above.

Accountability and Entitlement: Communal Power and the Moral Economy

"My own impression, for what it is worth, is not so much that Greece as a whole was poorer in the fourth century as that the wealthy class was now able to appropriate a greater share of the small available surplus than in the late fifth century – though probably less so in democratic Athens than in most other states" (De Ste Croix 1982, 294–5; see also Padgug 1975; Lekas 1988, 88–9). I have argued in this chapter that the trend identified here by De Ste Croix continued at an accelerated pace from the end of the fourth century onward, and as we saw earlier, it came to encompass Athens as well. This shift in the distribution of wealth was symptomatic of and integrally linked with broader changes in the fundamental basis of political, social, and economic relations between peasant households, their communities, local elites, and the state. And, moreover, "dearth . . . exposed [the] tensions set up by [these] more persistent structural changes between the economy and society" (Walter and Wrightson 1976, 23)

I harbor no illusion that the *polis* was a "moral" community wherein the better off saw unstintingly to the needs of the peasants in times of crisis and that this reflected a socially accepted *right* to a subsistence minimum (J.C. Scott 1976; G. Evans 1988, 248–9). The *polis* was rife with social and economic inequalities and wealth was maldistributed, but what did distinguish it from the consitutient communities in the Hellenistic kingdoms was the degree of accountability which the community had over its elite.

I argued in the previous chapter that a notion of communal patronage or paternalism was current in the Greek *polis* and that an ideology of obligation and reciprocity underlay it. The members of the elite were expected to tend to the needs of the community, particularly during a crisis. At times, through the institution of the liturgy, this became less of an expectation and more of a requirement (Finley 1983, 32–5; P.J. Rhodes 1982). Moreover, the community had at is disposable the means to compel compliance. The *polis* was a small-scale polity. Power was mediated directly and personally between local elites and the citizenry, most of whom were peasants. The community held those in power accountable for their actions in the following ways. In such a social environment, reputation was important, and through gossip and slander it could be sullied (J.C. Scott 1985, 22–7). A man who failed to perform to expectations or stinted on his liturgy could easily find himself before a jury, with his reputation and much more on the line (Adeleye 1983; Knox 1985; Roberts 1986; Lekas 1988, 88, 91). In the end, of course, accountability could have been enforced by brute violence, as the Argive incident cited earlier demonstrates.

"In the Hellenistic monarchies, however, a new type of liturgy became widespread and often oppressive; it was now a compulsory burden, in money or in corvée labor, covering a wide range of activities, no longer restricted to the wealthy, and wholly lacking in any element of honor or political advancement" (Finley 1983, 37; Veyne 1976; Gauthier 1985). Liturgy had changed from an obligation expected of the rich to a requirement laid on the rest, especially the peasantry. Wealthy powerbrokers were still honored as benefactors, indeed more so than ever before, but their actions were much more self-interested and exploitative.

The internal power relationship between rich and poor, elite and peasantry was transformed when they were integrated into centralized imperial polities. A common feature associated with the rise of such states is "the strengthening of the old local elite or the creation of a new elite class, and this weakens the reciprocal obligations of these elites to other segments of the population" (Minnis, 1985, 11). This observation finds wide support in the historical record (e.g. Arlacchi 1983; Moore 1966; Scott and Kerkvliet 1977, 439–40; Watts 1983; McCann 1987a; Greenough 1982; Tilly 1975; Migdal 1982, 72–3; Kaba 1984, 30–1). Because the local elite no longer needed to look solely to the community for legitimation of its power, the community lost the leverage it used to have over them. Instead power devolved downward from the king to his "friends" and others (Herman 1981; 1987; Le Bohec 1985; Lekas 1988, 91), and thus communal accountability dissipated.

Two major structural changes converged and together they necessitated a re-evaluation and redefinition of collective responsibility for subsistence risk. Peasants had to pay large sums in taxes, tithes, and tribute. This led to widespread indebtedness and to increased participation on unfavorable terms in a fickle market. Consequently, some of the main props of the domestic economy's risk minimization system were either incapacitated or removed. Peasants were rendered more vulnerable and subsistence crises rose in frequency (Gallant 1989). More than ever before the peasantry had to rely on members of the elite for subsistence support. But simultaneously the community lost its capacity for enforcing as rigorously as before its claim to the entitlement of crisis relief from the upper class because of changes in the nature of inter-class political relations. Nevertheless, the local elites, the subject states, and the Hellenistic empires all had a vested interest in ensuring the continued existence of a viable, tax-paying peasantry. Thus, dynasts did give gifts of grain during shortages. Eumenes 3, for example, gave the people of Miletos 160,000 *medimnoi* (6,400,000 kg) of grain (Burstein 1985, no. 40); Laodike 3, the wife of Antiochos 3, gave annually for a period of ten years 1,000 *medimnoi* of wheat to the people of Iasos (Burstein 1985, no. 36); Ptolemy one time provided Athens with 10,000 *medimnoi* of wheat (*IG* 2^2.834). Thus, on occasion, they remitted the taxes and tithes of those unable to pay. When Antiochos 3 found the people of Teos "weakened" both publicly and privately because of war and the "magnitude of the taxes" they were paying, he exempted them from tribute (Burstein 1985, no. 33). Ptolemy 2 relieved the people of Miletos of the "harsh and irksome" tribute imposed on them by his father (Burstein 1985, no. 71). Ptolemy 3 in response to the desperate pleas of the people of Telmessos stopped the collection of the tithe on wheat, legumes, millet, sesame, and lupines, and exempted them from the payment of the special tax on wheat he had recently levied (Burstein 1985, no. 100). Thus, local elites did furnish subsistence assistance during crises, in ways we examined earlier. But such relief was now provided on terms and in forms which were markedly different from the previous period. The result was that in the long run the peasantry paid a much steeper premium for its subsistence insurance.

Poverty became more profound and widespread. Famines did not. The system of coping mechanisms was not destroyed, only modified, and it still worked to reduce risk. The fragile equilibrium between the moral economy of the peasantry and the political economy of the elites and the state was not shattered, only transmogrified and the boundaries of what constituted "legitimate exploitation" redefined. The "razor-thin" line separating the bulk of the peasantry from destitution was shaved, not severed. The system of survival strategies continued to work, and they survived.

Notes

1. I can only scratch the surface of this very large body of literature. For more detailed discussion of it, the reader is advised to consult Arnold (1988, 29–46), Kates (1980a; 1981; 1985a; 1985b), Dando (1980), Vaughan (1987, 4–20). A detailed bibliography on the subject can be found in Rabb (1983, 77–114).
2. In her work in Brittany, Segalen found that (a) while there was a marked preference for nuclear residence, most families went through a stage when they were extended or even multiple, (b) that there were marked differences between wealthy and poor households, with the latter being more likely to be nuclear for longer periods of time, and (c) that even though the norm was for nuclear residence, wider kin and non-kin groupings were of vital importance: "In the nineteenth century in the Pays Bigouden Sud the norm was nuclear. Households should be nuclear but tightly bound by kin and neighbor relationships" (1984, 172).
3. Much of the earlier scholarship on slavery was mired in seemingly endless rounds of debate concerning the total number of slaves in Athens at any one time (Westermann 1955; Starr 1979; Gomme 1933; Hopper 1979). The ancient sources on this are few and contradictory, thus leaving ample room for debate. On numerous occasions, Finley has pointed out the shortcomings of the sources and, at times, the wrongheadedness of the debate (Finley 1985; Finley 1980). Assuredly the number of slaves is important, but when the sources permit estimates to vary from 20,000 to 110,000 (see, Wood 1983, 39–47 and Garlan 1988, 55–60 for recent assessments of the literature), alternative approaches need to be sought.
4. If we accept a price of 200 drachmai for a slave (Jameson 1977/78, 139) and a price of 5 drachmai for a *medimnos* of wheat, then the equivalency is 40 *medimnoi* per slave. Employing a figure of 40 per *medimnos*, this produces 1600 kg. Using the life cycle defined earlier and at the consumption rates discussed on page 73, we can conclude that the slave represents 19.8 months worth of grain.
5. McCloskey's results have met with some criticism, in particular from Stefano Fenoaltea. Some of their points of disagreement are caused by the fact that they are dealing with problems associated with open field farming and the impact of enclosure; this is irrelevant to my concerns. Fenoaltea would emphasize the role of scattered holdings as a means to maximize productivity by reducing transaction costs (1976; Fenoaltea 1977). Nonetheless, it would still stabilize individual output, and thus would provide some buffering of risk. Moreover, they both agree that diversification is enhanced by fragmentation and that it lowers risk. On the whole, I find much to agree with in both their work, but come down in favor of McCloskey's general conclusion.

6. Numerous cereals, like wheat and barley, send out secondary growths called tillers. A single parent seed may produce a number of interconnected stalks. More will be said about tillering shortly.

7. Most households, in fact, owned no sheep at all. Household number 12, however, had a flock of 200. Not surprisingly, it also had the most land under fallow (18.4 hectares).

8. Diamond cites as his source for the pre-WWII data the UNRRA mission in Athens. I initially suspected that he was referring to the Metaxas survey, but as the figures he presents differ from that survey, we have to assume that he relied on a different survey about which we know nothing.

9. This is, of course, quite possible, but other explanations come to mind as well. Quantitative analysis of data from around the Mediterranean seems to suggest greater consumption of vegetables. In Egypt, Israel, Lebanon, Jordan, Syria and Iraq, there is a correlation, as measured by the Pearson Correlation Coefficient (-0.75, significant at 0.05), between cereal and vegetable consumption (data taken from Clawson, Landsberg, and Alexander 1971, 156–7). Visual inspection of the data presented in Table 5.2 (given only 6 cases any more rigorous tests would be pointless), indicates that oil consumption is fairly consistent but that cereal and vegetable consumption are correlated negatively. This in turn suggests that greater consumption of vegetables might explain the seemingly lower levels of cereal consumption amongst modern Greek peasants. In any case, I agree with their main point that the figures from ancient Greece are too high and require adjustment.

10. These data were kindly provided by the National Statistical Service of Greece and were collected as part a larger project on agroclimatology under the direction of Peter Garnsey and funded by the Economic and Social Research Council.

11. In some of the analyses presented here, "fitted polynomial curves" were employed. These are a particular type of regression function which can be used, as here, to dampen the magnitude of the oscilations between data points (Agresti and Agresti 1979, 364–5).

12. There could, of course, be good reasons why these farms may have been larger than the averages from elsewhere. For example, the area in which they are located is extremely rocky and the soils are thin. If the authors are correct in associating these farms with the Athenian klerouchy of the 430, then the answer may be that the poor quality of the land required that settlers be given larger plots of land.

13. These estimates are slightly lower than the 14 to 16 months I published earlier (Gallant 1989, 401). Those calculations were based only on a cereal consumption rate of 175 kg/person/year and a household of five persons (Foxhall and Forbes 1982, 72; Garnsey, Gallant, and Rathbone 1984, 41; Garnsey 1988, 72). It seems to me that calculations based on total kilocalories and correlated to the life cycle are more likely to reflect reality and to allow more accurate assessments of ancient storage strategies. And so the lower estimates suggested here are to be preferred.

14. The following is a serviceable definition of "market": it is "a system of exchange in which the participants are a supply crowd offering certain goods and a demand crowd wanting those goods, all of whom are free to choose the

counterpart with whom the exchange will be made" (Carrasco 1983, 69; Polanyi 1957a, 254–70; Neale 1959; Bates 1983; Hodges 1988; Berdan 1983; Blanton 1983).

15. A number of recent studies have increased our knowledge of the ancients' views on the economy and exchange (Meikle 1979; Lowry 1987; Morpeth 1982; W.F. Campbell 1983; 1985). They focus more on the history of ideas than on the anaylsis of actual behavior. What is needed now is the integration of their results into a broader analytical framework, encompassing evidence of the types discussed here in tandem with comparative material from economic anthropology and history.

16. Some recent work on the organization of the grain trade in Africa can provide informative comparisons for the study of the Athenian grain market. Saul's study (1987), in particular, shows how itinerant middlemen can mobilize surplus grain from the countryside in the absence of rural markets: "where marketplaces are rare or nonexistent . . . the choice for the farmer who wants to sell large quantities of produce is restricted to two or three resident buyers or to the erratic visits of itinerant traders and of assemblies for city merchants; with greater involvement in the market, however, most such places are now establishing periodic markets" (Saul 1987, 78). He indicates that personal bonds between farmers and merchants were also of great importance (Saul 1987, 81–2).

17. *IG* 2^2 1672.289–290 contains a list of the prices paid by the cult at Eleusis in 329. The prices for sacrificial animals appear to be much higher than normal. While the precise chronology of the drought which affected Greece during the 320s is uncertain, it seems likely that there is a connection (Garnsey 1983; 1988, 99–101).

18. We do not have precise figures on this point, but the evidence we do have indicates that the numbers cited here are serviceable approximations. For example, during the Persian war of 480 BC, the Persian fleet alone encompassed 241,000 men drawn from around the eastern Mediterranean (Herodotos 7.184.1) During the later fifth and fourth centuries, we know warships each required between 170 and 870 rowers (Casson 1971, 93, 105, 302–3, 314–21). While the size of the combined fleets of all the Greek states is not known it seems to have been approximately on the order of a few thousand ships.

19. Using figures from Bengal over the period 1939–44, Sen shows how the exchange between wages and foodgrain prices fell from 100 (i.e., parity between the two) to 34 as the foodgrains price index rose to 385 while wages rose to only 130 (Sen 1981, 64–7).

20. Clearly not all loans were contracted in the socialized context of clientage. Theophrastos describes vividly such disinterested lending: "More than that he lends money to these fellows [low-lives] the moment they ask for a loan–collecting interest, to be sure, at a rate of three obols in twelve, not yearly or monthly but daily (i.e. 25% interest *per diem*). He gets interest from their businesses, too, and makes the rounds of bakers and fishmongers with money stuffed into his cheek" (*Char* 6.9).

But the fact that such behavior is described as being characteristic of a man devoid of morality simply proves my main point: whenever possible one borrowed from "friends" or "friends of friends" (Millett 1983, 45–6).

21. Thus Herman notes: "The reason for this [most loans that we know of being interest free] was that the partners to these transactions were tied by kinship, friendship and institutionalised friendship, and *philia* was the underlying principle of this primitive credit system" (1987, 94).

22. I have neither the time nor the space in this study to analyze in detail the problems associated with the rise of the Hellenistic kingdoms. It is a topic of great importance and one in need of work. I find fourth-century roots for many of the social and economic transformations, which appear so markedly in the Hellenistic period. I have touched on this topic in a preliminary manner already (Gallant 1989) and I shall return to it in another forum and address more baldly the question of the impact of empire formation on the Greek world.

23. The Samian grain distribution system discussed earlier bears some resemblance to the Athenian use of the cult of Demeter and Kore. At Samos, the officials appointed by the state purchased grain from the tithe given to the cult of Hera and then the quantity was distributed accordingly. In other words, the cult sells, the community buys and then distributes. At Athens, the cult gives and the community sells.

24. This incident probably dates to the fourth century BC; although Salmon questions its historicity (1984, 385, 76), it would be in keeping with what we know about civil disorder at Korinth around this time (Diodoros Sikeliotes, 15.40) and it is reminiscent of incidences recorded elsewhere during the fourth century; for other examples, see: Lintott 1982, 222–38; Fuks 1974; Gehrke 1985, 11–201.

Appendix 1

Pearson Correlation Coefficients of Crop Yields by Region. Greece, 1911, 1926–36, 1955–6, 1959–80

	Wheat	Barley	Broad beans	Lentils	Chickpeas
ACHAIA					
W	—	.9176*	.4746	.5947*	.7198*
B	.9176*	—	.5244*	.6204*	.6434*
BB	.4746	.5244*	—	.7565*	.4544
L	.5947*	.6204*	.7565*	—	.6236*
C	.7198*	.6434*	.4544*	.6236*	—
AITOLIA					
W	—	.8424*	.7604*	.7710*	.6529*
B	.8424*	—	.6278*	.7259*	.5768*
BB	.7604*	.6278*	—	.8199*	.7759*
L	.7710*	.7259*	.8199*	—	.6725*
C	.6529*	.5768*	.7759*	.6725*	—
ARGOLID					
W	—*	.9173*	.6051*	.5893*	.5150*
B	.9173*	—	.6354*	.5108*	.3380
BB	.6051*	.6354*	—	.2136	.3878
L	.5893*	.5108	.2136	—	.2088
C	.5150	.3380	.3878	.2088	—
ARKADIA					
W	—	.9559*	.8686*	.7029*	.8569*
B	.9559*	—	.8682*	.7000*	.8670*
BB	.8686*	.8682*	—	.6778*	.7709*
L	.7029*	.7000*	.6778*	—	.6566*
C	.8569*	.8670*	.7709*	.6566*	—
ATHENS					
W	—	.6627*	.1929	.2590	.0599
B	.6627*	—	.1318	.2433	− .0008
BB	.1929	.1318	—	.2481	− .1388
L	.2590	.2433	.2481	—	− .0140
C	.0599	− .0008	.1388	− .0140	—
EVROS					
W	—	.9534*	.7076*	.6688*	.6354*
B	.9534*	—	.6676*	.6735*	.6258*
BB	.7076*	.6676*	—	.5563*	.6455*
L	.6688*	.6735*	.5563*	—	.3564
C	.6354*	.6258*	.6455*	.3564	—

HERAKLEION (Crete)

W	—	.6791*	.6657*	.7452*	.5525*
B	.6791*	—	.5649*	.7214*	.5554*
BB	.6657*	.5649*	—	.7719*	.6812*
L	.7452*	.7214*	.7719*	—	.7477*
C	.5525*	.5554*	.6812*	.7477*	—

IOANNINA

W	—	.9831*	.8553*	.7631*	.7473*
B	.9831*	—	.8412*	.7496*	.7963*
BB	.8553*	.8412*	—	.8287*	.5758*
L	.7631*	.7496*	.8287*	—	.5385*
C	.7473*	.7963*	.5758*	.5385*	—

KALAMATA

W	—	.9436*	.6521*	.7687*	.7776*
B	.9436*	—	.5627*	.7139*	.7512*
BB	.6521*	.5627*	—	.6004*	.5845*
L	.7687*	.7139*	.6004*	—	.8225*
C	.7776*	.7512*	.5845*	.8225*	—

KAVALA

W	—	.9491*	.7151*	.3908	− .0520
B	.9491*	—	.7033*	.3746	− .0246
BB	.7151*	.7033*	—	.2534	.1202
L	.3908	.3746	.2534	—	.4343*
C	− .0520	− .0246	.1202	.4343	—

KOZANI

W	—	.9696*	.7409*	.7504*	.5514*
B	.9696*	—	.7336*	.7021*	.4872*
BB	.7409*	.7336*	—	.7395*	.2808
L	.7504*	.7021*	.7395*	—	.5279*
C	.7504*	.5514*	.4872*	.5279*	—

LARISA

W	—	.8638*	.1349*	.5585*	.3934
B	.8638*	—	.3102	.5159*	.2482
BB	.1359	.3102	—	.3385	.1586
L	.5585*	.5159*	.3385	—	.2019
C	.3934	.2428	.1586	.2019	—

LESBOS

W	—	.9243*	.8395*	.6795*	.2335
B	.9243*	—	.9004*	.6589*	.2114
BB	.8395*	.9004*	—	.6988*	.2175
L	.6795*	.6589*	.6988*	—	− .0210
C	.2335	.2114	.2175	− .0210	—

PHTHIOTIS

W	—	.9745*	.8403*	.8788*	.8123*
B	.9745*	—	.8255*	.9026*	.7772*
BB	.8403*	.8255*	—	.7552*	.7351*

L	.8788*	.9026*	.7552*	—	.7030*
C	.8123*	.7772*	.7351*	.7030*	—
SAMOS					
W	—	.7965*	.1444*	.3700	.2899
B	.7965*	—	− .1037	.4401	.1562
BB	.1444	− .1037	—	− .0803	.5162*
L	.3700	.4401	− .0803	—	− .0507
C	.2899	.1562	.5162*	− .0507	—
THESSALONIKI					
W	—	.7953*	.7607*	.7895*	.4536*
B	.7953*	—	.8092*	.6997*	.3457
BB	.7607*	.8092*	—	.7513*	.3014
L	.7895*	.6997*	.7513*	—	.3214
C	.4536*	.3457	.3014	.3214	—

*Statistical significance at 0.01 level

Bibliography

Abu-Shakra, S. and R. I. Tannous. 1982. Nutritional Value and Quality of Lentils. In *Lentils*, ed. C. Webb and G. Hawtin. London: Commonwealth Agricultural Bureau and the International Center for Agricultural Research in the Dry Areas, 191–202.

Abu-Zahra, N. 1976. Family and Kinship in a Tunisian Peasant Community. In *Mediterranean Family Structure*, ed. J. G. Peristiany. Cambridge: Cambridge University Press, 157–72.

Adams, Paul. 1971. Public and Private Interest in Hogar. In *Gifts and Poison: The Politics of Reputation*, ed. F. G. Bailey. Oxford: Basil Blackwell, 167–81.

Adeleye, G. 1983. The Purpose of *Dokimasia*. *Greek, Roman and Byzantine Studies* 24: 295–306.

Adkins, Arthur W. H. 1963. "Friendship" and "Self-Sufficiency" in Homer and Aristotle. *Classical Quarterly* 13: 30–45.

Adler, Jeffrey S. 1989. A Historical Analysis of the Law of Vagrancy. *Criminology* 27: 209–28.

Agresti, Alan and Barbara Finlay Agresti. 1979. *Statistical Methods for the Social Sciences*. San Francisco, Calif: Dellen.

Alamgir, Mohiuddin. 1981. An Approach toward a Theory of Famine. In *Famine: Its Causes, Effects and Management*, ed. John R. K. Robson. London: Gordon and Breach, 19–40.

Allbaugh, L. G. 1953. *Crete. A Case Study of an Underdeveloped Area*. Princeton, NJ: Princeton University Press.

Allen, Peter S. 1976. Aspida: A Depopulated Community. In *Regional Variation in Modern Greece and Cyprus: Toward a Perspective on the Ethnography of Greece*, ed. Muriel Dimen and Ernestine Friedl. New York: The New York Academy of Sciences. 168–98.

Amundsen, D. W. and C. J. Diers. 1969. The Age of Menarche in Classical Greece and Rome. *Human Biology* 41: 125–32.

Anders, Martha B. 1981. Investigation of State Storage Facilities in Pampa Grande, Peru. *Journal of Field Archaeology* 8: 391–404.

Anderson, E. 1924. *White Oak Acorns as Food*. St. Louis: Missouri Botanical Gardens.

Anderson, J. K. 1975. *Hunting in the Ancient World*. Berkeley: University of California Press.

Andrewes, Antony, 1957. The *Patriai* of Kamiros. *Annual of the British School at Athens* 52: 30–7.

Andrewes, Antony, 1961. Philochoros on Phratries. *Journal of Hellenic Studies* 91: 1–15.

Andreyev, V. N. 1974. Some Aspects of Agrarian Conditions in Attica in the Fifth to Third Centuries B. C. *Eirene* 12: 5–46.

Angel, J. Lawrence. 1945. Skeletal Material from Attica. *Hesperia* 14: 279–363.

—— 1972. Genetic and Social Factors in a Cypriote Village. *Human Biology* 44: 53–80.

—— 1975. Paleoecology, Paleodemography and Health. In *Population, Ecology and Social Evolution*, ed. Steven Polgar. The Hague: Mouton, 167–90.

Appleby, Andrew B. 1978. *Famine in Tudor and Stuart England*. Stanford, Calif.: Stanford University Press.

Arlacchi, Pino. 1983. *Mafia, Peasants and Great Estates: Society in Traditional Calabria*. Trans. Jonathan Steinberg. Cambridge: Cambridge University Press.

Arnold, David. 1988. *Famine: Social Crisis and Historical Change*. Oxford: Basil Blackwell.

Arnon, I. 1972. *Crop Production in Dry Regions*. Vol. ii: *Systematic Treatment of the Principal Crops*. London: Leonard Hill.

Arnould, Eric J. 1984. Marketing and Social Reproduction in Zinder, Niger Republic. In *Households: Comparative and Historical Studies of the Domestic Group*, ed. Robert M. Netting, Richard R. Wilk, and Eric J. Arnould. Berkeley: University of California Press, 130–62.

Aschenbrenner, Stanley E. 1972. A Contemporary Community. In *The Minnesota Messenia Expedition: Reconstructing a Bronze Age Regional Environment*, ed. William A. McDonald and G. R. Rapp. Minneapolis: University of Minnesota Press, 47–63.

—— 1976. Karpofora: Reluctant Farmers on a Fertile Land. In *Regional Variation in Modern Greece and Cyprus: Toward a Perspective on the Ethnography of Greece*, ed. Muriel Dimen and Ernestine Friedl. New York: The New York Academy of Sciences, 207–21.

Atkinson, K. M. T. 1968. The Seleucids and the Greek Cities of Western Asia Minor. *Antichthon* 2: 32–57.

—— 1972. A Hellenistic Land-Conveyance: The Estate of Mnesimachus in the Plain of Sardis. *Historia* 21: 45–74.

Attalides, A. 1977. Forms of Peasant Incorporation during the Last Century. In *Patrons and Clients in Mediterranean Societies*, ed. Ernest Gellner and James Waterbury. London: Duckworth, 137–55.

Ault, W. O. 1961/62. By-laws of Gleaning and the Problem of Harvest. *Economic History Review* 14: 19–31.

Austin, Michel. 1986. Hellenistic Kings, War and the Economy. *Classical Quarterly* 36: 450–66.

Aykroyd, A. B. 1974. *The Conquest of Famine*. London: Chatto and

Windus.

Back, K. W. 1977. Food, Sex and Theory. In *Nutrition and Anthropology in Action*, ed. T. K. Fitzgerald. Amsterdam: Van Gorcum, 24–34.

Bailey, F. G. 1971a. Gifts and Poison. In *Gifts and Poison: The Politics of Reputation*, ed. F. G. Bailey. Oxford: Basil Blackwell, 1–26.

—— 1971b. Changing Communities. In *Gifts and Poison*, 26–40.

—— 1971d. The Management of Reputations and the Process of Change. In *Gifts and Posion*, 281–301.

Baker, Randall. 1987. Linking and Sinking: Economic Externalities and the Persistence of Destitution and Famine in Africa. In *Drought and Hunger in Africa: Denying Famine a Future*, ed. Michael H. Glantz. Cambridge: Cambridge University Press, 49–170.

Bakker, J. I. 1988. Patrimonialism, Innvolution, and the Agrarian Question in Java: a Weberian Analysis of Class Relations and Servile Labour. In *State and Society: The Emergence and Development of Social Hierarchy and Political Centralization*, ed. John Gledhill, Barbara Bender, and Mogens Trolle Larsen. London: Unwin Hyman, 279–301.

Banfield, E. C. 1958. *The Moral Basis of a Backward Society*. University of Chicago, Ill.: The Free Press/Research Center in Economic Development and Cultural Change.

Bardan, Pranab and Ashok Rudra. 1986. Labour Mobility and the Boundaries of the Village Moral Economy. *Journal of Peasant Studies* 13: 90–115.

Barlett, Peggy F. 1980a. Introduction: Development Issues and Economic Anthropology. In *Agricultural Decision Making. Anthropological Contributions to Rural Development*, ed. Peggy F. Barlett. London: Academic Press, 1–16.

—— 1980b, Cost-Benefit Analysis: A Test of Alternative Methodologies. In *Agricultural Decision Making. Anthropological Contributions to Rural Development*, ed. Peggy F. Barlett. New York: Academic Press, 137–60.

—— 1980c. Adaptive Strategies in Peasant Agricultural Production. *Annual Review of Anthropology* 9: 545–73.

Barreveld, W. H. 1980. FAO's Action Programme for the Prevention of Food Losses, Its Scope and Objectives. In *Post Harvest Food Conservation*, ed. A. Herzka. Rome: Progress in Food and Nutrition Science, 4, 41–5.

Basler, Frank. 1982. Weeds and Their Control. In *Lentils*, ed. C. Webb and G. Hawtin. London: Commonwealth Agricultural Bureau and the International Centre for Agricultural Research in the Dry Areas, 143–52.

Bates, Robert A. 1983. Some Core Assumptions in Development Economics. In *Economic Anthropology: Topics and Theories*, ed, Sutti Ortiz. New York: University Press of America, 361–98.

Behar, Ruth. 1986. *Santa Maria del Monte. The Presence of the Past in a Spanish Village*. Princeton, NJ: Princeton University Press.

Beier, A. L. 1985. *Masterless Men: The Vagrancy Problem in England, 1560–1640*. New York: Metheun.

Bell III, Malcolm. 1988. Excavations at Morgantina, 1980–1985: Preliminary Report XII. *American Journal of Archaeology* 92: 313–42.

Bell, R. M. 1979. *Fate and Honor, Family and Village, Demographic and Cultural Change in Rural Italy since 1800*. Chicago, Ill.: University of Chicago Press.

Bender, A. E. 1979. *The Pocket Guide to Calories*. London: M. Beazley Pub.

Benedict, Peter. 1976. Aspects of the Domestic Cycle in a Turkish Provincial Town. In *Mediterranean Family Structure*, ed. J. G. Peristiany. Cambridge: Cambridge University Press, 219–42.

Bennett, John W. 1966. Further Remarks on Foster's Image of Limited Good. *American Anthropologist* 68: 206–9.

—— and Don Kanel. 1983. Agricultural Economics and Economic Anthropology: Confrontation and Accommodation. In *Economic Anthropology: Topics and Theories*, ed. Sutti Ortiz. New York: University Press of America, 201–48.

Berdan, Frances F. 1983. The Reconstruction of Ancient Economies: Perspectives from Archaeology and Ethnohistory. In *Economic Anthropology: Topics and Theories,* ed. Sutti Ortiz. New York: University Press of America, 83–98.

Berkner, Lutz. 1972. The Stem Family and the Development Cycle of the Peasant Household: An 18th Century Austrian Example. *American Historical Review* 77: 398–418.

Berkowitz, Susan G. 1984. Familism, Kinship and Sex Roles in Southern Italy: Contradictory Ideals and Real Contradictions. *Journal of Family History* 7: 289–98.

Bermus, E. 1988. Seasonality, Climatic Fluctuations, and Food Supplies (Sahelian Nomadic Pastoral Groups). In *Coping with Uncertainty in Food Supply*, ed. I. de Garine and G. A. Harrison. Oxford: Oxford University Press, 318–36.

Bhandari, M. M. 1974. Famine Foods in the Rajasthan Desert. *Economic Botany* 28: 73–81.

Bharati, P. and A. Basu. 1988. Uncertainties in Food Supply and Nutritional Deficiencies, in Relation to Economic Conditions in a Village Population of Southern West Bengal, India. In *Coping with Uncertainty in Food Supply,* ed. I. de Garine and G. A. Harrison. Oxford: Oxford University Press, 418–36.

Bialor, Perry. 1968. Tensions Leading to Conflict Resolution and the Avoidance of Conflict in a Greek Farming Community. In *Contributions to Mediterranean Sociology*, ed. J. G. Peristiany. The Hague: Mouton, 107–26.

Bialor, Perry. 1976. The Northwestern Corner of the Peloponnesos: Mavrikon and its Region. In *Regional Variation in Modern Greece and Cyprus: Toward a Perspective on the Ethnography of Greece,* ed. Muriel Dimen and Ernestine Friedl. New York: The New York Academy of Sciences, 222–35.

Binswanger, H. P. 1978. Risk Attitudes of Rural Households in Semi-arid Tropical India. *Economic and Political Weekly* 13: 49–62.

Birdwell-Pheasant, Donna. 1985. Economic Strategies and Personal Power Careers among Family Farmers in Northern Belize. *Research in Economic Anthropology* 7: 251–76.

Bisel, Sarah L. C. 1980. *A Pilot Study of Aspects of Human Nutrition in the Ancient Eastern Mediterranean, with Particular Attention to Trace Elements in Several Populations from Different Time Periods.* Ph. D. Dissertation: University of Minnesota. Ann Arbor, Mich.: University Microfilms.

Bland, B. F. 1971. *Crop Production: Cereals and Legumes.* New York: Academic Press.

Blanton, Richard E. 1983. Factors Underlying the Origin and Evolution of Market Systems. In *Economic Anthropology: Topics and Theories,* ed. Sutti Ortiz. New York: University Press of America, 51–66.

Blaxter, Lorraine. 1971. *Rendre service* and *Jalousie.* In *Gifts and Poison: The Politics of Reputation,* ed. F. G. Bailey. Oxford: Basil Blackwell, 119–38.

Bloch, Maurice. 1973. The Long Term and the Short Term: The Economic and Political Significance of the Morality of Kinship. In *The Character of Kinship,* ed. Jack Goody. Cambridge: Cambridge University Press, 75–88.

—— 1977. The Disconnection between Power and Rank as Process. *European Journal of Sociology* 18: 107–48.

Blok, Anton. 1966. Land Reform in a West Sicilian Latifondi Village: The Persistence of a Feudal Structure. *Anthropological Quarterly* 39: 1–16.

—— 1969. Peasants, Patrons, and Brokers in Western Sicily. *Anthropology Quarterly* 42: 155–70.

—— 1974. *The Mafia of a Sicilian Village.* Oxford: Blackwell.

Boardman, John. 1980. *The Greeks Overseas: Their Early Colonies and Trade.* London: Thames and Hudson.

Bocquet-Appel, Jean-Pierre and Claude Masset. 1982. Farwell to Paleo-demography. *Journal of Human Evolution* 11: 321–34.

Boehm de Lameiras, Brigitte. 1988. Subsistence, Social Control of Resources and the Development of Complex Society in the Valley of Mexico. In *State and Society: The Emergence and Development of Social Hierarchy and Political Centralization,* ed. John Gledhill and Mogens Trolle Larsen. London: Unwin Hyman, 91–102.

Boessneck, Joachim. 1986. Zooarchäologische Ergebnisse and den Tier-knochenund Molluskenfunden. In *Haus and Stadt in Klassichen Griech-enland. Wohnen in Klassichen Polis*, ed. Wilhelm Hoepfner and Ernst-L. Schwander. Munich: Deutscher Kunstverlag, 136–40.

Boessneck, Joachim. and Jonann Schaffer. 1973. *Die Tierknochenfunde aus dem Kabirenheiligtum bei Theben, Böotien*. München: Institut für Palae-oanatomie, Domestikations for schung und Greschichte der Tier-medizin.

—— 1986. Tierknochen aus Didyma II. *Archäologischer Anzeiger* 251–301.

Boissevain, Jeremy. 1974. *Friends of Friends: Networks, Manipulations and Coalitions*. Oxford: Basil Blackwell.

—— 1977. Factions, Parties, and Politics in a Maltese Village. In *Friends, Followers and Factions: A Reader in Political Clientism*, ed. Steffen W. Schmidt, Laura Guasti, Carl H. Landé, and James C. Scott. Berkeley: University of California Press, 279–86.

Bonfield, Lloyd. 1986. Normative Rules and Property Transmission: Reflections on the Link between Marriage and Inheritance in Early Modern England. In *The World We Have Gained: Histories of Population and Social Structure*, ed. Lloyd Bonfield, Richard M. Smith, and Keith Wrightson. Oxford: Basil Blackwell, 155–76.

Bose, Sugata. 1986. *Agrarian Bengal: Economy, Social Structure and Politics, 1919–1947*. Cambridge: Cambridge University Press.

Bosehart, H. W. 1973. Cultivation Intensity, Settlement Patterns, and Homestead Forms among the Matengo of Tanzania. *Ethnology* 12: 57–75.

Boserup, Esther. 1965. *The Conditions of Agricultural Growth*. Chicago, Ill: Aldine Publishing Company.

—— 1981. *Population and Technology*. Oxford: Basil Blackwell.

Bousquet, Jean. 1965. Convention entre Myania et Hypnia. *Bulletin de Correspondance Helléniqe* 89: 665–81.

Bratton, Michael. 1987. Drought, Food and the Social Organization of Small Farmers in Zimbabwe. In *Drought and Hunger in Africa: Denying Famine a Future*, ed. Michael H. Glantz. Cambridge: Cambridge University Press, 213–44.

Bremmer, Jan N. 1983. Scapegoat Rituals in Ancient Greece. *Harvard Studies in Classical Philology* 87: 299–320.

—— 1987. The Old Women of Ancient Athens. In *Sexual Asymmetry: Studies in Ancient Society*, ed. Josine Blok and Peter Mason. Amster-dam: Gieben, 191–216.

Briggs, D. E. 1978. *Barley*. London: Chapman and Hall.

Brodsky, Vivien. 1986. Widows in Late Elizabethan London: Remarriage, Economic Opportunity and Family Orientations. In *The World We Have Gained: Histories of Population and Social Structure*, ed. Lloyd Bonfield,

210   Bibliography

Richard M. Smith, and Keith Wrightson. Oxford: Basil Blackwell, 122–54.

Brögger, J. 1968. Conflict Resolution and the Role of the Bandit in Peasant Society. *Anthropology Quarterly* 41: 288–40.

—— 1971. *Montevarese. A Study of Peasant Society and Culture in Southern Italy.* Bergen: Universitetsforlaget.

Brookfield, H. C. 1972. Intensification and Disintensification in Pacific Agriculture: A Theoretical Approach. *Pacific Viewpoint* 13: 30–48.

Brown, P. and A. Podolefsky. 1976. Population Density, Agricultural Intensity, Land Tenure, and Group Size in the New Guinea Highlands. *Ethnology* 15: 211–39.

Brulé, Pierre. 1978. *La Piraterie Crétoise Hellénistique.* Paris: Centre de Recherches d'Histoire Ancienne, vol. 27, Annales Litteraire de l'Université de Basancon.

Brumfield, Allison Chandor. 1981. *The Attic Festivals to Demeter and Their Relation to the Agricultural Year.* Salem, NH: Ayer.

Bryceson, D. F. 1980. Changes in Peasant Food Production and Food Supply in Relation to the Historical Development of Commodity Production in Pre—Colonial and Colonial Tanganyika. *Journal of Peasant Studies* 7: 281–311.

—— 1981. Colonial Famine Responses – the Bagamoyo District of Tanganyika, 1920–61. *Food Policy* 6: 78–90.

Buikstra, Jane E. and J. H. Miekle. 1985. Demography, Diet and Health. In *The Analysis of Prehistoric Diets,* ed. R. I. Gilbert, Jr. and J. H. Miekle. New York: Academic Press, 360–422.

Buikstra, Jane E. and Lyle W. Konigsberg. 1985. Paleodemography: Critiques and Controversies. *American Anthropologist* 87: 316–33.

Burch, T. K. 1970. Some Demographic Determinants of Average Household Size: An Analytic Approach. *Demography* 7: 61–9.

Burford, Alison. 1972. *Craftsmen in Greek and Roman Society.* London: Thames and Hudson.

Burkert, Walter. 1979. *Structure and History in Greek Mythology and Ritual.* Berkeley: University of California Press.

—— 1983. *Homo Necans: The Anthropology of Ancient Greek Sacrificial Ritual and Myth.* Berkeley: University of California Press.

Burstein, Stanley M. 1978. IG II. 2.653, Demosthenes and the Athenian Relations with the Bosporus in the Fourth Century B.C. *Historia* 27: 428–36.

—— (ed. and transl.). 1985. *The Hellenistic Age from the Battle of Ipsos to the Death of Kleopatra* 7. Cambridge: Cambridge University Press.

Burton, Ian, Robert W. Kates, and Gilbert F. White. 1978. *The Environment as Hazard.* Oxford: Oxford University Press.

Cahill Jr., George F. 1981. Physiology of Acute Starvation in Man. In *Famine: Its Causes, Effects and Management,* ed. John R. K. Robson.

London: Gordon and Breach, 51–9.

Cairns, Francis. 1986. IG XII Suppl. 555, Reinmuth #15, and the Demes and Tribes of Eretria. *Zeitschrift für Papyrologie und Epigrahie* 64: 149–58.

Caiti, Vito. 1986. The Peasant Household under Tuscan Mezzadria: A Socioeconomic Analysis of Sienese Mezzadri Households. *Journal of Family History* 9: 111–26.

Calavan, Michael M. 1984. Prospects for a Probabilistic Reinterpretation of Chayanovian Theory: An Exploratory Discussion. In *Chayanov, Peasants, and Economic Anthropology,* ed. E. Paul Durrenberger. New York: Academic Press, 51–70.

Calhoun, George M. 1913. *Athenian Clubs in Politics and Litigation.* Austin, Tex.: University of Texas.

Campbell, Bruce M. S. 1984. Population Pressure, Inheritance and the Land Market in a Fourteenth Century Peasant Community. In *Land, Kinship, and the Life Cycle,* ed. Richard M. Smith. Cambridge: Cambridge University Press, 87–134.

Campbell, John K. 1964. *Honour, Family, and Patronage: A Study of Institutions and Moral Values in a Greek Mountain Community.* Oxford: Oxford University Press.

Campbell, William F. 1983. Pericles and the Sophistication of Economics. *History of Political Economy* 15: 112–35.

—— 1985. The Free Market for Goods and the Free Market for Ideas in the Platonic Dialogues. *History of Political Economy* 17: 187–97.

Cancian, F. 1980. Risk and Uncertainty in Agricultural Decision Making. In *Agricultural Decision Making. Anthropological Contributions to Rural Development,* ed. Peggy F. Barlett. London: Academic Press, 161–76.

Carbone, A. A. and B. C. Keel. 1985. Preservation of Plant and Animal Remains. In *The Analysis of Prehistoric Diets,* ed. R. I. Gilbert, Jr. and J. H. Miekle. New York: Academic Press, 1–20.

Carrasco, Pedro. 1983. Some Theoretical Considerations about the Role of the Market in Ancient Mexico. In *Economic Anthropology: Topics and Theories,* ed. Sutti Ortiz. New York: University Press of America, 67–82.

Carter, A. 1974. *Elite Politics in Rural India: Political Stratification and Political Alliances in Western Maharashtra.* Cambridge: Cambridge University Press.

Carter, Anthony T. 1984. Household Histories. In *Households: Comparative and Historical Studies of the Domestic Group,* ed. Robert M. Netting, Richard R. Wilk, and Eric J. Arnould, Berkeley: University of California Press, 44–83.

Carter, L. B. 1986. *The Quiet Athenian.* Oxford: Clarendon Press.

Cashdan, E. A. 1985. Coping with Risk: Reciprocity among the Basarwa of Northern Botswana. *Man* 20: 454–74.

Casimir, M. J. 1988. Nutrition and Socio-economic Strategies in Mobile Pastoral Societies in the Middle East with Special Reference to West Afghan Pashtuns. In *Coping with Uncertainty in Food Supply*, ed. I. de Garine and G. A. Harrison. Oxford: Clarendon, 337–59.

Casson, L. 1971. *Ships and Seamanship in the Ancient World.* Princeton, NJ: Princeton University Press.

Cattle, D. J. 1977. An Alternative to Nutritional Particularism. In *Nutrition and Anthropology in Action,* ed. T. K. Fitzgerald. Amsterdam: Van Gorcum, 35–45.

Caulk, Richard. 1979. Armies as Predators: Soldiers and Peasants in Ethiopia c. 1850–1935. *International Journal of African Historical Studies* 11: 457–93.

Chabot, Isabelle. 1988. Poverty and the Widow in Later Medieval Florence. *Continuity and Change* 3: 291–311.

Chang, K. 1977. *Food in Chinese Culture.* New Haven, Conn.: Yale University Press.

Chapman, C. Gower. 1971. *Milocca. A Sicilian Village.* Cambridge, Mass: Schenkman Publishing Company.

Charlton, P. J. 1976. The Use of Models in Systems Research. In *Food Production and Consumption. The Efficiency of Human Food Chains and Nutrient Cycles,* ed. A. N., Duckham, J. G. W. Jones and E. H. Roberts. Oxford: North-Holland Publishing Company, 385–404.

Charneux, P. 1984. Phratries et Komai d'Argos. *Bulletin de Correspondance Hellénique* 108: 207–27.

Chayanov, A. V. *The Theory of Peasant Economy.* 1986 [1966]. Madison: University of Wisconsin Press.

Chaytor, Miranda. 1980. Household and Kinship: Ryton in the Late 16th and Early 17th Centuries. *History Workshop* 10: 25–60.

Cherry, John F. 1988. Pastoralism and the Role of Animals in the Pre- and Protohistoric Economies of the Aegean. In *Pastoral Economies in Classical Antiquity,* ed. C. R. Whittaker. Cambridge: Cambrige Philosophical Society, 6–34.

Cheung, N. S. 1969. *The Theory of Share Tenancy.* Chicago, Ill.: The University of Chicago Press.

Chevalier, Jacques M. 1983. There is Nothing Simple about Simple Commodity Production. *Journal of Peasant Studies* 10: 153–86.

Chibnik, Michael. 1980. The Statistical Behavior Approach: The Choice between Wage Labor and Cash Cropping in Rural Belize. In *Agricultural Decision Making. Anthropological Contributions to Rural Development,* ed. Peggy F. Barlett. New York: Academic Press, 87–114.

Chroust, A. H. 1956. Treason and Patriotism in Ancient Greece. *Journal of the History of Ideas* 15: 280–8.

Clark, C. and M. Haswell. 1970. *The Economics of Subsistence Agriculture.* London: Macmillan and Co.

Clark, Mari H. 1976a. Farming and Foraging in Prehistoric Greece: A Cultural Ecological Perspective. In *Regional Variation in Modern Greece and Cyprus: Toward a Perspective on the Ethnography of Greece,* ed. Muriel Dimen and Ernestine Friedl. New York: The New York Academy of Sciences, 127–43.

—— 1976b. Gathering in the Argolid: A Subsistence Subsystem in a Greek Agricultural Community. In *Regional Variation in Modern Greece and Cyprus,* 251–64.

—— 1976c. The Pursuit of Wild Edibles, Present and Past. *Expedition* 19: 12–18.

—— 1977. Farming and Foraging in Prehistoric Greece: The Nutritional Ecology of Wild Resource Use. In *Nutrition and Anthropology in Action,* ed. T. K. Fitzgerald. Amsterdam: Van Gorcum, 46–61.

Clark, Stephen R. L. 1975. *Aristotle's Man: Speculations in Aristotelian Anthropology.* Oxford: Clarendon Press.

Clarke, A. L. and J. S. Russell. 1979. Crop Sequential Practices. In *Soil Factors in Crop Production in a Semi-Arid Environment,* ed. A. E. Hall, G. H. Cannell, and H. W. Lawton. Berlin: Springer-Verlag, 279–300.

Clawson, M., H. H. Landsberg, and L. T. Alexander. 1971. *The Agricultural Potential of the Middle East.* New York: American Elsevier Publishing Company, Inc.

Clinton, Kevin. 1974. *The Sacred Officials of the Eleusian Mysteries* Philadelphia, Pa.: American Philosophical Society.

Coale, A. J. 1981. The Importance of Remarriage in the Seventeenth and Eighteenth Centuries. In *Marriage and Remarriage in Populations of the Past,* ed. J. Dupaquier, E. Helin, P. Laslett, M. Livi-Bacci, and S. Sogner. New York: Academic Press, 163–76.

—— and P. Demeny. 1966. *Regional Model Life Tables and Stable Populations.* Princeton, NJ: Princeton University Press.

Codd, Nanneke. 1971. Reputation and Social Structure in a Spanish Pyrenean Village. In *Gifts and Poison: The Politics of Reputation,* ed. F. G. Bailey. Oxford: Basil Blackwell, 182–211.

Cohen, Abner. 1965. *Arab Border Villages in Israel. A Study of Continuity and Change in Social Organization.* Manchester: Manchester University Press.

—— 1977. The Social Organization of Credit in a West African Cattle Market. In *Friends, Followers and Factions: A Reader in Political Clientism,* ed. Steffen W. Schmidt, Laura Guasti, Carl H. Landé, and James C. Scott. Berkeley: University of California Press, 233–14.

Cohen, David William. 1984. Food Production and Food Exchange in the Precolonial Lakes Plateau Region. In *Imperialism, Colonialism and Hunger: East and Central Africa,* ed. Robert I. Rotberg. Lexington, Mass.: Lexington Books, 1–18.

Cohen, Getzel M. 1978. *The Seleucid Colonies: Studies in Founding,*

Administration and Organization. Wiesbaden: Historia Einzelschriften 30. Franz Steiner.

Cohen, John M. and David B. Lewis. 1987. Role of Government in Combatting Food Shortages: Lessons from Kenya, 1984–85. In *Drought and Hunger in Africa: Denying Famine a Future,* ed. Michael H. Glantz. Cambridge: Cambridge University Press, 269–96.

Cohen, Mark N. 1987. The Significance of Long-Term Changes in Human Diets and Food Economy. In *Food and Evolution: Toward a Theory of Human Food Habits,* ed. Marvin Harris and E. B. Ross. Philadelphia, Pa.: Temple Univeristy Press, 261–84.

Colclough, N. T. 1971. Social Mobility and Social Control in a South Italian Village. In *Gifts and Poison: The Politics of Reputation,* ed. F.G. Bailey. Oxford: Basil Blackwell, 212–31.

Cole, J. W. and E. R. Wolf. 1974. *The Hidden Frontier. Ecology and Ethnicity in an Alpine Valley.* New York: Academic Press.

Colson, E. 1979. In Good Years and in Bad: Food Strategies of Self-Reliant Societies. *Journal of Anthropological Research* 35: 18–29.

Connor, W. Robert. 1971. *The New Politicans of Fifth-Century Athens.* Princeton, NJ: Princeton University Press.

Coon, N. 1974. *The Dictionary of Useful Plants.* Emmaus, Pa.: Rodale Press.

Cooper, Allison Burford. 1977–8. The Family Farm in Greece. *Classical Journal* 73: 162–75.

Cooper, Frederick. 1981. Peasants, Capitalists and Historians: A Review Article. *Journal of Southern African Studies* 7: 284–314.

—— 1984. Subsistence and Agrarian Conflict: The Coast of Kenya after Slavery. In *Imperialism, Colonialism and Hunger: East and Central Africa,* ed. Robert I. Rotberg. Lexington Mass.: Lexington Books, 19–38.

Cooper, J. P. 1976. Patterns of Inheritance and Settlement by Great Landowners from the Fifteenth to the Eighteenth Centuries. In *Family and Inheritance: Rural Society in Western Europe, 1200–1800,* ed. Jack Goody, Joan Thirsk, and E. P. Thompson. Cambridge: Cambridge University Press, 192–327.

Cooper, John M. 1980. Aristotle on Friendship. In *Essays on Aristotle's Ethics,* ed. Amelie Okesenberg Rorty. Berkeley: University of California Press, 301–40.

Copping, A. 1976. Household Consumption and Human Nutrition. In *Food Production and Consumption. The Efficiency of Human Food Chains and Nutrient Cycles,* ed. A. N. Duckham, J. G. W. Jones, and E. H. Roberts. Oxford: North-Holland Publishing Company, 271–87.

Corkhill, N. L. 1949. Dietary Changes in a Sudan Village following Locust Visitation. *Africa* 19: 1–12.

Cornell, L. 1986. Household Studies. *Historical Methods* 19: 129–34.

Corsini, C. A. 1981. Why Is Remarriage a Male Affair? Some Evidence from Tuscan Villages during the Eighteenth Century. In *Marriage and Remarriage in Populations of the Past,* ed. J. Dupaquier, E. Helin, P. Laslett, M. Livi-Bacci, and S. Sogner. New York: Academic Press, 385–96.

Counihan, Carole M. 1984. Bread as World: Food Habits and Social Relations in Modernizing Sardinia. *Anthropological Quarterly* 57: 47–57.

Couroucli, Maria. 1985. *Les Oliviers du linéage. Une Grèce de tradition vénitienne.* Paris: Maisonneuve et Larose.

Cox, Cheryl Ann. 1988. Sibling Relationships in Classical Athens: Brother–Sister Ties. *Journal of Family History* 13: 377–95.

Crummet, Maria de los Angelos. 1987. Class, Household Structure and the Peasantry. *Journal of Peasant Studies* 14: 363–79.

Cubero, J. I. 1982. Origin, Taxonomy and Domestication. In *Lentils,* ed. C. Webb and G. Hawtin. London: Commonwealth Agricultural Bureau and the International Centre for Agricultural Research in the Dry Areas, 15–38.

Cummings, Robert F. 1987. Internal Factors that Generate Famine. In *Drought and Hunger in Africa: Denying Famine a Future,* ed. Michael H. Glantz. Cambridge: Cambridge University Press, 111–26.

Currey, Bruce. 1981. The Famine Syndrome: Its Definition for Relief and Rehabilitation in Bangladesh. In *Famine,* ed. John R. K. Robson. London: Gordon and Breach, 123–34.

Currie, J. M. 1981. *The Economic Theory of Agricultural Land Tenure.* Cambridge: Cambridge University Press.

Curtis, Noah and Cyril Gilbey. 1944. *Malnutrition: Quaker Work in Austria 1919–1924 and Spain 1930–1939.* Oxford: Oxford University Press.

Cutileiro, Jose. 1971. *A Portuguese Rural Society.* Oxford: Clarendon Press.

D'Altroy, Terence N. and Timothy Earle. 1985. Staple Finance, Wealth Finance, and Storage in the Inka Political Economy. *Current Anthropology* 26: 187–206.

Dahl, G. and A. Hjort. 1976. *Having Herds: Pastoral Herd Growth and Household Economy.* Stockholm: Stockholm Studies in Social Anthropology, 2.

Dalton, George. 1971. Peasants in Anthropology and History. In *Economic Anthropology and Development: Essays on Tribal and Peasant Economics,* ed. George Dalton. London: Basic Books, 217–68.

—— 1974. How Exactly are Peasants "Exploited"? *American Anthropologist* 76: 553–61.

—— 1975. Putting the Cat among the Red Herrings: A Reply to Newcomer and Rubenstein. *American Anthropologist* 77: 338–41.

—— 1977. Further Remarks on Exploitation: A Reply to Newcomer and

Derman and Levin. *American Anthropologist* 79: 125–33.

Damaskenides, A. N. 1965. Problems of the Greek Rural Economy. *Balkan Studies* 6: 21–34.

Dando, William A. 1980. *The Geography of Famine*. London: Edward Arnold.

Dareste, R., B. Haussoullier, and T. Reinach. 1965 [1895] *Recueil des inscriptions juridiques Grecques*. Rome: "L'Erma" di Bretschneider.

Datoo, Bashir A. 1976. Relationship between Population Density and Agricultural Systems in the Uluguru Mountains, Tanzania. *Journal of Tropical Geography* 41: 1–112.

Davies, John K. 1967. Demosthenes on Liturgies: A Note. *Journal of Hellenic Studies* 87: 33–40.

—— 1971. *Athenian Propertied Families, 600–300 B. C.* Oxford: Clarendon Press.

—— 1977/78. Athenian Citizenship: The Descent Group and the Alternatives. *Classical Journal* 73: 105–21.

—— 1984a. *Wealth and the Power of Wealth in Classical Athens*. Salem, NH: The Ayer Company.

—— 1984b. Cultural, Social and Economic Features of the Hellenistic World. *CAH* 8: 257–320.

Davis, J. 1969. Town and Country. *Anthropological Quarterly* 42: 171–85.

—— 1973. *Land and Family in Pisticci*. London: Athlone Press.

—— 1977. *People of the Mediterranean. An Essay in Comparative Social Anthropology*. London: Routledge & Kegan Paul.

De Garine, I. and G. Koppert. 1988. Coping with Seasonal Fluctuations in Food Supply among Savanna Populations: The Massa and Mussey of Chad and Cameroon. In *Coping with Uncertainty in Food Supply,* ed. I. de Garine and G. A. Harrison. Oxford: Oxford University Press. 210–59.

De Ligt, L. and P. W. de Neeve. 1988. Ancient Periodic Markets: Festivals and Fairs. *Athenaeum* 3–4: 391–416.

Degefu, Workineh 1987. Some Aspects of Meterological Drought in Ethiopia. In *Drought and Hunger in Africa: Denying Famine a Future,* ed. Michael H. Glantz. Cambridge: Cambridge University Press, 23–36.

Delano Smith, Caroline. 1979. *Western Mediterranean Europe*. New York: Academic Press.

Day, Leslie Preston. 1984. Dog Burials in the Greek World. *American Journal of Archaeology* 88: 21–32.

Den Hartog, Adel P. 1981. Adjustments of Food Behaviour during Famine. In *Famine,* ed. John R. K. Robson. London: Gordon and Breach, 155–62.

Dennell, Robin W. 1979. Prehistoric Diet and Nutrition: Some Food for

Thought. *World Archaeology* 2: 121–35.

Derman, William and Michael Levin. 1977. Peasants, Propoganda, Economics and Exploitation: A Reply to Dalton. *American Anthropologist* 79: 119–25.

Desai, Meghnad. 1987. The Economics of Famine. In *Famine*, ed. G. Ainsworth Harrison. Oxford: Oxford University Press, 107–38.

De Souza, Frances. 1987. Famine: Social Security and Analysis of Vulnerability. In *Famine*, ed. G. A. Harrison. Oxford: Oxford University Press, 1–56.

De Ste Croix, Geoffrey E. M. 1982. *The Class Struggle in the Ancient Greek World from the Archaic Age to the Arab Conquests.* Ithaca, NY: Cornell University Press.

Detienne, Marcel and Jean-Pierre Vernant (eds.). 1979. *La Cuisine du sacrifice en pays grec.* Paris: Gallimard.

De Vooys, A. C. 1959. Western Thessaly in Transition. *Tjidschrift van het Koninklijk Nederlandsch Aardrijkskundig Genootschap* 76: 29–55.

—— and J. J. C. Piket. 1958. A Geographical Analysis of Two Villages in the Peloponnesos. *Tjidschrift van het Koninklijk Nederlandsch Aardrijkskundig Genootschap* 75: 30–55.

De Vries, Jan. 1976. *Economy of Europe in an Age of Crisis 1500–1750.* Cambridge: Cambridge University Press.

—— 1980. Measuring the Impact of Climate on History: The Search for Appropriate Methodologies. *Journal of Interdisciplinary History* 10: 559–630.

Dewalt, K. M. and G. H. Pelto. 1977. Food Use and Household Economy in a Mexican Community. In *Nutrition and Anthropology in Action,* ed. T. K. Fitzgerald. Amsterdam: Van Gorcum, 79–139.

Diamond, W. 1947. Agriculture and Food in Greece. *UNRRA, Operational Analysis Paper* 19.

Diels, Herman and W. Kranz. 1934–7. *Die Fragmente der Vorsokratiker.* Berlin: Weidmann.

Diener, Paul, K. Moore, and R. Muttow. 1980. Meat, Markets and Mechanical Materialism: The Great Protein Fiasco in Anthropology. *Dialectical Anthropology* 5: 171–93.

Dirks, R. 1980. Social Responses during Severe Food Shortages and Famines. *Current Anthropology* 21: 21–44.

Donlan, Walter. 1980. *The Aristocratic Ideal in Ancient Greece: Attitudes of Superiority from Homer to the End of the Fifth Century B.C..* Lawrence, Kan.: Coronado Press.

—— 1981. Scale, Value and Function in the Homeric Economy. *American Journal of Ancient History* 6: 101–17.

—— 1985. The Social Groups of Dark Age Greece. *Classical Philology* 80: 293–308.

Douglass, William A. 1980. The South Italian Family: A Critique.

Journal of Family History 5: 338–59.

Dow, Sterling. 1976. Companionable Associates in the Athenian Government. In *In Memoriam Otto J. Brendel: Essays in Archaeology and the Humanities,* ed. Larissa Bonfante and Helga von Heintze. Mainz: Philipp von Zabern, 69–84.

Driesch A. von den and Joachim Boessneck. 1983. Schneckengehause und Muschelschaken. *Archäologischer Anzeiger* 653–72.

Du Boulay, Juliet. 1974. *Portrait of a Greek Mountain Village.* Oxford: Oxford University Press.

—— 1976. Lies, Mockery and Family Integrity. In *Mediterranean Family Structure,* ed. J. G. Peristiany. Cambridge: Cambridge University Press, 389–406.

—— 1984. The Blood: Symbolic Relationships between Descent, Marriage, Incest Prohibitions and Spiritual Kinship in Greece. *Man* 19: 533–56.

—— and Rory Williams. 1987. Amoral Familism and the Image of Limited Good. *Anthropological Quarterly* 60: 12–24.

Duby, Georges. 1974. *The Early Growth of the European Economy: Warriors and Peasants from the Seventh to the Twelfth Century.* Trans. Howard B. Clarke. Ithaca, NY: Cornell University Press.

Duckham, A. N. 1976. Environmental Constraints. In *Food Production and Consumption. The Efficiency of Human Food Chains and Nutrient Cycles,* ed. A. N. Duckham, J. G. W. Jones, and E. H. Roberts. Oxford: North-Holland Publishing Company, 61–81.

—— and G. B. Masefield. 1970. *Farming Systems of the World.* London: Chatto and Windus.

Ducrey, P. 1983. Les Cyclades a l'époque hellénistique. La pirateris, symptôme d'un maladie économique et social. In *Les Cyclades. Matériaux pour une étude de géographie historique,* ed. G. Rougemont. Paris: CNRS, 143–8.

Duncan-Jones, Richard. 1972. *The Economy of the Roman Empire: Quantitative Studies,* 2nd edn. Cambridge: Cambridge University Press.

Durrenberger, E. Paul. 1984. Operationalizing Chayanov. In *Chayanov, Peasants, and Economic Anthropology,* ed. E. Paul Durrenberger. New York: Academic Press, 39–50.

Earle, Timothy K. and T. N. D'Altroy. 1982. Storage Facilities and State Finance in Upper Mantaro Valley, Peru. In *Contexts for Prehistoric Exchange,* ed. J. E. Ericson and T. K. Earle. New York: Academic Press, 265–90.

Ehrenberg, Victor. 1951. *The People of Aristophanes: A Sociology of Old Attic Comedy.* Oxford: Basil Blackwell.

Eisenstadt, S. N. and Luis Roniger. 1980. Patron–Client Relations as a Model of Structuring Social Exchange. *Comparative Studies in Society and History* 22: 42–77.

Eisenstadt, S. N. and Luis Roniger. 1981. The Study of Patron–Client Relations and Recent Developments in Sociological Theory. In *Political Clientism: Patronage and Development,* ed. S. N. Eisenstadt and René Lemarchand. London: Sage Publications, 271–95.

—— 1984. *Patrons, Clients, and Friends: Interpersonal Relations and the Structure of Trust in Society.* Cambridge: Cambridge University Press.

Elder Jr, Glen H. 1978. Family History and the Life Course. In *Transitions: The Family and the Life Course in Historical Perspective,* ed. T. K. Hareven, New York: Academic Press, 17–64.

—— 1987. Families and Lives: Some Development in Life-Course Studies. In *Family History at the Crossroads,* ed. Tamara Hareven and Andrejs Plakans, Princeton, NJ: Princeton University Press, 179–200.

Ellen, Roy F. 1982. *Environment, Subsistence, and System: The Ecology of Small Scale Systems.* Cambridge: Cambridge University Press.

Elliott, J. G. 1980. Weed Control: Past, Present and Future–A Historical Perspective. In *Opportunities for Increasing Crop Yields,* ed. R. G. Hurd, P. V. Biscoe, and C. Dennis. London: Pitman Advanced Publishing Program, 285–95.

Engelmann, Helmut and Reinhold Merkelbach. 1972. *Die Inschriften von Erythrai und Klazomenai Teil I.* Bonn: Rudolf Habelt.

—— 1973. *Die Inschriften von Erythrai und Klazomenai Teil II.* Bonn: Rudolf Habelt.

Engels, Donald. 1980. The Problem of Female Infanticide in the Graeco-Roman World. *Classical Philology* 75: 112–20.

—— 1984. The Use of Historical Demography in Ancient History. *Classical Quarterly* 34: 386–93.

Errico, F. D. and A. M. Moigne. 1985. La faune classique et hellenistique de Locres. Ecologie, elevage, depecage. *Mélanges d' Archeologie et d' Histoire de l'Ecole Française de Rome* 97: 719–50.

Evans, Grant. 1988. "Rich Peasants" and Cooperatives in Socialist Laos. *Journal of Anthropological Research* 44: 229–50.

Evans, John K. 1980a. *Plebs Rustica.* The Peasantry of Classical Italy I. *American Journal of Ancient History* 5: 16–47.

—— 1980b. *Plebs Rustica.* The Peasantry of Classical Italy II. *American Journal of Ancient History* 5: 134–73.

—— 1981. Wheat Production and its Social Consequences in the Roman World. *Classical Quarterly* 312: 428–42.

Eyben, E. 1980/81. Family Planning in Graeco-Roman Antiquity. *Ancient Society* 5–81.

Faber, Bernard. 1981. *Conceptions of Kinship.* New York: Elsevier.

Fenoaltea, Stefano. 1975. The Rise and Fall of a Theoretical Model of the Manorial System. *Journal of Economic History* 35: 386–409.

—— 1976. Risk, Transaction Costs, and the Organization of Mediaeval

Agriculture. *Explorations in Economic History* 13: 129–51.

Fenoaltea, Stefano. 1977. Fenoaltea on Open Fields: A Reply. *Explorations in Economic History* 14: 405–10.

Ferguson, William S. 1910. The Athenian Phratries. *Classical Philology* 5: 257–84.

―― 1938. The Salaminioi of Heptaphylai and Sounion. *Hesperia* 7: 1–76.

―― 1944. The Attic Orgeones. *The Harvard Theological Review* 37: 62–140.

―― 1972. *Athenian Festivals*. London: Thames and Hudson.

Ferro-Luzzi, A. and M. A. Spadoni. 1978. Protein-Energy Malnutrition. *Progress in Food and Nutritional Science* 2: 515–41.

Fidanza, Flamminio. 1979. Diets and Dietary Recommendations in Ancient Greece and Rome and the School of Salerno. *Progress in Food and Nutritional Science* 3: 79–99.

Figueira, Thomas J. 1984. Mess Contributions and Subsistence at Sparta. *Transactions of the American Philological Association* 114: 87–109.

―― 1985. The Theognidae and Megarian Society. In *Theognis of Megara: Poetry and the Polis,* ed. Thomas J. Figueira and Gregory Nagy. Baltimore, Md.: The Johns Hopkins Press, 112–57.

―― 1986. *Sitopolai* and *Sitophylakes* in Lysias' "Against The Graindealers": Governmental Intervention in the Athenian Economy. *Phoenix* 40: 149–71.

Finley, M. I. 1951. *Studies in Land and Credit in Ancient Athens 500–200 B.C. The "Horos" Inscriptions.* New Brunswick, NJ: Rutgers University Press.

―― 1960. Was Greek Civilization Based on Slave Labour? In *Slavery in Classical Antiquity,* ed. M. I. Finley, Cambridge: W. Heffer & Sons, 53–72.

―― 1974. Aristotle and Economic Analysis. In *Studies in Ancient Society,* ed. Moses I. Finley, London: Routledge & Kegan Paul, 26–52.

―― 1977. *The World of Odysseus,* 2nd edn. London: Chatto & Windus.

―― 1980. *Ancient Slavery and Modern Ideology.* London: Chatto & Windus.

―― 1981a. Land, Debt and the Man of Property in Classical Athens. In *Economy and Society in Ancient Greece,* ed. Brent D. Shaw and Richard P. Saller. London: Chatto & Windus, 62–76.

―― 1981b. The Elderly in Classical Antiquity. *Greece and Rome* 28: 156–71.

―― 1983. *Politics in the Ancient World.* Cambridge: Cambridge University Press.

―― 1985. *The Ancient Economy,* 2nd edn. Berkeley: University of California Press.

Firth, R. 1969. Social Structure and Peasant Economy: The Influence of

Social Structure upon Peasant Economies. In *Subsistence Agriculture and Economic Development,* ed. C. R. Wharton. Chicago, Ill.: Aldine, 23–37.

Fisher, N. R. E. 1976. *Social Values in Classical Athens.* London: Dent.

Fisher, P. and A. Bender. 1979. *The Value of Food.* Oxford: Oxford University Press.

Fisher, R. A. 1973. The Effect of Water Stress at Various Stages of Development on Yield Processes in Wheat. In *Plant Responses to Climatic Factors,* ed. R. O. Slayter. Paris: UNESCO, 233–42.

Forbes, Hamish A. 1976a. "We Have a Little of Everything": The Ecological Basis of Some Agricultural Practices in Methana, Trizinia. In *Regional Variation in Modern Greece and Cyprus: Toward a Perspective of the Ethnography of Greece,* ed. M. Dimen and E. Friedl. New York: The New York Academy of Sciences, 236–50.

—— 1976b. The "Thrice-Ploughed Field": Cultivation Techniques in Ancient and Modern Greece. *Expedition* 19: 5–11.

—— 1982. *Strategies and Soils: Technology, Production, and Environment in the Peninsula of Methana, Greece.* Ph.D. Dissertation: University of Pennsylvania.

—— and Harold A. Koster. 1976. Fire, Axe and Plow: Human Influence on Local Plant Communities in the Southern Argolid. In *Regional Variation in Modern Greece and Cyprus: Toward a Perspective on the Ethnography of Greece,* ed. Muriel Dimen and Ernestine Friedl. New York: The New York Academy of Sciences, 109–26.

Fortes, Meyer. 1949. *The Web of Kinship among the Tallensi.* Oxford: Oxford University Press.

—— 1969. *Kinship and the Social Order. The Legacy of Lewis Henry Morgan.* London: Routledge & Kegan Paul.

Foster, Brian L. 1984. Family Structure and the Generation of Thai Social Exchange Networks. In *Households: Comparative and Historical Studies of the Domestic Group,* ed. Robert M. Netting, Richard R. Wilk, and Eric J. Arnould. Berkeley: University of California Press, 84–108.

Foster, George M. 1965. Peasant Society and the Image of the Limited Good. *American Anthropologist* 67: 293–315.

—— 1972. A Second Look at Limited Good. *Anthropological Quarterly* 45: 57–64.

—— 1977. The Dyadic Contract: A Model for the Social Structure of a Mexican Peasant Village. In *Friends, Followers and Factions: A Reader in Political Clientism,* ed. Steffen W. Schmidt, Laura Giusti, Carl H. Landé, and James C. Scott. Berkeley: University of California Press, 15–27.

Foucart, Paul F. 1873. *Des associations religieuses chez les Grecs: Thiases, Eranes, Orgeones.* Paris: Klincksieck.

Fox, John W. 1988. Hierarchization in Maya Segmentary States. In *State and Society: The Emergence and Development of Social Hierarchy and*

Political Centralization, ed. John Gledhill, Barbara Bender, and Mogens Trolle Larsen. London: Unwin Hyman, 103–12.

Foxhall, Lin. 1989. Household, Property and Gender in Classical Athens. *Classical Quarterly* 39: 22–44.

Foxhall, Lin. and Hamish A. Forbes. 1982. *Sitometria:* The Role of Grain as a Staple Food in Classical Antiquity. *Chiron* 12: 41–90.

Fraisse, Jean-Claude. 1974. *Philia: La Notion d'amitie dans la philosophie antique. Essai sur un problème perdu et retrouvé.* Paris: Librairie Philsophique J. Vrin.

Franke, Richard W. 1987. The Effects of Colonialism and Neocolonialism on the Gastronomic Patterns of the Third World. In *Food and Evolution: Toward a Theory of Human Food Habits,* ed. Marvin Harris and E. B. Ross. Philadelphia: Temple University Press, 455–80.

Franklin, P. 1986. Peasant Widows' "Liberation" and Remarriage before the Black Death. *Economic History Review* 39: 188–204.

Frayn, Joan. 1979. *Subsistence Farming in Roman Italy.* Fonwell: Centaur Press.

Frederick, R. F. 1965. *Wheat: Botany, Cultivation and Utilization.* London.

Fredrickson, George M. 1981. *White Supremacy: A Comparative Study in American and South African History.* Oxford: Oxford University Press.

Freedman, R. L. 1977. Nutritional Anthropology: An Overview. In *Nutrition and Anthropology in Action,* ed. T. K. Fitzgerald. Amsterdam: Van Gorum, 1–23.

Freeman, Derek. 1973. Kinship, Attachment Behaviour and the Primary Bond. In *The Character of Kinship,* ed. Jack Goody. Cambridge: Cambridge University Press, 109–20.

Freeman, Susan Tax. 1970. *Neighbors: The Social Contract in a Castillian Hamlet.* Chicago, Ill.: University of Chicago Press.

French, Valerie. 1986. Midwives and Maternity Care in the Graeco-Roman World. In *Rescuing Creusa: New Methodological Approaches to Women in Antiquity,* ed. Marilyn Skinner. *Helios,* ns 12(2), 69–84.

Frey, G. F. 1985. Analysis of Fecal Material. In *The Analysis of Prehistoric Diets,* ed. R. I. Gilbert, Jr. and J. H. Miekle. New York: Academic Press, 127–54.

Friedl, Ernestine. 1962. *Vasilika. A Village in Modern Greece.* New York: Holt, Rinehart, and Winston.

Friedl, H. 1984. *Tierknochen aus Kassope, Griechenland (4.-1. Jh. v. Chr).* University of München: Ph.D. Dissertation.

Frier, Bruce. 1982. Roman Life Expectancy: Ulpian's Evidence. *Harvard Studies in Classical Philology* 86: 213–51.

—— 1983. Roman Life Expectancy: The Pannonian Evidence. *Phoenix* 37: 328–44.

Fuchs, R. 1984. *Abandoned Children: Foundlings and Child Welfare in 19th Century France.* Albany, NY: SUNY Press.

Fuks, Alexander. 1972. Isokrates and the Social-Economic Situation in Greece. *Ancient Society* 3: 17–44.

—— 1974. Patterns and Types of Social-Economic Revolution in Greece from the Fourth to the Second Century B. C. *Ancient Society* 5: 51–81.

—— 1979. Plato and the Social Question: The Problem of Poverty and Riches in the *Laws*. *Ancient Society* 10: 33–78.

—— 1984. *Social Conflict in Ancient Greece*. Leiden: E. J. Brill.

Gabbert, J. J. 1986. Piracy in the Early Hellenistic Period: A Career Open to Talents. *Greece & Rome* 33: 156–63.

Gabrielson, Vincent. 1987a. The *Diadikasia*-Documents. *Classica et Mediaevalia* 37: 39–52.

—— 1987b. The *Antidosis* Procedure in Classica Athens. *Classica et Mediaevalia* 37: 7–38.

Gair, R., J. E. E. Jenkins, and E. Lester. 1978. *Cereal Pests and Diseases*. Ipswich: Farming Press.

Gallant, Thomas W. 1982a. Agricultural Systems, Land Tenure and the Reforms of Solon. *Annual of the British School at Athens* 77: 111–24.

—— 1982b. *An Examination of Two Island Polities in Antiquity: the Lefkas-Pronnoi Surveys*. Ph.D. Dissertation: Cambridge University.

—— 1982c. Coping with Uncertainty: The Agroclimatology of Athens, Melos, Thera and the Black Sea. Economic and Social Research Council, Working Paper No. 1.

—— 1985a. *A Fisherman's Tale: An Analysis of the Potential Productivity of Fishing in the Ancient Mediterranean*. Brussels: Miscellanea Graeca.

—— 1985b. The Agronomy, Production and Utilization of Sesame and Linseed in the Graeco-Roman World. *Bulletin on Sumerian Agriculture* 2: 153–8.

—— 1986a. "Background Noise" and Site Definition: A Contribution to Survey Methodology. *Journal of Field Archaeology* 13: 403–18.

—— 1986b. Currant Production and Social Relations in the Ionian Islands during the 18th & 19th Centuries: Some Preliminary Thoughts. *Proceedings of the Ies Jornades Sobres la Viticultura de la Conca Mediterrania*. Tarragona: University of Tarragona, 515–32.

—— 1988. Greek Bandit Gangs: Lone Wolves or a Family Affair? *Journal of Modern Greek Studies* 6: 269–90.

—— 1989. Crisis and Response: Risk-Buffering Behavior in Hellenistic Greek Communities. *Journal of Interdisciplinary History* 19: 393–413.

Galt, Anthony H. 1974. Rethinking Patron-Client Relationships: The Real System and the Official System in South Italy. *Anthropological Quarterly* 47: 182–202.

—— 1975. Social Organization, Land Tenure and Ecological Adaptation on the Island of Pantelleria, Sicily. *Paper Presented at the 74th Meeting of the American Anthropological Association*

—— 1979. Exploring the Cultural Ecology of Field Fragmentation and

Scattering on the Island of Pantelleria, Italy. *Journal of Anthropological Research* 35: 93–108.

Gamble, C. 1982. Animal Husbandry, Population and Urbanism. In *An Island Polity: The Archaeology of Exploitation in Melos,* ed. Colin Renfrew and Malcolm Wagstaff. Cambridge: Cambrige University Press, 161–72.

Gamst, Fredrick C. 1974. *Peasants in Complex Societies.* New York: Holt, Rinehart and Winston.

Garbarino, M. S. 1976. *Native American Heritage.* Boston, Mass.: Little, Brown and Company.

Garcia, Rolando V. 1981. *Drought and Man: the 1972 Case History.* Oxford: Pergamon Press.

Garlan, Yvon. 1974. *Recherches de Poliorcetique Grecque.* Paris: Diffusion de Boccard.

—— 1975. *War in the Ancient World: A Social History.* London: Chatto and Windus.

—— 1978. Signification historique de la piraterie grecque. *DHA* 4: 1–14.

—— 1980. Le Travail Libre en Grèce Ancienne. In *Non-Slave Labor in the Graeco-Roman World,* ed. Peter Garnsey. Cambridge: Cambridge Philological Society, 6–22.

—— 1988. *Slavery in Ancient Greece.* Ithaca, NY: Cornell University Press.

Garland, Robert. 1987. *The Piraeus from the Fifth to the First Century BC.* Ithaca, NY: Cornell University Press.

Garnsey, Peter. 1984. Grain for Athens. In *Crux,* ed. Paul Cartledge and F. D. Harvey. London: Imprint, 62–75.

—— 1988a. *Famine and Food Supply in the Graeco-Roman World: Responses to Risk and Crisis.* Cambridge: Cambridge University Press.

—— 1988b. Mountain Economies in Europe: Thoughts on the Early History, Continuity and Individuality of Mediterranean Upland Pastoralism. In *Pastoral Economies in Classical Antiquity,* ed. C. R. Whittaker. Cambridge: Cambridge Philosophical Society, 196–209.

—— T. Gallant and D. Rathbone. 1984. Thessaly and the Grain Supply of Rome during the Second Century B. C. *Journal of Roman Studies* 74: 30–44.

Gauthier, Philippe. 1972. *Symbola: Les Étrangers et la justice dans les cités grecques.* Nancy: Annales de l'Est.

—— 1985. *Les Cités Grecques et leurs bienfaiteurs (iv-i siècle avant J.C.). Contribution a' l'histoire des insititutions.* Paris: BCH Supplement XII. Boccard.

Gautier, A. 1965. Analyse des restes osseaux de l'insula 3. *Thorikos* 3: 72–5.

Gavazzi, Milovan. 1982. The Extended Family in Southeastern Europe.

Journal of Family History 7: 89–102.

Gavrielides, Nicholas. 1976. The Impact of Olive Growing on the Landscape in the Fourni Valley. In *Regional Variation in Modern Greece and Cyprus: Toward a Perspective on the Ethnography of Greece,* ed. Muriel Dimen and Ernestine Friedl. New York: The New York Academy of Sciences, 143–57.

Gehrke, Hans-Joachim. 1985. *Stasis: Untersuchungen zu den inneren Kriegen in den griechischen Staaten des 5. und 4. Jahrhunderts v. Chr.* München: C. H. Beck'sche Verlagsbuchhandlung.

Gellner, Ernest. 1977. Patrons and Clients. In *Patrons and Clients in Mediterranean Societies,* ed. Ernest Gellner and James Waterbury. London: Duckworth, 1–6.

Georges-Roegen, N. 1970. The Institutional Aspects of Peasant Communities: An Analytical View. In *Subsistence Agriculture and Economic Development,* ed. C. R. Wharton. Chicago, Ill.: Aldine, 61–93.

Georgoudi, Stella. 1974. Quelques problèmes de la transhumance dans la Grece ancienne. *Revue des Études Grecques* 87: 155–85.

Gernet, L. 1981a. Mortgage *horoi.* In *The Anthropology of Ancient Greece* Trans. by John Hamilton, S. J. and Blaise Nagy. Baltimore, Md.: The Johns Hopkins University Press, 303–11.

—— 1981b. Ancient Feasts. In *The Anthropology of Ancient Greece,* 13–47.

Ghatak, Subrata and Ken Ingersent. 1984. *Agriculture and Economic Development.* Baltimore, Md: The Johns Hopkins University Press.

Gibbs, J. A. C. and V. C. Nielson. 1976. Farm Wastes: Animal Excreta. In *Food Production and Consumption. The Efficiency of Human Food Chains and Nutrient Cycles,* ed. A. N. Duckham, J. G. W. Jones, and E. H. Roberts. Oxford: North-Holland Publishing Company, 319–29.

Gilbert, Jr., R. I. 1985. Stress, Paleonutrition, and Trace Elements. In *The Analysis of Prehistoric Diets,* ed. R. I. Gilbert, Jr. and J. H. Miekel. New York: Academic Press, 339–59.

Gilmore, David D. 1987. *Aggression and Community: The Paradoxes of Andalusian Culture.* New Haven, Conn.: Yale University.

Galdwin, Christina H. 1980. A Theory of Real-Life Choice: Applications to Agricultural Decisions. In *Agricultural Decision Making. Anthropological Contributions to Rural Development,* ed. Peggy F. Barlett. New York: Academic Press, 45–85.

Glantz, Michael H. 1987. Drought and Economic Development in Sub-Saharan Africa. In *Drought and Hunger in Africa: Denying Famine a Future,* ed. Michael H. Glantz. Cambridge: Cambridge University Press, 37–58.

Gledhill, John W. 1988. Legacies of Empire: Political Centralization and Class-Formation in the Hispanic American World. In *State and Society: The Emergence and Development of Social Hierarchy and Political*

Centralization, ed. John Gledhill, Barbara Bender, and Mogens Trolle Larsen. London: Unwin Hyman, 302–19.

Glotz, G. 1913. Le Prix des denrées ä Delos. *Journal des savants* 16–29.

—— 1916. L'histoire de Delos arpës les prix d'une denre. *Revue des Études Grecques* 29: 281–325.

Golden, Mark. 1979. Demosthenes and the Age of Majority at Athens. *Phoenix* 33: 25–38.

—— 1981. Demography and the Exposure of Girls at Athens. *Phoenix* 35: 316–31.

—— 1988. Did the Ancients Care When Their Children Died? *Greece and Rome* 35: 152–63.

Goldhill, Simon. 1986. *Reading Greek Tragedy.* Cambridge: Cambridge University Press.

Gomme, A. W. 1967. *The Population of Athens in the Fifth and Fourth Centuries B. C.* (repr.). Chicago: Argonaut Inc.

Goode, William J. 1978. *The Celebration of Heroes: Prestige as a Social Control System.* Berkeley: University of California Press.

Goodell, G. E. 1986. Paternalism, Patronage, and Potlatch: The Dynamics of Giving and Being Given To. *Current Anthropology* 26: 247–66.

Goodhart, Robert S. and Maurice E. Shils. 1973. *Modern Nutrition in Health and Disease.* Philadelphia, Pa.: Lees and Febiger.

Goodman, David and Michael Redclift. 1981. *From Peasant to Proletarian: Capitalist Development and Agrarian Transitions.* Oxford: Basil Blackwell.

Goody, J. 1976. *Production and Reproduction. A Comparative Study of the Domestic Domain.* Cambridge: Cambridge University Press.

—— (ed.) 1958. *The Development Cycle in Domestic Groups.* Cambridge: Cambridge University Press.

Goubert, Pierre. 1987. *The French Peasantry in the Seventeenth Century.* Trans. Ian Patterson. Cambridge: Cambridge University Press.

Gould, John. 1980. Law, Custom, and Myth: Aspects of the Social Position of Women in Classical Athens. *Journal of Hellenic Studies* 100: 38–59.

Gouldner, Alvin W. 1977. The Norm of Reciprocity: A Preliminary Statement. In *Friends, Followers and Factions: A Reader in Political Clientism,* ed. Steffen W. Schmidt, Laura Guasti, Carl H. Landé, and James C. Scott. Berkeley: University of California Press, 28–42.

Goure, L. 1962. *The Siege of Leningrad.* Stanford Calif.: Stanford University Press.

Graves, Adrian. 1983. Truck and Gifts: Melanesian Immigrants and the Trade Box System in Colonial Queensland. *Past & Present* 101: 87–124.

Graziano, Luigi. 1977. Patron–Client Relationships in Southern Italy. In *Friends, Followers and Factions: A Reader in Political Clientism,* ed.

Steffen W. Schmidt, Laura Guasti, Carl H. Landé, and James C. Scott. Berkeley: University of California Press, 360–77.

Greece Basic Statistics. 1941. Unpublished report: Greek Office of Information. Copy available at Cambridge University Library Reference Collection.

Greenough, Paul R. 1982. *Prosperity and Misery in Modern Bengal: The Famine of 1943–44.* Oxford: Oxford University Press.

Gregory, Christopher A. 1982. *Gifts and Commodities.* New York: Academic Press.

Gregory, J. R. 1975. Image of Limited Good or Expectation of Reciprocity. *Current Anthropology* 16: 73–92.

Griffith, Guy T. 1935. *The Mercenaries of the Hellenistic World.* Cambridge: Cambridge University Press.

Grigg, D. B. 1974. *The Agricultural Systems of the World. An Evolutionary Approach.* Cambridge: Cambridge University Press.

—— 1976. Population Pressure and Agricultural Change. In *Progress in Geography,* ed. C. Beard *et al.* London: Edward Arnold, 133–77.

—— 1980. *Population Growth and Agrarian Change. An Historical Perspective.* Cambridge: Cambridge University Press.

Gross, Daniel. 1983. The Ecological Perspective in Economic Anthropology. In *Economic Anthropology: Topics and Theories,* ed. Sutti Ortiz. New York: University Press of America, 147–54.

Guggenheim, Scott E. and Robert P. Weller. 1982. Introduction: Moral Economy, Capitalism and State Power in Rural Protest. In *Power and Protest in the Countryside: Studies of Rural Unrest in Asia, Europe and Latin America,* ed. Robert P. Weller and Scott E. Guggenheim. Durham: Duke University Press, 3–12.

Guiraud, Paul. 1979 [1893]. *La Propriété foncière en Grèce jusqu'a la conquête romaine.* New York: Arno Press.

Habicht, Christian. 1976. Eine hellenistische Urkunde aus Larisa. In *Demetrias I,* ed. V. Milojcic and D. Theocaris. Bonn: R. Habelt Verlag, 157–74.

Hajnal, J. 1965. European Marriage Patterns in Perspective. In *Population in History: Essays in Historical Demography,* ed. D. V. Glass and D. E. C. Eversley. London: Edward Arnold, 101–143.

—— 1983. Two Kinds of Pre-Industrial Household Formation System. In *Family Forms in Historic Europe,* ed. R. Wall, J. Robin, and P. Laslett. Cambridge: Cambridge University Press, 65–104.

Hale, W. 1981. *The Political and Economic Development of Modern Turkey.* London: Croom Helm.

Hall, D. W., G. A. Haswell, and T. Q. Oxley. 1956. *Underground Storage of Grain.* London: Colonial Office.

Halpern, J. M. 1958. *A Serbian Village.* New York: Columbia University Press.

Halstead, Paul. 1981a. Counting Sheep in Neolithic and Bronze Age Greece. In *Pattern of the Past: Studies in Honour of David Clarke,* ed. I. Hodder, G. Isaac, and N. Hammond. Cambridge: Cambridge University Press, 307–38.

—— 1981b. From Determinism to Uncertainty: Social Storage and the Rise of the Minoan Palace. In *Economic Archaeology* ed. A. Sheridan and G. Bailey. Oxford: BAR no. 96, 187–213.

—— 1987a. Traditional and Ancient Rural Economy in Mediterranean Europe: plus ça change? *Journal of Hellenic Studies* 107: 77–87.

—— 1987b. Man and Other Animals on Later Greek Prehistory. *Annual of the British School at Athens* 82: 71–83.

—— and J. O'Shea. 1982. A Friend in Need Is a Friend Indeed: Social Storage and the Origins of Social Ranking. In *Ranking, Resource and Exchange. Aspects of the Archaeology of Early European Society,* ed. C. Renfrew and S. Shennan. Cambridge: Cambridge University Press, 92–9.

Hamer, John H. 1982. Rivalry and Taking Kinsmen for Granted: Limiting Factors in the Development of Voluntary Associations. *Journal of Anthropological Research* 38: 303–14.

Hamilton, F. E. I. 1968. *Yugoslavia. Patterns of Economic Activity.* London: G. Bell & Sons.

Hammel, Eugene A. 1968. *Alternative Social Structures and Ritual Relations in the Balkans.* Englewood Cliffs, NJ: Prentice Hall.

—— 1972. The Zadruga as Process. In *Household and Family in Past Time,* ed. P. Laslett and R. Wall. Cambridge: Cambridge University Press, 335–74.

—— 1980a. Household Structure in Fourteenth Century Macedonia. *Journal of Family History* 5: 242–73.

—— 1980b. Sensitivity Analysis of Household Structure in Medieval Serbian Censuses. *Historical Methods* 13: 105–18.

—— 1984. On the ### of Studying Household Form and Function. In *Households: Comparative and Historical Studies of the Domestic Group,* ed. Robert M. Netting, Richard R. Wilk, and Eric J. Arnould. Berkeley: University of California Press, 29–43.

—— and Kenneth W. Wachter. 1977. Primonuptiality and Ultimonuptiality: Their Effects on Stem Family Household Frequencies. In *Population Patterns in the Past,* ed. R. D. Lee. New York: Academic Press, 113–34.

Hanawalt, Barbara A. 1981. Childbearing among the Lower Classes of Late Medieval Europe. In *Marriage and Fertility,* ed. R. I. Rotberg and T. K. Rabb. Princeton, NJ: Princeton University Press, 19–40.

Handy, E. S. Craighill and Elizabeth Handy. 1972. *Native Planters in Old Hawaii.* Maui: Bernice P. Bishop Museum.

Hankins, T. D. 1974. Response to Drought in Sukumaland. In *Natural*

Hazards: Local, National, Global, ed. G. White. Oxford: Oxford University Press, 98–104.

Hanks, L. M. 1975. The Thai Social Order as Entourage and Circle. In *Change and Persistence in Thai Society: Essays in Honor of Lauristan Sharp,* ed. G. W. Skinner and A. T. Kirsch. Ithaca, NY: Cornell University Press, 197–218.

Hansen, E. C. 1969. The State and Land Tenure Conflicts in Rural Catania. *Anthropological Quarterly* 42: 214–43.

Hansen, Marianne V. 1984. Athenian Maritime Trade in the 4th Century B. C. Operation and Finance. *Classical et Mediaivalia* 33: 71–92.

Hansen, Mogen 1981–2. The Athenian *Heliaia* from Solon to Aristotle. *Classica et Mediaevalia* 33: 9–48.

——— 1983. *The Athenian Ecclesia. A Collection of Articles, 1976–1983.* Copenhagen: Museum Tusculanum Press.

Hareven, T. K. 1978. Introduction: The Historical Study of the Life Course. In *Transitions: The Family and the Life Course in Historical Perspective,* ed. T. K. Hareven, New York: Academic Press, 1–26.

Harper, F. 1983. *Principles of Arable Crop Production.* London: Granada.

Harris, Marvin. 1979. *Cultural Materialism.* New York: Randon House.

——— 1987. Cultural Materialism: Alarums and Excursions. In *Waymarks: The Notre Dame Inaugural Lectures in Anthropology,* ed. Kenneth Moore. Notre Dame, Ind.: University of Notre Dame Press, 107–26.

——— and E. B. Ross. 1987a. Foodways: Historical Overview and Theoretical Prolegomenon. In *Food and Evolution: Toward a Theory of Human Food Habits,* ed. Marvin Harris and E. B. Ross. Philadelphia, Penn.: Temple University Press, 57–90.

——— 1987b. *Death, Sex and Fertility: Population Regulation in Preindustrial and Developing Societies.* New York: Columbia University Press.

Harris, Olivia. 1982. Households and Their Boundaries. *History Workshop* 13: 143–52.

Harris, William V. 1982. The Theoretical Possibility of Extensive Infanticide in the Graeco-Roman World. *Classical Quarterly* 32: 114–16.

Harrison, Alick R. W. 1968. *The Law of Athens: The Family and Property.* Oxford: Clarendon Press.

Harrison, B. R. M. 1974. *Chayanov and the Economics of the Russian Peasantry.* Warwick: University of Warwick, Economic Research Papers, No. 55.

——— 1976. *The Peasant Mode of Production in the Work of A. V. Chayanov.* Warwick: University of Warwick, Economic Research Papers, No. 56.

Haviland, John B. 1977. *Gossip, Reputation and Knowledge in Zinacantan.* Chicago, Ill.: University of Chicago Press.

Hay, Roger W. 1981. The Concept of Food Supply System with Special Reference to the Management of Famine. In *Famine: Its Causes, Effects and Management,* ed. John R. K. Robson. London: Gordon and Breach, 81–8.

Heath, D. C. 1973. New Patrons for Old: Changing Patron–Client Relationships in the Bolivian Yungas. *Ethnology* 12: 75–98.

Hedrick Jr, Charles W. 1983. Old and New Information on the Attic Phratry of the Therrikleidai. *Hesperia* 52: 299–302.

—— 1988. The Thymaitian Phratry. *Hesperia* 57: 81–6.

—— 1989. The Phratry from Paiania. *Classical Quarterly* 39: 114–25.

Heisserer, A. J. 1980. *Alexander the Great and the Greeks.* Norman: University of Oklahoma Press.

Heitland, William E. 1921. *Agricola. A Study of Agriculture and Rustic Life in the Greco-Roman World from the Point of View of Labor.* Cambridge: Cambridge University Press.

Henderson, D. W. 1979. Soil Management in Semi-Arid Environments. In *Agriculture in Semi-Arid Environments,* ed. A. E. Hall, G. H. Cannell, and H. W. Lawton. Berlin: Springer-Verlag, 224–37.

Heppenstall, M. A. 1971. Reputation, Criticism and Information in an Austrian Village. In *Gifts and Poison: The Politics of Reputation,* ed. F. G. Bailey. Oxford: Basil Blackwell, 139–66.

Herlihy, D. and C. Klapisch-Zuber. 1985. *Tuscans and their Families. A Study of the Florentine Catasto of 1427.* New Haven, Conn.: Yale University Press.

Herman, Gabriel. 1981. The "Friends" of the Early Hellenistic Rulers: Servants or Officials? *Talanta* 103–49.

—— 1987. *Ritualised Friendship and the Greek City.* Cambridge: Cambridge University Press.

Herzfeld, Michael. 1984. The Significance of the Insignificant: Blasphemy as Ideology. *Man* 19: 653–64.

—— 1985. *The Poetics of Manhood: Contest and Ideology in a Cretan Mountain Village.* Princeton, NJ: Princeton University Press.

Hill, Polly. 1982. *Dry Grain Farming Families: Hausaland (Nigeria) and Karnataka (India).* Cambridge: Cambridge University Press.

Hillman, G. 1973a. Agricultural Resources and Settlement in the Asvan Region. *Anatolian Studies* 23: 217–24.

—— 1973b. Agricultural Productivity and Past Population Potential at Asvan. *Anatolian Studies* 23: 225–40.

Hilton, Rodney. 1973. *Bond Men Made Free: Medieaval Peasant Movements and the English Rising of 1381.* London: Temple Smith.

Hirsch, Eva. 1970. *Poverty and Plenty on the Turkish Farm: A Study of Income Distribution in Turkish Agriculture.* New York: Columbia University Press.

Hirschmann, John D. 1979. *Nutrition Almanac.* New York: McGraw-Hill Book Company.

Hodges, Richard. 1988. *Primitive and Peasant Markets.* Oxford: Basil

Blackwell.

Hodkinson, Stephen. 1983. Social Order and the Conflict of Values in Classical Sparta. *Chiron* 13: 239–81.

—— 1986. Land Tenure and Inheritance in Classical Sparta. *Classical Quarterly* 36: 378–406.

—— 1988. Animal Husbandry in the Greek Polis. In *Pastoral Economies in Classical Antiquity,* ed. C.R. Whittaker. Cambridge: Cambridge Philological Society, 35–74.

—— and Hilary Hodkinson. 1981. Mantineia and the Mantinike: Settlement and Society in a Greek Polis. *Annual of the British School at Athens* 76: 239–96.

Holderness, B. A. 1984. Widows in Pre-Industrial Society: An Essay upon their Economic Functions. In *Land, Kinship, and the Life Cycle,* ed. Richard M. Smith. Cambridge: Cambridge University Press, 423–42.

Hopkins, Keith. 1965. The Age of Roman Girls at Marriage. *Population Studies* 18: 309–27.

—— 1980. Taxes and Trade in the Roman Empire (200 BC – AD 400). *Journal of Roman Studies* 70: 101–25.

—— and Graham Burton. 1983. Political Succession in the Late Republic (249–50 BC). In *Death and Renewal,* ed. Keith Hopkins. Cambridge: Cambridge University Press, 31–119.

Hopper, Robert J. 1979. *Trade and Industry in Classical Greece.* London: Thames and Hudson.

Horne, Lee. 1982. The Household in Space: Dispersed Holdings in an Iranian Village. In *Archaeology of the Household: Building a Prehistory of Domestic Life,* ed. Richard R. Wilk and William J. Rathje. New York: *American Behavioral Scientist,* vol. 25, 677–85.

Houliarkis, M. 1975. *Yiographiki, Diikiti Kai Plithismiaki Ekseleksis tis Ellados, 1821–1917.* Athens: Karanisi.

Huang, Philip C. C. 1985. *The Peasant Economy and Social Change in North China.* Stanford, Calif.: Stanford University Press.

Hufton, Olwen. 1972. Begging, Vagrancy, Vagabondage and the Law: An Aspect of the Problem of Poverty in Eighteenth Century France. *European Studies Review* 2: 97–124.

—— 1974. *The Poor of Eighteenth-Century France.* Oxford: Oxford University Press.

—— 1983. Social Conflict and the Grain Supply in Eighteenth-Century France. *Journal of Interdisciplinary History.* 14: 303–31.

Hughes, Dennis D. 1986. *Human Sacrifice in Ancient Greece.* Ph.D. Dissertation: Ohio State University.

Hull, Dennison Bingham. 1964. *Hounds and Hunting in Ancient Greece.* Chicago, Ill.: University of Chicago Press.

Humphreys, Sally. 1983. The Family in Classical Athens: Search for a Perspective. In *The Family, Women and Death,* ed. S. Humphreys.

Boston: Routledge & Kegan Paul, 58–77.

Humphreys, Sally. 1986. Kinship Patterns in Athenian Courts. *Greek, Roman and Byzantine Studies* 27: 57–92.

Hunter, F. A. 1980. Problems Encountered When Protecting Stored Grain from Damage by Rodents, Birds, Insects and Mites in England and Wales. In *Post Harvest Food Conservation,* ed. A. Herzka. Progress in Food and Nutrition Science, 4, 79–90.

Hunter, Virginia. 1989. Women's Authority in Classical Athens. *Classical Views* 23: 389–408.

Huss-Ashmore, R. and R. B. Thomas. 1988. A Framework for Analysing Uncertainty in Highland Areas. In *Coping with Uncertainty in Food Supply,* ed. I. de Garine and G. A. Harrison. Oxford: Oxford University Press, 452–68.

Huss-Ashmore, R., G. J. Goodman, and G. J. Armelagos. 1982. Nutritional Inferences from Paleopathology. In *Advances in Archaeological Method and Theory,* ed. M. B. Schiffer. New York: Academic Press, 365–474.

Hutson, S. 1971. Social Ranking in a French Alpine Community. In *Gifts and Poison: The Politics of Reputation,* ed. F. G. Bailey. Oxford: Basil Blackwell, 41–69.

Isager, S. 1981–2. Marriage Patterns in Classical Athens – Men and Women in Isaios. *Classica et Mediaevalia* 33: 81–96.

Isom, W. H. and G. F. Worker. 1979. Crop Management in Semi-Arid Environments. In *Agriculture in Semi-Arid Environments,* ed. A. E. Hall, G. H. Cannell, and H. W. Lawtaon. Berlin: Springer Verlag, 200–23.

Jackson, Kennell A. 1985. The Family Entity and Famine among the Nineteenth-Century Akamba of Kenya: Social Responses to Environmental Stress. *Journal of Family History* 10: 193–216.

Jalil, M. 1977. Importance of Food Legumes in Human Nutrition. *Food Legume Crops* 3: 63–72.

Jameson, Michael H. 1977/78. Agriculture and Slavery in Classical Athens. *Classical Journal* 73: 122–46.

—— 1982. The Leasing of Land in Rhamnous. *Studies in Attic Epigraphy, History, and Topography* Hesperia Supplement 19: 66–74.

—— 1988. Sacrifice and Animal Husbandry in Classical Greece. In *Pastoral Economies in Classical Antiquity,* ed. C. R. Whittaker. Cambridge: Cambridge Philosophical Society, 87–119.

Jardé, Auguste. 1979 [1925]. *Les Cereales dans l'antiquité grecque.* Paris: Editions E. de Boccard.

Jenness, D. 1962. *The Economics of Cyprus. A Survey to 1914.* Montreal: McGill University Press.

Johnson, Allen. W. 1980. The Limits of Formalism in Agricultural Decision Research. In *Agricultural Decision Making: Anthropological Contributions to Rural Development,* ed. Peggy F. Barlett. New York:

Academic Press, 19–44.

Johnson, Allen. W. and Timothy Earle. 1987. *The Evolution of Human Societies: From Foraging Group to Agrarian State.* Stanford, Calif: Stanford University Press.

Johnson, Allen. W. and Michael Bakash. 1987. Ecological and Structural Influences on the Proportions of Wild Foods in the Diets of Two Machiguenga Communities. In *Food and Evolution: Toward a Theory of Human Food Habits,* ed. Marvin Harris and E. B. Ross. Philadelphia, Pa.: Temple University Press, 387–406.

Jones, A. H. M. 1960. Slavery in the Ancient World. In *Slavery in Classical Antiquity,* ed. M. I. Finley. Cambridge: W. Heffer & Sons Ltd., 1–16.

—— 1974. Taxation in Antiquity. In *The Roman Economy: Studies in Ancient Economic and Administrative History,* ed. P. A. Brunt. Oxford: Basil Blackwell, 151–86.

Jones, Douglas L. 1975. The Strolling Poor: Transciency in Eighteenth Century Massachusetts. *Journal of Social History* 8: 28–54.

Jones, Glynis. 1987. Agricultural Practice in Greek Prehistory. *Annual of the British School at Athens* 82: 115–24.

Jones, John E. 1975. Town and Country Houses of Attica in Classical Times. In *Thorikos and Lavrion in Archaic and Classical Times,* ed. H. Mussche and Paul Spitaels. Brussels: Miscellanea Graeca, 63–140.

Jones, Nicholas F. 1987. *Public Organizaion in Ancient Greece: A Documentary Study.* Philadelphia: American Philosophical Society.

Jordan, B. 1975. *The Athenian Navy in the Classical Period.* Berkeley: University of California Press.

Jordan, L. S. and D. L. Shaner. 1979. Weed Control. In *Agriculture in Semi-Arid Environments,* ed. A. E. Hall, G. H. Cannell, and H. W. Lawton, 266–96. New York: Springer-Verlag.

Jordan, W. C. 1988. Women and Credit in the Middle Ages: Problems and Direction. *Journal of European Economic History* 17: 33–62.

Kaba, Lansine. 1984. Power, Prosperity and Social Inequality in Songhay (1464–1591). In *Life Before the Drought,* ed. Earl P. Scott. Boston, Mass.: Allen & Unwin, 29–48.

Kalcyk, Hansjorg. 1988. Der Damm van Akraiphia. Landsicherung und Landgewinnung in der Bucht van Akraiphia am Kopaissee, in Boeotein, Griecheland. *Boreas* 11: 5–14.

Kaplan, D. and B Saler. 1966. Foster's Image of the Limited Good: An Example of Anthropological Explanation. *American Anthropologist* 68: 202–5.

Kates, Robert W. 1980. Climate and Society: Lessons from Recent Events. *Weather* 35: 17–25.

—— 1981. Drought in the Sahel: Competing Views as to What Really Happened in 1910–14 and 1968–74. *Mazingira* 5: 72–83.

Kates, Robert W. 1985a. *Climate Impact Assessment.* New York: John Wiley & Sons.

—— 1985b. Success, Strain, and Surprise. *Issues in Science and Technology* 2: 46–58.

Kawerau, Georg and Albert Rehm. 1914. *Das Delphinion in Milet. Milet: Ergebnisse der Ausgrabungen und Untersuchungen seit dem Jahre 1899, Heft III.* Berlin: Georg Reimer.

Keene, A. S. 1985. Nutrition and Economy: Models for the Study of Prehistoric Diet. In *The Analysis of Prehistoric Diets,* ed. R. I. Gilbert, Jr. and J. H. Miekle. New York: Academic Press, 155–90.

Keller, D. R. and M. B. Wallace. 1988. The Canadian Karystia Project: Two Classical Farmsteads. *Classical Views* 7: 151–7.

Kenna, Margaret. 1976a. The Idiom of Family. In *Mediterranean Family Structure,* ed. J. G. Peristiany. Cambridge: Cambridge University Press. 347–62.

—— 1976b. Houses, Fields, and Graves: Property and Ritual Obligation on a Greek Island. *Ethnology* 15: 21–34.

Kenny, Michael. 1977. Patterns of Patronage in Spain. In *Friends, Followers and Factions: A Reader in Political Clientism,* ed. Steffen W. Schmidt, Laura Guasti, Carl H. Landé, and James C. Scott. Berkeley: University of California Press, 355–9.

Kent, John H. 1948. The Temple Estates of Delos, Rheneia, and Mykonos. *Hesperia* 17: 243–338.

Kertze, David I. 1984. *Family Life in Central Italy, 1880–1910: Sharecropping, Wage Labor and Coresidence.* New Brunswick, NJ: Rutgers University Press.

—— 1985. European Peasant Household Structure: Some Implications from a Nineteenth Century Italian Community. *Journal of Family History* 10: 333–49.

—— 1989. The Joint Family Household Revisited: Demographic Constraints and Household Complexity in the European Past. *Journal of Family History* 14: 1–16.

—— and Caroline Bretell. 1987. Advances in Italian and Iberian Family History. In *Family History at the Crossroads,* ed. Tamara Hareven and Andrejs Plakans. Princeton, NJ: Princeton University Press, 87–120.

Khan, A. R. 1963. Tillage–Its Traditional Lore and Rational Practice. *World Crops* 15: 68–74.

Khayrallah, W. A. 1982. The Mechanization of Lentil Harvesting. In *Lentils,* ed. C. Webb and G. Hawtin. London: Commonwealth Agricultural Bureau and the International Centre for Agricultural Research in the Dry Areas, 131–9.

Kiefer, Thomas M. 1968. Institutional Friendship and Warfare among the Tausug of Jolo. *Ethnology* 7: 255–44.

Kiray, M. and J. Hinderink. 1968. Interdependencies between Agroeconomic Development and Social Change: A Comparative Study Conducted in the Cukuroua Region of Southern Turkey. *The Journal of Development Studies* 4: 497–528.

Kirby, Anne V. 1974. Individual and Community Responses to Rainfall Variability in Oaxace, Mexico. In *Natural, Hazards: Local, National, Global,* ed. G. White. Oxford: Oxford University Press, 119–28.

Kirkham, M. B. and E. T. Kanemasu. 1983. Wheat. In *Crop-Water Relations,* ed. I. D. Teare and M. M. Peet. New York: John Wiley and Sons, 482–520.

Klaffenbach, G. 1960. *Bemerkungen zum griechischen Urkundenwesen.* Berlin: SDAW, no. 6.

Klapisch-Zuber, C. 1985. *Women, Family and Ritual in Renaissance Italy.* Chicago, Ill.: University of Chicago Press.

Knackfuss, Hubert. 1924. *Der Sudmarket und die denachbarten Bauanlagen. Milet I.* 7. Berlin: Schoetz und Parrhysius.

Knapp, Charles. 1919. Irrigation among the Greeks and the Romans. *The Classical Weekly* vol. 12, no. 10, January 6: 73–4.

Knodel, John E. 1988. *Demographic Behavior in the Past: A Study of Fourteen German Village Populations in the Eighteenth and Nineteenth Centuries.* Cambridge: Cambridge University Press.

Knox, Ronald A. 1985. "So Mischievous a Beaste"? The Athenian *Demos* and Its Treatment of Its Politicians. *Greece & Rome* 32: 132–61.

Kondomihis, Pandazi. 1985. *Ta Gioryika tis Lefkadas.* Athens: Ekdoseis Griyori.

Kramer, Carol. 1982a. *Village Ethnoarchaeology: Rural Iran in Archaeological Perspective.* New York: Academic Press.

—— 1982b. Ethnographic Households and Archaeological Interpretations: A Case from Iranian Kurdistan. In *Archaeology of the Household: Building a Prehistory of Domestic Life,* ed. Richard R. Wilk and William J. Rathje. New York: *American Behavioral Scientist,* vol. 25, 663–75.

Kreissig, H. 1977. Landed Property in "Hellenistic" Orient. *Eirene* 15: 5–26.

—— 1980. Free Labor in the Hellenistic Age. In *Non-Slave Labor in the Graeco-Roman World,* ed. Peter Garnsey. Cambridge: Cambridge Philological Society, 30–3.

Kriedte, Peter. 1983. *Peasants, Landlords, and Merchant Capitalists: Europe and the World Economy 1500–1800.* Lemington Spa: Berg Publishing Ltd.

Kroll, H. 1984. Bronze Age and Iron Age Agriculture in Kastanas, Macedonia. In *Plants and Ancient Man. Studies in Paleoethnobotany,* ed. W. Van Zeist and W. A. Caspari. Boston, Mass.: Reidel, 243–6.

Kunstadter, Peter. 1984. Cultural Ideals, Socioeconomic Change, and Household Composition: Karen, Lua', Hmong, and Thai in Northwestern Thailand. In *Households: Comparative and Historical Studies of the Domestic Group,* ed. Robert M. Netting, Richard R. Wilk, and Eric

J. Arnould. Berkeley: University of California Press, 299–329.

Lacey, W. K. 1968. *The Family in Classical Greece.* London: Thames and Hudson.

La Lone, D. E. 1982. The Inca as a Non-Market Economy: Supply on Command versus Supply and Demand. In *Contexts for Prehistoric Exchange,* ed. J. E. Ericson and T. K. Earle. New York: Academic Press, 291–316.

Lamberton, Robert. 1988. *Hesiod.* New Haven, Conn.: Yale University Press.

Landé, Carl. 1977. Networks and Groups in Southeast Asia: Some Observations on the Group Theory of Politics. In *Friends, Followers and Factions: A Reader in Political Clientism,* ed. Steffen W. Schmidt, Laura Guasti, Carl H. Landé, and James C. Scott. Berkeley: University of California Press, 75–99.

Lane Fox, R. 1983. Aspects of Inheritance in the Greek World. In *Crux,* ed. P. Cartledge and H. D. Harvey. London: Academic Imprint, 208–32.

Langholm, Odd. 1984. *The Aristotelian Analysis of Usury.* Bergen: Universitetsforlaget As.

Laslett, Peter. 1972. Introduction: The History of the Family. In *Household and Family in Past Time,* ed, P. Laslett and R. Wall. Cambridge: Cambridge University Press, 1–89.

——— 1978. The Stem-Family Hypothesis and Its Privileged Position. In *Statistical Studies of Historical Social Structure,* ed. K. W. Wachter, E. A. Hammel, and P. Laslett. New York: Academic Press, 89–112.

——— 1981. Age at Menarche in Europe since the Eighteenth Century. In *Marriage and Fertility,* ed. R. I. Rotberg and T. K. Rabb. Princeton, NJ: Princeton University Press, 285–300.

——— 1983. Family and Household as Work Group and Kin Group: Areas of Traditional Europe Compared. In *Family Forms in Historic Europe,* ed. R. Wall, J. Robin, and P. Laslett. Cambridge: Cambridge University Press, 513–63.

——— 1984a. The Family as a Knot of Individual Interests. In *Households: Comparative and Historical Studies of the Domestic Group,* ed. Robert M. Netting, Richard R. Wilk, and Eric J. Arnould. Berkeley: University of California Press, 353–82.

——— 1984b. *The World We Have Lost: England before the Industrial Age.* 3rd ed. New York: Charles Scribner's Sons.

——— 1988. Family, Kinship and Collectivity as Systems of Support in Preindustrial Europe: A Consideration of the "Nuclear-hardship" Hypothesis. *Continuity and Change* 3: 153–76.

Lawless, Richard I. 1977. The Economy and Landscapes of Thessaly during Ottoman Rule. In *An Historical Geography of the Balkans,* ed. F. W. Carter. New York: Academic Press, 501–33.

Lawton, H. W. and P. J. Wilke. 1979. Ancient Agricultural Systems in Dry Regions. In *Agriculture in Semi-Arid Environments,* ed. A. E. Hall, G. H. Cannell, and H. W. Lawton. New York: Springer-Verlag, 1–44.

Le Bohec, S. 1985. Les philoi des rois antigonides. *Revue de Étude Grèce* 98: 93–124.

Le Bras, H. and Kenneth W. Wachter. 1978. Living Forebears in Stable Populations. In *Statistical Studies of Historical Social Structure,* ed. Kenneth W. Wachter, Eugene A. Hammel, and Peter Laslett. New York: Academic Press, 163–88.

Lee, R. D. 1977. Methods and Models for Analyzing Historical Series of Births, Deaths, and Marriages. In *Population Patterns in the Past,* ed. R. D. Lee. New York: Academic Press, 337–70.

Lees, Susan H. 1983. Environmental Hazards and Decision Making: Another Perspective from Human Ecology. In *Economic Anthropology: Topics and Theories,* ed. Sutti Ortiz. New York: University Press of America, 183–94.

Lekas, Padelis. 1988. *Marx on Classical Antiquity: Problems of Historical Methodology.* New York: St. Martin's Press.

Lemarchand, René. 1981. Comparative Political Clientism: Structure, Process and Optic. In *Political Clientism: Patronage and Development,* ed. S. N. Eisenstadt and René Lemarchand. London: Sage Publications, 7–32.

Leone, M. L. and M. Palkovicj. 1985. Ethnographic Inference and Analogy in Analyzing Prehistoric Diets. In *The Analysis of Prehistoric Diets,* ed. R. I. Gilbert, Jr. and J. H. Miekle. New York: Academic Press, 423–32.

Lepore, E. 1980. Grecia: Il Lavoro Urbano. In *Non-Slave Labor in the Graeco-Roman World,* ed. Peter Garnsey. Cambridge: Cambridge Philological Society, 26–9.

Le Roy Ladurie, Emmanuel. 1974. *The Peasants of Languedoc.* Trans. by John Day. Urbana: University of Illinois Press.

—— 1979. *Montaillou: The Promised Land of Error.* Trans. by Barbara Bray. New York: Vintage.

Levy, Harry L. 1956. Property Distribution by Lot in Present Day Greece. *Transactions of the American Philological Association* 87: 42–6.

Lewis, David M. 1973. The Athenian Rationes Centesimarum. In *Problème de la terre en Grèce ancienne,* ed. M. I. Finley. Paris: Mouton, 187–212.

Lewis, Naphtali. 1982. *Aphairesis* in Athenian Law and Custom. In *Symposion 1977. Vortraege sur griechischen und hellenistischen Rechtsgeschichte,* ed. Joseph Modrzejewski und Detlef Liebs. Koln: Bohlau Verlag, 161–78.

Lewis, Oscar. 1949. Plow Culture and Hoe Culture – A Study in Contrasts. *Rural Sociology* 14: 116–27.

Lianres, Olga F. 1984. Households among the Diola of Senegal: Should Norms Enter by the Front or the Back Door? In *Households: Comparative and Historical Studies of the Domestic Group,* ed. Robert M. Netting, Richard R. Wilk, and Eric J. Arnould. Berkeley: University of California Press, 407–45.

Liebenow, J. Gus. 1987. Food Self-Sufficiency in Malawi: Are Successes Transferable? In *Drought and Hunger in Africa: Denying Famine a Future,* ed. Michael H. Glantz. Cambridge: Cambridge University Press, 367–90.

Lintott, Andrew. 1982. *Violence, Civil Strife and Revolution in the Classical City.* London: Croom Helm.

Lipton, M. 1968. The Theory of the Optimizing Peasant. *The Journal of Development Studies* 4: 327–51.

Lis, Catherina and Hugo Soly. 1979. *Poverty and Capitalism in Preindustrial Europe.* Bristol: Harvester.

Littlewood, P. 1981. Patrons or Bigshots? Paternalism, Patronage and Clientist Welfare in Southern Italy. *Sociologia Ruralis* 21: 1–18.

Littman, Robert J. 1979. Kinship in Athens. *Ancient Society* 10: 5–32.

Litwak, E. and I. Szelwymi. 1969. Primary Group Structures and Functions: Kin, Neighbors, and Friends. *American Sociological Review* 34: 465–81.

Livvi-Bacci, M. 1981. On the Frequency of Remarriage in Nineteenth-Century Italy: Methods and Results. In *Marriage and Remarriage in Populations of the Past,* ed. J. Dupaquier, E. Helin, P. Laslett, M. Livi-Bacci, and S. Sogner. New York: Academic Press, 347–62.

Lockwood, W. G. 1975. *European Moslems. Economy and Ethnicity in Western Bosnia.* New York: Academic Press.

Lofchie, Michael F. 1987. The Decline of African Agriculture: An Internalistic Perspective. In *Drought and Hunger in Africa: Denying Famine a Future,* ed. Michael H. Glantz. Cambridge: Cambridge University Press, 85–110.

Lonsdale, J. and B. Berman. 1979. Coping with Contradictions. *Journal of African History* 20: 487–505.

Lopez, R. E. 1986. Structural Models of the Farm Household That Allow for Interdependent Utility and Profit-Maximization Decisions. In *Agricultural Household Models: Extensions, Applications, and Policy,* ed. I. Singhan, L. Squire, and J. Strauss. Baltimore, Md.: The Johns Hopkins Press, 306–26.

Lowry, S. Todd. 1987. *The Archaeology of Economic Ideas: The Classical Greek Tradition.* Durham, NC: Duke University Press.

Ludden, David. 1985. *Peasant History in South India.* Princeton, NJ: Princeton University Press.

Lynch, Joseph H. 1986. *Godparents and Kinship in Early Medieval Europe.* Princeton, NJ: Princeton University Press.

Malhotra, K. C. and M. Gadgil. 1988. Coping with Uncertainty in Food Supply: Case Studies among the Pastoral and Non-pastoral Nomads of Western India. In *Coping with Uncertainty in Food Supply*, ed. I. de Garine and G. A. Harrison. Oxford: Clarendon, 379–404.

Maraspini, A. L. 1968. *The Study of an Italian Village*. Paris: Mouton.

Marinovich, I. 1962. The Socio-Political Struggle and the Use of Mercenaries in 4th Century Greece in the Treatise of Aeneas Tacticus. *VDI* 49–77.

Martin, D. L., A. H. Goodman, and G. J. Armelagos. 1985. Skeletal Pathologies as Indicators of Quality and Quantity of Diet. In *The Analysis of Prehistoric Diets,* ed. R. I. Gilbert, Jr. and J. H. Miekle. New York: Academic Press, 227–80.

Martinez-Alier, Juan. 1971. *Labourers and Landowners in Southern Spain*. Totowa, NJ: Rowman and Littlefield.

Marx, Karl. 1976. [1867] *Capital I*. Harmondsworth: Penguin.

May, J. M. 1963. *The Ecology of Malnutrition in Five Countries of Eastern and Central Europe. East Germany, Poland, Yugoslavia, Albania, Greece.* London: Hafner Publishing Company, Studies in Medical Geography, No. 4.

Mayer, Adrian C. 1977. The Significance of Quasi-Groups in the Study of Complex Societies. In *Friends, Followers and Factions: A Reader in Political Clientism*, ed. Steffen W. Schmidt, Laura Guasti, Carl H. Landé, and James C. Scott. Berkeley: University of California Press, 43–54.

Mayer, J. 1974. Coping with Famine. *Foreign Affairs* 53: 98–120.

McAlpin, Michelle B. 1979. Dearth, Famine and Risk: The Changing Impact of Crop Failures in Western India, 1870–1920. *Journal of Economic History* 31: 143–57.

―― 1983. *Subject to Famine: Food Crisis and Economic Change in Western India, 1860–1920*. Princeton, NJ: Princeton University Press.

―― 1987. Famine Relief Policy in India: Six Lessons for Africa. In *Drought and Hunger in Africa: Denying Famine a Future*, ed. Michael H. Glantz. Cambridge: Cambridge University Press, 391–414.

McCann, James. 1987a. *From Poverty to Famine in Northeast Ethiopia: A Rural History, 1900–1935*. Philadelphia, Pa.: University of Pennsylvania Press.

―― 1987b. The Social Impact of Drought in Ethiopia: Oxen, Households and Some Implications for Rehabilitation. In *Drought and Hunger in Africa: Denying Famine a Future*, ed. Michael H. Glantz, Cambridge: Cambridge University Press, 245–68.

McCloskey, Donald N. 1972. The Enclosure of Open Fields: Preface to a Study of its Impact on the Efficiency of English Agriculture in the Eighteenth Century. *Journal of Economic History* 32: 15–35.

―― 1976. English Open Fields as Behavior towards Risk. *Research in*

Economic History 1: 124–70.

McCloskey, Donald N. 1977. Fenoaltea On Open Fields: A Comment. *Explorations in Economic History* 14: 402–5.

MacCromack, G. 1976. Reciprocity. *Man* 11: 89–104.

MacDowell, Douglas M. 1989. The *Oikos* in Athenian Law. *Classical Quarterly* 39: 10–21.

Macfarlane, Alan. 1970. *The Family Life of Ralph Josselin: An Essay in Historical Anthropology*. Cambridge: Cambridge University Press.

McGrew, William. 1985. *Land and Revolution in Modern Greece. The Transformation in the Tenure of Land from Ottoman to Independence*. Kent, OH: Kent State University Press.

McInnis, R. M. 1977. Childbearing and Land Availability: Some Evidence from Individual Household Data. In *Population Patterns in the Past*, ed. R. D. Lee. New York: Academic Press, 201–28.

McIntosh, Majorie K. 1988. Local Responses to the Poor in Late Medieval and Tudor England. *Continuity and Change* 3: 209–46.

McNall, Scott G. 1974. *The Greek Peasant*. Washington DC: American Sociological Association.

McNeill, William H. 1957. *Greece: American Aid in Action, 1947–1956*. New York: The Twentieth Century Fund.

Medick, Hans. 1976. The Proto-Industrial Family Economy: The Structural Function of Household and Family during the Transition from Peasant Society to Industrial Capitalism. *Social History* 3: 291–316.

Meiggs, R. 1972. *The Athenian Empire*. Oxford: Clarendon Press.

—— 1982. *Trees and Timber in the Ancient Mediterranean World*. Oxford: Oxford University Press.

—— and David Lewis. 1969. *A Selction of Greek Historical Inscriptions to the End of the Fifth Century BC*. Oxford: Clarendon Press.

Meikle, Scott. 1979. Aristotle and the Political Economy of the Polis. *Journal of Hellenic Studies* 79: 57–73.

Mendels, F. 1986. Family Forms in Historic Europe. *Social History* 11: 81–7.

Metochis, C. 1980. Irrigation of Lucerne under Semi-Arid Conditions. *Irrigation Science* 1: 247–52.

Migdal, Joel S. 1982. Capitalist Penetration in the Nineteenth Century: Creating Conditions for New Patterns of Social Control. In *Power and Protest in the Countryside: Studies of Rural Unrest in Asia, Europe and Latin America*, ed. Robert P. Weller and Scott E. Guggenheim. Durham, NC: Duke Unversity Press, 57–74.

Migeotte, L. 1984. *L'Emprunt Public dans les cités grecques. Recueil des documents et analyse critique*. Paris: Les Belles Lettres.

Mikalson, Jon D. 1983. *Athenian Popular Religion*. Chapel Hill: University of North Carolina Press.

Miller, Harvey F. 1984. The Practical and Economic Background to the

Greek Mercenary Explosion. *Greece and Rome* 31: 153–9.

Miller, R. A. 1974. Are Familists Amoral? A Test of Banfield's Amoral Familism Hypothesis in a South Italian Village. *American Ethnologist* 1: 515–35.

Millett, Paul. 1983. Maritime Loans and the Structure of Credit in Fourth-Century Athens. In *Trade and Politics in the Ancient Economy*, ed. Keith Hopkins, Peter Garnsey, and C. R. Whittaker. Berkeley: University of California Press, 36–52.

—— 1984. Hesiod and His World. *Proceedings of the Cambridge Philological Society* 210: 84–116.

Milthorpe, F. L. and J. Moorby. 1979, 2nd edn; 1974, 1st edn *An Introduction to Crop Physiology*. Cambridge: Cambridge University Press.

Minnis, P. E. 1985. *Social Adaptation to Food Stress. A Prehistoric Southwestern Example*. Chicago, Ill.: University of Chicago Press.

Mintz, Sidney and Eric R. Wolf. 1971. Ritual Co-Parenthood (*compadrazgo*). In *Kinship*, ed. Jack Goody. Harmondsworth: Penguin, 346–71.

Miskimin, Harry A. 1977. *The Economy of Late Renaissance Europe 1460–1600*. Cambridge: Cambridge University Press.

Modell, John and Tamara K. Hareven. 1978. Transitions: Patterns of Timing. In *Transitions: The Family and the Life Course in Historical Perspective*, ed. Tamara K. Hareven. New York: Academic Press, 245–69.

Montgomery, Hugo. 1986. "Merchants Fond of Corn": Citizens and Foreigners in the Athenian Grain Trade. *Symbolae Osloenses* 61: 43–61.

Moore Jr., Barrington. 1966. *Social Origins of Dictatorship and Democracy: Lord and Peasant in the Making of the Modern World*. Boston, Mass. Beacon Press.

Moretti, Luigi. 1966. Epigraphica. *Rivista di Filologia e di Istruzione Classica* 94: 290–301.

Morpeth, N. A. 1982. Aristotle, Plato, and Self-Sufficiency. Ancient and Modern Controversy in Economic History and Theory. *Ancient Society* 12: 34–6.

Morris, Ian. 1986a. The Use and Abuse of Homer. *Classical Antiquity* 5: 81–129.

—— 1986b. Gift and Commodity in Archaic Greece. *Man* 21: 1–17.

Morrison, John S. and R. T. Williams. 1968. *Greek Oared Ships 990–322 BC*. Cambridge: Cambridge University Press.

Morrison, John S. and John F. Coates. 1986. *The Athenian Triereme: The History and Reconstruction of an Ancient Greek Warship*. Cambridge: Cambridge University Press.

Mosse, Claude. 1983. The "World of the Emporium" in the Private Speeches of Demosthenes. In *Trade and Politics in the Ancient Economy*, ed. Keith Hopkins, Peter Garnsey, and C. R. Whittaker. Berkeley: University of California Press, 53–62.

Murray, William M. 1984. The Ancient Dam of the Mytikas Valley. *American Journal of Archaeology* 88: 195–203.

Mylonas, George. 1961. *Eleusis and the Eleusian Mysteries.* Princeton, NJ: Princeton University Press.

Myrick. D. C. and L. A. Witucki. 1971. *How Greece Developed Its Agriculture, 1947–1967.* Washington DC: USDA Economic Research Service.

Neale, Walter C. 1959. The Market in Theory and History. In *Trade and Market in the Early Empires: Economies in History and Theory,* ed. Karl Polanyi, Conrad M. Arensberg, and Harry W. Pearson. Glencoe, Ill.: The Free Press, 357–72.

—— and Anne Mayhew. 1983. Polanyi, Institutional Economics, and Economic Anthropology. In *Economic Anthropology: Topics and Theories,* ed. Sutti Ortiz. New York: University Press of America, 11–20.

Netting, Robert M. 1981. *Balancing on an Alp: Ecological Change and Continuity in a Swiss Mountain Community.* Cambridge: Cambridge University Press.

—— 1982. Some Home Truths on Household Size and Wealth. In *Archaeology of the Household: Building a Prehistory of Domestic Life,* ed. Richard R. Wilk and Willam J. Rathie, New York: *American Behavioral Scientist,* vol. 25, 641–62.

—— Richard R. Wilk, and Eric J. Arnould 1984. Introduction. In *Households: Comparative and Historical Studies of the Domestic Group,* ed. Robert M. Netting, Richard R. Wilk, and Eric J. Arnould, Berkeley: University of California Press, iii–xxiii.

Newcomer, Peter J. 1977. Toward a Scientific Treatment of "Exploitation": A Critique of Dalton. *American Anthropologist* 79: 114–19.

—— and Hymie Rubenstein. 1975. Peasant Exploitation: A Reply to Dalton. *American Anthropologist* 77: 337–8.

Nicholls, W. H. 1970. Development in Agrarian Economies: The Role of Agricultural Surplus, Population Pressures, and Systems of Land Tenure. In *Subsistence Agriculture and Economic Development,* ed. C. Wharton. Chicago, Ill.: Aldine, 296–319.

Noland, Susan. 1980. Dispute Settlement and Social Organization in Two Iranian Communities. *Anthropological Quarterly* 53: 190–201.

Nunti, Hugo G. and Betty Bell. 1980. *Ritual Kinship: The Structure and Historical Development of the Compadrazgo System in Rural Tlaxcala.* Princeton, NJ: Princeton University Press.

Okigbo, B. N. 1980. The Importance of Mixed Stands in Tropical Agriculture. In *Opportunities for Increasing Crop Yields,* R. G. Hurd, P. V. Biscoe, and C. Dennis. London: Pitman Advanced Publishing Program, 233–45.

Oldenziel, Ruth. 1987. The Historiography of Infanticide in Antiquity: A Literature Stillborn. In *Sexual Asymmetry: Studies in Ancient Society*, ed. Josine Blok and Peter Mason. Amsterdam: Gieben, 87–108.

Orenstein, Henry. 1980. Asymmetrical Reciprocity: A Contribution to the Theory of Political Legitimacy: *Current Anthropology* 21: 69–91.

O'Neill, Brian Juan. 1987. *Social Inequality in a Portuguese Hamlet: Land, Late Marriage, and Bastardy, 1870–1978*. Cambridge: Cambridge University Press.

Ormerod, Henry A. 1924. *Piracy in the Ancient World. An Essay in Mediterranean History*. Liverpool: University of Liverpool Press.

Ortiz, Sutti. 1980. Forecasts, Decisions, and the Farmer's Response to Uncertain Environment. In *Agricultural Decision Making: Anthropological Contribution to Rural Development*, ed. Peggy F. Barlett. New York: Academic Press, 177–202.

—— 1983. What is Decision Analysis About? The Problem of Formal Representations. In *Economic Anthropology: Topics and Theories*, ed. Sutti Ortiz. New York: University Press of American, 249–300.

Osborne, Robin. 1985. *Demos: The Discovery of Classical Attika*. Cambridge: Cambridge University Press.

—— 1987. *Classical Landscape with Figures: The Ancient Greek City and its Countryside*. London: George Philip.

—— 1988. Social and Economic Implications of the Leasing of Land and Property in Classical and Hellenistic Greece. *Chiron* 18: 279–323.

O'Shea, J. 1981. Coping with Scarcity: Exchange and Social Storage. In *Economic Archaeology*, ed. A. Sheridan and G. Bailey. Oxford: BAR no. 96, 167–83.

Padgug, R. A. 1975. Classes and Society in Classical Greece. *Arethusa* 8: 85–118.

Palmer, Robin and Niel Parsons. 1977. *The Roots of Rural Poverty in Central and Southern Africa*. Berkeley: University of California Press.

Panayiotopoulos, Vasili. 1985. *Plithisomos kai Ikismi tis Peloponnisoy 13os–18os Eonas*. Athens: Emboriki Trapeza tis Ellados.

Panayiotous, G. S. and S. Papachristodoulou. 1983. *Agroeconomic Analysis of Farms in the North-West Region of Cyprus (Khrysokhou Project Area)*. Nicosia: Agricultural Research Institute, Miscellaneous Reports, 8.

Parke, Herbert W. 1933. *Greek Mercenary Soldiers from the Earliest Times to the Battle of Ipsus*. Oxford: Clarendon Press.

Parker, Robert. 1983. *Miasma: Pollution and Purification in Early Greek Religion*. Oxford: Oxford University Press.

Parmalee, P. W. 1985. Identification and Interpretation of Archaeologically Derived Remains. In *The Analysis of Prehistoric Diets*, ed. R. I. Gilbert, Jr. and J. H. Miekle. New York: Academic Press, 61–96.

Parrack, Dwain W. 1981. Ecosystems and Famine. In *Famine: Its Causes, Effects and Management*, ed. John R. K. Robson. London: Gordon and

Breach, 41–9.

Parry, Martin L. 1978. *Climatic Change, Agriculture and Settlement.* Kent: Dawson and Sons.

—— 1981. Climatic Change and the Agricultural Frontier: A Research Strategy. In *Climate and History: Studies in Past Climates and Their Impact on Man,* ed. Thomas M. L. Wigley, Michael J. Ingram, and George Farmer. Cambridge: Cambridge University Press, 319–36.

Patterson, Cynthia. 1985. "Not Worth the Rearing": The Causes of Infant Exposure in Ancient Greece. *Transactions of the American Philological Association* 115: 103–23.

Paul, A. A. and D. A. T Southgate. 1983. *McCance and Widdowson's The Composition of Foods.* Oxford: Elsevier/North Holland Biomedical Press.

Payiatas, A. and S. Papachristodoulou. 1973. *Economics of Wheat and Barley Production in Cyprus.* Nicosia: Agricultural Research Institute, Agricultural Economics Report, No. 1.

Payne, P. and E. Dowler. 1980. Crop Conservation and the Third World: Famine and Plenty. In *Post Harvest Food Conservation,* ed. A. Herzka. Progress in Food and Nutrition Science, 4, 123–6.

Pearce, R. 1983. Sharecropping: Towards a Marxist View. *Journal of Peasant Studies* 2–3: 42–70.

Pearson, Lionel. 1962. *Popular Ethics in Ancient Greece.* Stanford, Calif.: Stanford University Press.

Pečirka, Jan. 1973. Homestead Farms in Classical and Hellenistic Hellas. In *Problèmes de la terre en Grece ancienne,* ed. M. I. Finley. Paris: Mouton, 113–49.

Pedlow, Gregory W. 1982. Marriage, Family Size and Inheritance among Hessian Nobles, 1650–1900. *Journal of Family History* 7: 333–52.

Pelto, Gretel. 1987. Social Class and Diet in Contemporary Mexico. In *Food and Evolution: Toward a Theory of Human Food Habits,* ed. Marvin Harris and E. B. Ross. Philadelphia, Penn.: Temple University Press, 517–40.

Pennington, Jean A. T. and Helen Nichols Church. 1985. *Bowes and Church's Food Values of Portions Commonly Used,* 14th edn. New York: Harper and Row.

Pepelasis, A. A and P. A. Yotopoulos. 1962. *Surplus Labor in Greek Agriculture 1953–1960.* Athens: Center for Economic Research.

Perisynakis, Ioannis. 1986. Hesiod's Treatment of Wealth. *Metis* 1: 97–119.

Pertev, Rashid. 1986. A New Model for Sharecropping and Peasant Economy. *Journal of Peasant Studies* 14: 27–49.

Peterson, Rudolph F. 1965. *Wheat: Botany, Cultivation, Utilization.* London: L. Hill Books.

Pfister, F. 1951. *Die Reisenbilder des Herakleides.* Wien: Rohrer.

Piker, S. 1966. The Image of the Limited Good: Comments of an Excercise in Description and Interpretation. *American Anthropologist* 68: 202–11.

Pingle, U. 1988. Central Indian Tribal Society Under Stress of Modern Socioeconomic Pressure: Strategies to Face the Challenge. In *Coping with Uncertainty in Food Supply*, ed. I. de Garine and G. A. Harrison. Oxford: Oxford University Press, 405–17.

Pitt-Rivers, Julian. 1973. The Kith and the Kin. In *The Character of Kinship*, ed. Jack Goody. Cambridge: Cambridge University Press, 89–106.

—— 1976. Ritual Parenthood in the Mediterranean: Spain and the Balkans. In *Mediterranean Family Structure*, ed. J. G. Peristiany, Cambridge: Cambridge University Press, 317–34.

Plakans, Andrejs. 1984. *Kinship in the Past. An Anthropology of European Family Life, 1500–1900*. Oxford: Basil Blackwell.

—— 1987. Interaction between the Household and the Kin Group in the Eastern European Past: Posing the Problem. In *Family History of the Crossroads*, ed. Tamara Hareven and Andrejs Plakans, Princeton, NJ: Princeton University Press, 1963–75.

Polanyi, Karl. 1957a. The Economy as Instituted Process. In *Trade and Market in the Early Empires: Economies in History and Theory*, ed. Karl Polanyi, Conrad M. Arensberg, and Harry W. Pearson. Glencoe, Ill.: The Free Press, 243–69.

—— 1957b. Aristotle Discovers the Economy. In *Trade and Market in the Early Empires*, 64–97.

Pomeroy, Sarah B. 1975. *Goddesses, Whores, Wives, and Slaves: Women in Classical Antiquity*. New York: Schocken Books.

—— 1983. Infanticide in Hellenistic Greece. in *Images of Women in Antiquity*, ed. a. Cameron and A. Kuhrt. London: Croom Helm, 207–20.

—— 1984. *Women in Hellenistic Egypt*. New York: Schocken Books.

Popkin, Samuel L. 1979. *The Rational Peasant. The Political Economy of Rural Society in Vietnam*. Berkeley: University of California Press.

Post, John D. 1977. *The Last Great Subsistence Crisis in the Western World*. Baltimore, Md.: The Johns Hopkins University Press.

—— 1985. *Food Shortage, Climatic Variability, and Epidemic Disease in Preindustrial Europe: The Mortality Peak in the Early 1740s*. Ithaca, NY: Cornell University Press.

Postan, M. M. 1966. Medieval Agrarian Society in Its Prime: England. In *The Cambridge Economic History of Europe*, ed. M. M. Postan, Cambridge: Cambridge University Press.

Pound, John. 1971. *Poverty and Vagrancy in Tudor England*. London: Longman.

Pounder, Robert L. 1983. A Hellensitic Arsenal at Athens. *Hesperia* 52:

233–56.

Powell, John Duncan. 1977. Peasant Society and Clientelist Politics. In *Friends, Followers and Factions: A Reader in Political Clientism,* ed. Steffen W. Schmidt, Laura Guasti, Carl H. Landé, and James C. Scott. Berkeley: University of California Press, 147–61.

Powell, S. 1985. The Analysis of Dental Wear and Carries for Dietary Reconstruction. In *The Analysis of Prehistoric Diets,* ed. R. I. Gilbert, Jr. and J. H. Miekle. New York: Academic Press, 307–38.

Price, Sally. 1978. Reciprocity and Social Distance: A Reconsideration. *Ethnology* 17: 339–50.

Pritchett, W. K. 1953. The Attic Stelai, Part I. *Hesperia* 22: 225–99.

—— 1956. The Attic Stelai, Part II. *Hesperia* 25: 178–317.

Pullan, Brian. 1988. Support and Redeem: Charity and Poor Relief in Italian Cities from the 14th c to the 17th c. *Continuity and Change* 3: 177–208.

Purcell, Susan Kaufman. 1981. Mexico: Clientism, Corporatism and Political Stability. In *Political Clientism: Patronage and Development*, ed. S. N. Eisenstadt and Rene Lemarchand. London: Sage Publications, 191–216.

Pusey, Nathan Marsh. 1940. Alcibiades and *to Philopoli. Harvard Studies in Classical Philology* 51: 215–31.

Qviller, Bjorn. 1981. The Dynamics of Homeric Society. *Symbloae Osloenses* 56: 109–56.

Rabb, Theodore K. 1983. Climate and Society in History: A Research Agenda. In *Social Science Research and Climate Change: An Interdisciplinary Appraisal,* ed. R. S. Chen and S. H. Schneider, Boston: D. Reidel, 62–76.

Rackham, Oliver. 1983. Observations on the Historical Ecology of Boiotia. *Annual of the British School at Athens* 78: 291–352.

Raepsaet, George. 1971. Les motivations de la natalité Athènes aux Ve et IVe siècles avant notre. *L'Antiquite Classique* 40: 80–110.

—— 1973. À Propos de l'utilisation de statistique en démographie grecqu. Le nombre d'enfants par famille. *L'Antiquité Classique* 42: 536–43.

Rathje, William J. and Randall H. McGuire. 1982. Rich Men . . . Poor Men. In *Archaeology of the Household: Building a Prehistory of Domestic Life,* ed. Richard R. Wilk and William J. Rathje. New York: *America Behavioral Scientist,* vol. 25, 705–15.

Razi, Zvi. 1984. The Erosion of the Family–Land Bond in the Late Fourteenth and Fifteenth Centuries: A Methodological Note. In *Land, Kinship, and the Life Cycle*, ed. Richard M. Smith. Cambridge: Cambridge University Press, 295–304.

Reese, David S. 1987. A Bone Assemblage at Corinth of the Second Century after Christ. *Hesperia* 56: 255–74.

Reid Jr, Joseph D. 1987. The Theory of Sharecropping: Occam's Razor and Economic Analysis. *History of Political Economy* 19: 551–69.

Rheubottam, David B. 1988. "Sisters First": Betrothal Order and Age at Marriage in Fifteenth-Century Ragusa. *Journal of Family History* 13: 359–76.

Rhodes, M. C. 1980. The Physiological Basis for the Conservation of Food Crops. In *Post Harvest Food Conservation,* ed. A. Herzka. Progress in Food and Nutrition Science, 4, 11–20.

Rhodes, Peter J. 1981. *Commentary on the Aristotelian Athenaion Politeia.* Oxford: Clarendon.

—— 1982. Problems in Athenian *Eisphora* and Liturgies. *American Journal of Ancient Historians* 7: 1–19.

Richards, Paul. 1986. *Coping with Hunger: Hazard and Experiment in an African Rice-Farming System.* Boston, Mass.: Allen & Unwin.

Rickman, Geoffrey. 1971. *Roman Granaries and Store Buildings.* Cambridge: Cambridge University Press.

—— 1980. *Corn Supply of Ancient Rome.* Oxford: Clarendon.

Ring, Richard R. 1979. Early Medieval Peasant Households in Central Italy. *Journal of Family History* 4: 2–23.

Roberts, Jennifer T. 1986. Aristocratic Democracy: The Perseverance of Timocratic Principles in Athenian Government. *Athenaeum* 3–4: 355–70.

Robinson, David M. 1934. New Inscriptions from Olynthus, 1934. *Transactions of the American Philological Society* 65: 103–37.

—— 1941. *Excavations at Olynthus X. Metal and Minor Miscellaneous Finds, An Original Contribution to Greek Life.* Baltimore, Md.: The Johns Hopkins University Press.

—— 1946. *Excavations at Olynthus XII. Domestic and Public Architecture.* Baltimore, Md.: The Johns Hopkins University Press.

—— and J. Walter Graham. 1938. *Excavations at Olynthus VIII. The Hellenic House.* Baltimore, Md.: The Johns Hopkins University Press.

Roe, J. and T. Graham-Tomasi. 1986. Yield Risk in a Dynamic Model of the Agricultural Household. In *Agricultural Household Models: Extensions, Applications, and Policy,* ed. I. Singh, L. Squire, and J. Strauss. Baltimore, Md.: The Johns Hopkins Press, 255–76.

Roeder, Philip G. 1984. Legitimacy and Peasant Revolution: An Alternative to Moral Economy. *Peasant Studies* 11: 149–68.

Roosevelt, Anna. 1987. The Evolution of Human Subsistence. In *Food and Evolution: Toward a Theory of Human Food Habits,* ed. Marvin Harris and E. B. Ross. Philadelphia, Pa.: Temple University Press, 565–78.

Root, Hilton L. 1987. *Peasant and King in Burgundy: Agrarian Foundations of French Absolutism.* Berkeley: University of California Press.

Rose, J. E., K. W. Condon, and A. H. Goodman. 1985. Diet and Dentition: Developmental Disturbances. In *The Analysis of Prehistoric*

Diets, ed. R. I. Gilbert, Jr. and J. H. Miekle. New York: Academic Press, 281–306.

Rostovtzeff, Michael. 1923. Notes on the Economic Policy of the Pergamene Kings. In *Anatolian Studies Presented to Sir William Mitchell Ramsay,* ed. W. H. Buckler and W. M. Calder. Manchester: Manchester University Press, 359–90.

—— 1941. *The Social and Economic History of the Hellenistic World.* Oxford: Clarendon Press.

Roussel, Denis. 1976. *Tribu et cité.* Paris: Annales Litteraires de l'Université de Besançon.

Roy, J. 1967. The Mercenaries of Cyrus. *Historia* 16: 287–323.

Ruggles, Steven. 1987. *Prolonged Connections: The Rise of the Extended Family in Nineteenth-Century England and America.* Madison: University of Wisconsin Press.

Ruschenbusch, Edouard. 1984a. Die Bevolkerungszahl Griechenland im 5 und 4 Jh. v. Chr. *Zeitschrift für Papyrologie und Epigraphie* 56:55–7.

—— 1984b. Modell Amorgos. In *Aux Origines de l'Hellénisme le Crète et la Grèce. Hommages à Henri van Effenterre.* Paris: Publications de la Sorbonne, 265–71.

—— 1985. Ein Beitrag zur Leiturgie und zur Eisphora. Die Hohe des Vermogens, das die Pflicht zur Leistung einer Leiturgie und zur Zahlung der Eisphora begrundete. *Zeitschrift für Papyrologie und Epigrahie* 59: 237–40.

Russell, Susan D. 1987. Middlemen and Moneylending: Relations of Exchange in a Highland Philippine Economy. *Journal of Anthropological Research* 43: 139–61.

Rutman, Darrett B. 1986. History and Anthropology: Clio's Dalliances. *Historical Methods* 19: 120–23.

—— and Anita H. Rutman. 1984. *A Place in Time: Explicatus.* New York: W. W. Norton and Company.

—— 1984. *A Place in Time: Middlesex Country, Virginia 1650–1750.* New York: W. W. Norton and Company.

Sahlins, Marshall. 1972. *Stone Age Economics.* Chicago, Ill.: Aldine.

Saller, Richard P. 1987. Men's Age at Marriage and its Consequences in the Roman Family. *Classical Philology* 82: 21–34.

Salmanzadeh, Cyrus. 1980. *Agricultural Change and Rural Society in Southern Iran.* Cambridge: Middle Eastern and North African Studies Press Ltd.

Salmon, John B. 1984. *Wealthy Corinth: A History of the City to 338 B. C.* Oxford: Clarendon Press.

Salviat, F. and C. Vatin. 1974. Le Cadastre de Larissa. *Bulletin de Correspondance Hellénique* 98: 247–62.

Samuel, A. E. 1983. *From Egypt to Alexandria: Hellenism and Social Goals in Ptolemaic Egypt.* Louvain.

Sandars, G. D. R. 1985. Reassessing Ancient Populations. *Annual of British School at Athens* 80: 251–62.

Sarti, Roland. 1985. *Long Live the Strong: A History of Rural Society in the Apennine Mountains*. Amherst: University of Massachusetts Press.

Sauerwein, Freidrich. 1968. *Landschaft, Siedlung und Wirtschaft Inner-messeniens (Griechenland)*. Frankfurt: Frankfurter Wirtschafts- und Sozialgeographische Schriften.

—— 1971. *Die moderne Argolis. Probleme des Strukturwandels in einer griechischen Landschaft*. Frankfurt: Frankfurter Wirtschafts- und Sozial-geographische Schriften.

Saul, Mahir. 1987. The Organization of a West African Grain Market. *American Anthropologist* 89: 74–95.

Saxena, M. C. 1982. Agronomoy of Lentils. In *Lentils,* ed. C. Webb and G. Hawtin. London: Commonwealth Agricultural Bureaux and the International Center for Agricultural Research in the Dry Areas, 111–29.

Schaps, D. M. 1979. *The Economic Rights of Women in Ancient Greece*. Edinburgh: University of Edinburgh Press.

Schlegal, Alice and Rohn Eloul. 1988. Marriage Transactions: Labor, Property, and Status. *American Anthropologist* 90: 291–309.

Schmidt, Steffen W. 1977. The Transformation of Clientism in Rural Columbia. In *Friends, Followers and Factions: A Reader in Political Clientism,* ed. Steffen W. Schmidt, Laura Guasti, Carl H. Landé, and James C. Scott. Berkeley: University of California Press, 305–22.

Schneider, Jane. 1969. Family Patrimonies and Economic Behavior in Western Sicily. *Anthropological Quarterly* 42: 109–29.

Schneider, Peter. 1969. Honor and Conflict in a Sicilian Town. *Anthropological Quarterly* 42: 130–53.

—— Jane Schneider, and Edward Hansen. 1977. Modernization and Development: The Role of Regional Elites and Noncorporate Groups in the European Mediterranean. In *Friends, Followers and Factions: A Reader in Political Clientism,* ed. Steffen W. Schmidt, Laura Guasti, Carl H. Landé, and James C. Scott. Berkeley: University of California Press, 467–82.

Schofield, Richard and E. A. Wrigley. 1981. Remarriage Intervals and the Effect of Marriage Order on Fertility. In *Marriage and Remarriage in Populations of the Past,* ed. J. Dupaquier, E. Helin, P. Laslett, M. Livi-Bacci, and S. Sogner. New York: Academic Press, 211–28.

Schofield, Roger. 1986. Did Mothers Really Die? Three Centuries of Maternal Mortality in "The World We Have Lost". In *The World We Have Gained: Histories of Population and Social Structure,* ed. Lloyd Bonfield, Richard M. Smith, and Keith Wrightson. Oxford: Basil Blackwell, 231–60.

Schumann, Debra A. 1985. Family Labor Resources and Household

Economic Strategy in a Mexican Ejido. *Research in Economic Anthropology* 7: 277–87.

Schwimmer, E. 1979. Reciprocity and Structure: A Semiotic Analysis of Some Orokaiva Exchange Data. *Man* 14: 271–85.

Scott, Earl P. 1984a. Introduction: Life and Poverty in the Savanna-Sahel Zones. In *Life Before the Drought,* ed. Earl P. Scott. Boston, Mass.: Allen & Unwin, 1–28.

—— 1984b. Life Before the Drought: A Human Ecological Perspective. In *Life Before the Drought,* 49–76.

Scott, James C. 1976. *The Moral Economy of the Peasant: Rebellion and Subsistence in Southeast Asia.* New Haven, Conn.: Yale University Press.

—— 1977a. Patronage of Exploitation?. In *Patrons and Clients in Mediterranean Societies,* ed. Ernest Gellner and James Waterbury. London: Duckworth, 21–40.

—— 1977b. Patron-Client Politics and Political Change in Southeast Asia. In *Friends, Followers and Factions: A Reader in Political Clientism,* ed. Steffen W. Schmidt, Laura Guasti, Carl H. Landé, and James C. Scott. Berkeley: University of California Press, 123–46.

—— 1985. *Weapons of the Weak: Everyday Forms of Peasant Resistance.* New Haven, Conn.: Yale University Press.

—— and Benedict J. Kerkvliet. 1977. How Traditional Rural Patrons Lose Legitimacy: A Theory with Special Reference to Southeast Asia. In *Friends, Followers and Factions: A Reader in Political Clientism,* ed. Steffen W. Schmidt, Laura Guasti, Carl H. Landé and James C. Scott. Berkeley: University of California Press, 439–57.

Seavoy, Ronald E. 1986. *Famine in Peasant Societies.* Westport, Conn.: Greenwood Press.

Segalen, Martine. 1984. Nuclear Is Not Independent: Organization of the Household in the Pays Bigouden Sud in the Nineteenth and Twentieth Centuries. In *Households: Comparative and Historical Studies of the Domestic Group,* ed. Robert M. Netting, Richard R. Wilk, and Eric J. Arnould. Berkeley: University of California Press, 163–86.

—— 1987. Life-Course Patterns and Peasant Culture in France: A Critical Assessment. In *Family History at the Crossroads,* ed. Tamara Hareven and Andrejs Plakans. Princeton, NJ: Princeton University Press, 213–24.

Segre, A. 1934. Grano di Tessaglio a Coo. *Rivista di Filologia* 12: 169–93.

Semple, E. C. 1932. *The Geography of the Mediterranean Region: Its Relation to Ancient History.* London: Constable.

Sen, Amartya. 1977. Starvation and Exchange Entitlements: A General Approach and Its Application to the Great Bengal Famine. *Cambridge Journal of Economics* 1: 33–59.

—— 1980. Famine Mortality: A Study of the Bengal Famine of 1943. In

Peasants in History: Essays in Memory of Daniel Thorner, ed. Eric Hobsbawm and A. Thorner. Calcutta: Oxford University Press, 194–220.

Sen, Amartya. 1981. *Poverty and Famines: An Essay on Entitlement and Deprivation.* Oxford: Oxford University Press.

Shaw, Brent D. 1987. The Age of Roman Girls at Marriage: Some Reconsiderations. *Journal of Roman Studies* 77: 30–46.

Shaw, Timothy. 1987. Towards a Political Economy of the African Crisis: Diplomacy, Debates and Dialectics. In *Drought and Hunger in Africa: Denying Famine a Future,* ed. Michael H. Glantz. Cambridge: Cambridge University Press, 127–48.

Shear J., T. Leslie. 1975. The Athenian Agora: Excavations of 1973–1974. *Hesperia* 44: 331–74.

———— 1978. *Kallias of Sphettos and the Revolt of Athens in 186 B. C.* Hesperia Supp. 17.

Sherwin-White, Susan. 1978. *Ancient Cos: An Historical Study from the Dorian Settlement to the Imperial Period.* Gottingen: Vandenhoeck and Ruprecht.

Shipley, Graham. 1987. *A History of Samos 800–188 BC.* Oxford: Clarendon Press.

Shubik, Martin. 1987. *Game Theory in the Social Sciences: Concepts and Solutions.* Cambridge, Mass.: The MIT Press.

Sicular, T. 1986. Using a Farm-Household Model to Analyze Labor Allocation on a Chinese Collective Farm. In *Agricultural Household Models: Extensions, Applications, and Policy,* ed. I. Singh, L. Squire, and J. Strauss. Baltimore, Md.: The Johns Hopkins Press, 277–305.

Silverman, Sydel. 1966. At Ethnographic Approach to Social Stratification: Prestige in a Central Italian Community. *American Anthropologist* 68: 899–921.

———— 1968. Agricultural Organization, Social Structure and Values in Italy: Amoral Familism Reconsidered. *American Anthropologist* 70: 1–20.

———— 1970. Exploitation in Rural Central Italy: Structure and Ideology in Stratification Study. *Comparative Studies in Society and History* 12: 327–39.

———— 1975. *Three Bells of Civilization: The Life of an Italian Hill Town.* New York: Columbia University Press.

———— 1977. Patronage and Community–Nation Relationships in Central Italy. In *Friends, Followers and Factions: A Reader in Political Clientism,* ed. Steffen W. Schmidt, Laura Guasti, Carl H. Landé, and James C. Scott. Berkeley: University of California Press, 293–304.

———— 1981. Rituals of Inequality: Stratification and Symbol in Central Italy. In *Social Inequality: Comparative and Developmental Approaches,* ed. Gerald D. Berreman. New York: Academic Press, 163–81.

Silverman, Sydel. 1986. Anthropology and History: Understanding the Boundaries. *Historical Methods* 19: 123–6.

Simon, Erika. 1983. *Festivals of Attica: An Archaeological Commentary*. Madison: University of Wisconsin Press.

Simoni, Peter. 1979. Agricultural Change and Landlord–Tenant Relations in Nineteenth Century France: The Canton of Apt (Vaucluse). *Journal of Social History* 13: 115–35.

Singer, D. P. 1980. Post-Harvest Food Losses: World Overview. In *Post Harvest Food Conservation*, ed. A. Herzka. Progress in Food and Nutrition Science, 4, 3–9.

Singh, I., L. Squire, and J. Strauss. 1986a. The Basic Model: Theory, Empirical Results and Policy Conclusions. In *Agricultural Household Models: Extensions, Applications, and Policy*, ed. I. Singh, L. Squire, and J. Strauss. Baltimore, Md.: The Johns Hopkins Press, 17–47.

—— 1986b. Methodological Issues. In *Agricultural Household Models*, 48–70.

Singh, I. L. and J. Subramanian. 1986. Agricultural Household Modeling in a Multicrop Environment: Case Studies in Korea and Nigeria. In *Agricultural Household Models: Extensions, Applications, and Policy*, ed. I. Singh, L. Squire, and J. Strauss. Baltimore, Md.: The Johns Hopkins Press, 95–115.

Sinha, S. K. 1977. *Food Legumes: Distribution, Adaptibility, and Biology of Yield*. Rome: FAO Plant Production and Protection Paper, No. 3.

Sjöqvist, Eric. 1960. Excavations at Morgantina (Serra Orlando) 1959– Preliminary Report IV. *American Journal of Archaeology* 64: 125–36.

Skerman, P. J. 1977. *Tropical Forage Legumes*. Rome: FAO.

Skocpol, Theda. 1982. What Makes Peasants Revolutionary. In *Power and Protest in the Countryside: Studies of Rural Unrest in Asia, Europe and Latin America*, ed. Robert P. Weller and Scott E. Guggenheim. Durham: Duke University Press, 157–79.

Skydsgaard, Jens Erik. 1988. Transhumance in Ancient Greece. In *Pastoral Economies in Classical Antiquity*, ed. C. R. Whittaker. Cambridge: Cambridge Philosophical Society, 75–86.

Slack, Paul A. 1974. Vagrants and Vagrancy in England, 1598–1664. *Economic History Review* 27: 360–79.

Slaughter, Cliff and Charalambos Kasimis. 1986. Some Social-Anthropological Aspects of Boeotian Rural Society: A Field-Report. *Byzantine and Modern Greek Studies* 10: 103–60.

Sloan, Robert E. and Mary Ann Duncan. 1978. Zooarchaeology of Nichoria. In *Excavations at Nichoria in Southwest Greece*. Vol. 1. *Site, Environs and Techniques*, ed. George Rapp Jr. and S. E. Aschenbrenner. Minneapolis: University of Minnesota Press, 60–77.

Smartt, J. 1976. *Tropical Pulses*. London: Longman.

Smith Jr., C. E. 1985. Recovery Processing of Botanical Remains. In *The*

Analysis of Prehistoric Diets, ed. R. I. Gilbert, Jr. and J. H. Miekle. New York: Academic Press, 97–126.

Smith, C. V. 1969. *Meteorology and Grain Storage.* Geneva: World Meteorological Organization Technical Note No. 101.

Smith, Gavin. 1985. Reflections on the Social Relations of Simple Commodity Production. *Journal of Peasant Studies* 13: 99–108.

Smith, J. E. 1981. How First Marriage and Remarriage Markets Mediate the Effects of Declining Mortality and Fertility. In *Marriage and Remarriage in Populations of the Past,* ed. J. Dupaquier, E. Helin, P. Laslett, M. Livi-Bacci, and S. Sogner. New York: Academic Press, 229–46.

Smith, Richard M. 1984. Some Issues concerning Families and Their Property in Rural England 1250–1800. In *Land, Kinship, and the Life Cycle,* ed. Richard M. Smith. Cambridge: Cambridge University Press, 1–86.

Smith, V. E. and J. Strauss. 1986. Simulating the Rural Economy in a Subsistence Environment: Sierra Leone. In *Agricultural Household Models: Extensions, Applications, and Policy,* ed. I. Singh, L. Squire, and J. Strauss. Baltimore, Md.: The Johns Hopkins Press, 206–32.

Snaydon, R. W. and J. Elston. 1976. Flows, Cycles and Yields in Agricultural Ecosystems. In *Food Production and Consumption. The Efficiency of Human Food Chains and Nutrient Cycles,* ed. A. N. Duckham, G. W. Jones, and E. H. Roberts. Oxford: North-Holland Publishing Company, 43–60.

Snodgrass, Anthony. 1980. *Archaic Greece: The Age Of Experiment.* London: J. M. Dent and Sons.

—— 1987. *An Archaeology of Greece: The Present State and Future Scope of a Discipline.* Berkeley: University of California Press.

Snowden, Frank M. 1986. *Violence and Great Estates in the South of Italy. Apulia 1900–1922.* Cambridge: Cambridge University Press.

Spencer, J. E. and Norman R. Stewart. 1973. The Nature of Agricultural Systems. *Annals of the Association of American Geographers* 63: 529–44.

Spiertz, J. H. J. 1980. Grain Production of Wheat in Relating to Nitrogen, Weather and Diseases. In *Opportunities for Increasing Crop Yields,* ed. R. G. Hurd and C. Dennis. London: Pitman Advanced Publishing Program, 97–113.

Spitters, C. T. T. 1980. Competition Effects within Mixed Stands. In *Opportunities for Increasing Crop Yields,* ed. R. G. Hurd, P. V. Briscoe, and C. Dennis. London: Pitman Advanced Publishing Program, 219–31.

Springbord, P. 1986. Political Primordialism and Orientalism: Marx, Aristotle and the Myth of Gemeinschaft. *American Political Science Review* 80: 185–211.

Spurr, M. S. 1983. The Cultivation of Millet in Roman Italy. *Papers of the*

British School at Rome 51: 1–15.

Spurr, M. S. 1986. *Arable Cultivation in Roman Italy c. 200 B.C. – c. A.D. 100.* London: Society for the Promotion of Roman Studies.

Stanton, G. R. 1986. The Territorial Tribes of Korinth and Phleious. *Classical Antiquity* 5: 139–53.

Stark, B. L. and B. Voorhies (eds). 1978. *Prehistoric Cosatal Adaptations.* New York: Academic Press.

Starr, Chester G. 1979. An Overdose of Slavery. In *Essays on Ancient History. A Selection of Articles and Essays,* ed. Athrur Ferrill and Thomas Kelly. Leiden: E. J. Brill, 43–58.

Stone, Lawrence. 1981. Family History in the 1980s: Past Achievements and Future Trends. *Journal of Interdisciplinary History* 11: 51–87.

Strauss, Barry S. 1986. *Athens after the Peloponnesian War: Class, Faction and Policy 403–386 B. C.* Ithaca, NY: Cornell University Press.

Strauss, J. 1986a. The Theory and Comparative Statics of Agricultural Household Models. In *Agricultural Household Models: Extensions, Applications, and Policy,* ed. I. Singh, I. Squire, and J. Strauss. Baltimore, Md.: The Johns Hopkins Press, 71–94.

—— 1986b. Estimating the Determinants of Food Consumption and Caloric Availability in Rural Sierra Leone. In *Agricultural Household Models, 95–115.*

Styles, B. W. 1985. Reconstruction of Availability and Utilization of Food Resources. In *The Analysis of Prehistoric Diets,* ed. R. I. Gilbert Jr. and J. H. Miekle. New York: Academic Press, 21–60.

Surridge, B. J. 1930. *A Survey of Rural Life in Cyprus.* Nicosia: Government Printing Office.

Sutherland, D. 1981. Weather and the Peasantry of Upper Brittany, 1780–1789. In *Climate and History: Studies in Past Climates and Their Impact on Man,* ed. Thomas M. L. Wigley, Michael J. Ingram, and George Farmer. Cambridge: Cambridge University Press, 434–49.

Sweet-Escott, B. 1954. *Greece: A Political and Economic Survey.* London: Royal Institute of International Affairs.

Sweetman, John. 1978. Class-Based and Community-Based Ritual Organizations in Latin America. *Ethnology* 17: 425–38.

Thaxton, Ralph. 1982. Mao Zadong, Red *Misérables,* and the Moral Economy of Peasant Rebellion in Modern China. In *Power and Protest in the Countryside: Studies of Rural Unrest in Asia, Europe and Latin America,* ed. Robert P. Weller and Scott. E. Guggenheim, Durham: Duke University Press, 132–56.

Thompson, E. P. 1971. The Moral Economy of the English Crowd in the Eighteenth Century. *Past & Present* 50: 76–136.

—— 1975. *Whigs and Hunters: The Origin of the Black Act.* New York: Pantheon.

—— 1978. *The Poverty of Theory and Other Essays.* New York: Monthly

Review Press.

Thompson, Kenneth. 1963. *Farm Fragmentation in Greece*. Athens: Center of Economic Research, Research Monographs Series, No. 5.

Thomspon, W. E. 1972. Athenian Marriage Patterns: Remarriage. *California Studies in Classical Antiquity* 5: 211–25.

Tilly, Charles. 1975. Food Supply and Public Order in Modern Europe. In *The Formation of National States in Europe*, ed. Charles Tilly. Princeton, NJ: Princeton University Press, 380–455.

—— 1982. Routine Conflicts and Peasant Rebellions in Seventeenth-Century France. In *Power and Protest in the Countryside: Studies of Rural Unrest in Asia, Europe and Latin America*, ed. Robert P. Weller and Scott E. Guggenheim. Durham: Duke University Press, 13–41.

Tilly, L. 1983. Food Entitlement, Famine, and Conflict. *Journal of Interdisciplinary History* 14: 333–49.

Timmerman, Peter. 1981. *Vulnerability, Resilience and the Collapse of Society: A Review of Models and Possible Climatic Applications*. Toronto: Institute for Environmental Studies, University of Toronto.

Tod, Marcus N. 1932. *Sidelights on Greek History*. Oxford: Basil Blackwell.

Torry, William I. 1979. Anthropological Studies in Hazardous Environments: Past Trends and New Horizons. *Current Anthropology* 20: 511–40.

—— 1983. Anthropological Perspectives on Climate Change. In *Social Science Research and Climatic Change: An Interdisciplinary Appraisal*, ed. Robert S. Chen and Stephen Schneider. Boston, Mass.: D. Reidel, 208–27.

—— 1987. Evolution of Food Rationing Systems with Reference to African Group Farms in the Context of Drought. In *Drought and Hunger in Africa,* ed. Michael H. Glantz. Cambridge: Cambridge University Press, 323–48.

Tremolieres, J. 1963. Nutrition and Public Health. *World Review of Nutrition and Dietetics* 4: 1–24.

Uhlenberg, P. 1978. Changing Configurations of the Life Course. In *Transitions: The Family and the Life Course in Historical Perspectives*, ed. Tamara K. Hareven. New York: Academic Press, 65–98.

Van Apeldoorn, G. Jan. 1981. *Perspective on Drought and Famine in Nigeria*. London: George Allen & Unwin.

Van Gerven, Dennis P., and George J. Armelagos. 1983. "Farewell to Paleodemography"? Rumors of Its Death Have Been Exaggerated. *Journal of Human Evolution* 12: 353–60.

Van Soesbergen, P. G. 1983. Colonisation as a Solution to Social-Economic Problems in Fourth-Century Greece: A Confrontation of Isocrates with Xenophon. *Ancient Society* 14: 131–46.

Van Wersch, H. J. 1972. The Agricultural Economy. In *The Minnesota Messenia Expedition: Reconstructing a Bronze Age Regional Environment*, ed. William A. McDonald and G. R. Rapp. Minneapolis: University of Minnesota Press, 177–87.

Vaughn, Megan. 1982. Food Production and Family Labor in Southern Malawi: The Shire Highlands and Upper Shire Valley in the Early Colonial Period. *Journal of African History* 23: 351–64.

—— 1983. Which Family? Problems in the Reconstruction of the History of the Family as an Economic and Cultural Unit. *Journal of African History* 24: 275–84.

—— 1985. Famine Analysis and Family Relations: 1949 in Nyasaland. *Past & Present* 108: 177–205.

—— 1987. *The Story of an African Famine: Gender and Famine in Twentieth-Century Malawi*. Cambridge: Cambridge University Press.

Veyne, Paul. 1976. *Le Pain et le cirque: sociologic historigue d'un pluralisme politique*. Paris: Editions du Seuil.

Vinovskis, Maris. 1977. From Household Size to Life Course: Some Observations on Recent Trends in Family History. *American Behavioral Scientist* 21: 263–387.

von Szalay, A. and E. Boerhinger. 1937. *Die Hellenistischen Arsenale. Ausgrabgungun von Pergamon X.* Berlin: Walter de Gruyter.

Wachter, Kenneth W. and Peter Laslett. 1978. Measuring Patriline Extinction for Modelling Social Mobility in the Past. In *Statistical Studies of Historical Social Structure,* ed. Kenneth W. Wachter, Eugene A. Hammel, and Peter Laslett. New York: Academic Press, 113–37.

Wachter, Kenneth W., Eugene A. Hammel, and Peter Laslett (eds.). 1978. *Statistical Studies of Historical Social Structure*. New York: Academic Press.

Wade, Robert. 1971. Political Behaviour and World View in a Central Italian Village. In *Gifts and Poison: The Politics of Reputation,* ed. F. G. Bailey. Oxford: Basil Blackwell, 252–80.

Wagstaff, Malcom and Siv Augustson. 1982. Traditional Land Use. In *An Island Polity: The Archaeology of Exploitation in Melos,* ed. Colin Renfrew and Malcom Wagstaff. Cambridge: Cambridge University Press, 105–34.

Wagstaff, Malcolm, Siv Auguston and Clive Gamble. 1982. Alternative Subsistence Strategies. In *An Island Polity,* 172–80.

Wagstaff, Malcolm and John Cherry. 1982a. Settlement and Resources. In *An Island Polity,* 246–63.

—— 1982b. Settlement and Population Change. In *An Island Polity,* 136–55.

Wagstaff, Malcom and Clive Gamble. 1982. Island Resources and Limitations. In *An Island Polity,* 95–105.

Walbank, Frank W. 1981. *The Hellenistic World*. London: Fontana.

Walbank, Michael B. 1987. Athens Grants Citizenship to a Benefactor: IG II.2 398a + 438. *The Ancient History Bulletin* 1: 10–12.

Walcot, Peter. 1970. *Greek Peasants, Ancient and Modern: A Comparison of Social and Moral Values.* Manchester: Manchester University Press.

———— 1977. *Envy and the Greeks: A Study of Human Behaviour.* Warminster, Wilts.: Aris & Phillips Ltd.

Wales, Tim. 1984. Poverty, Poor Relief and the Life-Cycle: Some Evidence from Seventeenth Century Norfolk. In *Land, Kinship, and the Life Cycle,* ed. Richard M. Smith. Cambridge: Cambridge University Press, 351–404.

Wall, Richard. 1984. Real Property, Marriage and Children: The Evidence from Four Pre-industrial Communities. In *Land, Kinship, and the Life Cycle,* ed. Richard M. Smith. Cambridge: Cambridge University Press, 443–80.

———— 1986. Work, Welfare and the Family: An Illustration of the Adaptive Family Economy. In *The World We Have Gained: Histories of Population and Social Structure,* ed. Lloyd Bonfield, Richard M. Smith, and Keith Wrightson. Oxford: Basil Blackwell, 261–95.

Wallace, Michael B. 1970. Early Greek Proxenoi. *Phoenix* 24: 198–208.

Walter, John and Keith Wrightson. 1976. Dearth and the Social Order in Early Modern England. *Past & Present* 71: 22–42.

Wasserman, Mark. 1984. *Capitalists, Caciques, and Revolution: The Native Elite and Foreign Enterprise in Chihuahua, Mexico, 1854–1911.* Chapel Hill:University of North Carolina Press.

Wasserstrom, Robert. 1982. Indian Uprisings under Spanish Colonialism: Southern Mexico in 1712. In *Power and Protest in the Countryside: Studies of Rural Unrest in Asia, Europe and Latin America,* ed. Robert P. Weller and Scott E. Guggenheim. Durham: Duke University Press, 42–56.

Wasson, Margaret O. 1973 [1947]. *Class Struggle in Ancient Greece.* New York: Howard Fertig.

Watts, Michael. 1983. *Silent Violence: Food, Famine and Peasantry in Northern Nigeria.* Berkeley: University of California Press.

———— 1984. The Demise of the Moral Economy: Food and Famine in a Sudano-Sahelian Region in Historical Perspective. In *Life Before the Drought,* ed. Earl P. Scott. Boston, Mass.: Allen & Unwin, 124–48.

———— 1987. Drought, Environment and Food Security: Reflections on Peasants, Pastoralists and Commoditization in Drylands West Africa. In *Drought and Hunger in Africa: Denying Famine a Future,* ed. Michael H. Glantz. Cambridge: Cambridge University Press, 171–212.

———— 1988. Coping with the Market: Uncertainty of Food Security among Hausa Peasants. In *Coping with Uncertainty in Food Supply,* ed. I. De Garine and G. A. Harrison. Oxford: Oxford University Press, 260–89.

Webster, Hutton. 1968. *Primitive Secret Societies: A Study in Early Politics and Religion.* New York: Octagon Books.

Weiner, Annette B. 1985. Inalienable Wealth. *American Ethnologist* 12: 210–27.

Weingrod, Alexander. 1977. Patronage and Power. In *Patrons and Clients in Mediterranean Societies,* ed. Ernest Gellner and James Waterbury. London: Duckworth, 41–52.

Weinstein, Matina. 1973. Household Structures and Activities. *Anatolian Studies* 23: 271–6.

Welles, C. Bradford. 1938. New Texts from the Chancery of Philip V of Macedonia and the Problem of the "Diagramma". *American Journal of Archaeology* 42: 245–60.

—— 1974 [1934]. *Royal Correspondence in the Hellenistic Period: A Study in Greek Epigraphy.* Chicago, Ill.: Ares Press.

Wells, Calvin. 1975. Prehistoric and Historical Changes in Nutritional Diseases and Associated Conditions. *Progress in Food and Nutritional Science* 1: 729–79.

Welskopf, E. C. 1980. Free Labor in the City of Athens. In *Non-Slave Labor in the Graeco-Roman World*, ed. Peter Garnsey. Cambridge: Cambridge Philological Society, 23–5.

Welwei, Karl-Wilhelm. 1979. Abhangige Landbevolkerungen auf "Tempel-territotien" im hellenistischen Kleinasian und Syrien. *Ancient Society* 10: 97–118.

West, M. L. 1972. *Iambi et elegi graeci ante Alexandrum cantati.* Oxford: Clarendon.

Westermann, W. L. 1955. *The Slave Systems of Greek and Roman Antiquity.* Philadelphia, Pa: American Philosophical Society.

Wevers, R. F. 1969. *Isaeus: Chronology, Prosopography, and Social History.* The Hague: Mouton.

Wharton, C. R. 1969. Subsistence Agriculture: Concepts and Scope. In *Subsistence Agriculture and Economic Development,* ed. C. Wharton. Chicago, Ill.: Aldine, 12–20.

Wheaton, Robert. 1975. Family and Kinship in Western Europe: The Problem of the Joint Family Household. *Journal of Interdisciplinary History* 5: 601–28.

Wheeler, E. F. and M. Abdullah. 1988. Food Allocation within the Family: Response to Fluctuating Food Supply and Food Needs. In *Coping with Uncertainty in Food Supply,* ed. I. de Garine and G. A. Harrison. Oxford: Oxford University Press, 437–51.

Whitaker, I. 1976. Familial Roles in the Extended Patrilineal Kin-Group in Northern Albania. In *Mediterranean Family Structure*, ed. J. G. Peristiany. Cambridge: Cambridge University Press, 195–204.

White, C. 1980. *Patrons and Partisans: A Study of Politics in Two Southern Italian Communes.* Cambridge: Cambridge University Press.

White, K. D. 1965. The Productivity of Labour in Roman Agriculture.

Antiquity 39: 102–7.

White, K. D. 1974. *Roman Farming*. London: Thames and Hudson.

—— 1976. Food Requirements and Food Supplies in Classical Times in Relation to the Diet of the Various Classes. *Progress in Food and Nutritional Science* 2: 143–91.

Whitehead, David. 1983. Competitive Outlay and Community Profit: *Philotimia* in Democratic Athens. *Classica et Mediaevalia* 34: 55–74.

—— 1986. *The Demes of Attica, 508/7–ca. 250 B.C.* Princeton, NJ: Princeton University Press.

Wichers, A. J. 1964. Amoral Familism Reconsidered. *Sociologia Ruralis* 4: 167–81.

Wiedmann, T. 1984. *Greek and Roman Slavery*. Baltimore, Md.: The Johns Hopkins University Press.

Wilk, Richard R. 1984. Households in Process: Agricultural Change and Domestic Transformation among the Kekchi Maya of Belize. In *Households: Comparative and Historical Studies of the Domestic Group*, ed. Robert M. Netting, Richard R. Wilk, and Eric J. Arnould. Berkeley: University of California Press, 217–44.

—— and Robert M. Netting. 1984. Households: Changing Forms and Functions. In *Households: Comparative and Historical Studies of the Domestic Group*, ed. Robert M. Netting, Richard R. Wilk, and Eric J. Arnould. Berkeley: University of California Press, 1–28.

—— and William J. Rathje. 1982. Household Archaeology. In *Archaeology of the Household: Building a Prehistory of Domestic Life*, ed. Richard R. Wilk and William J. Rathje. New York: *American Behavioral Scientist*, vol. 25, 617–39.

Wilkens, Gene. 1970. The Ecology of Gathering in a Mexican Farming Region. *Economic Botany* 24: 286–95.

Willetts, Ronald F. 1967. *The Law Code of Gortyn*. Berlin: Walter de Gruyter.

Wilmsen, E. N. and D. Durham. 1988. Food as Function of Seasonal Environment and Social History. In *Coping with Uncertainty in Food Supply*, ed. I. de Garine and G. A. Harrison. Oxford: Oxford University Press, 52–87.

Wilson, C. S. 1977. Research Methods in Nutritional Anthropology. In *Nutrition and Anthropology in Action*, ed. T. K. Fitzgerald. Amsterdam: Van Gorcum, 62–8.

Wing, Elizabeth S. and Antoinette B. Brown. 1979. *Paleonutrition*. New York: Academic Press.

Winterhalter, Bruce. 1986. Diet Choice, Risk and Food Sharing in a Stochastic Environment. *Journal of Anthropological Archaeology* 5: 368–92.

—— 1987. The Analysis of Hunter-Gatherer Diets: Stalking an Optimal Foraging Model. In *Food and Evolution: Toward a Theory of Human Food*

Habits, ed. Marvin Harris and E. B. Ross. Philadelphia, Pa.: Temple University Press, 311–40.

Wisner, B. and A. Mbithi. 1974. Drought in Eastern Kenya: Nutritional Status and Farmer Activity. In *Natural Hazards: Local, National, Global,* ed. G. White. Oxford: Oxford Univeristy Press, 87–97.

Wolf, Arthur P. 1981. Women, Widowhood, and Fertility in Pre-Modern China. In *Marriage and Remarriage in Populations of the Past*, ed. J. Dupaquier, E. Helin, P. Laslett, M. Livi-Bacci, and S. Sognar. New York: Academic Press, 139–50.

—— 1984. Family Life and the Life Cycle in Rural China. In *Households: Comparative and Historical Studies of the Domestic Group,* ed. Robert M. Netting, Richard R. Wilk, and Eric J. Arnould. Berkeley: University of California Press. 279–98.

Wolf, Eric R. 1966. *Peasants*. Englewood Cliffs, NJ: Prentice-Hall.

—— 1977. Kinship, Friendship, and Patron–Client Ties in Complex Societies. In *Friends, Followers and Factions: A Reader in Political Clientism*, ed. Steffen W. Schmidt, Laura Guasti, Carl H. Landé, and James C. Scott. Berkeley: University of California Press, 167–77.

Wolff, Hans J. 1944. Marriage Law and Family Organization in Ancient Athens. *Traditio* 2: 43–95.

Wood, Ellen Meiskins. 1983. Agricultural Slavery in Classical Athens. *American Journal of Ancient History* 8: 1–47.

—— 1988. *Peasant-Citizen and Slave: The Foundations of Athenian Democracy*. New York: Verso.

Woolf, Stuart J. 1986. *The Poor in Western Europe in the Eighteenth and Nineteenth Centuries*. London: Methuen.

Worcello, W. W. 1969. Cultural Studies on Yield and Quality of Field Crops in Lebanon. In *Man, Food, and Agriculture in the Middle East*, ed. T. S. Stickley *et al.* Beirut: The American University of Beirut, 491–515.

Wrightson, Keith. 1984. Kinship in an English Village: Terling, Essex 1550–1700. In *Land, Kinship, and the Life Cycle*, ed. Richard M. Smith. Cambridge: Cambridge University Press, 313–32.

Wrigley, E. A. 1987. *People, Cities and Wealth: The Transformation of Traditional Society*. Oxford: Basil Blackwell.

Wylie, Diana. 1989. The Changing Face of Hunger in Southern Africa. *Past & Present* 122: 159–99.

Yanagisako, Sylvia Junko 1979. Family and Household: The Analysis of Domestic Groups. *Annual Review of Anthropology* 8: 161–205.

—— 1984. Explicating Residence: A Cultural Analysis of Changing Households among Japanese-Americans. In *Households: Comparative and Historical Studies of the Domestic Group*, ed. Robert M. Netting, Richard R. Wilk, and Eric J. Arnould. Berkeley: University of California Press, 330–52.

Yesner, David R. 1987. Life in the "Garden of Eden": Causes and Consequences of the Adoption of Marine Diets by Human Societies. In *Food and Evolution: Toward a Theory of Human Food Habits,* ed. Marvin Harris and E. B. Ross. Philadelphia, Pa.: Temple University Press, 285–310.

Zanetti, D. E. 1977. The Patriziato of Milan from the Domination of Spain to the Unification of Italy: An Outline of the Social and Demographic History. *Social History* 6: 745–60.

—— 1982. *La Demografía del Patriziato Milanese nei secoli XVII, XVIII, XIX.* Pavia: Universite dí Pavia.

Zimmermann, H. D. 1974. Die freie Arbeit in Griechenland wahrend des 5. und 4. Jahrhunderts v.u.z. *Klio* 56: 337–52.

Index